# Data Science for Business With

Sara Miller McCune founded SAGE Publishing in 1965 to support the dissemination of usable knowledge and educate a global community. SAGE publishes more than 1000 journals and over 800 new books each year, spanning a wide range of subject areas. Our growing selection of library products includes archives, data, case studies and video. SAGE remains majority owned by our founder and after her lifetime will become owned by a charitable trust that secures the company's continued independence.

Los Angeles | London | New Delhi | Singapore | Washington DC | Melbourne

# Data Science for Business With R

**Jeffrey S. Saltz**
*Syracuse University*

**Jeffrey M. Stanton**
*Syracuse University*

Los Angeles | London | New Delhi
Singapore | Washington DC | Melbourne

FOR INFORMATION:

SAGE Publications, Inc.
2455 Teller Road
Thousand Oaks, California 91320
E-mail: order@sagepub.com

SAGE Publications Ltd.
1 Oliver's Yard
55 City Road
London, EC1Y 1SP
United Kingdom

SAGE Publications India Pvt. Ltd.
B 1/I 1 Mohan Cooperative Industrial Area
Mathura Road, New Delhi 110 044
India

SAGE Publications Asia-Pacific Pte. Ltd.
18 Cross Street #10-10/11/12
China Square Central
Singapore 048423

Printed and bound by CPI Group (UK) Ltd, Croydon, CR0 4YY

ISBN: 978-1-5443-7045-3

Acquisitions Editor:  Leah Fargotstein
Editorial Assistant:  Kenzie Offley
Production Editor:  Gagan Mahindra
Copy Editor:  diacriTech
Typesetter:  diacriTech
Proofreader:  Eleni Maria Georgiou
Indexer:  diacriTech
Cover Designer: Karine Hovsepian
Marketing Manager: Victoria Velasquez

This book is printed on acid-free paper.

21 22 23 24 25 10 9 8 7 6 5 4 3 2

# BRIEF CONTENTS

# DETAILED CONTENTS

# INSTRUCTOR PREFACE

Data science has continued to grow in importance within many different organizational contexts. As data science tools improve, a larger and larger number of students will need to possess a basic level of data science skills and knowledge. With this in mind, our goal of creating this book was to provide an easy to understand introductory data science text that provides an intuitive understanding of how to apply data science concepts within a variety of organizational contexts. As such, we've worked to make the book easy to read and to provide students with hands on learning opportunities that will prepare them for the workplace. We chose to use the R programming language, because it is freely available to all students and instructors, it is relatively easy to learn as a first language, the R-Studio development environment is superior to most of the alternatives, and it connects conveniently with common spreadsheet formats.

We've tested the content of this book thoroughly over many semesters with a diverse range of students. In teaching our introductory data science course, we have noticed an increase in the number of business majors taking the course. In response, this book has a specific focus on how to use data science within business contexts. We leverage one business case across the whole book – this includes a realistic data set that we use to illustrate a variety of data science techniques. As such, our book will help students gain an appreciation of not only the different strategies that a data scientist can use to get insight in the data, but also allows students to understand the full life cycle of executing a data science project – from reading and cleaning data, to exploratory analysis, to using machine learning insights to provide actionable advice to a client or business partner.

The case focuses on customer satisfaction at a national airline and specifically focuses on how to provide actionable insight to improve the company's Net Promoter Score. The dataset includes 27 attributes (ranging from departure city/time to the customer's frequent flyer status).

Beyond the integrated case study, there are several other important updates as compared to the previous edition of *An Introduction to Data Science:*

- First, there is an entire new chapter focused on explaining deep learning, which is growing in use across a range of application areas. Similar to other chapters, we keep the discussion of deep learning at a high conceptual level while also showing an example of how to use deep learning within an R program.

- Another key improvement results from the consistent use of the 'tidyverse' set of packages. Among other capabilities, tidyverse provides the ability to 'pipe' results from one command / function to another command / function, making code more readable.

- The third key update is the use of the 'caret' package, which provides a robust framework for easily trying different machine learning algorithms. The package raises the abstraction level and, as such, makes it easier to write R code.

- Finally, we refined the length and layout of the chapters such that they now map more easily to weeks within a semester.

In short, the book provides a survey of the major concepts within practice areas of data science, including how to:

- Read and clean a dataset

- Use simple statistics to do initial exploratory analysis of a dataset

- Create visualizations to aid in exploratory analysis

- Leverage location data to create map visualizations

- Use machine learning techniques such as association rules and support vector machines

- Apply advanced deep learning techniques

- Explore text data via sentiment analysis

In addition, for each chapter, we provide clearly articulated learning objectives, the R functions used in the chapter, chapter challenge questions that can be used in class or as a homework exercise, and additional resources students can use to explore a specific area in more detail. Finally, there are supporting instructional tools for use with our book, including slides for the instructor, datasets for use in the course, and a sample homework assignment for each chapter (with solutions).

## TEACHING RESOURCES

This text includes an array of instructor teaching materials designed to save you time and to help you keep students engaged. To learn more, visit **sagepub.com** or contact your SAGE representative at **sagepub.com/findmyrep**.

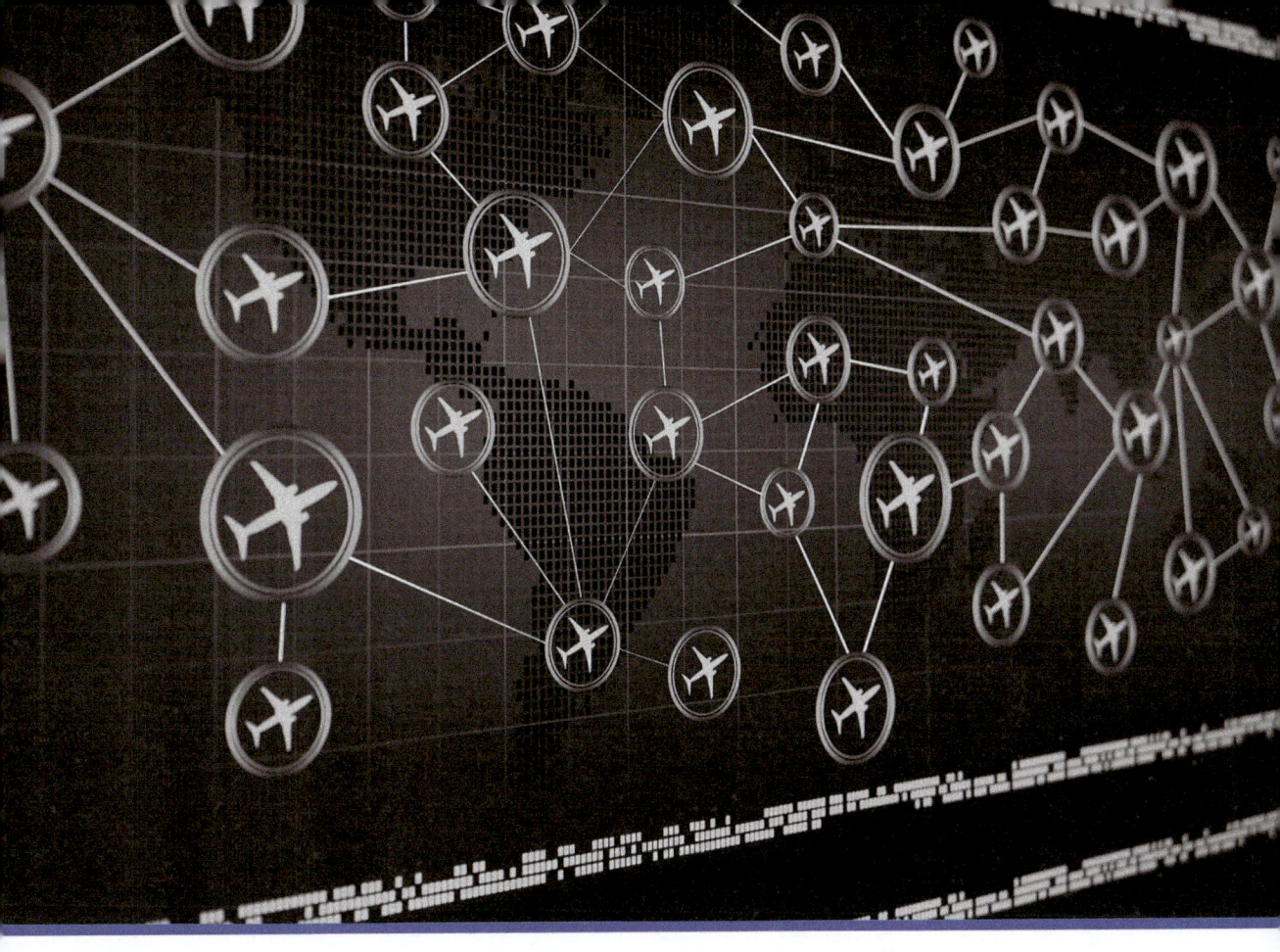

# INTRODUCTION: DATA SCIENCE, MANY SKILLS

## LEARNING OBJECTIVES

Articulate what data science is.

Describe the applicability of data science to business.

Understand the steps, at a high level, of doing data science.

Describe the roles and skills of a data scientist.

# WHAT IS DATA SCIENCE?

For some, the term "data science" evokes images of statisticians in white lab coats staring fixedly at blinking computer screens filled with scrolling numbers. Nothing could be further from the truth. First, statisticians do not wear lab coats: this fashion statement is reserved for biologists, physicians, and others who have to keep their clothes clean in environments filled with unusual fluids. Second, much of the data in the world is non-numeric and unstructured. In this context, unstructured means that the data are not arranged in neat rows and columns. Think of a web page full of photographs and short messages among friends: very few numbers to work with there. Although it is certainly true that businesses use plenty of numeric information—sales of products, financial reports, and customer satisfaction are a few examples—there are lots of other kinds of information in the world that mathematicians and statisticians look at and cringe. So, although it is always useful to have great math skills, there is much to be accomplished in the world of data science for those of us who are presently more comfortable working with words, lists, photographs, sounds, and other kinds of information.

In addition, data science is much more than simply analyzing data. There are many people who enjoy analyzing data and who could happily spend all day looking at histograms and averages, but for those who prefer other activities, data science offers a range of roles and requires a range of skills. Let's consider this idea by thinking about some of the data involved in buying a box of cereal.

Whatever your cereal preferences—fruity, chocolaty, fibrous, or nutty—you prepare for the purchase by writing "cereal" on your grocery list. Already your planned purchase is a piece of data, also called a datum, albeit a pencil scribble on the back of an envelope that only you can read. When you get to the grocery store, you use your datum as a reminder to grab that jumbo box of FruityChocoBoms off the shelf and put it in your cart. At the checkout line, the cashier scans the barcode on your box and the cash register logs the price. Back in the warehouse, a computer tells the stock manager that it is time to request another order from the distributor, because your purchase was one of the last boxes in the store. You also have a coupon for your big box and the cashier scans that, giving you a predetermined manufacturer discount. At the end of the week, a report of all the scanned manufacturer coupons gets uploaded to the cereal company so they can issue a reimbursement to the grocery store for all of the coupon discounts they have handed out to customers. Finally, at the end of the month a store manager looks at a colorful collection of pie charts showing all the different kinds of cereal that were sold, and, on the basis of strong sales of fruity cereals, decides to offer more varieties of these on the store's limited shelf space next month.

The small piece of information that began as a scribble on your grocery list ended up in many different places, but most notably on the desk of a manager as an aid to decision-making. On the trip from your pencil to the manager's desk, the datum went through many transformations. In addition to the computers where the datum might have stopped by or stayed on for the long term, lots of other pieces of hardware—such as the barcode scanner—were involved in collecting, manipulating, transmitting, and storing the datum. Many different pieces of software also were used to organize, aggregate, visualize, and present the datum. Finally, many different human systems were involved in working with the datum. People decided which systems to buy and install, who should get access to what kinds of data, and what would happen to the data after its immediate purpose was fulfilled. The personnel of the grocery chain and its partners made a thousand other detailed decisions and negotiations before the scenario described above could become reality.

## THE STEPS IN DOING DATA SCIENCE

Obviously, data scientists are not involved in all these steps. Data scientists don't design and build computers or barcode readers, for instance. So where would the data scientists play the most valuable role? Generally speaking, data scientists play the most active roles in the four A's of data: data architecture, data acquisition, data analysis, and data archiving. Using our cereal example, let's look at these roles one by one. First, with respect to architecture, it was important in the design of the point-of-sale system (what retailers call their cash registers and related gear) to think through in advance how different people would make use of the data coming through the system. The system architect, for example, had a keen appreciation that both the stock manager and the store manager would need to use the data scanned at the registers, albeit for somewhat different purposes. A data scientist would help the system architect by providing input on how the data would need to be routed and organized to support the analysis, visualization, and presentation of the data to the appropriate people.

Next, acquisition focuses on how the data are collected, and, importantly, how the data are represented prior to analysis and presentation. For example, each barcode represents a number that, by itself, is not very descriptive of the product it represents. At what point after the barcode scanner does its job should the number be associated with a text description of the product or its price or its net weight or its packaging type? Different barcodes are used for the same product (e.g., for different-sized boxes of cereal). When should we make note that purchase X and purchase Y are the same product, just in different packages? Representing, transforming, grouping, and linking the data are all tasks that need to occur before the data can be profitably analyzed, and these are all tasks in which the data scientist is actively involved.

The analysis phase is where data scientists are most heavily involved. In this context, we are using analysis to include summarization of the data, using portions of data (samples) to make inferences about the larger context, and visualization of the data by presenting it in tables, graphs, and even animations. Although there are many technical, mathematical, and statistical aspects to these activities, keep in mind that the ultimate audience for data analysis is always a person or people. These people are the data users, and fulfilling their needs is the primary job of a data scientist. This point highlights the need for excellent communication skills in data science. The most sophisticated statistical analysis ever developed will be useless unless the results can be effectively communicated to the data user.

Finally, the data scientist must become involved in the archiving of the data. Preservation of collected data in a form that makes it highly reusable—what you might think of as data curation—is a difficult challenge because it is so hard to anticipate all the future uses of the data. For example, when the developers of Twitter were working on how to store tweets, they probably never anticipated that tweets would be used to pinpoint earthquakes and tsunamis, but they had enough foresight to realize that geocodes—data that show the geographical location from which a tweet was sent—could be a useful element to store with the data.

## THE SKILLS NEEDED TO DO DATA SCIENCE

All in all, our cereal box and grocery store example helps to highlight where data scientists get involved and the skills they need. Here are some of the skills that the example suggested:

- Learning the application domain: The data scientist must quickly learn how the data will be used in a particular context.

- Communicating with data users: A data scientist must possess strong skills for learning the needs and preferences of data users. The ability to translate back and forth between the technical terms of computing and statistics and the vocabulary of business is a critical skill.

- Seeing the big picture of a complex system: After developing an understanding of the application domain within a business, the data scientist must imagine how data will move around among all the relevant systems and people.

- Knowing how data can be represented: Data scientists must have a clear understanding about how data can be stored and linked, as well as about metadata (data that describe how other data are arranged).

- Data transformation and analysis: when data become available for the use of managers, data scientists must know how to transform, summarize, and make inferences from the data. As noted above, being able to communicate the results of analyses to data users is also a critical skill here.

- Visualization and presentation: Although numbers often have the edge in precision and detail, a good data display (e.g., a bar chart) can often be a more effective means of communicating results to data users.

- Attention to quality: No matter how good a set of data might be, there is no such thing as perfect data. Data scientists must know the limitations of the data they work with, know how to quantify its accuracy, and be able to make suggestions for improving the quality of the data in the future.

- Ethical reasoning: If data are important enough to collect, they are often important enough to affect the lives of employees, customers, and others. Data scientists must understand important ethical issues such as privacy, and must be able to communicate the limitations of data to try to prevent misuse of data or analytical results.

The skills and capabilities noted above are just the tip of the iceberg, of course, but notice what a wide range is represented here. Although a keen understanding of numbers and mathematics is important, particularly for data analysis, the data scientist also needs to have excellent communication skills, be a great systems thinker, have a good eye for visual displays, and be highly capable of thinking critically about how data will be used to make decisions and affect people's lives. Of course, there are very few people who are good at all these things, so some of the people interested in data will specialize in one area, whereas others will become experts in another area. This highlights the importance of teamwork, as well.

# IDENTIFYING DATA PROBLEMS

Apple farmers live in constant fear, first for their blossoms and later for their fruit. A late spring frost can kill the blossoms. Hail or extreme wind in the summer can damage the fruit. More generally, farming is an activity that is first and foremost in the physical world, with complex natural processes and forces, such as weather, that are beyond the control of humankind.

In this highly physical world of unpredictable natural forces, is there any role for data science? On the surface, there does not seem to be. But how can we know for sure? Having a nose for identifying data problems requires openness, curiosity, creativity, and a willingness to ask a lot of questions. In fact, if you took away the impression that a data scientist sits in front of a computer all day and works a crazy program like R, that is a mistake. Every data scientist must (eventually) become immersed in the problem domain where she is working. The data scientist might never actually become a farmer, but if you are going to identify a data problem that a farmer has, you have to learn to think like a farmer, to some degree.

To get this domain knowledge you can read or watch videos, but the best way is to ask subject matter experts (in this case, farmers) about what they do. The whole process of asking questions deserves its own treatment, but for now there are three things to think about when asking questions. First, you want the subject matter experts, or SMEs, as they are sometimes called, to tell stories of what they do. Then you want to ask them about anomalies: the unusual things that happen for better or for worse. Finally, you want to ask about risks and uncertainty: about the situations where it is hard to tell what will happen next, when what happens next could have a profound effect on whether the situation ends badly or well. Each of these three areas of questioning reflects an approach to identifying data problems that might turn up something good that could be accomplished with data, information, and the right decision at the right time.

The purpose of asking about stories is that people mainly think in stories. From farmers to teachers to managers to CEOs, people know and tell stories about success and failure in their particular domain. Stories are powerful ways of communicating wisdom between different members of the same profession and they are ways of collecting a sense of identity that sets one profession apart from another profession. The only problem is that stories can be wrong.

If you can get a professional to tell the main stories that guide how she/he conducts her/his work, you can then consider how to verify those stories. Without questioning the veracity of the person that tells the story, you can imagine ways of measuring the different aspects of how things happen in the story with an eye toward eventually verifying (or sometimes debunking) the stories that guide professional work.

For example, the farmer might say that in the deep spring frost that occurred five years ago, the trees in the hollow were spared frost damage, whereas the trees around the ridge of the hill had frost damage. For this reason, on a cold night the farmer places most of the smudge pots (containers that hold a fuel that creates a smoky fire) around the ridge. The farmer strongly believes that this strategy works, but does it? It would be possible to collect time-series temperature data from multiple locations within the orchard on cold and warm nights, and on nights with and without smudge pots. The data could be used to create a model of temperature changes in the different areas of the orchard and this model could support, improve, or debunk the story. Of course, just as the story could be wrong, we also have to keep in mind that the data might be wrong. For example, a thermometer might not be calibrated correctly, and hence, provide incorrect temperature data. In summary, there is no one correct way of understanding and representing the situation that is inherently more truthful than others. We have to develop a critical lens to be able to assess the possible situations where information might be correct or incorrect.

A second strategy for problem identification is to look for the exception cases, both good and bad. A little later in the book we will learn about how the core of classic methods of statistical inference is to characterize the center—the most typical cases that occur—and then examine the extreme cases that are far from the center for information that could help us understand an intervention or an unusual combination of circumstances. Identifying unusual cases is a powerful way of understanding how things work, but it is first necessary to define the central or most typical occurrences in order to have an accurate idea of what constitutes an unusual case.

Coming back to our farmer friend, in advance of a thunderstorm late last summer a powerful wind came through the orchard, tearing the fruit off the trees. Most of the trees lost a small amount of fruit: the dropped apples could be seen near the base of the trees. One small grouping of trees seemed to lose a much larger amount of fruit, however, and the drops were apparently scattered much farther from the trees. Is it possible that some strange wind conditions made the situation worse in this one spot? Or is it just a matter of chance that a few trees in the same area all lost more fruit than would be typical?

A systematic count of lost fruit underneath a random sample of trees would help to answer this question. The bulk of the trees would probably have each lost about the same amount, but, more importantly, that typical group would give us a yardstick against which we could determine what would really count as unusual. When we found an unusual set of cases that was truly beyond the limits of typical, we could rightly focus our attention on these to try to understand the anomaly.

A third strategy for identifying data problems is to find out about risk and uncertainty. A basic function of information is to reduce uncertainty. It is often valuable to reduce uncertainty because of how risk affects the things we all do. At work, at school, and at home, life is full of risks: making a decision or failing to do so sets off a chain of events that could lead to something good or something not so good. In general, we would like to narrow things down in a way that maximizes the chances of a good outcome and minimizes the chance of a bad one. To do this, we need to make better decisions, and to make better decisions we need to reduce uncertainty. By asking questions about risks and uncertainty (and decisions), a data scientist can zero in on the problems that matter. You can even look at the previous two strategies—asking about the stories that comprise professional wisdom and asking about anomalies/unusual cases—in terms of the potential for reducing uncertainty and risk.

In the case of the farmer, much of the risk comes from the weather, and the uncertainty revolves around which countermeasures will be cost-effective under prevailing conditions. Consuming lots of expensive oil in smudge pots on a night that turns out to be quite warm is a waste of resources that could make the difference between a profitable or an unprofitable year. So more-precise and more-timely information about local weather conditions might be a key focus area for problem-solving with data. What if a live stream of national weather service Doppler radar could appear on the farmer's smartphone? The app could provide the predicted wind speed and temperature for the farm in general. But, as this example has shown, it is typically helpful to have more data. So, predicting the wind and temperature across the different locations within the farm might be much more useful to the farmer.

Of course, there are many other situations where data science (and big data science) could prove useful. For example, banks have used data science for many years to perform credit analysis for a consumer when they want to take out a loan or obtain a credit card. Retailers have used data science to try to predict inventory and the related concept of pricing their inventory. Online retailers can use data science to cluster people, so that the retailer can suggest a related product to someone who liked a certain product (such as a movie). Finally, smart devices can use data science to learn a person's habits, such as a thermostat that can predict when a person will be home or away. Although it would take an entire book to describe the many different situations where data science has been or could be used, hopefully these examples give you a feel for what is possible when data science is applied to real-world challenges.

To recap, there are many different contexts in which a data scientist might work and doing data science requires much more than sitting in front of a computer and doing R coding. The data scientist needs to understand the domain and data in that domain. Often the data scientist gets this knowledge by talking to or observing SMEs. One strategy for problem identification is to interact with an SME and get that person to tell a story about the situation. A second strategy is to look for good and bad exceptions. Finally, a third strategy is to explore risk and uncertainty.

## ADDITIONAL INTRODUCTORY THOUGHTS

Note that the idea of "big data" is a very closely related area of focus. In brief, big data is data science that is focused on processing and analysis of very large datasets. Of course, there's no particular size threshold that defines a "very large dataset," but for our purposes we define big data as trying to analyze datasets that are so large that one cannot use RStudio on a personal computer. As an example of a big data problem to be solved, one clothing retailer adjusts its pricing in near real time for 73 million items, based on demand and inventory (http://searchcio.techtarget.com/opinion/Ten-big-data-case-studies-in-a-nutshell). As one might guess, the amount of data and calculations required for this type of analysis is too large for one computer running RStudio. However, the techniques covered in this book are conceptually similar to how one would approach the retailer's challenge and the chapter 7 in the book provides an overview of some big data concepts.

No one book can cover the wide range of activities and capabilities involved in a field as diverse and broad as data science. Throughout the book, references to other guides and resources provide the interested reader with access to additional information. In the open source spirit of R and RStudio, these are, wherever possible, web-based and free. In fact, one of the guides that appears most frequently in these pages is Wikipedia, the free, online, user-sourced encyclopedia. Although some have legitimate complaints and concerns about Wikipedia, and it is admittedly not perfect, it is a very useful learning resource. Because it is free, because it covers about 50 times more topics than a printed encyclopedia, and because it keeps up with fast-moving topics (such as data science) better than printed sources, Wikipedia is very useful for getting a quick introduction to a topic. You can't become an expert on a topic by consulting only Wikipedia, but you can certainly become smarter by starting there.

Another very useful resource is Khan Academy. Most people think of Khan Academy as a set of videos that explain math concepts to middle and high school students, but thousands of adults around the world use Khan Academy as a refresher course for a range of topics or as a quick introduction to a topic that they never studied before. All the lessons at Khan Academy are free, and if you log in with a Google or Facebook account, you can do exercises and keep track of your progress.

At the end of each chapter of this book, a list of Wikipedia sources and Khan Academy lessons (and other resources too!) shows the key topics relevant to the chapter. These sources provide a great place to start, if you want to learn more about any of the topics the chapter does not explain in detail.

It is valuable to have access to the Internet while you are reading, so that you can follow some of the many links this book provides. Also, as you move into the sections in the book where open source software such as the R data analysis system is used, you will sometimes want to have access to a desktop or laptop computer where you can run these programs.

We think that the book presents topics in an order that should work well for people with little or no prior experience in areas like computer science. Relatedly, most business schools offer, or require, an essential course in statistics, but you may not have taken that course. If you already have knowledge, training, or experience in computer science and/ or statistics, you should feel free to skip over some of the introductory material and move right into the topics and chapters that interest you most.

One last thing: In this book we use a large airline customer survey dataset as a case to illustrate how to turn data into actionable insight, while at the same time, showing the skills and capabilities needed by data scientists. Specifically, at the end of each chapter, we tackle a different aspect of this case: opening up the data, describing the kinds of challenges that businesses want to address, and using the data as a demonstration of how data science might help. The open source data analysis programming language, known as R, and its graphical user interface companion RStudio are used to work with this data to illustrate both the challenges of data science and some of the techniques used to address those challenges. In the next section, we provide the background context and information for the case.

# CASE STUDY OVERVIEW: CUSTOMER CHURN IN THE AIRLINE INDUSTRY

```
Case Key Points:
-  Southeast airlines has surveyed their customers
-  Each survey has 27 attributes (e.g., flight and customer
   info)
-  Each survey also has a question, on a scale of 1 to 10:
   "How likely are you to recommend this airline to your
   friends?"
-  Net promoter score (NPS) is calculated as  percentage
   of promoters (9 or 10) minus  percentage of detractors
   (below 7)
-  Can Southeast leverage the NPS surveys to reduce churn?
-  Do any of Southeast's regional airline partners impact
   NPS?
```

Southeast Airlines needed to lower their customer churn (sometimes referred to as customer attrition). Like many airlines, Southeast has, up until now, believed that the best way to minimize customer churn was to have a robust loyalty program for frequent flyers. The basics of Southeast's loyalty program were similar to other airlines. In short, the airline rewarded repeat business and as a customer flew more, they would rise through levels of service and "bank" miles that could be redeemed for free or discounted travel. There were no data to back up this line of thinking, however, as it was just the "accepted industry best practice." However, their customers were valuing the loyalty program less, which was one reason why just relying on their loyalty program might not be sufficient in keeping low customer churn. In fact, according to a recent International Air Transport Association (IATA) study, airlines carry $12B in "loyalty debt" and frequent flier mileage and points are slowly devaluing, while the overall balance (or debt) is increasing.

Additionally, customer churn is actually a lagging indicator, meaning the loss has already occurred. As such, it was a measurement of the damage inflicted. The real goal is to reduce churn by getting ahead of the loss (of the customer) by identifying some leading indicators, or metrics, that might help keep a customer. In other words, these leading indicators, or metrics, could help identify when a customer was about to stop flying Southeast. These insights could provide actionable suggestions as to how to avoid having the customers leave and go to another airline. In thinking about customer churn, several key facts are relevant:

## Net Promoter Score

NPS asks customers to respond, on a scale of 1–10, to one simple question: "How likely is it that you will recommend our airline to a friend or colleague?" If respondents score less than 7, they're detractors. If they score above an 8, they're promoters. In the middle range (a score of 7 or 8), they're "passive." In a given group, subtracting the percent of respondents who are detractors from the percent of respondents who were promoters provides the overall NPS score. The concept of NPS is that customers who are promoters are good customers to keep. Such customers may sometimes even provide free "word of mouth" advertising. Customers who are detractors are really problematic in that they may actively tell their social connections not to use the product or service (i.e., they would be telling people not to fly Southeast). It has often been suggested that NPS provides a good proxy for understanding how likely a customer is to churn. For example, according to one source, NPS is nearly three times more sensitive at predicting customer churn than customer satisfaction. In addition, detractors are 1.5 times more likely to stop using a service as compared to promoters. In short, analytics could be a key to the success of Southeast.

## Southeast and Its Regional Airline Partners

The airline had many regional airline partners that operated quasi-independently. Southeast Airlines is one of the top four airlines in the United States. Like the other large airlines in the United States, customers buying a Southeast plane ticket fly on Southeast Airlines primary routes as well as on Southeast's regional partner airlines. Regional airlines act as feeder airlines to major airlines by connecting smaller airports to the airline's main hubs. Hub airports are always located in major cities, whereas the regionals serve smaller cities and rural areas. Like other airlines, Southeast contracted out to regional carriers because it allowed them to lower their risks related to capacity and pricing. Specifically, regional airline contracts last for a number of years, after which, Southeast can renegotiate to adjust (up or down) the number of flights provided by that partner. This enables Southeast to more easily reflect their current market conditions. It is possible, for example, that if demand falls, Southeast would not renew some of their regional contracts. On the other hand, if demand rises, Southeast can expand their contract and bring more planes into service more quickly than they could on their own. Note that NPS was not currently used as part of Southeast's partner airline strategy (i.e., it was not part of the data Southeast used to help decide which partners to keep, which partners to drop, and which regional airlines should become new partners).

## The Data Available

Southeast often surveyed their customers, and in fact, possessed thousands of recently completed customer surveys. Southeast has been using the surveys to calculate NPS. Southeast would increase their focus on providing good customer service when their NPS score went down. This was typically via a memo to customer-facing staff, where they were encouraged to "smile more." The survey dataset contained thousands of observations of flight segment data collected by Southeast. Each row represents one flight segment, by one airline (either Southeast or one of its partner airlines), for a specific customer. Each column represents an attribute of that particular flight segment. Each row captures 26 characteristics of the flight (e.g., day of month, date, airline, origin, and destination city, if the flight was delayed), the customer (e.g., age, gender, price sensitivity, the person's frequent flyer status). The row also contains a simple survey-based rating of each customer's likelihood to recommend the airline that they just flew as well as a field for open-ended text comments. It should be noted that there are some missing values in the dataset. The list below provides a short description for each attribute.

## Attribute Names

1. ***Likelihood to Recommend***—*rated on a scale of 1 to 10, which shows how likely the customer is to recommend the airline to their friends (10 is very likely, and 1 is not very likely).*

2. ***Airline Flyer Status***—*each customer has a different type of airline status, which are platinum, gold, silver, and blue (based on level of travel with the airline)*

3. ***Age***—*the specific customer's age. Ranging from 15 to 85 years old.*

4. ***Gender***—*male or female.*

5. ***Price Sensitivity***—*the grade to which the price affects the customers purchasing. The price sensitivity has a range from 0 to 5.*

6. ***Year of First Flight***—*this attribute shows the first flight of each single customer. The range of year of the first flight for each customer has been started in 2003 until 2012.*

7. ***Flights per Year***—*the number of flights that each customer has taken in the most recent 12 months. The range starting from 0 to 100.*

8. ***Loyalty***—*an index of loyalty ranging from -1 to 1 that reflects the proportion of flights taken on other airlines versus flights taken on this airline. A higher index means more loyalty.*

9. *Type of Travel*—one of business travel, mileage tickets, or personal travel (e.g., vacation).

10. *Total Frequent Flyer Accounts*—how many frequent flyer accounts the customer has.

11. *Shopping Amount at Airport*—the spending on non-food and services at the airport (in $).

12. *Eating and Drinking at Airport*—the spending on food/drink at the airport (in $).

13. *Class*—three different kinds of service level (business, economy plus, and economy).

14. *Day of Month*—the traveling day of each customer (ranges from 1 to 31).

15. *Flight date*—the passenger's flight date of travel.

16. *Partner Code*—this airline works with wholly and partially owned subsidiary companies to deliver regional flights. For example, AA, AS, B6, and DL.

17. *Partner Name*—these are the full names of the partner airline companies.

18. *Origin City*—the place where passenger departed from. For example, Boston, Massachusetts.

19. *Origin State*—the place where passenger departed from. For example, Texas.

20. *Destination City*—the place to which passenger travels to. For example, Boston, Massachusetts.

21. *Destination State*—the place to which passenger travels to. For example, Texas.

22. *Scheduled Departure Hour*—the specific time at which the plane was scheduled to depart.

23. *Departure Delay in Minutes*—how long the flight's departure was delayed, when compared to schedule.

24. *Arrival Delay in Minutes*—how long the arrival was delayed.

25. *Flight Cancelled*—occurs when the airline does not operate the flight.

26. *Flight Time in Minutes*—the length of time, in minutes, to reach the destination.

27. ***Flight Distance***—*the distance between the departure and arrival destination.*

28. ***Comment***—*a free-form text field of the passenger comment, with respect to the flight.*

The overall goal of the case is to provide actionable insight, based on the data available.

## Chapter Challenges

1. If you were hired to help Southeast Airlines, what are some questions that might be appropriate to ask the leadership team at Southeast? For each question, explain the reason why the question is being asked. Below are some questions to help get you started:

   - Are there additional datasets that have been collected and are available that might be useful (e.g., tweets)?

   - During the time when the survey was given, were there specific customer promotions that might have impacted Southeast's NPS?

   - Has there been any previous analysis of NPS by Southeast (beyond a high-level NPS calculation)?

2. To help structure discussions with SMEs, an interview guide can be useful. Create a general interview guide to ask questions of an SME.

3. Create an interview guide that you can use for those at Southeast.

## Sources

http://en.wikipedia.org/wiki/E-Science
http://en.wikipedia.org/wiki/E-Science_librarianship
http://en.wikipedia.org/wiki/Wikipedia:Size_comparisons
http://en.wikipedia.org/wiki/Statistician
http://en.wikipedia.org/wiki/Visualization_(computer_graphics)
http://www.khanacademy.org/
http://www.r-project.org/
http://rstudio.org/

### Case Sources

http://www.genroe.com/blog/net-promoter-score-is-2-7-times-more-sensitive-than-customer-satisfaction/1470
http://www.chicagotribune.com/news/nationworld/ct-regional-airlines-outdo-rivals-20180925-story.html
http://www.bloomberg.com/news/articles/2018-05-04/american-air-to-end-regional-deals-with-expressjet-trans-states
http://customercarebg.com/customer-support/customer-churn-rate-in-the-airlines
http://medium.com/@dfee/managing-churn-with-nps-8719b2ca27f1
http://blog.datAvery.com/loyalty-time-to-feel-the-burn-and-drop-the-churn
http://conversionxl.com/blog/customer-churn/
http://hbr.org/2003/12/the-one-number-you-need-to-grow.
http://onemileatatime.com/regional-airlines/
http://www.aerocrewnews.com/education-2/contract-talks/the-regional-airline-concept/
http://customergauge.com/blog/2017-customer-experience-lessons-from-the-airline-industry-so-far

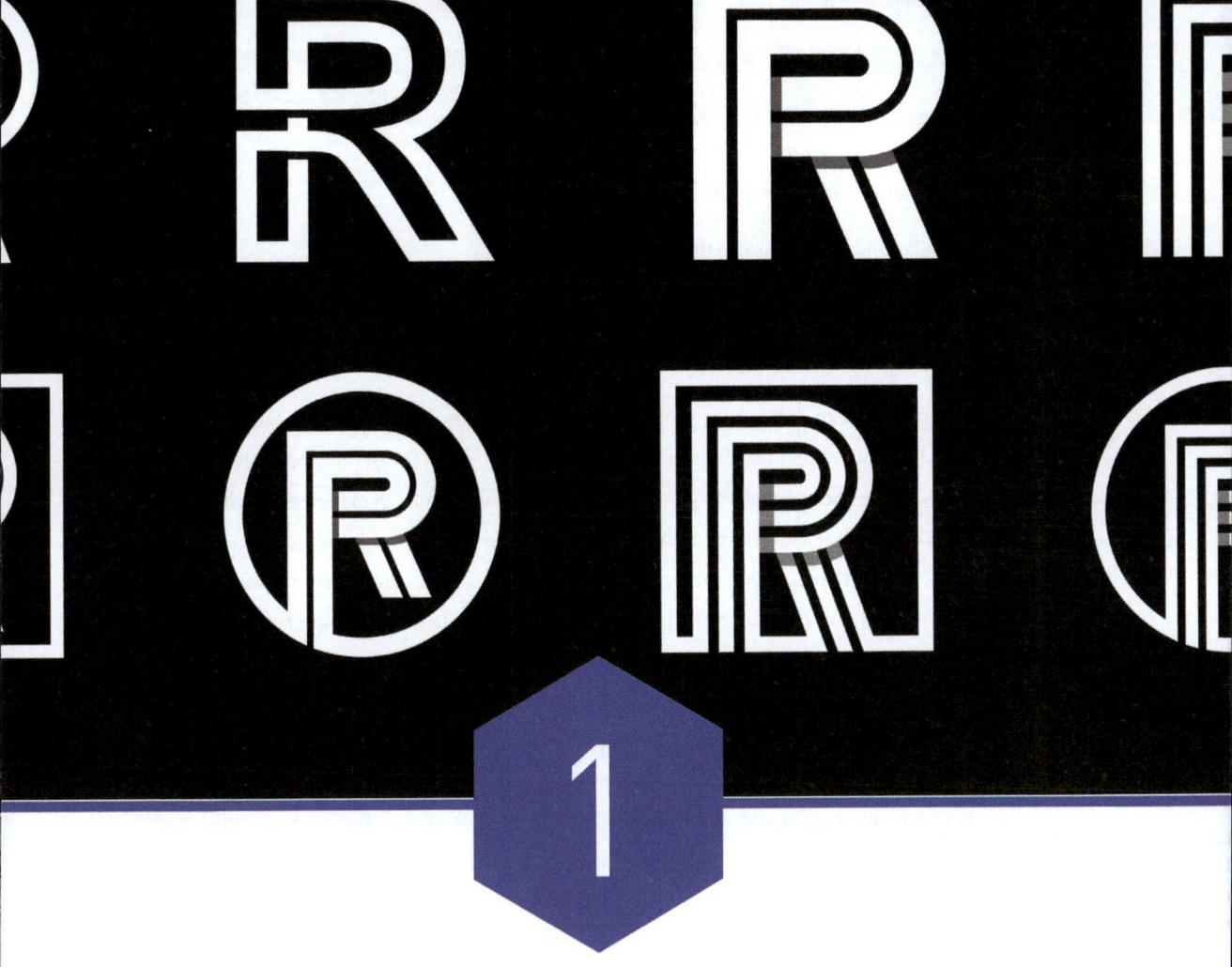

# 1

# BEGIN AT THE BEGINNING WITH R

## LEARNING OBJECTIVES

Know how to install the R software package.

Gain familiarity with using the R command line.

Build and manipulate vectors in R.

If you are new to computers, programming, and/or data science, welcome to an exciting world that will open the door to the most powerful free data analytics tool ever created anywhere in the universe, no joke. On the other hand, if you are experienced with spreadsheets, statistical analysis, or accounting software you are probably thinking, as you start this chapter, that this book has gone off the deep end, never to return to sanity and all that is good and right in user interaction design. Both perspectives are reasonable. The R open source data analysis programming language is immensely powerful, flexible, and extensible (meaning that people can create new capabilities for it quite easily). At the same time, R is code-oriented, meaning that most of the work that one needs to perform is done through carefully crafted text instructions, many of which have very specific syntax (the punctuation and related rules for creating a command that works). Additionally, like many programming languages, R is not especially good at giving feedback or error messages that help the user to fix mistakes or figure out what is wrong when results look funny.

But there is a method to the madness here. One of the virtues of R as a teaching tool is that it hides very little. A successful user must fully understand what the data situation is or else the R commands will not work. With a spreadsheet, it is easy to type in a lot of numbers and a formula like =FORECAST and a result pops into a cell like magic, whether the results make any sense or not. With R you have to know your data, know what you can do with it, know how it must be transformed, and know how to check for trouble. Because R is a programming language, it also forces users to think about problems in terms of data objects, methods that can be applied to those objects, and procedures for applying those methods. These are important metaphors used in modern programming languages, and no data scientist can succeed without having at least a rudimentary understanding of how software is programmed, tested, and integrated into working systems.

The extensibility of R means that new packages are being added all the time by volunteers: for example, R was among the first analysis programs to integrate capabilities for drawing data directly from Internet sources such as web pages and social media posts. You can be sure that, whatever the next big development is in the world of data, someone in the R community will start to develop a new package for R that will make use of it.

Finally, the lessons we can learn by working with R have nearly universal applicability to other programs and environments. If you have mastered R, it is a small step to get the hang of Python, another important data science language. Similarly, SAS® and SPSS®, two of the most widely used commercial statistical analysis programs, both have languages that will be easier to understand after you use R. Because R is open source, there are no licensing fees paid by schools, students, or teachers. As a result, it is possible to learn the most powerful data analysis system in the universe for free and take those lessons with you no matter where you go. It will take some patience though, so please hang in there!

## INSTALLING R

Let's get started. Obviously, you will need a computer. If you are working on a tablet device or smartphone, you might want to skip to the section on RStudio, because plain old R has not yet been reconfigured to work on tablet devices (there is a workaround for this that uses RStudio). There are a few experiments with web-based interfaces to R, like Jupyter Notebooks—but for now, we will focus on R and RStudio. If your computer has the Windows®, Mac-OS-X®, or a Linux operating system, there is a version of R waiting for you at http://cran.r-project.org/. Download and install your own copy. If you have difficulties with installing new software and you need some help, there is a wonderful little book by Thomas P. Hogan called *Bare-Bones R: A Brief Introductory Guide* (2009, Thousand Oaks, CA: SAGE) that you might want to buy or borrow from your library. There are lots of sites online that also give help with installing R, although many of them are not oriented toward the inexperienced user. We searched online using the term "help installing R" and got a few good hits. One site that was quite informative for installing R on Windows was readthedocs.org, and you can try to access it at this TinyUrl: http://tinyurl.com/872ngtt. YouTube also has videos that provide brief tutorials for installing R. Try searching for "install R" in the YouTube search box. The rest of this chapter assumes that you have installed R and can run it on your computer as shown in the first screenshot. Note that this screenshot is from the Mac version of R: if you are running Windows or Linux, your R screen could appear slightly different from this. If you are having trouble installing R and RStudio, you can also try https://rstudio.cloud, which is a web-based version of RStudio.

## USING R

The following screenshot shows a simple command to type that shows the most basic method of interaction with R. Notice near the bottom of the screenshot a greater than (>) symbol. This is the command prompt: When R is running and it is the active application on your desktop, if you type a command it appears after the > symbol. If you press the enter or return key, the command is sent to R for processing. When the processing is done, a result appears just under the >, if the command you used creates a result. When R is done processing, another command prompt (>) appears and R is ready for your next command. In the screenshot, the user has typed "1+1" and pressed the enter key. The formula 1+1 is used by elementary school students everywhere to insult each other's math

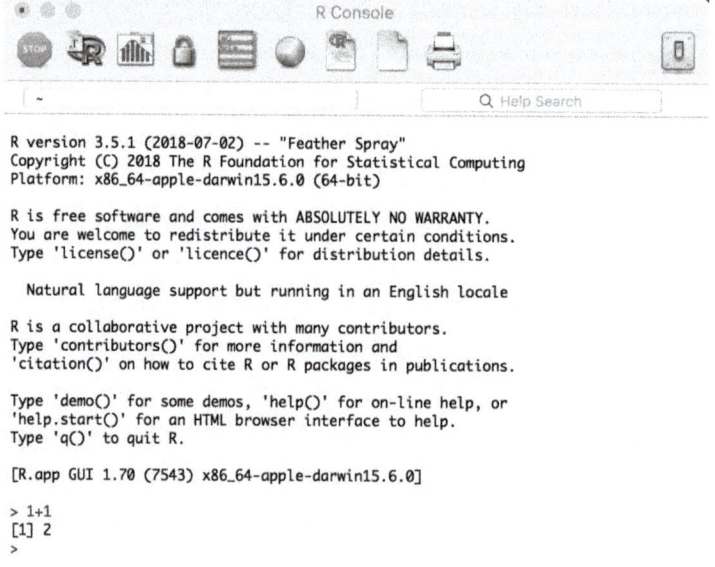

skills, but R dutifully reports the result as 2. If you are a careful observer, you will notice that just before the 2 there is a 1 in square brackets, like this: [1]. That [1] is an index that helps to keep track of the results that R displays. Pretty pointless when only showing one result, but R likes to be consistent, so we will see quite a lot of those numbers in square brackets as we dig deeper.

## CREATING AND USING VECTORS

Here is a list of ages of family members: 43, 42, 12, 8, 5, for Dad, Mom, Sis, Bro, and their Dog, respectively. This is a list of items, all of the same mode (or type), namely an integer. They are integers because there are no decimal points and therefore nothing after the decimal point. We can create a vector of integers in R using the c() command. Take a look at the screen shot just below.

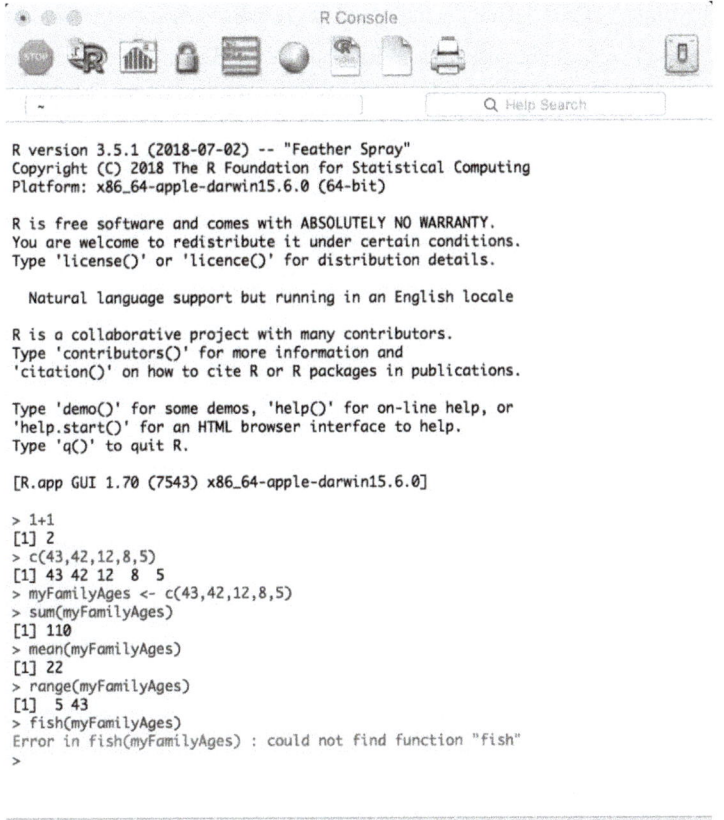

```
R version 3.5.1 (2018-07-02) -- "Feather Spray"
Copyright (C) 2018 The R Foundation for Statistical Computing
Platform: x86_64-apple-darwin15.6.0 (64-bit)

R is free software and comes with ABSOLUTELY NO WARRANTY.
You are welcome to redistribute it under certain conditions.
Type 'license()' or 'licence()' for distribution details.

  Natural language support but running in an English locale

R is a collaborative project with many contributors.
Type 'contributors()' for more information and
'citation()' on how to cite R or R packages in publications.

Type 'demo()' for some demos, 'help()' for on-line help, or
'help.start()' for an HTML browser interface to help.
Type 'q()' to quit R.

[R.app GUI 1.70 (7543) x86_64-apple-darwin15.6.0]

> 1+1
[1] 2
> c(43,42,12,8,5)
[1] 43 42 12  8  5
> myFamilyAges <- c(43,42,12,8,5)
> sum(myFamilyAges)
[1] 110
> mean(myFamilyAges)
[1] 22
> range(myFamilyAges)
[1]  5 43
> fish(myFamilyAges)
Error in fish(myFamilyAges) : could not find function "fish"
>
```

This is the last time that the whole screenshot from the R console will appear in the book. From here on out, we will just look at commands and output so we don't waste so much space on the page. The first command line creates a vector:

```
> c(43, 42, 12, 8, 5)
```

As you can see, when we show a short snippet of code we will make blue and bold what we type, and not blue and not bold what R is generating. So, in the above example, R generated the >, and then we typed c(43, 42, 12, 8, 5). You don't need to type the > because R provides it whenever it is ready to receive new input. From now on in the book, there will be examples of R commands and output that are mixed together. The code will always be in blue and the output will be in black. In order to make it easier for you to reuse our code, we will be leaving out the > character from now on.

You might notice that on the following line in the screenshot, R dutifully reports the vector that you just typed. After the line number [1], we see the list 43, 42, 12, 8, and 5. This is because R echoes this list back to us, because we didn't ask it to store the vector anywhere. In the rest of the book, we will show that output from R as follows:

```
[1] 43, 42, 12, 8, 5
```

Combining these two lines, our R console snippet would look as follows:

```
c(43, 42, 12, 8, 5)
[1] 43, 42, 12, 8, 5
```

In contrast, the next command line is as follows:

```
myFamilyAges <- c(43, 42, 12, 8, 5)
```

We have typed in the same list of numbers, but this time we have assigned it, using the left-pointing arrow, into a storage area that we have named myFamilyAges. This time, R responds just with an empty command prompt. That's why the third command line requests a report of what myFamilyAges contains. This is a simple but very important tool.

Any time you want to know what is in a data object in R, just type the name of the object and R will report it back to you. In the next command, we begin to see the power of R:

```
sum(myFamilyAges)
[1] 110
```

This command asks R to add together all of the numbers in myFamilyAges, which turns out to be 110 (you can check it yourself with a calculator if you want). This is perhaps a weird thing to do with the ages of family members, but it shows how with a very short and simple command you can unleash quite a lot of processing on your data. In the next line (of the screenshot image), we ask for the mean (what non-data people call the average) of all of the ages and this turns out to be 22 years. The command right afterward, called range, shows the lowest and highest ages in the list. Finally, just for fun, we tried to issue the command fish(myFamilyAges). Pretty much as you might expect, R does not contain a fish() function and so we received an error message to that effect. This shows another important principle for working with R. You can freely try things out at any time without fear of breaking anything. If R can't understand what you want to accomplish, or you haven't quite figured out how to do something, R will calmly respond with an error message and will not make any other changes until you give it a new command. The error messages from R are not always super helpful, but with some strategies that we will discuss in future chapters, you can break down the problem and figure out how to get R to do what you want.

Finally, it's important to remember that R is case sensitive. This means that myFamilyAges is different from myFamilyages. If we misspell the name of the data object by messing up the capitalization, we will get an error:

```
myFamilyages
Error: object 'myFamilyages' not found
```

Let's take stock for a moment. First, you should definitely try all of the commands noted above on your own computer. You can read about the commands in this book all you want, but you will learn a lot more if you actually try things out. Second, if you try a command that is shown in these pages and it does not work for some reason, you should try to figure out why. Begin by checking your spelling and punctuation, because R is very picky about how commands are typed. Remember that capitalization matters in R: myFamily Ages is not the same as myFamilyages. If you verify that you have typed a command just as you see in the book and it still does not work, try to go online and look for some help. There's lots of help at http://stackoverflow.com, at http://www.statmethods.net/, and at many other web sites. If you can figure out what went wrong on your own, you will probably learn something very valuable about working with R. Third, you should take a moment to experiment with each new set of commands that you learn. For example, just using the commands discussed earlier in the chapter you could do this totally new thing:

```
myRange <- range(myFamilyAges)
myRange
```

What would happen if you did these two commands? What would you see? Think about how that worked and try to imagine some other experiments that you could try. The more you experiment on your own, the more you will learn. Some of the best stuff ever invented for computers was the result of just experimenting to see what was possible.

## SUBSETTING VECTORS

We can use the ability to access individual elements within a vector to select a subset of the elements in the vector. For example, we can select the third, the second, and the fifth elements of the myFamilyAges vector:

```
myFamilyAges[ c(3,2,5) ]
[1] 12 42 5
```

We can also define a sequential range of values (indices) and select those elements of the vector. The colon operator, as used in the following, creates the inclusive list of integers 3, 4, 5:

```
myFamilyAges[ c(3:5) ]
[1] 12 8 5
```

As you can see below, if the indices are negative, those vector elements are removed and whatever is left over is returned:

```
myFamilyAges[ c(-3:-5) ]
[1] 43 42
```

In addition to defining specific indices to select or remove elements from the vector, we can also tell R, via a list of TRUEs and FALSEs, which vector elements to include: either directly with a vector of TRUE and FALSE (once for each element in the vector) or by using a variable that contains a TRUE or FALSE for each element of the vector. As you can see, both approaches create the same result:

```
myFamilyAges[ c(TRUE, FALSE, TRUE, FALSE, FALSE) ]
[1] 43 12

selectedFamily <- c(TRUE, FALSE, TRUE, FALSE, FALSE)
myFamilyAges[ selectedFamily ]
[1] 43 12
```

Next, if we combine these concepts with a conditional evaluation, we can get a subset of a vector based on a conditional test of the data itself. In the example below, we test which family members are older than 21. The expression myFamilyAges>21 applies that conditional test to every element of myFamilyAges and produces a vector of TRUEs and FALSEs that is exactly the same length as myFamilyages. Take the time to get a clear understanding of how this works, because it is a very powerful feature that we will use over and over again as we repair and transform data sets:

```
myFamilyAges > 21
[1] TRUE TRUE FALSE FALSE FALSE

selectedFamily <- myFamilyAges > 21
myFamilyAges[ selectedFamily ]
[1] 43 42
```

We can also do the conditional evaluation directly inside the square brackets. For example, we can identify all the family members that are a specific age (use two equal signs together to test equality in the conditional). We can also identify all the family members that are not a specific age (using the exclamation point "!" symbol. We can see that in R, the exclamation point in a conditional means "not." Examine the output created by this conditional and explain in an R comment what happened.

```
myFamilyAges[ myFamilyAges == 12]
[1] 12


myFamilyAges[ myFamilyAges != 12]
[1] 43 42 8 5


myFamilyAges[ !(myFamilyAges == 12)]
[1] 43 42 8 5
```

Finally, we can also construct an expression that performs multiple conditional tests within the same line, such as all the family members older than 6 but younger than 20:

```
myFamilyAges[ myFamilyAges > 6 & myFamilyAges < 20 ]
[1] 12 8
```

Don't forget that one way to make sure that your conditional works correctly or to figure out the problem if it does not is to copy just the conditional expression and run it by itself to look at the map of TRUE and FALSE that it produces.

## THE COMMAND CONSOLE

For all of the commands shown above, we used the R console. Console is an old technology term that dates back to the days when computers were so big that they each occupied their own air-conditioned room. Within that room, there was often one master control station where a computer operator could do just about anything to control the giant computer by typing in commands. That station was known as the console. The term "console" is now used in many cases to refer to any interface where you can directly type in commands. We've typed commands into the R console in an effort to learn about the R language as well as to illustrate some basic principles about data structures and statistics. If we really want to "do" data science, though, we can't sit around typing commands all day. First, it will become boring very fast. Second, whoever is paying us to be a data scientist will get suspicious when he or she notices that we are *retyping* some of the same commands we typed yesterday. Third, and perhaps most important, it is way too easy to make a mistake—to create what computer scientists refer to as a bug—if you are doing every little task by hand.

# USING AN INTEGRATED DEVELOPMENT ENVIRONMENT

To promote quality and efficiency in the R code that we create, one of our big goals within this book is to build something that is reusable: where we can do a few clicks or type a couple of things and unleash the power of many processing steps. Every software engineer knows that if you want to get serious about building something out of code, you must use an integrated development environment (IDE). Using an IDE, we can build these kinds of reusable pieces.

Starting in 2009, Joseph J. Allaire, a serial entrepreneur, software engineer, and the originator of some remarkable software products, began working with a small team to develop an open-source program to enhance the usability and power of R. As mentioned previously, R is an open-source program, meaning that the source code that is used to create a copy of R to run on a Mac, Windows, or Linux computer is available for all to inspect and modify. As with many open-source projects, there is an active community of developers who work on R, both on the basic program itself and on the many pieces and parts that can be added on to the basic program.

If you think of R as a piece of canvas lying on the table, RStudio is like an elegant picture frame where you can mount your canvas. R hangs in the middle of RStudio, and, like any good picture frame, RStudio enhances our appreciation of what is inside it. The IDE gives us the capability to open up the process of creation, to peer into the component parts when we need to, and to close the hood and hide them when we don't. Because we are working with data, we also need ways of inspecting the data, both its structure and its contents. As you probably noticed, it gets tedious doing this at the R console, where almost every piece of output is a chunk of text and longer chunks scroll off the screen before you can see them. As an IDE for R, RStudio allows us to control and monitor our code, our data, our output, and our graphics in a way that supports the creation of reusable code sequences.

## INSTALLING RSTUDIO

Before we can get there, though, we have to have RStudio installed on a computer. Perhaps the most challenging aspect of installing RStudio is having to install R first, but if you've already done that, then installing RStudio should be a piece of cake. Make sure that you have the latest version of R installed before you begin with the installation of RStudio. There is ample documentation on the RStudio website, http://www.rstudio.org/, so if you follow the instructions there, you should have minimal difficulty. If you reach a page where you are asked to choose between installing RStudio server and installing RStudio as a desktop application on your computer, choose the latter. If you run into any difficulties or you just want some additional guidance about RStudio, you might want to have a look at the book entitled, *Getting Started with RStudio*, by John Verzani (2011, Sebastopol, CA: O'Reilly Media). The first chapter of that book has a general orientation to R and RStudio as well as a guide to installing and updating RStudio. There is also a YouTube video that introduces RStudio here: http://www.youtube.com/watch?v=7sAmqkZ3Be8

If you search for other YouTube videos, be aware that there is a disk recovery program as well as a music group that share the RStudio name: you will get a number of these videos if you search on "RStudio" without any other search terms.

Once you have installed RStudio, you can run it immediately in order to get started with the activities in the later parts of this chapter. Unlike other introductory materials, we will not walk through all of the different elements of the RStudio screen. Rather, as we need each feature we will highlight the new aspect of the application. When you run RStudio, you will see three or four sub-windows. Use the File menu to select New, and in the sub-menu for New, select "R Script." This should give you a screen that looks something like this:

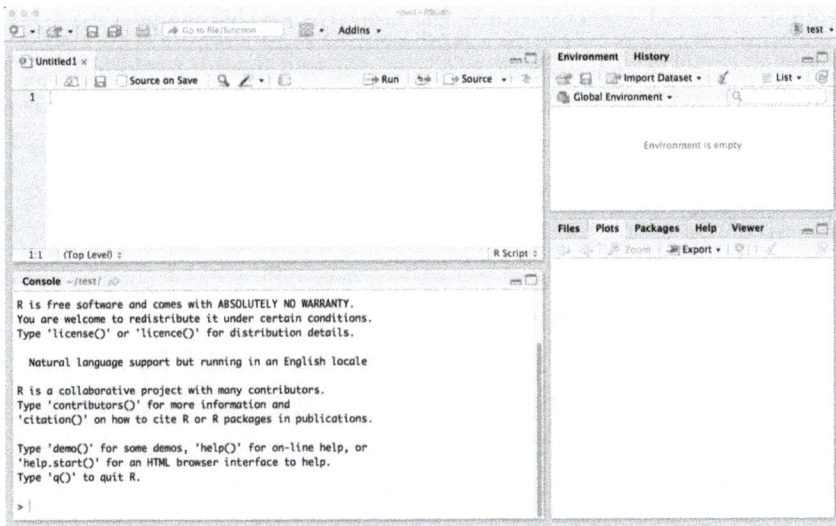

# CREATING R SCRIPTS

Now let's use RStudio! In the lower-left-hand pane (another name for a sub-window) of RStudio, you will notice that we have a regular R console running. You can type commands into this console, just like we did earlier using plain old R:

Click in the console pane and type the following:

```
tinyData <- c(1,2,1,2,3,3,3,4,5,4,5)
mean(tinyData)
[1]  3
```

As you can see, this behaves the exact same way as just using the R console! However, it gets much more interesting if we use the upper-left-hand pane, which displays a blank space under the tab title Untitled1. This is the pane that contains your R source code file. Click on the source code pane (upper left pane), and then enter the following code:

```
tinyData <- c(1,2,1,2,3,3,3,4,5,4,5)

min(tinyData)
mean(tinyData)
sum(tinyData)
```

You can see, we are still writing R code, and rather than typing things at the ">" console prompt, we are just putting them in an R source code file that can be saved. Once we have the R source code, we can click on the Run button to run the commands that you wrote into the R script file (upper-left-hand pane). The Run button also has an icon with a little green arrow next to it—if you make the code window very small, sometimes all you will see is the icon! There are two ways to use the run button. You can highlight the piece of code that you want to run. You have to highlight carefully in order to choose the complete piece of code that you want to run. The other way to do it is that if you simply click in a line of code without highlighting anything and then press the Run button, you will run that whole line of code. Once you click Run, R will copy your code into the Console and the output (if any) will appear just below the code that was copied into the Console. R will then move the cursor to the next line of code in the source code file. So, clicking on Run again will execute the next line of code in your source code file.

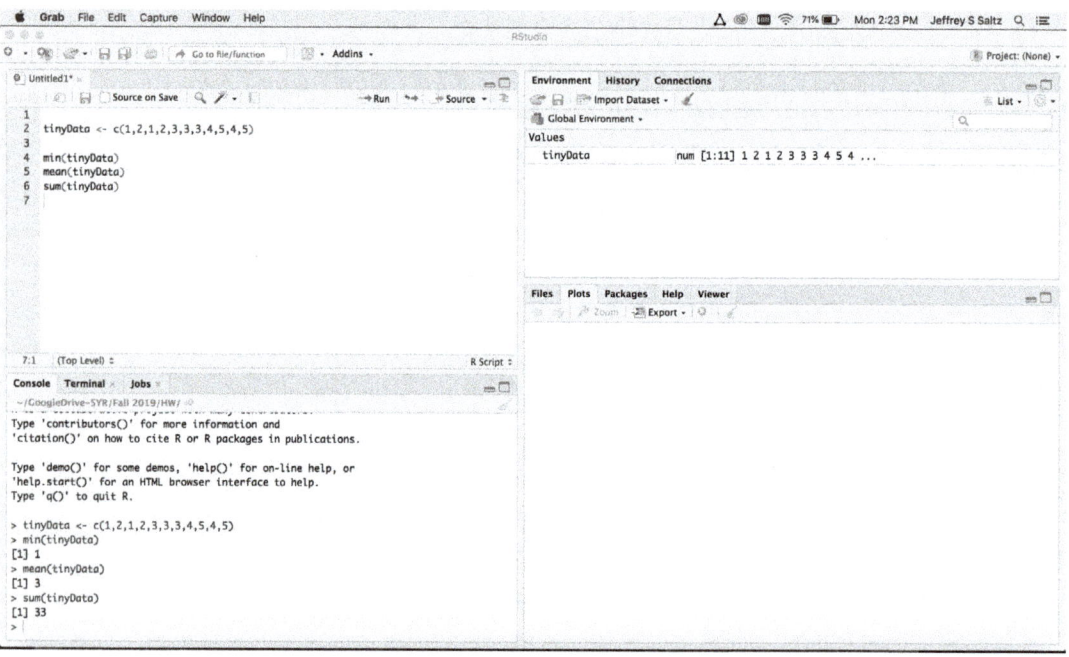

Try it: it is just as if we had typed the commands into the console window, and that the output of min, mean, and sum commands show up in the R console pane. The advantage of this is that the code you just ran in the code window sticks around and can be saved. You can fix problems in the code, make copies of it, add comments, and do other things that will help you be a more productive data scientist. You should also be able to see in the upper right pane (under the Environment tab) that there is a new data element tinyData. Your RStudio display should now look like this:

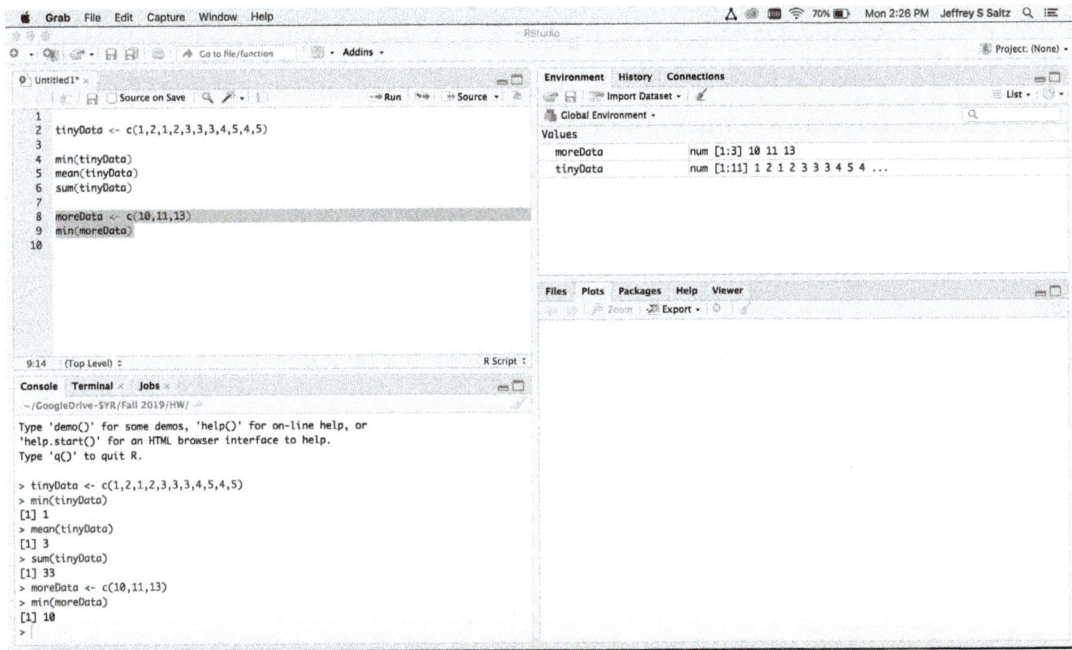

Let's practice highlighting code in the R source code window, and then clicking the "run" button. Here are two additional lines of code to type in: highlight and run:

```
moreData <- c(10,11,13)
min(moreData)
[1] 10
```

Note that in the upper right, the environment window now has the vector moreData as well as the vector tinyData. Another tab in the upper right is the History tab. This is useful to see the list of previous R commands we have executed. Although we have not yet discussed the lower-right window, we will use that window later to see the results of our visualizations.

To recap, this chapter provided a basic introduction to some basic R commands via the R Console and RStudio, an IDE for R. An IDE is useful for helping to build reusable components for handling data and conducting data analysis. From this point forward, we will use RStudio, rather than plain old R, in order to save and be able to reuse our work. Among other things, RStudio makes it easy to manage packages in R, and packages are the key to R's extensibility. In future chapters, we will be routinely using R packages to get access to specialized capabilities. These specialized capabilities come in the form of extra functions that are created by developers in the R community.

To summarize what we have discussed so far, you now know the following things about R (and about data):

- Installing and running R and RStudio on your computer.

- Typing commands on the R console.

- Using the c() function. Remember that c stands for combine, which just means to join things together. You can put a list of items inside the parentheses, separated by commas.

- A vector is the most basic form of data storage in R, and it consists of a list of items of the same type (such as numeric).

- A vector can be stored in a named location using the assignment arrow (a left-pointing arrow made of a dash and a less than symbol).

- You can get a report of the data object that is in any named location just by typing that name at the command line.

- Running a function, such as mean(), on a vector of numbers can transform them into something else. For example, mean() calculates the average, which is one of the most basic numeric summaries.

- sum(), mean(), and range() are all legal functions in R, whereas fish() is not.

- R is case sensitive.

# CASE STUDY: CALCULATING NPS

> **Case Key Points:**
> - **Define a vector that represents likelihood to recommend**
> - **Calculate the number of promoters and detractors—**
>   **Calculate net promoter score (NPS)**

Let's take what we have learned in this chapter about using vectors, and write some R code that can calculate an overall NPS for a vector of data. As we discussed in the Case Overview (in the previous chapter), NPS is a measurement that many businesses use to quickly summarize the attitudes of a set of consumers toward the product or service that the business offers. To calculate NPS, we need a vector of numbers where each number represents a *likelihood to recommend* an answer to the question: "on a scale of 1 to 10, how likely are you to recommend this [product or service]." For our case study, we have asked flyers how likely they were to recommend the airline that provided their flight.

Below is the code to calculate NPS (in the source code window). There are several ideas to note with this first real code example. First, note the use of comments (starting with the "#" character). Second, note that numPromoters was calculated differently than numDetractors. This was done to show two alternative ways to do the same calculation. We could have used either approach for the number of detractors or the number of promoters. Finally, make sure you understand the trick in summing a vector of TRUE and FALSE values. The reason this works is that R represents TRUE as "1" and FALSE as "0." As a result, calculating a sum on a vector of TRUE and FALSE values (often called Boolean values) results in a count of the number of TRUEs.

```
# define a test vector
ltr <- c(9,8,3,9,7,8,9,6,7,8,9)

# what is the range of the ltr vector
range(ltr)

# create a new vector with just the promoters
# then calculate the length of the promoters vector
promoters <- ltr[ltr>8]
numPromoters <- length(promoters)
```

```
# calculate the number of detractors by summing the
# elements that are less than 7
detractorsTrueFalse <- ltr < 7
numDetractors <- sum(detractorsTrueFalse)


# calculate NPS, based on the length of the ltr vector
# and the number of promoters and detractors
total <- length(ltr)
nps <- (numPromoters/total - numDetractors/total)*100


# output NPS
nps
```

This code is in the source code editor, so highlight all of the code and then click the "Run" button. After selecting and running the code, you should see, in the console window, the range of the ltr vector and the actual NPS value:

```
range(ltr)
[1]  6 9


nps
[1]  18.18182
```

## Chapter Challenges

1.  Use the c() function to add another family member's age onto the end of the myFamilyAges vector.

2.  Use square brackets subsetting to show just the first element of the myFamilyAges vector.

3.  Use square brackets subsetting together with the c() command to show just the odd numbered items from the myFamilyAges vector (i.e., just the first, third, and fifth items from this vector).

4.  Create a conditional expression that outputs a set of TRUEs and FALSEs. The expression should show TRUE when an element of the myFamilyAges vector is equal to 12.

5.  Using the code from the previous item, put an exclamation point in front of the conditional expression.

6.  Use the conditional expression from the previous item within the square brackets to select those elements of the myFamilyAges vector that are not equal to 12.

7.  **Power User:** Using the built-in Nile dataset, create a conditional expression that shows TRUE for every observation where the level of the Nile was over 900. Then use the sum() command to count up how many times the Nile dataset had observations higher than 900.

## Sources

https://en.wikipedia.org/wiki/R_(programming_language)
http://en.wikipedia.org/wiki/Joseph_J._Allaire
http://www.youtube.com/watch?v=7sAmqkZ3Be8
https://www.rstudio.com/products/rstudio/features/
http://a-little-book-of-r-for-biomedical-statistics.readthedocs.org/en/latest/src/installr.html
http://cran.r-project.org/
http://en.wikibooks.org/wiki/R_Programming
http://stackoverflow.com
http://www.statmethods.net/

## R Functions Used in This Chapter

| | |
|---|---|
| c() | Creates a vector. |
| min() | Finds the minimum number in a vector. |
| mean() | Finds the average for the entire vector. |
| range() | Finds the min and max values for the vector. |
| sum() | Finds the total for the entire vector. |
| length() | Finds the length (number of elements) of the vector. |

This text includes access to datasets and select student resources. To learn more, visit sagepub.com

# 2

# ROWS AND COLUMNS

# LEARNING OBJECTIVES

Explain what a dataframe is and how data are organized in a dataframe.

Create and use dataframes in R.

Access rows and columns in a dataframe.

Gain experience using the following R functions: c, data.frame, str, summary, head, tail.

Although we live in a three-dimensional world, where a box of cereal has height, width, and depth, it is a sad fact of modern life that pieces of paper, chalkboards, whiteboards, and computer screens are still only two dimensional. As a result, most of the statisticians, accountants, computer scientists, and engineers who work with lots of numbers tend to organize them in rows and columns. There's really no good reason for this other than that it makes it easy to fill a rectangular display with numbers. Rows and columns can be organized any way that you want, but the most common way is to have the rows be cases or instances, and the columns be attributes or variables. Take a look at this nice, two-dimensional representation of rows and columns in Table 2.1:

| TABLE 2.1 ● MYFAMILY DATAFRAME | | | |
|---|---|---|---|
| Name | Age | Gender | Weight |
| Dad | 43 | Male | 188 |
| Mom | 42 | Female | 136 |
| Sis | 12 | Female | 83 |
| Bro | 8 | Male | 61 |
| Dog | 5 | Female | 44 |

Pretty obvious what's going on, right? The top line, in bold, is not really part of the data. Instead, the top line contains the attribute or variable names. Note that computer scientists tend to call them attributes, whereas statisticians call them variables. Either term is OK. For example, age is an attribute that every living thing has, and you could count it in minutes, hours, days, months, years, or other units of time. Here we have the age attribute calibrated in years. Technically speaking, the variable names in the top line are metadata, or what you could think of as data about data. Imagine how much more difficult it would be to understand what was going on in that table without the metadata. There's lot of different kinds of metadata: variable names are just one simple type of metadata.

So if you ignore the top row, which contains the variable names, each of the remaining rows is an instance or a case. Again, computer scientists might call them instances, and statisticians might call them cases, but either term is fine. The important thing is that each row refers to an actual thing. In this case, all of our things are living creatures in a family. You could think of the Name column as case labels, in that each of these labels refers to one and only one row in our data. Most of the time when you are working with a large dataset, there is a number used for the case label, and that number is unique for each case (i.e., the same number would never appear in more than one row). Computer scientists sometimes refer to this column of unique numbers as a key. A key is very useful, particularly for matching things up from different data sources, and we will run into this idea again later. For now, though, just take note that the Dad row can be distinguished from the Bro row, even though they are both Males. Even if we added an Uncle row that had the same Age, Gender, and Weight as Dad, we would still be able to tell the two rows apart because one would have the name Dad and the other would have the name Uncle.

One other important note: look at how each column contains the same kind of data all the way down. For example, the Age column is all numbers. There's nothing in the Age column like Old or Young. This is a really valuable way of keeping things organized. After all, we could not run the mean() function on the Age column if it contained a little piece of text, like Old or Young. On a related note, every cell (i.e., an intersection of a row and a column, such as Sis's Age) contains just one piece of information. Although a spreadsheet or a word processing program might allow us to put more than one thing in a cell, a real data handling program will not. Finally, see that every column has the same number of entries, so that the whole forms a nice rectangle. When statisticians and other people who work with databases work with a data set, they expect this rectangular arrangement.

# CREATING DATAFRAMES

Now let's figure out how to get these rows and columns into R. One thing you will quickly learn about R is that there is almost always more than one way to accomplish a goal. Sometimes the quickest or most efficient way is not the easiest to understand. In this case, we will build each column one by one and then join them together. This is somewhat labor intensive, and not the usual way that we would work with a dataset, but it is easy to understand. First, we run this command to make the column of names:

```
myFamilyNames <- c("Dad","Mom","Sis","Bro","Dog")
```

One thing you might notice is that every name is placed within double quotes. This is how you signal to R that you want it to treat something as a string of characters rather than the name of a storage location. If we had asked R to use Dad instead of "Dad" it would have looked for a storage location (a data object or variable) named Dad. Another thing to notice is that the commas separating the different values are outside of the double quotes. If you were writing a regular sentence this is not how things would look, but for computer programming the comma can only do its job of separating the different values if it is not included inside the quotes. Once you have typed the line above, remember that you can check the contents of myFamilyNames by typing it on the next command line:

```
myFamilyNames
```

The output should look like this:

```
[1] "Dad" "Mom" "Sis" "Bro" "Dog"
```

Next, you can create a vector of the ages of the family members, like this:

```
myFamilyAges <- c(43, 42, 12, 8, 5)
```

Note that this is exactly the same command we used in Chapter 1, so if you have kept R running between then and now you would not even have to retype this command because myFamilyAges would still be there. Actually, if you closed R since working the examples from Chapter 1, you will have been prompted to save the workspace. If you did so, then R restored all of the data objects you were using in the last session. You can always check by typing myFamilyAges on a blank command line. The output should look like this:

```
[1] 43 42 12 8 5
```

Hey, now you have used the c() function and the assignment arrow to make myFamilyNames and myFamilyAges. If you look at the data table earlier in the chapter, you should be able to figure out the commands for creating myFamilyGenders and myFamilyWeights. In case you run into trouble, these commands also appear soon, but you should try to figure them out for yourself. After you type the command to create the new data object, you should also type the name of the data object at the command line to make sure that it looks the way it should. There are four variables, each with five values in it. Two of the variables are character data and the other two are integer data.

Before we show you the R code to create myFamilyGenders and myFamilyWeights, let's explore myFamilyAges some more. We now know that myFamilyAges is a variable, and that is a vector, which means it is a list of numbers. We can access each number individually, using square brackets. For example, if we want to output just the second element in myFamilyAges, we could do the following:

```
myFamilyAges[2]
[1]  42
```

Here are those two extra commands, to define myFamilyGenders and myFamilyWeights in case you need them:

```
myFamilyGenders <-
        c("Male","Female","Female","Male","Female")

myFamilyWeights <- c(188,136,83,61,44)
```

Look out! We're starting to get commands that are long enough that they break onto more than one line. In your code window you can type the code just as you see it above.

R knows what to do when it gets to the end of a line, but the command is not yet finished. If you type the first line above at the console and press enter, R will respond with a + to show that it is still expecting more input—you can type the second line and press enter again to run the whole command.

Now we are ready to tackle the dataframe. In R, a dataframe is a list (of columns), where each element in the list is a vector. Each vector is the same length, which is how we get our nice rectangular row and column setup, and generally each vector also has its own name. The command to make a dataframe is very simple:

```
myFamily <- data.frame(myFamilyNames, myFamilyAges,
        myFamilyGenders, myFamilyWeights)
```

The data.frame() function makes a dataframe from the four vectors that we listed. Notice that we have also used the assignment arrow to make a new stored location where R puts the dataframe. This new data object, called myFamily, is our dataframe. Once you have gotten that command to work, type myFamily at the command line to get a report back of what the dataframe contains.

```
myFamily
```

Here's the output you should see:

```
  myFamilyNames myFamilyAges myFamilyGenders
1          Dad           43            Male
2          Mom           42          Female
3          Sis           12          Female
4          Bro            8            Male
5          Dog            5          Female

  myFamilyWeights
1             188
2             136
3              83
4              61
5              44
```

This looks great. Notice that R has put row numbers in front of each row of our data. These are different from the output line numbers we saw in square brackets before, because these are actual indices into the dataframe. Later on, we will use row numbers like these to extract single rows or groups of rows from dataframes.

## EXPLORING DATAFRAMES

With a small data set like this one, only five rows, it is pretty easy just to take a look at all of the data. But when we get to a bigger data set, this won't be practical. We need to have other ways of summarizing what we have. The first method reveals the type of structure that R has used to store a data object.

```
str(myFamily)

'data.frame': 5 obs. of 4 variables:
$ myFamilyNames : Factor w/ 5 levels
                 "Bro","Dad","Dog",..: 2 4 5 1 3
$ myFamilyAges : num 43 42 12 8 5
$ myFamilyGenders: Factor w/ 2 levels
                 "Female","Male": 2 1 1 2 1
$ myFamilyWeights: num 188 136 83 61 44
```

OK, so the function str() reveals the structure of the data object that you name between the parentheses. In this case, we pretty well knew that myFamily was a dataframe because we just set that up in a previous command. In the future, however, we will run into many situations where we are not sure how R has created a data object, so it is important to know str() so that you can ask R to report what an object is at any time.

In the first line of output, we have the confirmation that myFamily is a dataframe as well as an indication that there are five observations (obs., which is another word that statisticians use instead of cases or instances) and four variables. After that first line of output, we have four sections that each begin with $. For each of the four variables, these sections describe the component columns of the myFamily dataframe object.

Each of the four variables has a mode or type that is reported by R right after the colon on the line that names the variable:

```
$ myFamilyGenders: Factor w/ 2 levels
```

For example, myFamilyGenders is shown as Factor. In the terminology that R uses, Factor refers to a special type of label that can be used to identify and organize groups of cases. R has organized these labels alphabetically and then listed out the first few cases (because our dataframe is so small it actually is showing us all of the cases). For myFamilyGenders we see that there are two levels, meaning that there are two different options: female and male. R assigns a number, starting with 1, to each of these levels, so every case that is Female gets assigned a 1 and every case that is Male gets assigned a 2 (Female comes before Male in the alphabet, so Female is the first Factor label, and gets a 1). If you have your thinking cap on, you might be wondering why we started out by typing in small strings of text, like Male, but then R has gone ahead and converted these small pieces of text into numbers that it calls Factors. The reason for this lies in the statistical origins of R. For years, researchers have done things like calling an experimental group Exp and a control group Ctl without intending to use these small strings of text for anything other than labels. So R assumes, unless you tell it otherwise, that when you type in a short string like Male that you are referring to the label of a group, and that R should prepare for the use of Male as a Level of a Factor. When you don't want this to happen you can instruct R to stop doing this by using the option on the data.frame() function stringsAsFactors=FALSE. We will look with more detail at options and defaults a little later on.

Phew, that was complicated! By contrast, our two numeric variables, myFamilyAges and myFamilyWeights, are very simple. You can see that after the colon the mode is shown as num (which stands for numeric) and that the first few values are reported:

```
$ myFamilyAges : num 43 42 12 8 5
```

Putting it all together, we have pretty complete information about the myFamily dataframe and we are just about ready to do some more work with it. We have seen firsthand that R has some kind of cryptic labels for things as well as some obscure strategies for converting this to that. R was designed for experts, rather than novices, so we will just have to take our lumps so that one day we can be experts, too.

Next, we will examine another very useful function called summary(). The summary command provides some overlapping information to the str command but also goes a little further, particularly with numeric variables. Here's what we get:

```
summary(myFamily)

myFamilyNames   myFamilyAges
Bro: 1          Min.     : 5
Dad: 1          1st Qu.  : 8
Dog: 1          Median   : 12
Mom: 1          Mean     : 22
Sis: 1          3rd Qu.  : 42
                Max.     : 43


myFamilyGenders    myFamilyWeights
Female: 3          Min.     : 44
Male  : 2          1st Qu.  : 61.0
                   Median   : 83.0
                   Mean     : 102.4
                   3rd Qu.  : 136.0
                   Max      : 188.0
```

In order to fit on the page properly, these columns have been reorganized somewhat. The name of a column/variable sits up above the information that pertains to it, and each block of information is independent of the others (so it is meaningless, for instance, that Bro: 1 and Min. happen to be on the same line of output). Notice, as with str(), that the output is quite different depending on whether we are talking about a factor, like myFamilyNames or myFamilyGenders, versus a numeric variable like myFamilyAges and myFamilyWeights. The columns for the Factors list out a few of the factor names along with the number of occurrences of cases that are coded with that factor. So, for instance, under myFamilyGenders it shows three females and two males. In contrast, for the numeric variables we get five different calculated quantities that help to summarize the variable. There's no time like the present to start to learn about what these are, so here goes:

- Min. refers to the minimum or lowest value among all the cases. For this dataframe, five is the age of Dog and it is the lowest age of all of the family members.

- 1st Qu. refers to the dividing line at the top of the first quartile. If we took all the cases and lined them up side by side in order of age (or weight) we could then divide up the whole into four groups, where each group had the same number of observations. Just like a number line, the smallest cases would be on the left with the largest on the right. If we're looking at myFamilyAges, the leftmost group, which contains one quarter of all the cases, would start with five on the low end (Dog) and would have eight on the high end (Bro). So the first quartile is the value of age (or another variable) that divides the first quarter of the cases from the other three quarters. Note that if we don't have a number of cases that divides evenly by four, the value is an approximation.

- Median refers to the value of the case that splits the whole group in half, with half of the cases having higher values and half having lower values. If you think about it, the median is also the dividing line that separates the second quartile from the third quartile.

- Mean, as we have learned before, is the numeric average of all of the values. For instance, the average age in the family is reported as 22.

- 3rd Qu. is the third quartile. If you remember back to the first quartile and the median, this is the third and final dividing line that splits up all of the cases into four equal-sized parts. You might be wondering about these quartiles and what they are useful for. Statisticians like them because they give a quick sense of the shape of the distribution. Everyone has the experience of sorting and dividing things up—pieces of pizza, playing cards into hands, a bunch of players into teams—and it is easy for most people to visualize four equal-sized groups and useful to know how high you need to go in age or weight (or another variable) to get to the next dividing line between the groups.

- Finally, Max is the maximum value and, as you might expect, displays the highest value among all of the available cases. For example, in this dataframe Dad has the highest weight: 188. Seems like a pretty trim guy.

Wow, that was a lot of info! Taking a step back, in statistics, central tendency is a key concept that is used to explain the center of a probability distribution. The most common measures of central tendency are the mean, median, and mode. Another key concept in statistics is dispersion (also called variability, scatter, or spread), which denotes how stretched or squeezed a distribution is. Common examples of measures of dispersion are the variance, standard deviation, and quartiles. As you just saw, in R we can use the summary function to get the first two measures of central tendency (mean and median) and the quartiles for a measure of dispersion. Mode refers to the most common occurring element in the dataset. We will explore mode, variance, and standard deviation in more detail later in this book.

While both the str and summary functions are very useful, sometimes we just want to look at a couple of rows in the dataframe. Previously, we typed myFamily at the command line and saw all the rows in the dataframe. However, if the dataframe has many rows, a better way is to use head or tail.

```
head(myFamily, 2)
myFamilyNames myFamilyAges myFamilyGenders myFamilyWeights
1            Dad           43            Male             188
2            Mom           42          Female             136


tail(myFamily, 2)
myFamilyNames myFamilyAges myFamilyGenders myFamilyWeights
4            Bro            8            Male              61
5            Dog            5          Female              44
```

You can see in the code that head() lists the first rows in the dataframe and tail() lists the last rows in the dataframe. The number of rows to display is the second argument to both head() and tail(). In our case, we used head() to show the first two rows and tail() to show the last two rows in the myFamily dataframe.

## ACCESSING COLUMNS IN A DATAFRAME

Just one more topic to pack in before ending this chapter: how to access the stored variables in our new dataframe? R stores the dataframe as a list of vectors and we can use the name of the dataframe together with the name of a vector to refer to each one using the $ to connect the two labels like this:

```
myFamily$myFamilyAges
[1] 43 42 12 8 5
```

If you're alert, you might wonder why we went to the trouble of typing out that big long thing with the $ in the middle, when we could have just referred to myFamilyAges as we did earlier when we were setting up the data. Well, this is a very important point. When we created the myFamily dataframe, we *copied* all the information from the individual vectors that we had before into a brand-new storage space. So now that we have created the myFamily dataframe, myFamily$myFamilyAges actually refers to a completely separate (but so far identical) vector of values. You can prove this to yourself very easily, and you should, by adding some data to the original vector, myFamilyAges:

```
myFamilyAges <- c(myFamilyAges, 11)
myFamilyAges
[1]  43 42 12 8 5 11


myFamily$myFamilyAges
[1]  43 42 12 8 5
```

Look very closely at the five lines above. In the first line, we use the c() command to add the value 11 to the original list of ages that we had stored in myFamilyAges (perhaps we have adopted an older cat into the family). In the second line, we ask R to report what the vector myFamilyAges now contains. Dutifully, on the third line above, R reports that myFamilyAges now contains the original five values and the new value of 11 on the end of the list. When we ask R to report myFamily$myFamilyAges, however, we still have the original list of five values only. This shows that the dataframe and its component columns/vectors is now a completely independent piece of data. We must be very careful, if we established a dataframe that we want to use for subsequent analysis, that we don't make a mistake and keep using some of the original data from which we assembled the dataframe.

Here's a puzzle that follows on from this question. We have a nice dataframe with five observations and four variables. This is a rectangular dataset, as we discussed at the beginning of the chapter. What if we tried to add on a new piece of data on the end of one of the variables? In other words, what if we tried something like the following command?

```
myFamily$myFamilyAges<-c(myFamily$myFamilyAges, 11)
```

If this worked, we would have a pretty weird situation: the variable in the dataframe that contained the family members' ages would all of a sudden have one more observation than the other variables: no more perfect rectangle! Try it out and see what happens. The error message you will receive shows how R approaches situations like this.

So what new skills and knowledge do we have at this point? Here are a few of the key points from this chapter:

- In R, as in other programs, a vector is a list of elements/things that are all of the same kind, or what R refers to as a mode. For example, a vector of mode numeric would contain only numbers.

- Statisticians, database experts, and others like to work with rectangular datasets where the rows are cases or instances and the columns are variables or attributes.

- In R, one of the typical ways of storing these rectangular structures is in an object known as a dataframe. Technically speaking, a dataframe is a list of vectors where each vector has the exact same number of elements as the others (making a nice rectangle).

- In R, the data.frame() function organizes a set of vectors into a dataframe. A dataframe is a conventional, rectangular data object where each column is a vector of uniform mode and having the same number of elements as the other columns in the dataframe. Data are copied from the original source vectors into a new storage area. The variables/columns of the dataframe can be accessed using $ to connect the name of the dataframe to the name of the variable/column.

- The str() and summary() functions can be used to reveal the structure and contents of a dataframe (as well as of other data objects stored by R). The str() function shows the structure of a data object, whereas summary() provides numerical summaries of numeric variables and overviews of non-numeric variables.

- The head() and tail() functions can be used to reveal the first or last rows in a dataframe.

- A factor is a labeling system often used to organize groups of cases or observations. In R, as well as in many other software programs, a factor is represented internally with a numeric ID number, but factors also typically have labels such as Male and Female or Experiment and Control. Factors always have levels, and these are the different groups that the factor signifies. For example, if a factor variable called Gender codes all cases as either Male or Female, then that factor has exactly two levels.

- Min and max are often used as abbreviations for minimum and maximum; these are the terms used for the highest and lowest values in a vector. Bonus: the range of a set of numbers is the maximum minus the minimum.

- The mean is the same thing that most people think of as the average. Bonus: the mean and the median are both measures of what statisticians call central tendency.

- Quartiles are a division of a sorted vector into four evenly sized groups. The first quartile contains the lowest-valued elements, for example, the lightest weights, whereas the fourth quartile contains the highest-valued items. Because there are four groups, there are three dividing lines that separate them. The middle dividing line that splits the vector exactly in half is the median. The term "first quartile" often refers to the dividing line to the left of the median that splits up the lower two quarters, and the value of the first quartile is the value of the element of the vector that sits right at that dividing line. Third quartile is the same idea, but to the right of the median and splitting up the two higher quarters. Bonus: quartiles is a measure of dispersion.

## CASE STUDY: CALCULATING NPS USING A DATAFRAME

Let's practice working with dataframes by setting up a small number of survey responses. Specifically, six surveys with likelihood to recommend (LTR) values of 9,9,7,6,8,7 and the type of travel also defined as follows: "Business travel", "Business travel", "Business travel", "Mileage tickets", "Personal Travel", "Personal Travel". Given this, is there a difference in net promoter score (NPS), comparing all the survey responses to just the business travel tickets?

In order to do this analysis, we first need to create a dataframe that represents the six surveys. Then, we can calculate and compare the overall NPS, with the NPS value for business travel tickets. Here is the code:

```
# Six surveys
ltr <- c(9,9,7,6,8,7)
TypeOfTravel <- c("Business travel",
     "Business travel", "Business travel", "Mileage",
     "Personal Travel", "Personal Travel")
survey <- data.frame(ltr, TypeOfTravel)

# look at the newly created dataframe
str(survey)

# Calculate number of promoters and detractors
numP <- sum(survey$ltr > 8)
numD <- sum(survey$ltr < 7)

# Now calculate NPS
total <- nrow(survey)
nps <- (numP/total - numD/total) * 100
nps

# do same analysis, but for the business travel tickets
busTravelDF <-
     survey[survey$TypeOfTravel=="Business travel",]

# Calculate number of promoters and detractors
numP <- sum(busTravelDF$ltr > 8)
numD <- sum(busTravelDF$ltr < 7)

# calculate NPS
total <- nrow(busTravelDF)
bus.nps <- (numP/total - numD/total) * 100
bus.nps
```

One thing to see is that, when we created the dataframe, R turned the type of travel into a factor. The code below shows this explicitly, and also shows the specific levels for the factor. A factor is a categorical variable with a defined set of choices. R stores a list of the categories and makes sure that every element of a factor variable fits one of those defined categories.

```
str(survey$TypeOfTravel)
 Factor w/ 3 levels "Business travel",..: 1 1 1 2 3 3

levels(survey$TypeOfTravel)
[1] "Business travel" "Mileage" "Personal Travel"
```

Finally, as we can see from the output (below), with this dataset, people flying with business class tickets have a higher NPS, as compared to all their passengers. Note that we would need to talk to SMEs to understand if this was expected, and if so, why.

```
nps
[1] 16.66667

bus.nps
[1] 66.66667
```

## Chapter Challenges

1. Use the c() command to create a new variable containing the favorite food of each family member. For example, your list could contain the entry "Pizza." Make sure that your new variable includes exactly five values. Call the new variable myFoods. Use str() on your new variable to show what kind of variable it is.

2. Add your new variable to the myFamily dataframe. If you were running the code while reading this chapter, you will have myFamilyNames, myFamilyAges, myFamilyGenders, and myFamilyWeights already available. Otherwise, you will need to type in the data for those variables as shown in this chapter.

3. Rerun the summary() function on myFamily to get descriptive information on all of the variables including your new variable. Take note of the data type for your new variable and report it in a comment.

4. Create an expression that shows a list of TRUE and FALSE values based on the age of each family member. The variable should be TRUE if myFamily$myFamilyAges is less than 40. In other words, your index will be TRUE for kids and FALSE for adults. Assign the results of your expression to a new variable called myIndex.

5. Use myIndex from the previous problem to show the favorite foods for each kid in the family. If you used the variable name suggested in problem 1, the expression would be myFamily$myFoods[myIndex].

6. The ! character is used to invert a set of Boolean values by changing each TRUE to FALSE and vice versa. Adapt the expression from the previous problem to show the favorite foods for each kid in the family.

## Sources

http://en.wikipedia.org/wiki/Central_tendency

http://en.wikipedia.org/wiki/Median

http://en.wikipedia.org/wiki/Relational_model

http://stat.ethz.ch/R-manual/R-devel/library/base/html/data.frame.html

http://www.burns-stat.com/pages/Tutor/hints_R_begin.html

http://www.khanacademy.org/math/statistics/v/mean-median-and-mode

## R Functions Used in This Chapter

| | |
|---|---|
| c() | Combines data elements together. |
| <- | Indicates an assignment arrow. |
| data.frame() | Makes a dataframe from separate vectors. |
| head() | Lists the first rows in a dataframe. |
| levels() | Shows the levels for a factor variable. |
| nrow() | Reports the number of rows for a dataframe. |
| str() | Reports the structure of a data object. |
| sum() | Calculates the sum of a set of values. |
| summary() | Reports data modes/types and a data overview. |
| tail() | Lists the last rows in a dataframe. |

This text includes access to datasets and select student resources. To learn more, visit sagepub.com

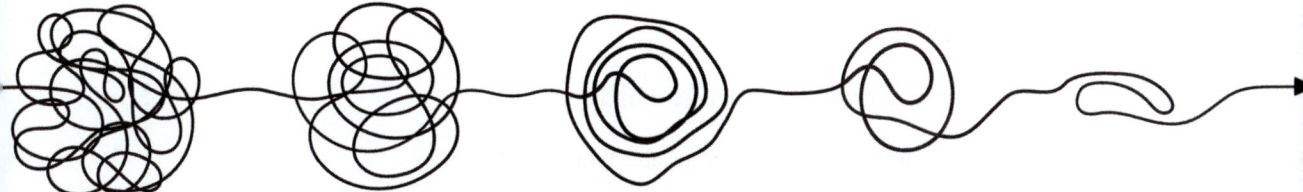

# 3

# DATA MUNGING

## LEARNING OBJECTIVES

Describe what data munging is.

Describe how to read a comma separated variable (CSV) data file.

Use RStudio to import data.

Select, filter, remove, and rename rows and columns.

Assess why data scientists need to be able to munge data.

Be able to use R packages, specifically Tidyverse.

Gain experience munging data in R using the base R functions well as with Tidyverse data manipulation functions.

Data munging is the process of turning a data set with a bunch of junk in it into a nice clean data set. Why is data munging required and why is it important? Well, often R does not guess correctly the structure of the dataset, or perhaps R reads a number or a date and thinks it is a simple string. Another issue might be that the data file might have additional information that is useful for humans, but not for R. If you think about it, so far we have only explored simple data sets that we created within R. Clearly, with larger data sets, it will not be practical to just type data into R. We need to be able to read in a large data set and use various tools in R to clean the data set and get it ready to analyze. This kind of work may not be glamorous, but it is a big part of data science, and very important to get right. If you're an aspiring data scientist, you may want a data munging coffee mug. Just visit the website http://www.cafepress.com/mf/17972553/i-love-munging_mugs. Money for the sale of mugs does not go to any authors of this book—we just like the mug!

## READING A CSV TEXT FILE

In this chapter, we will explore how to read in a dataset that is stored as a comma-delimited text file (known as a CSV file—which stands for comma-separated values) that needs to be cleaned up. As we will see in Chapter 7, there are many formats that we might have to be able to process to get data into R, but for now we will focus on a very common, human-readable file format. Our first real data set will be U.S. census data. The U.S. Census Bureau has stored population data in many locations on its website, with many interesting data sets to explore. We will use one of the simpler data sets available from the list shown at this website: www2.census.gov/programs-surveys/popest/tables/2010-2011/state/totals/

Click on the CSV link for nst-est2011-01.csv; you will either download a CSV or your browser will show a bunch of text information, with the first few lines looking like this:

```
table with row headers in column A and column headers in
rows 3 through 4. (leading dots indicate sub-parts),,,,,,,,,
"Table 1. Annual Estimates of the Population for the
United States, Regions, States, and Puerto Rico: April
1, 2010 to July 1, 2011",,,,,,,,, Geographic Area,"April 1,
2010",,Population Estimates (as of July 1)
,,,,,, ,Census,Estimates Base,2010,2011,,,,, United Sta
tes,"308,745,538","308,745,538","309,330,219","311,591,917",,,,,
Northeast,"55,317,240","55,317,244","55,366,108","55,521,598",,,,,
Midwest,"66,927,001","66,926,987","66,976,458","67,158,835",,,,,
South,"114,555,744","114,555,757","114,857,529","116,046,736",,,
,, West,"71,945,553","71,945,550","72,130,124","72,864,748",,,,,
.Alabama,"4,779,736","4,779,735","4,785,401","4,802,740",,,,,
```

Now, having the data in the browser isn't useful, so let's create some R code to read in this data set.

```
library(readr)

urlToRead <-
    "http://www2.census.gov/programs-surveys/popest/
    tables/2010-2011/state/totals/nst-est2011-01.csv"

testFrame <- read_csv(url(urlToRead))
```

The first command makes the readr package available. If you have not previously installed it, you will need to run install.packages("readr") first. The readr package provides a modern, straightforward way of reading in a CSV file and should be used in place of the older read.csv() function whenever possible. The second command just defines the location (on the web) of the file to load. Make sure that the URL is one continuous string with no spaces or line breaks. The third command reads the file, using the read_csv() command from the readr package. Note we also use the url() function, so R knows that the filename is a URL (as opposed to a local file on the computer).

Next, let's take a look at what we got back. We can use the str() function to create a summary of the structure of testFrame:

```
str(testFrame)
Classes 'spec_tbl_df', 'tbl_df', 'tbl' and 'data.frame':
   66 obs. of 10 variables:
 $ table with row headers in column A and column headers
   in rows 3 through 4. (leading dots indicate sub-parts):
   chr "Table 1. Annual Estimates of the Population for the
   United States, Regions, States, and Puerto Rico: April 1,
   "|__ truncated__ "Geographic Area" NA "United States"
   ...
 $ X2
   : chr NA "April 1, 2010" "Census" "308,745,538" ...
 $ X3
   : chr NA NA "Estimates Base" "308,745,538" ...
 $ X4
   : chr NA "Population Estimates (as of July 1)" "2010"
   "309,330,219" ...
 $ X5
   : num NA NA 2.01e+03 3.12e+08 5.55e+07 ...
 $ X6
   : logi NA NA NA NA NA NA ...
 $ X7
   : logi NA NA NA NA NA NA ...
 $ X8
   : logi NA NA NA NA NA NA ...
```

```
  $ X9
    : logi NA NA NA NA NA NA ...
  $ X10
    : logi NA NA NA NA NA NA ...
  - attr(*, "spec")=
  .. cols(
  ..    `table with row headers in column A and column head-
   ers in rows 3 through 4. (leading dots indicate sub-
   parts)` = col_character(),
  ..    X2 = col_character(),
  ..    X3 = col_character(),
  ..    X4 = col_character(),
  ..    X5 = col_number(),
  ..    X6 = col_logical(),
  ..    X7 = col_logical(),
  ..    X8 = col_logical(),
  ..    X9 = col_logical(),
  ..    X10 = col_logical()
  .. )
```

There is some stuff in that output reminiscent of that 1960s song entitled, "Na Na Hey Hey Kiss Him Goodbye." Setting aside all the NA NA NA NAs, however, the overall structure is 66 observations of 10 variables, signifying that the spreadsheet contained 66 rows and 10 columns of data. Note the "class" designations at the beginning of the output: 'spec_tbl_df', 'tbl_df', 'tbl' and 'data.frame'. The first three of these refer to an especially useful type of dataframe called a "tibble," which we will be using quite often in the rest of the book. The variable names that follow are pretty bizarre. Now you understand what data scientists mean by junk in their data. The first variable name is a complete mess:

```
table with row headers in column A and column headers in
rows 3 through 4. (leading dots indicate sub-parts): chr
"Table 1. Annual Estimates of the Population for the United
States, Regions, States, and Puerto Rico: April 1,
"|__ truncated__ "Geographic Area" NA "United States".
```

# REMOVING ROWS AND COLUMNS

It is clear that read_csv() treated the upper-left-most cell as a variable label, but was flummoxed by the fact that this was really just a note to human users of the spreadsheet (the variable labels, such as they are, came on lower rows of the spreadsheet). Subsequent variable names include X, X.1, and X.2: clearly the read_csv() function did not have an easy time getting the variable names out of this file.

The other worrisome finding from str() is that our data types are a strange mix of character, numeric, and logical data. Clearly, we have some work to do if we are to make use of these data. This is common for data scientists, in that sometimes the data are available, but need to be cleaned up before they can be used. In fact, data scientists often use the phrase "data munging" as the verb to describe the act of cleaning up data sets. So, let's get data munging!

First, let's review one way to access a list, a vector, or a dataframe. As mentioned briefly in Chapter 2, in R, square brackets allow indexing into a list, vector, or dataframe. For example, myList[3] would give us the third element of myList. Keeping in mind that a dataframe is a rectangular, two-dimensional structure, we can address any element of a dataframe with both a row and column designator: myFrame[4,1] would give the fourth row and the first column. A shorthand for taking the whole column of a dataframe is to leave the row index empty: myFrame[ , 6] would give every row in the sixth column. Likewise, a shorthand for taking a whole row of a dataframe is to leave the column index empty: myFrame[10, ] would give every column in the 10th row. We can also supply a list of rows instead of just one row, like this: myFrame[ c(1,3,5), ] would return rows 1, 3, 5 (including the data for all columns, because we left the column index blank).

Using this knowledge, we will use an easy trick to get rid of stuff we don't need. The Census Bureau put in header rows that we can eliminate like this:

```
testFrame <- testFrame[-1:-8,]
```

The minus sign used inside the square brackets refers to the index of rows that should be eliminated from the dataframe. So the notation -1:-8 gets rid of the first eight rows. We also leave the column designator empty so that we can keep all columns for now. We assign the result back to the same data object, thereby replacing the original with our new, smaller, cleaner version.

Next, we can see that of the 10 variables we got from read_csv(), only the first five are useful to us (the last five seem to be blank). How can we know that the last columns are not useful? Well, we can use the summary command we saw in Chapter 2 to explore testFrame, but only look at the summary for the last five columns:

```
summary(testFrame[,6:10])

    X.4            X.5            X.6            X.7            X.8
Mode:logical  Mode:logical  Mode:logical  Mode:logical  Mode:logical
NA's:58       NA's:58       NA's:58       NA's:58       NA's:58
```

Using the summary command, we can see those five columns are all just missing data (NA), and so can be removed without removing any data from testFrame. We can use the following command to keep the first five columns of the dataframe:

```
testFrame <- testFrame[,1:5]
```

Next, we can use the tail() function to show us the last five rows. These rows contain some Census Bureau notes that we don't need.

```
tail(testFrame,5)
```

Let's eliminate those rows like this:

```
testFrame <- testFrame[-54:-58,]
```

You may have noticed that we could have combined some of these commands, but for the sake of clarity we have done each operation individually. The result is a dataframe with 53 rows and five observations/columns. There is still one bad entry, row 52, that is all missing data. We can get rid of any rows that contain missing data using the complete.cases() command. This command analyzes each row of the dataframe and returns the value of TRUE for every row that has all of its data. We can use the output of complete.cases() as a row selector to indicate the rows we want to keep:

```
testFrame <- testFrame[complete.cases(testFrame), ]
```

# RENAMING ROWS AND COLUMNS

Now we are ready to perform a couple of data transformations. Let's rename the columns, using the colnames() function. If this function is just called with a dataframe as a parameter, then it returns the column names in the dataframe, as shown below:

```
colnames(testFrame)
[1] "table with row headers in column A and column headers
    in rows 3 through 4. (leading dots indicate sub-parts)"
[2] "X2"
[3] "X3"
[4] "X4"
[5] "X5"
```

We also can use colnames to update the column names in the dataframe. We do this by having the colnames function on the left side of the assignment statement. We set this up by creating a character vector called cnames and listing the five-column names we want using the c() command. Note that these column names are similar to those shown in the documentation that appeared in the first few lines of the CSV file:

```
cnames <- c("Region","Census","Estimate",
                        "April2010","April2011")
colnames(testFrame) <- cnames

colnames(testFrame)
[1] "Region" "Census" "Estimate" "April2010" "April2011"
```

We could also have named the columns one at a time and if we worked really hard we probably could have extracted the census bureau's names from the original CSV file rather than typing them in by hand. This points out one of the good (and bad) aspects of using R—there is usually more than one way to get something done. Sometimes there is a better way and sometimes there is a quick way!

# CLEANING UP THE ELEMENTS

Next, we can change formats and data types as needed. We can remove the dots in front of the state names very easily with the gsub() command, which replaces all occurrences of a pattern with a new string. The "g" in gsub() stands for global substitution. We want all the dots to be removed, so the gsub() function is perfect because it will repeat the substitution process for every row.

```
testFrame$Region <- gsub("\\.","",
                         as.character(testFrame$Region))
```

The two backslashes in the string expression above are called escape characters and they force the dot that follows to be treated as a literal dot rather than as a wildcard character. The dot on its own is a wildcard that matches one instance of any character.

Next, we can use gsub() and as.numeric() to convert the data contained in the population columns to usable numbers. Remember that those columns are now represented as character data and what we are doing is taking out the commas and making the digits that remain into numeric data:

```
testFrame$Census <- as.numeric(gsub(",",
                       "", testFrame$Census))
testFrame$Estimate <- as.numeric(gsub(",",
                        "", testFrame$Estimate))
testFrame$April2010 <- as.numeric(gsub(",",
                        "", testFrame$April2010))
```

In each of these cases, we are combining two steps: on the inside of the expression on the right, we are using gsub() to remove the commas, whereas on the outside of that we are running as.numeric() to do the type coercion. You may note that we did not need to convert the April2011 column because that came in as numeric without any intervention by us. We can confirm that the new columns on the dataframe are numeric by using str() to accomplish this.

```
str(testFrame)
Classes 'tbl_df', 'tbl' and 'data.frame': 52 obs. of 5
   variables:
$ Region   : chr  "Alabama" "Alaska" "Arizona" "Arkansas"
   ...
$ Census   : num  4779736 710231 6392017 2915918 37253956 ...
$ Estimate : num  4779735 710231 6392013 2915921 37253956 ...
$ April2010: num  4785401 714146 6413158 2921588 37338198 ...
$ April2011: num  4802740 722718 6482505 2937979 37691912 ...
```

Perfect! Let's take a look at the first five rows:

```
head(testFrame,5)
# A tibble: 5 x 5
  Region          Census Estimate April2010 April2011
  <chr>            <dbl>    <dbl>     <dbl>     <dbl>
1 Alabama        4779736  4779735   4785401   4802740
2 Alaska          710231   710231    714146    722718
3 Arizona        6392017  6392013   6413158   6482505
4 Arkansas       2915918  2915921   2921588   2937979
5 California    37253956 37253956  37338198  37691912
```

These data look great! Notice that we've spent a lot of time just conditioning the data we got in order to make it usable for later analysis. Herein lies a key lesson: an important, and sometimes time-consuming, aspect of what data scientists do is to make sure that data are fit for the purpose to which they are going to be used. We had the convenience of importing a nice dataset directly from the web with one simple command, and yet getting those data actually ready to analyze took several additional steps.

# SORTING AND SUBSETTING DATAFRAMES

Now that we have a real data set, let's do something with it! How about showing the states with the largest increase in population? We can do this by first calculating the change in population and adding that column to our dataframe. We then can list only the states with above-average changes. Finally, we can order this dataframe by the new column in the dataset. Wow that's a lot to do, but let's break it down step by step. The first step is to create a new column, which is the increase in population:

```
testFrame$Change <- testFrame$April2011 -
                            testFrame$April2010
```

Next, we need to calculate the average change, across all the states.

```
avgChange <- mean(testFrame$Change)
```

The third step is to make a new dataframe that only has the states with an above-average increase. This part is a bit tricky and takes advantage of a powerful feature of R. We can supply a list of TRUE and FALSE to represent each row, and then R will only return the rows that have a TRUE value. Here's a miniature example: myFrame[ c(TRUE, TRUE, FALSE, TRUE), ] would return rows 1, 2, 4 (but not row 3). This would include the data for all columns, because we left the column index blank. This line of code will produce the data for the above-average states:

```
testFrame[testFrame$Change > avgChange, ]
# A tibble: 11 x 6
  Region           Census    Estimate  April2010  April2011  Change
  <chr>            <dbl>     <dbl>     <dbl>      <dbl>      <dbl>
1 Arizona          6392017   6392013   6413158    6482505    69347
2 California        37253956  37253956  37338198   37691912   353714
3 Colorado         5029196   5029196   5047692    5116796    69104
4 Florida          18801310  18801311  18838613   19057542   218929
5 Georgia          9687653   9687660   9712157    9815210    103053
6 New York         19378102  19378104  19395206   19465197   69991
7 North Carolina   9535483   9535475   9560234    9656401    96167
```

| | | | | | | |
|---|---|---|---|---|---|---|
| 8 | Tennessee | 6346105 | 6346110 | 6357436 | 6403353 | 45917 |
| 9 | Texas | 25145561 | 25145561 | 25253466 | 25674681 | 421215 |
| 10 | Virginia | 8001024 | 8001030 | 8023953 | 8096604 | 72651 |
| 11 | Washington | 6724540 | 6724540 | 6742950 | 6830038 | 87088 |

Using this command, only the TRUE rows (where the state has an above-average population) will be shown. We get all columns because we left the column index blank. Let's store that dataset for later use:

```
growingStates <-
        testFrame[testFrame$Change > avgChange, ]
```

Now we just have to sort. Although we can sort a vector easily with the sort() command, sorting a dataframe requires a new function called order(). If we want to sort a dataframe, what we provide is an ordered list that shows which rows should appear in which order. We use this list together with R's built-in square bracket notation to put the rows in order. As a reminder, we can supply a list of row indices to access any dataframe: myFrame[ c(3, 2, 1), ] would return the first three rows in reverse order. We tell order() which variable we want to sort on, and it will give back a list of row indices in the order we requested. Putting it all together yields this command:

```
growingStates <-
        growingStates[order(growingStates$Change), ]
```

Working our way from the inside to the outside of the expression above, we want to sort in the order of the growingStates$Change column. We wrap this column reference inside the order() function. The order() function will spit out a list of row indices that reflects the change in the population of the states. We use the square brackets notation to address the rows in the growingStates dataframe, taking all of the columns by leaving the index after the comma empty. Finally, we stored sorted dataframe back into growingStates. Let's take a look at our results by looking at the first five rows:

```
head(growingStates, 5)
# A tibble: 5 x 6
  Region      Census    Estimate  April2010 April2011 Change
  <chr>       <dbl>     <dbl>     <dbl>     <dbl>     <dbl>
1 Tennessee   6346105   6346110   6357436   6403353   45917
2 Colorado    5029196   5029196   5047692   5116796   69104
3 Arizona     6392017   6392013   6413158   6482505   69347
4 New York    19378102  19378104  19395206  19465197  69991
5 Virginia    8001024   8001030   8023953   8096604   72651
```

Well, that is very close, but it's showing the states in increasing order of the Change column. We can redo the sort, but tell R to sort largest to smallest. We tell R we want the largest populations first by adding an additional parameter to the order function, stating that it should be in decreasing order, which is done as follows:

```
growingStates <- growingStates[
        order(growingStates$Change, decreasing = TRUE), ]
head(growingStates, 5)
# A tibble: 5 x 6
  Region          Census    Estimate  April2010 April2011 Change
  <chr>           <dbl>     <dbl>     <dbl>     <dbl>     <dbl>
1 Texas           25145561  25145561  25253466  25674681  421215
2 California       37253956  37253956  37338198  37691912  353714
3 Florida          18801310  18801311  18838613  19057542  218929
4 Georgia          9687653   9687660   9712157   9815210   103053
5 North Carolina   9535483   9535475   9560234   9656401   96167
```

That's it! We can see Texas has the highest increase, followed by California. Of course, this is only for the states with above-average population changes.

## TIDYVERSE: AN INTRODUCTION AND HOW TO INSTALL THE PACKAGE

The "tidyverse" is a collection of R packages that helps reorganize and visualize data. Developed by RStudio's chief scientist Hadley Wickham, the tidyverse uses a consistent approach to build an ecosystem of packages. The tidyverse consists of many packages to help with data manipulation (e.g., dplyr), working with data types (e.g., stringr for strings) and data visualization (e.g., ggplot2). If you remember the mention earlier in the chapter of "tibbles," that is a very useful data class from the tidyverse. In short, the tidyverse helps us do data manipulation by providing easy to use functions to sort, filter, and summarize datasets. We will explore the dataframe manipulation functions now, and later, explore tidyverse visualizations via the use of ggplot2.

Let's get started. To install the tidyverse package, look in the lower-right-hand pane of RStudio. There are several tabs there, and one of them is Packages. Click on this and you will get a list of every package that you already have available in your copy of R (it might be a short list) with checkmarks for the ones that are ready to use. It is unlikely that tidyverse is already on this list, so click on the button that says Install Packages. This will give a dialog that looks like what you see on the screenshot above. Type the beginning of the package name in the appropriate area, and RStudio will start to prompt you with matching choices. Finish typing "tidyverse" or choose it from the list. There might be a checked box for Install Dependencies, and if so leave this checked. In some cases, an R package will depend on other packages and R will install all of the necessary packages in the correct order if it can. Once you click the Install button in this dialog, you will see some commands running on the R console (the lower-left pane). Generally, this works without a hitch and you should not see any warning messages. Once the installation is complete, you will see tidyverse added to the list in the lower-right pane (assuming you have clicked the Packages tab). One last step is to click the checkbox next to it. This runs the library() function on the package, which prepares it for further use.

Another way to install tidyverse is to go into an R session and type:

```
install.packages("tidyverse")
```

Note that, just as through RStudio, this can take a while, but is only required once on your machine. Then, to load tidyverse into your current R session, simply type

```
library(tidyverse)
```

You will need to do the library command any time you clean up/clear your environment. Of course, that raises the question what is an environment and how do I clear it? As you might remember, we discussed the environment in Chapter 1, where we discussed

RStudio. As a quick reminder, it is the computer memory where all your variables, such as the vector "familyAges," are stored, and can be cleared via the environment tab in RStudio.

Note that by installing and using tidyverse (either of the ways we just explained), we get easy access to most of the tidyverse packages, so we don't typically have to worry about which package we are using.

# SORTING AND SUBSETTING DATAFRAMES USING TIDYVERSE

Let's explore how we would show the five states that are above average with respect to their population change. The following code accomplishes roughly the same moves as we did above, but this time using tidyverse functions. A little later we will show a more compact way of using the same tidyverse functions.

Similar to before, we first calculate the Change using mutate(). Then, we pull the Change column (pull creates a vector from the column), and use that vector to calculate the mean change in population. After that, we create a new dataframe called growingStates, where we filter (create a subset) where the only rows in the dataframe are those with Change greater than the avgChange. The growingStates dataframe is next sorted via arrange, in descending order of the Change column. The slice command slices the dataset down to the first five rows. Finally, we select the columns we want to display.

```
testFrame <- mutate(testFrame,
                    Change = (April2011 - April2010))
avgChange <- mean( pull(testFrame, Change))
growingStates <- filter(testFrame, Change > avgChange)
growingStates <- arrange(growingStates, desc(Change))
growingStates <- slice(growingStates, 1:5)
select(growingStates, Region, April2011, Change)
# A tibble: 5 x 3
```

```
  Region          April2011 Change
  <chr>              <dbl>  <dbl>
1 Texas           25674681 421215
2 California      37691912 353714
3 Florida         19057542 218929
4 Georgia          9815210 103053
5 North Carolina   9656401  96167
```

You're probably looking at that code and thinking it's not much better than before, or maybe it's even a bit more confusing than the original code. Now let's add a cool tidyverse feature called "pipes" and see how it looks. The pipe operator (two percent signs with a greater than in the middle: %>% ) passes data from one command to the next one, enabling us to chain the commands together without the need for intermediate variables. Below is the code—which we think is much easier to read and follow:

```
testFrame %>%
  mutate(Change =(April2011 - April2010)) %>%
  filter(Change > mean(Change)) %>%
  arrange(desc(Change)) %>%
  slice(1:5) %>%
  select(Region, April2011, Change)
# A tibble: 5 x 3
  Region          April2011 Change
  <chr>              <dbl>  <dbl>
1 Texas           25674681 421215
2 California      37691912 353714
3 Florida         19057542 218929
4 Georgia          9815210 103053
5 North Carolina   9656401  96167
```

The result of the final command shows the top five growth states on the console. It is also possible to take the result of the final command and assign it to a new object with a right-pointing assignment arrow as shown here:

```
testFrame %>%
  mutate(Change = (April2011 - April2010)) %>%
  filter(Change > mean(Change)) %>%
```

```
    arrange(desc(Change)) %>%
    slice(1:5) %>%
    select(Region, April2011, Change) -> growingStates
```

In summary, the tidyverse provides a powerful set of data munging tools to help work with dataframes, which in turn allow us to get out data into a format that is usable for later analyses. Although we have explored some common challenges related to data munging, there are other challenges we did not get to in this chapter. One classic challenge is working with dates, in that there are many formats such as a year with two or four digits, and dates where the month or day is listed first. Another challenge often seen is when we want to combine or merge two datasets. Combining them can be useful, for example, when you have a dataset with an account identifier and a transaction history. A related dataset might have the same identifier along with information about a customer such as name an address. Later in the book, we will explore commands that help us join datasets on key fields like customer identifiers.

## CASE STUDY: READING, CLEANING, AND EXPLORING A SURVEY DATASET

```
Case Key Points:
-   Read a CSV file that has survey data
-   Clean the dataset (survey) by removing NAs
-   Explore likelihood to recommend (LTR), calculating the
    mean of LTR across different groups with in the survey
```

Let's explore a small airline survey dataset. First, we need to read in the small airline survey CSV datafile, using the Import Dataset within RStudio. Now that we have a survey dataset, let's explore it by first calculating the overall mean likelihood to recommend (noted as LTR in this dataset). The code to begin this analysis is below:

```
# Use RStudio's data import:
#   File -> Import Dataset -> From Text (readr...)
#   the following code was created
library(readr)
smallSurvey <- read_csv("smallSurvey.csv")
```

```
#Explore the small survey using str
str(smallSurvey)
```

You have used str() to examine data structures before. The tidyverse provides an alternative to str() called glimpse(), which we use below. In looking at the output (below), we note one issue with the dataset. Specifically, there are some NAs, at least one for Type.of.Travel, and at least one as an LTR value.

```
glimpse(smallSurvey)
Observations: 500
Variables: 5
$ Type.of.Travel <chr> NA, "Business…
$ Airline.Status <chr> "Blue", "Blue", "Blue", …
$ Gender         <chr> "Female", "Female", "Male"…
$ Age            <dbl> 22, 45, 39, 64, 26, 50, 36, …
$ LTR            <dbl> 8, NA, 8, 7, 9, 7, 10, 4, 5, …
mean(smallSurvey$LTR)
[1] NA
```

In order to clean this dataset, we will remove any survey without an LTR response, because without an LTR response, that survey will not be helpful in understanding drivers for improving LTR. However, we will leave NAs in the other columns since it's not clear what to do (e.g., if someone doesn't provide their age). This strategy will also allow us to keep as much of the data as possible (specific later calculations could remove NAs in a different column if needed).

So, we will remove the NA from the LTR column as well as the mean by the type of travel. We can also explore the average likelihood to recommend based on the age of the passenger. However, to make the age analysis easier to understand, we round the age to the nearest decade. Finally, within our age analysis, we can sort the output based on the average likelihood to recommend for that decade (in descending order). Note that when running the summarize, we use "n()" to show the number of instances in that specific group. The code to do the rest of this analysis is below:

```
#Remove NAs from the LTR column
smallSurvey <- filter(smallSurvey, !is.na(LTR))
```

```
#What is the average Likelihood.to.recommend?
mean(smallSurvey$LTR)
[1] 7.290581


#The mean Likelihood.to.recommend by Type.of.Travel
smallSurvey %>%
  group_by(Type.of.Travel) %>%
  summarize(mean=mean(LTR), count=n())


# A tibble: 4 x 3
 Type.of.Travel    mean count
 <chr>            <dbl> <int>
1 NA                  7     1
2 Business travel  8.14   303
3 Mileage tickets  8.05    39
4 Personal Travel  5.46   156
```

In the code below, where we analyze LTR by age, we can see a definite trend where those over 70, on average, have a lower likelihood to recommend.

```
smallSurvey %>%
  mutate(Age, Age=round(Age, digits=-1)) %>%
  group_by(Age) %>%
  summarize(mean=mean(LTR), count=n()) %>%
  arrange(desc(mean))
# A tibble: 7 x 3
   Age mean count
 <dbl> <dbl> <int>
1    50  8.12    85
2    30  8.06    79
3    40  7.82   120
4    20  6.75    57
5    60  6.67    79
6    70  6       36
7    80  5.67    43
```

Although there is clearly more analysis that would need to be done before understanding the drivers of higher and lower net promoter score (NPS), this high-level analysis starts to provide some clues that could be explored.

## Chapter Challenges

1. The built-in R data set called "InsectSprays" has 72 rows and two columns. Use the str() command on this dataset to reveal this information and the names and data types of the columns.

2. Sticking with InsectSprays, use the square brackets notation to select the second observation in the second column.

3. Continuing to work with InsectSprays, use the $ notation to select the spray column. Run the head() command on this column.

4. Use a pipe (%>%) to connect the InsectSprays dataframe to the select() command. Use select() to choose the count variable from the dataframe. All 72 values of the count variable should display on the console.

5. Connect the result of the previous item to the filter() command with a pipe, using count > 20 as the filtering expression.

6. Connect the result of the previous item to the glimpse() command with another pipe. Describe the result in a comment.

7. Create your own CSV file on your computer. Include five rows and two columns of data. The first column should be called Number and should contain the numbers 1 through 5. The second column should be called Letter and should contain the letters A through E. Make sure to put the letters in double quotes. Read your CSV into R and use str() to examine the resulting dataframe.

8. Use a pipe and the arrange() function with the desc() function to sort your dataframe in descending order of the Number column.

9. Go to the lendingClub website (https://www.lendingclub.com/info/download-data.action), download a CSV file and then read in the file using read_csv(). Then, clean up the data set, making sure all the columns have useful information. This means you must explore the dataset to understand what needs to be done! One trick to get you started is that you might need to skip one or more lines (before the header line in the CSV file). There is a skip parameter that you can use in your read_csv() command.

## Sources

http://www2.census.gov/programs-surveys/popest/tables/2010-2011/state/totals
https://s3.amazonaws.com/assets.datacamp.com/blog_assets/Tidyverse+Cheat+Sheet.pdf

## R Functions Used in This Chapter

arrange()        Returns the sorted observations in a dataset in ascending or descending order based on one of its variables.*

c()              Concatenates/combines items into a vector.

colnames()       Gets/sets the column names for the dataframe.

desc()           Organizes a vector in descending order—useful with arrange().*

filter()         Returns a selected subset of rows in a dataframe, based on evaluating a condition.*

glimpse()        Shows basic information about a vector or dataframe.*

group_by()       Organizes data into groups.*

gsub()           Substitutes one string for another.

head()           Shows the first few observations in a vector or dataframe.

library()        Makes a package available for use.

mean()           Calculates the arithmetic average of a set of numbers.

mutate()         Returns a new dataframe with an updated or new column.*

order()          Returns the indices in the order of the vector supplied.

read_csv()       Reads in a CSV file.*

select()         Returns a subset of columns within a dataframe.*

slice()          Returns a subset of row within a dataframe.*

summary()        Summarizes a vector or dataframe.

summarize()      Summarizes data with selected functions.*

tail()           Shows the last few observations in a vector or dataframe.

url()            Makes sure R knows that the file is a URL (not a local file).

*Indicates a tidyverse function.

This text includes access to datasets and select student resources. To learn more, visit sagepub.com

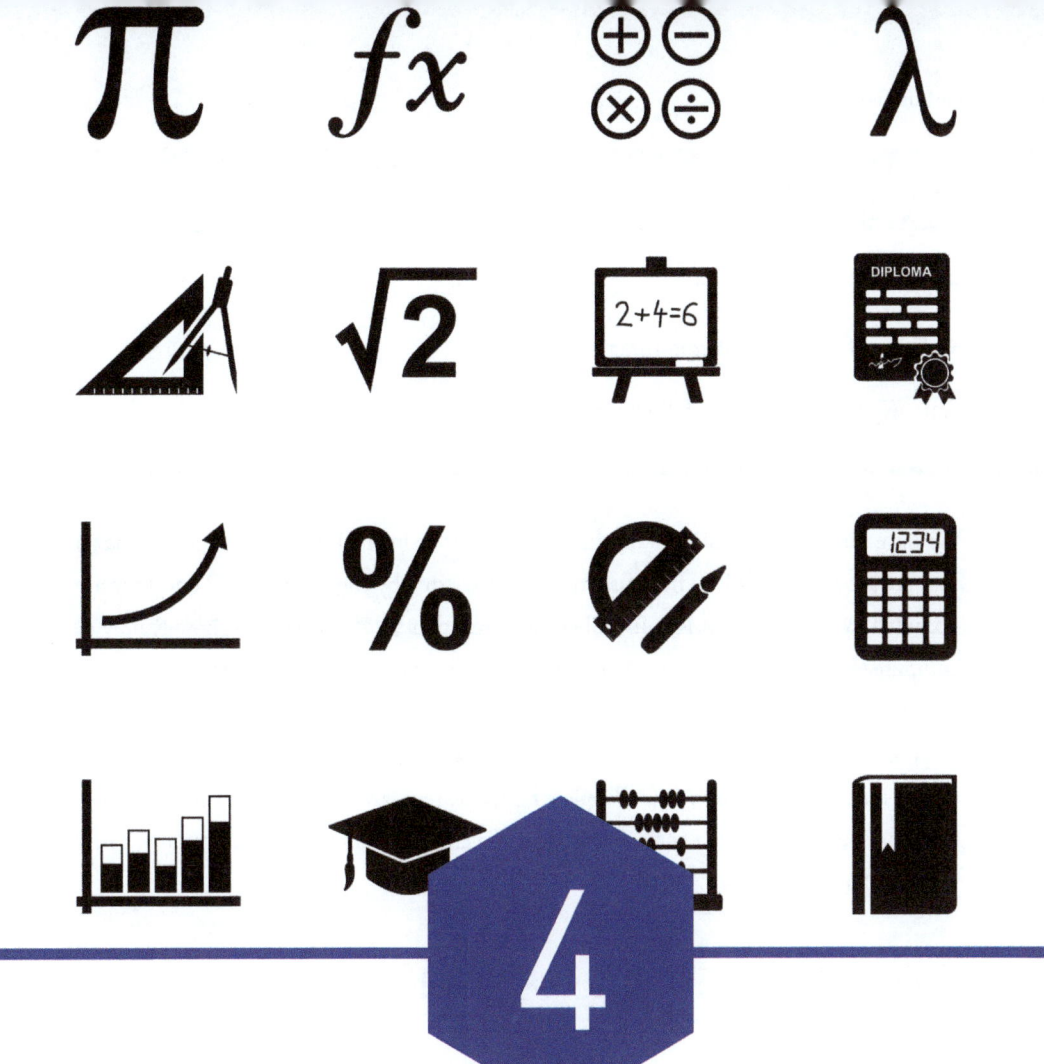

# 4

# WHAT'S MY FUNCTION?

## LEARNING OBJECTIVES

Explain the benefits of writing and using functions.

Write, verify, and use custom functions in R.

Gain experience using the following R capabilities: function and return.

We have already been using many functions, such as mean(), hist(), min(), and max(), that are provided with R. Those functions were written by the creators of R and they are provided by default when R is installed, meaning that we don't have to show R how to compute the mean, min, or max with detailed code—we can simply call these functions instead. Because these functions are already written and are known to R, we can simply call them in our R code whenever we need them, without worrying about how they work on the inside. Super convenient! People who use R regularly often create their own new functions so that they can achieve that same level of convenience by automating a new process or a calculation.

## WHY CREATE AND USE FUNCTIONS?

This idea of automation highlights the two most important reasons that people use functions. The first reason is reusability. Once a function is defined, it can be used over and over again. We can invoke the same function many times in our program and this saves us work. The second reason is a concept from software engineering known as abstraction. Abstraction means that after a function has been created, we don't need to remember the details of how it works in order to use it. Once a function has been created and is known to R, we only need to know the following four things:

1. The name of the function;

2. Its purpose (i.e., why and when we would want to use it);

3. What arguments must be supplied to the function; and

4. What kind of result the function returns.

We have already used arguments a little while ago with functions such as mean() and sum(). For these two functions, we had to supply a vector of numbers to either of these functions so that they could do the necessary calculations. However, we did not talk about the concept of arguments then—we just used the function. "Argument" (also known as "parameter") is a term used by computer scientists to refer to some information that is sent into a function to help it do its job. For mean(), we passed in one argument, the vector on which we should calculate the mean. Other functions take more than one argument. One such function is head(), which can takes two arguments. The second argument to head() is optional, which means that R only needs it in certain circumstances and/or R can supply a default value if the user does not pass in a value.

## CREATING FUNCTIONS IN R

Most functions in R have a common set of components: a name, some optional arguments, some code to run, and an optional return value. Figure 4.1 shows a simple example of a function and points out its key components.

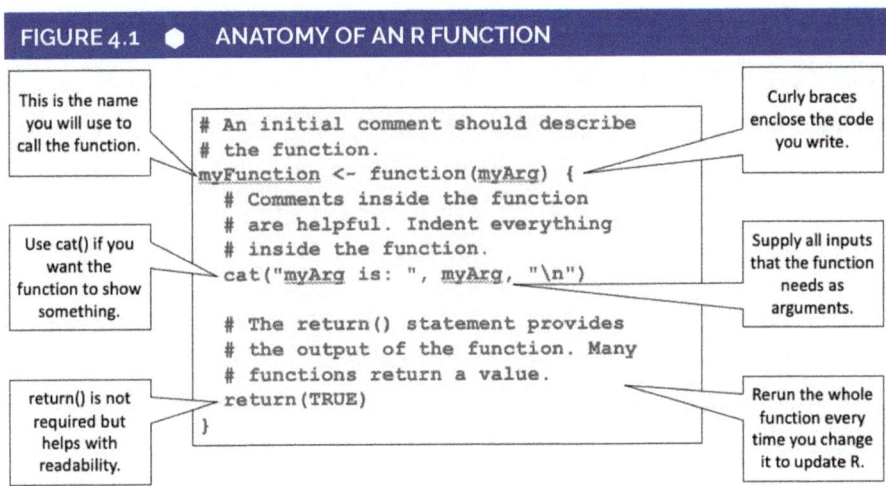

**FIGURE 4.1 ● ANATOMY OF AN R FUNCTION**

This is the name you will use to call the function.

Curly braces enclose the code you write.

```
# An initial comment should describe
# the function.
myFunction <- function(myArg) {
    # Comments inside the function
    # are helpful. Indent everything
    # inside the function.
    cat("myArg is: ", myArg,  "\n")

    # The return() statement provides
    # the output of the function. Many
    # functions return a value.
    return(TRUE)
}
```

Use cat() if you want the function to show something.

Supply all inputs that the function needs as arguments.

return() is not required but helps with readability.

Rerun the whole function every time you change it to update R.

Figure 4.1 illustrates the features a function must have. The name of this function is "myFunction" and that is what we would use to call it. The function has one argument, called "myArg," that we can use to supply some information to the function. The function does a little bit of work—specifically it contains a call to cat() that will print some information on the console. Finally, the function ends with a return statement: in this case we return the same thing every time, and that is the value TRUE. Other than serving as an illustration, this is not a useful function, so let's build our own function to perform a simple but useful trick: alphabetically sort the column names of a dataframe. As a start, click in that R source code pane (or create a new R Script file) and type the following:

```
# Create a function to sort a dataframe's columns
# alphabetically by column name
colNameSort <- function(inputDF) {
}
```

You have just created your first function in R! As we previously mentioned, a function is a bundle of R code that can be used over and over again without having to retype it. Other programming languages also have functions: sometimes they are called "procedures" or "subroutines," although these terms can have slightly different meanings in other languages. We have called our function colNameSort(). Our new function has just one argument, called inputDF. We have not said anything about what inputDF will contain and R is flexible about that.

Note the curly braces that are used on final two lines above. These curly braces hold together all of the code that goes in our function. At this time, we have no code inside the curly braces, so our function doesn't actually do anything. By the way, this is a very common way to develop code, building up a little at a time, each time more closely approximating what we want the completed function to do.

Let's test out what we have accomplished so far. We can use the built-in mtcars dataframe to test our function. In the lower-left-hand pane of RStudio you will notice that we have a regular R console running. You can type commands into this console, just as we did in Chapters 2 and 3 just using R. So let's try out our new colNameSort() function:

```
colNameSort(mtcars)
Error: could not find function "colNameSort"
```

Oops! R doesn't know about our new function yet. We typed our colNameSort() function into the code window, but we didn't tell R about it. If you look above the code window, you will see a few small buttons on a tool bar. One of the buttons looks like a little right-pointing arrow with the word "Run" next to it. First, use your mouse to select all of the code for colNameSort(), all the way to the last curly brace. Then click the Run button. You will immediately see the same code appear in the R console window just below. If you have typed everything correctly, there should be no errors or warnings. Now R knows about the colNameSort() function and is ready to use it. Let's try the following code again:

```
colNameSort(mtCars)
NULL
```

This did exactly what we expected: nothing! Actually, we got a return value of NULL, which is R's way of saying that nothing was returned. Now we are ready to add some code to our function:

```
# Create a function to sort a dataframe's columns
# alphabetically by column name
colNameSort <- function(inputDF) {
  nameList <- colnames(inputDF) # What are the names?
  cat(nameList)
}
```

Let's see what this code does. First, don't forget to select the code again and click on the Run button. Then, in the R console, try the colNameSort() function again:

```
colNameSort(mtcars)
mpg cyl disp hp drat wt qsec vs am gear carb
```

Pretty easy to see what the new code does, right? We called the colnames() function, and that returned a list of the column names from the dataframe that we specified in the argument. Then we used cat() to report that list of names to the console. Now let's build a little more code:

```
# Create a function to sort a dataframe's columns
# alphabetically by column name
colNameSort <- function(inputDF) {
  nameList <- colnames(inputDF) # What are the names?
  nameList <- sort(nameList)
  cat(nameList)
}
```

Don't forget to select all of this code and Run it before testing it out. This time we extract the column names from the dataframe supplied as the argument and we sort the list alphabetically before we display the list on the console:

```
colNameSort(mtcars)
am carb cyl disp drat gear hp mpg qsec vs wt
```

Let's now rearrange the columns in the dataframe, using the sorted list. This turns out to be incredibly easy, because the square brackets notation will happily accept a list of the column names in whatever order we want to supply them. In this next version of our function, we are also using cat() to report the list of column names from our new copy of the dataframe, which we have named outputDF:

```
# Create a function to sort a dataframe's columns
# alphabetically by column name
colNameSort <- function(inputDF) {
  nameList <- colnames(inputDF) # What are the names?
  nameList <- sort(nameList)
  outputDF <- inputDF[nameList]
  cat(colnames(outputDF))
}
```

Let's retest this version of the function. Don't forget to select and rerun the code to make sure that R is aware of our new version:

```
colNameSort(mtcars)
am carb cyl disp drat gear hp mpg qsec vs wt
```

There's one last step that we need to take. Remember that most functions have a return value. In this case we want to return the outputDF that we created in the most recent version of our function:

```
# Create a function to sort a dataframe's columns
# alphabetically by column name
colNameSort <- function(inputDF) {
  nameList <- colnames(inputDF) # What are the names?
  nameList <- sort(nameList)
  outputDF <- inputDF[nameList]
  return(outputDF)
}
```

Let's do one final test of the function, this time by checking that the return value was what we expected. Don't forget to select and rerun the code to make sure that R is aware of our new version:

```
alphaMtcars <- colNameSort(mtcars)
str(alphaMtcars)
'data.frame': 32 obs. of 11 variables:
 $ am: num 1 1 1 0 0 0 0 0 0 0...
 $ carb: num 4 4 1 1 2 1 4 2 2 4...
 $ cyl: num 6 6 4 6 8 6 8 4 4 6...
 $ disp: num 160 160 108 258 360...
 $ drat: num 3.9 3.9 3.85 3.08 3.15 2.76 3.21 3.69...
 $ gear: num 4 4 4 3 3 3 3 4 4 4...
 $ hp: num 110 110 93 110 175 105 245 62 95 123...
 $ mpg: num 21 21 22.8 21.4 18.7 18.1 14.3 24.4...
 $ qsec: num 16.5 17 18.6 19.4 17...
 $ vs: num 0 0 1 1 0 1 0 1 1 1...
 $ wt: num 2.62 2.88 2.32 3.21 3.44...
```

Perfect! The dataframe that our function returned has all of the original columns from mtcars, but now they are in alphabetical order!

# DEFENSIVE CODING

R is a very flexible language that allows users and coders to use a variety of types of data in many different situations. One unfortunate side effect of this flexibility, however, is that there are no rules enforced for what kind of data an argument must receive. We designed colNameSort() to accept a dataframe as input and to return a dataframe as its output. What if we gave our function something it did not expect? Let's try it with the built-in Titanic data, which is stored as a table rather than a dataframe:

```
colNameSort(Titanic)
 [1] NA NA
```

Wow, that's weird. Instead of returning a dataframe, our function did something strange and returned two NA values. Perhaps more importantly, we got no warning or notification that the function failed to do its job. Let's add a feature to our function that checks to make sure that the incoming argument is a dataframe:

```
# Create a function to sort a dataframe's columns
# alphabetically by column name
colNameSort <- function(inputDF) {

  if (is.data.frame(inputDF)) {
    nameList <- colnames(inputDF) #What are the names?
    nameList <- sort(nameList)
    outputDF <- inputDF[nameList]
    return(outputDF)
  } else {
    warning("Expecting a dataframe as input.\n")
    return(NULL)
  }
}
```

We've added an if-else statement to this function. The if statement uses is.data.frame() to test whether the input is what we expect. This returns TRUE if inputDF is a dataframe and FALSE if it is anything else. If TRUE, we proceed with the same code as before. The else statement handles the FALSE condition and you can see that we generate a warning message explaining what happened and return a NULL instead of an output dataframe. Let's test this with the built-in Titanic data:

```
colNameSort(Titanic)
NULL
Warning message:
In colNameSort(Titanic):
  Expecting a dataframe as input.
```

Depending upon how mission critical your function is, you can include any number of tests of the assumptions that the function makes. R even provides ways of trying out a piece of code and grabbing any error that the code generates before it causes any problems. RStudio also offers debugging features that allow you to step through code one line at a time to see where something goes wrong. For now, our functions will be simple enough that we won't need these advanced features.

Two other points deserve our attention. First, notice that when we created our own function we had to do some testing to make sure it ran the way we wanted it to. This is a common situation when working on anything related to computers, including spreadsheets, macros, and pretty much anything else that requires precision and accuracy. Second, we introduced new functions in this exercise, such as warning() and return(). Where did these come from and how did we know where to find them and how to use them? R has so many functions that it is very difficult to memorize them all. There's almost always more than one way to do something, as well. It can be quite confusing to create a new function if you don't know all of the ingredients. This is where the data science community comes in. Search online and you will find dozens of instances where people have probably tried to solve similar problems to the one you are solving, and you will also find that they have posted the R code for their solutions. These code fragments are free to borrow and test. In fact, learning from other people's examples is a great way to expand your horizons and learn new techniques.

Second, we went through several steps to create our colNameSort() function and we are still not sure that it will work perfectly on every variation of data it might encounter. Maybe someone else has already solved the same problem. If they did, we might be able to find an existing package to add onto our copy of R to extend its functions. In the next section, let's next take a look at how to install packages and find out about new functions.

# INSTALLING A PACKAGE TO ACCESS A FUNCTION

The dplyr package contains several very helpful functions for helping to manipulate data. Let's write another implementation of our colNameSort() code using the select() function from the dplyr package. To install this package, look in the lower-right-hand pane of RStudio. There are several tabs there, and one of them is "Packages." Click on this and you will get a list of every package that you already have available in your copy of R (it might be a short list) with checkmarks for the ones that are ready to use. If you followed along with Chapter 3, you probably have the dplyr package already installed. This was a side effect of installing the tidyverse. If not, then click on the Install button at the top of the window and type dplyr in the dialog box. There might be a checked box for Install Dependencies, and if so, leave this checked. In some cases, an R package will depend on other packages and R will install all of the necessary packages in the correct order if it can. Once you click the Install button in this dialog, you will see some commands running on the R console (the lower-left pane). Generally, this works without a hitch and you should not see any warning messages. Once the installation is complete you will see dplyr added to the list in the lower-right pane (assuming you have clicked the Packages tab). One last step is to click the check box next to it. This runs the library() function on the package, which prepares it for further use. Instead of the point-and-click strategy above, you could also use the install.packages() and library() functions in the code window or on the console command line.

Let's look at the help for the select() function. There are three ways to get the help: (1) type help("select") at the command line; (2) use a shortcut for the same command by typing ?select at the command line; or (3) click on the name dplyr in the Packages window and navigate to the function you want using the topical index. The help shows that the long title for the function is "Select/rename variables by name" and the brief description of the function is "Choose or rename variables from a tbl. select() keeps only the variables you mention." The help page goes on to describe the inputs and outputs of the function and gives some examples of how to use it. These help pages can be a little hard to read at first, but the more you practice this skill the more "helpful" you will find these pages to be. We're going to use the select() function together with sort() and names() to rebuild our colNameSort() function. Try this code:

```r
# To access the select() function we need dplyr
library(dplyr)

colNameSort <- function(inputDF) {
  inputDF %>% select(sort(names(.)))
}
```

The first line, a call to library() is often included by R programmers when they are about to use a function from a new library. There is no harm in running the library() command on a package more than once and this practice serves as a reminder to readers of the code that the specified package is needed for the code to work. Here, with library(dplyr), we are making it possible to use the select() function.

You will notice that we have shrunk our function down to a single line of code by piping inputDF into our select() expression. There are a couple of advanced features at work here. The innermost expression, names(.), returns a list of the column names from the data structure that was received from the pipe. The dot in that expression is just a shortcut for, "that thing we just got," and it can be used whenever needed within a pipe expression. So when we run sort(names(.)) we get a nice alphabetical list of the column names from the inputDF. We are supplying that list to select() so that it will know what columns to keep and the order in which to present them. Finally, we are taking advantage of a handy feature of R functions, which is that, without a call to return(), the output value of the function is whatever the last expression in the function produced. It would also have been fine to enclose that whole line of code—inputDF %>% select(sort(names(.)))—inside the return() function, but it looks a little nicer without that extra clutter.

You should test our new function by calling colNameSort() with mtcars or another dataframe. Also retest with the Titanic tables or some other non-dataframe object to see what happens. Remember that we did not build any special error handling code for this version of colNameSort() so it will be interesting to see how the function handles a data structure that it was not designed for.

To recap, by creating our own function we learned that functions take arguments as their inputs and provide a return value as their output. A return value can be any R data object, so it could be a single number (technically a vector of length one) or it could be a set of values of the same type (a vector) or even a more complex data object like a list or a dataframe. We can write and reuse our own functions, which we will do again later in the book, or we can use other people's functions by installing their packages and using the library() function to make the contents of the package available.

## CASE STUDY: CREATING AND USING A CALCULATE NPS FUNCTION

> **Case Key Points:**
> - Define a function that accepts a vector of likelihood-to-recommend values, and returns the NPS value.
> - Test the function to ensure it is working correctly.
> - Use the function to explore the survey dataset.

We can use the code that we created in Chapter 1, which calculates a net promoter score (NPS) for a vector of data, to create a function to do this calculation. This way, we can calculate NPS as easily as calculating the mean of likelihood to recommend values. As we discussed in the Case Overview (and in Chapter 1), NPS is a measurement that many businesses use to quickly summarize the attitudes of a set of consumers toward the product or service that the business offers. To calculate NPS, we need a vector of numbers where each number represents a *likelihood to recommend* answer to the question: "On a scale of 1 to 10, how likely are you to recommend this [product or service]?" Below is the code that creates a function to calculate NPS (in the source code window):

```
# CalcNPS function - calculate a net promoter score
# ltr - a vector of likelihood-to-recommend values
# neutral - the range, below which someone
# is considered a detractor and above which
# someone is considered a promoter (default is 7 to 8)

CalcNPS <- function(ltr, neutral=c(7,8)) {

  # create a new vector with just the promoters
  # then calculate the length of the promoters vector
  promoters <- ltr[ltr > max(neutral)]
  numPromoters <- length(promoters)
```

```
# calculate the number of detractors
detractorsTrueFalse <- ltr < min(neutral)
numDetractors <- sum(detractorsTrueFalse)

# calculate NPS, based on the length of LTR
# and the number of promoters and detractors
total <- length(ltr)
nps <- (numPromoters/total -
        numDetractors/total)*100

#return the NPS value
return(nps)
}
```

Put this code in the code editing window and don't forget to highlight all of the code and then click the "Run" button. After selecting and running the code, you can test the function with the following values:

```
ltr <- c(9,8,3,9,7,8,9,6,7,8,9)
CalcNPS(ltr)
[1] 18.18182
```

One of the things you may have noticed about this function is that it takes two arguments. The second argument, called neutral, can be used to specify the neutral zone where a respondent is considered neither a promoter nor a detractor. To make the function easier to use we have supplied a default value in the function specification. In the first line of the function where we mention neutral, we also use an equal sign and provide the default range of 7 to 8 (this range is consistent with our initial consideration of NPS scores in Chapter 2). Providing these default values means that when the function is called, it is optional to provide values for neutral. If the call to CalcNPS() does not provide the neutral argument, then 7 and 8 will be used. Other values can be provided to override these defaults. Next let's reuse the CalcNPS function to explore the small survey dataset, that we started to explore in Chapter 3. First, as a reminder, we will redo the analysis of the mean values for likelihood to recommend (LTR) by type of travel:

```
library(readr)
smallSurvey <- read_csv("smallSurvey.csv")

#remove the NAs from the LTR column
smallSurvey <- filter(smallSurvey, !is.na(LTR))

#The mean Likelihood.to.recommend by Type.of.Travel
smallSurvey %>%
  group_by(Type.of.Travel) %>%
  summarize(mean=mean(LTR), count=n())

# A tibble: 4 x 3
  Type.of.Travel    mean count
  <chr>            <dbl> <int>
1 NA                   7     1
2 Business travel   8.14   303
3 Mileage tickets   8.05    39
4 Personal Travel   5.46   156
```

In the code above, we read in the survey from the CSV file, filter out all of the rows that have missing data for LTR and then calculate a mean for each type of travel. The output shows that there is one row that has a missing code for type of travel, but we can ignore that for now. Based on this analysis, we can see that, collectively, people who do personal travel have lower LTR, as compared to business and mileage rewards travelers. Next, let's calculate net promoter scores (NPS), first for all of the respondents and then broken down by group. Don't forget that by leaving out the neutral argument, we are accepting the defaults of 7 and 8 for the neutral zone:

```
CalcNPS(smallSurvey$LTR)
[1] 9.018036

smallSurvey %>%
    group_by(Type.of.Travel) %>%
    summarize(nps=CalcNPS(LTR), count=n())
# A tibble: 4 x 3
  Type.of.Travel    nps count
  <chr>            <dbl> <int>
```

```
1 NA                     0       1
2 Business travel      40.3    303
3 Mileage tickets      30.8     39
4 Personal Travel     -57.1    156
```

These results show that NPS is highest for business travelers and lowest for personal travelers. In fact, the value for personal travelers is negative, indicating that there are more detractors than promoters in this group. Obviously, this is a finding that bears further exploration: figuring out how to improve the customer experience for personal travelers should be a priority for this airline.

## Chapter Challenges

1. Create a new function that accepts one argument and returns that same argument. In addition to your new function, include at least one line of code that tests the function.

2. Create a new function that accepts one argument. The function should test whether the argument is numeric or not, using the is.numeric() function. If the incoming argument is numeric, the function should return that number. If the incoming argument is not numeric, the function should return NULL. In addition to your new function, include at least one line of code that tests the function.

3. Write and test a new function called MyVectorInfo() that takes as input a vector and displays the key characteristics of the vector, namely the min, max, and mean of the vector. Hint: You will need to use cat() inside of your function so that it can produce output on the console. Make sure that you test the incoming vector to ensure that it is numeric. In addition to your new function, include at least one line of code that tests the function.

4. Create a function that accepts the name of a CSV file as its input. The function should read in that file using read_csv() and then remove any rows that have missing data. Hint: The complete.cases() function can help you find all of the rows that have no missing data. The function should return a dataframe. Make sure to test your function on a CSV file such as the smallSurvey.csv file used in this chapter.

5. Modify the function from the previous problem so that it uses na.omit() rather than comple.cases() to help remove cases with missing data.

6. Modify the function from the previous problem so that it uses pipes and the filter() command to remove rows with NA values.

7. Create a function that reads and cleans the population dataset using the repairs that were accomplished in Chapter 3.

8. Modify the CalcNPS() function developed in this chapter so that the total count of cases used in the NPS calculation is the sum of all of the promoters and detractors (rather than the total number of cases). Test your code by redoing the calculations by type of travel shown in this chapter.

## Sources

https://www.cs.utah.edu/~zachary/computing/lessons/uces-10/uces-10/node11.html

## R Functions Used in This Chapter

| | |
|---|---|
| cat() | Concatenate and print information to the console (or a file). |
| colnames() | Displays a lit of the column names in a dataframe. |
| filter() | Selectively returns rows from a dataframe based on a criterion (dplyr package). |
| function() | Creates a new function. |
| group_by() | Divides a dataframe into groups (dplyr package). |
| is.data.frame() | Tests whether a data object is a dataframe. |
| n() | Shows the number of observations in a group (dplyr package). |
| names() | Produces a list of names of the elements of a structure such as a dataframe. |
| return() | Completes a function by returning a value. |
| select() | Chooses a subset of a dataframe (dplyr package). |
| sort() | Sorts the input vector alphabetically or numerically. |
| str() | Shows the structure of a data object. |
| sum() | Calculates the total of a numeric vector. |
| summarize() | Produces summary statistics for groups (dplyr package). |
| warning() | Produces a warning message on the console. |

This text includes access to datasets and select student resources. To learn more, visit sagepub.com

   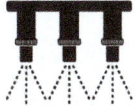

# 5

# BEER, FARMS, PEAS, AND THE USE OF STATISTICS

## LEARNING OBJECTIVES

Explain why we need to sample from a population.

Compare the basic concepts of descriptive statistics such as mean, median, range, mode, variance, and standard deviation.

Use histograms to explain the concepts of central tendency and measures of dispersion.

Understand and be able to generate a normal distribution.

Gain experience using the following R functions: mean, median, var, sd, hist, rnorm.

## HISTORICAL PERSPECTIVE

The end of the 1800s and the early 1900s were a time of astonishing progress in mathematics and science. Given enough time, paper, and pencils, scientists and mathematicians of that age imagined that just about any problem facing humankind—including the limitations of people themselves—could be measured, broken down, analyzed, and made more efficient. Four Englishmen who epitomized both this scientific progress and these idealistic beliefs were Francis Galton, Karl Pearson, William Sealy Gosset, and Ronald Fisher.

First on the scene was Francis Galton, a half-cousin to the more widely known Charles Darwin. Galton was a gentleman of independent means who studied Latin, Greek, medicine, and mathematics, and who made a name for himself as an explorer in Africa. He created the statistical concepts of correlation and regression. He applied statistical methods to the study of differences among people and the influence of inheritance, which led to him coining the term "nature vs. nurture." Alas, he also introduced the concept of eugenics. Eugenics was the idea that the human race could be improved through selective breeding. Galton studied heredity in peas, rabbits, and people, and concluded that certain people should be paid to get married and have children because their offspring would improve the human race. These repugnant ideas were later used, most notably by the Nazis during the Second World War, as a justification for killing people based on their ethnic backgrounds.

For all his theorizing, Galton was not much of a mathematician, but he had a partner, Karl Pearson, who is often credited with founding the field of mathematical statistics. Pearson refined the math behind correlation and regression and did a lot else besides to contribute to our modern abilities to manage numbers. Like Galton, Pearson was a proponent of eugenics, but he also is credited with inspiring some of Einstein's thoughts about relativity and was an early advocate of women's rights.

Next to the statistical party was William Sealy Gosset, a wizard of math and chemistry. It was his expertise with chemistry that led the Guinness Brewery in Dublin, Ireland, to hire Gosset after he finished college. The brewery was on the lookout for ways of making batches of beer more consistent in quality. Gosset developed what we now refer to as small sample statistical techniques—ways of generalizing from the results of a relatively few observations. Of course, brewing a batch of beer is time-consuming and expensive, so to draw conclusions from experimental methods applied to just a few batches, Gosset had to figure out the role of chance in determining how each batch of beer turned out. Guinness frowned on academic publications, so Gosset published his results under the modest pseudonym, "Student." If you ever hear someone discussing the "Student's t-Test," that is where the name came from.

Last but not least was Ronald Fisher, another mathematician who also studied the natural sciences, in his case biology and genetics. Unlike Galton, Fisher was not a gentleman of independent means. In fact, during his early married life he and his wife struggled as subsistence farmers. One of Fisher's later jobs was at an agricultural research farm called Rothamsted Experimental Station. Here, he analyzed variations in crop yield that led to his development of a widely used statistical technique known as the analysis of variance. Fisher also pioneered the area of experimental design, which includes factors, levels, experimental groups, and control groups that we discuss elsewhere in the book.

Of course, these four are not the only mathematicians and researchers to have made substantial contributions to practical statistics, but they are notable with respect to the applications of statistics to the other sciences, engineering, and agriculture. In some ways, these guys were the grandfathers of data science.

# SAMPLING A POPULATION

One of the critical distinctions woven throughout the work of these four is between the sample of data that you have available to analyze versus the larger population of cases that might or do exist. When Gosset ran batches of beer at the brewery, he knew that it was impractical to run every possible batch of beer with every possible variation in recipe and preparation. Gosset knew that he had to run a few batches, describe what he had found, and then generalize or infer what might happen in future batches. This is a fundamental aspect of working with all kinds of data: **whatever data you have, there's always more out there**. There's data that you might have collected by changing the way things are done or the way things are measured. There's future data that hasn't been collected yet and might never be collected. There's data that is inaccessible to us because of the expense or impracticality of collecting it. There's even data that we might have gotten using the exact same strategies we did use, but that would have come out subtly different just due to randomness. Whatever data you have, it is just a snapshot, or sample, of what might be out there. This means that we can never, ever 100% trust the data we have. We must remember that there is always uncertainty in data. A lot of the power and goodness in statistics comes from the techniques that people like Fisher developed to help us understand that uncertainty and to know when to guard against putting too much stock in what a sample of data has to say. Remember that while we can always *describe* the sample of data we have, the real trick is to *infer* what the data could mean when generalized to the larger population of data that we don't have. This is the key distinction between descriptive and inferential statistics.

# UNDERSTANDING DESCRIPTIVE STATISTICS

We have already encountered several descriptive statistics in Chapters 2, 3, and 4, but for the sake of practice here they are again, this time with the more-detailed definitions:

> The mean (technically the arithmetic mean), is a measure of central tendency that is calculated by adding together all of the observations and dividing by the number of observations.

> The median is another measure of central tendency, but one that cannot be directly calculated. Instead, you make a sorted list of all of the observations in the sample,

then go halfway up that list. Whatever the value of the observation is at the halfway point, that is the median.

The range is a measure of dispersion—how spread out a bunch of numbers in a sample are—calculated by subtracting the lowest value from the highest value.

The mode is another measure of central tendency. The mode is the value that occurs most frequently in a sample of data. Like the median, the mode cannot be directly calculated. You just have to count up how many of each number there are and then pick the category that has the most.

To this list we should add two more descriptive statistics that you will encounter in a variety of situations. The first is the variance. Like the range, the variance describes the "spread" of a sample of numbers. Unlike the range, though, which uses just two numbers to calculate dispersion, the variance is obtained by including all of the numbers in a simple calculation that compares each value to the mean.

Let's do some simple calculations with family ages, which was also used earlier in the book. Here's the code we used to create the vector, as well as the calculation of the mean, which you can see is 22.

```
myFamilyAges <- c(43, 42, 12, 8, 5)
mean(myFamilyAges)
[1] 22
```

Now take a close look at the following table:

**TABLE 5.1 ◆ CALCULATION OF THE VARIANCE**

| Who | Age | Age–Mean | (Age–Mean)$^2$ |
|---|---|---|---|
| Dad | 43 | 43 – 22 = 21 | 21 × 21 = 441 |
| Mom | 42 | 42 – 22 = 20 | 20 × 20 = 400 |
| Sis | 12 | 12 – 22 = –10 | –10 × –10 = 100 |
| Bro | 8 | 8 – 22 = –14 | –14 × –14 = 196 |
| Dog | 5 | 5 – 22 = –17 | –17 × –17 = 289 |
| | | Total: | 1426 |
| | | Total/4: | 356.5 |

Table 5.1 shows the calculation of the variance, which begins by obtaining the deviations from the mean and then squaring them (multiplying each one times itself) to take care of the negative deviations (e.g., –14 from the mean for Bro). We add up all of the squared deviations and then divide by the number of observations to get a kind of average squared deviation. It was not a mistake to divide by 4 instead of 5—the reasons for this comes from a concept called the "degrees of freedom" that affects calculations on samples of data. The result of this calculation is the variance, a very useful mathematical concept that appears often in statistics. While variance is mathematically useful, it is not easy to describe to other people. For instance, in this example we are looking at the 356.5 squared-years of deviation from the mean. Who measures anything in squared years? Squared feet maybe, but that's a different discussion. So, to address this weirdness, statisticians have also provided us with the next descriptive statistic, the standard deviation.

The standard deviation is another measure of dispersion and a cousin to the variance. The standard deviation is simply the square root of the variance, which puts us back in regular units like years. In the example above, the standard deviation would be about 18.88 years (rounding to two decimal places, which is plenty in this case). Let's have R calculate the variance and the standard deviation for us:

```
var(myFamilyAges)
[1] 356.5

sd(myFamilyAges)
[1] 18.88121
```

## USING DESCRIPTIVE STATISTICS

This was a pretty boring example and not super useful for the rest of the chapter, so let's analyze our previously discussed U.S. population dataset. Since we will use this dataset many times, let's create a readCensus() function. In the code below, note how comments are used (anything after the #), so that if we go back to this code, we can understand what was done. Note that we are also now using tidyverse functions and pipes. As you can see, for this function, the key tidyverse dataframe manipulation functions were *select,* which selects or removes columns, *slice,* which selects or removes rows, *mutate,* which updates/creates a new column, which renames a column, and *str_replace_all,* which replaces all the occurrences of specified characters. You can also see how the dataframe is passed via pipes (rather than being the first element of each of the functions). If some of this code does not make sense, go back to the chapter on data munging (Chapter 3) and review how we worked on this data set to get the data file into a useful dataframe, and then created a subset of the dataframe.

```
#read in the census data set
readCensus <- function(urlToRead) {

  #read the data from the web
  testFrame <- read_csv(url(urlToRead))

  #use pipes to keep updating testFrame
  testFrame <- testFrame %>%

    #only keep the first 5 columns
    select(1:5) %>%

    #convert columns to numbers & rename columns
    mutate(april10census=Numberize(testFrame$X2))%>%
    mutate(april10base=Numberize(testFrame$X3)) %>%
    mutate(july10pop=Numberize(testFrame$X4)) %>%
    mutate(july11pop=Numberize(testFrame$X5)) %>%

    #remove the old columns that have been updated
    select(-X2, -X3, -X4, -X5) %>%

    #remove the first 8 rows ('header information')
    slice(-1:-8) %>%

    #rename the first column to StateName
    rename(stateName=1) %>%

    #remove the last rows (tail info to see)
    slice(c(-52, -54:-n())) %>%

    #remove the 'dot' from the state name
    mutate(stateName=
```

```
        str_replace_all(stateName, "\.",""))

  #remove the old row names, which are now confusing
  rownames(testFrame) <- NULL
  return(testFrame)
}
```

Note that we used an additional custom function, Numberize(). The code appears below. This is because some of the code to remove commas and spaces from a string, and then convert it into a number, was sufficiently repetitive that it seemed to make sense to create a function call to do it—and it also might be useful with other R data munging that we might need to do. A lesson from our chapter on functions is that it is important and valuable to try to automate as many of these steps as possible. So when we saw that numbers had gotten stored as factor labels, we moved to create a general function that would convert these to numbers. Not only does this save a lot of future typing, but it also prevents mistakes from creeping into our processes.

```
# Numberize() - Gets rid of commas and other junk and
# converts to numbers
# Assumes that the inputVector is a list of data that
# can be treated as character strings
Numberize <- function(inputVector)
{
  # Get rid of commas and spaces
  inputVector<-str_replace_all(inputVector,"[,]","")

  #convert to a number and then return that number
  return(as.numeric(inputVector))
}
```

Now that we have the two custom functions we need, let's call them to read in and process the census data:

```
library(tidyverse)
USregionPops <- readCensus(
  "http://www2.census.gov/programs-surveys/popest/
   tables/2010-2011/state/totals/nst-est2011-01.csv")
USregionPops$april10census[1:3]
[1] 4779736 710231 6392017
```

Note that you will get some warning messages when you run this code because of the way the incoming CSV file is formatted. This would be a great moment to practice your skills from Chapter 2 by using the str() and summary() functions on our new data object called USregionPops. Now we're ready to have some fun with a good-sized list of numbers. Here are the basic descriptive statistics on the population of the U.S. regions:

```
mean(USregionPops$april10census)
[1] 6009064

median(USregionPops$april10census)
[1] 4085220

mode(USregionPops$april10census)
[1] "numeric"

var(USregionPops$april10census)
[1] 4.575791e+13

sd(USregionPops$april10census)
[1] 6764460
```

Some great summary information there, but wait—a couple things look funny. First, the mode() function has returned the data type of our vector of numbers instead of the statistical mode. The basic R package does not have a statistical mode function! This is partly due to the fact that the mode is only useful in a very limited set of situations. If you ever need the mode, there are simple code examples online that show how to create your own function.

Second, the variance is reported as 4.656676e+13. This is the first time that we have seen scientific notation in R. If you haven't seen scientific notation before, the way you interpret it is to imagine 4.656676 multiplied by 10,000,000,000,000 (also known as 10 raised to the 13th power). You can see that this is 10 trillion, a huge and unwieldy number, and that is why scientific notation is used. If you would prefer not to type all of that into a calculator, another trick to see what number you are dealing with is just to move the decimal point 13 digits to the right.

## USING HISTOGRAMS TO UNDERSTAND A DISTRIBUTION

Other than these two issues, we now know that the average population of a U.S. region is 6,009,064 with a standard deviation of 6,764,460. You might be wondering, what does it mean to have a standard deviation of almost 7 million? The mean and standard deviation are OK, and they certainly are mighty precise, but for most of us, it would make much more sense to have a *picture* that shows the central tendency and the dispersion of a large set of numbers. The picture we need is called a frequency histogram—one of the most common and useful statistical visualizations. Run this command:

```
hist(USregionPops$april10census)
```

Here's the output you should get:

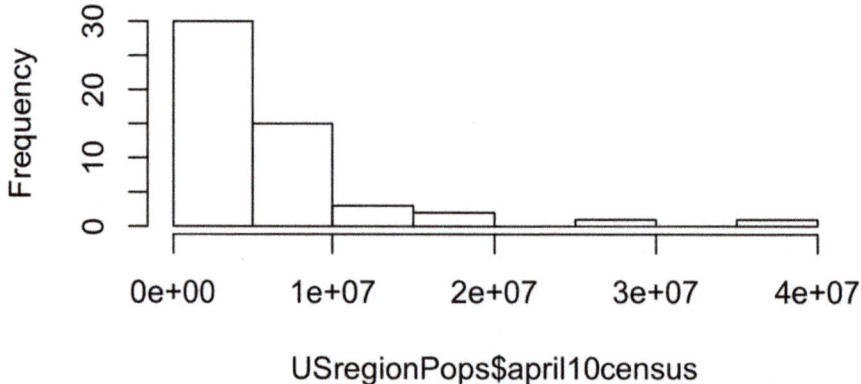

A histogram is a specialized type of bar graph designed to show how often data points occur when they are organized into a set of equal-sized ranges, called "bins." The word "frequencies" here means how often a particular value or range of values occurs in a dataset. This histogram shows a very interesting picture. There are nearly 30 states or regions with populations under 5 million, another 15 with populations under 10 million, and then a very small number with populations greater than 10 million. Having said all that, how do we glean this kind of information from the graph? First, look along the Y-axis (the vertical axis on the left) for an indication of how often the data occur in a given category. The tallest bar is just to the right of this and it is nearly up to the 30 mark. To know what this tall bar represents, look along the X-axis (the horizontal axis at the bottom) and see that there is a tick mark for every two bars. We see scientific notation under each tick mark. The first tick mark is 1e+07, which translates to 10,000,000. So each new bar (or an empty space where a bar would go) goes up by 5 million in population. With these points in mind it should now be easy to see that there are nearly 30 states with populations under 5 million.

If you think about presidential elections, or the locations of schools and businesses, or how a single U.S. state might compare with other countries in the world, it is interesting to know that there are two really giant states in the United States and then lots of much smaller states and regions. Once you have some practice reading histograms, all of the knowledge becomes apparent at a glance.

On the other hand, there is something a bit unsatisfying about this diagram. With more than 40 of the states and regions clustered into the first couple of bars, there might be some more details hiding in there that we would like to know about. This concern translates into the number of bars shown in the histogram. There are eight shown here, so why did R pick eight?

The answer is that the hist() function has an algorithm, or recipe, for deciding on the number of categories/bars to use by default. The number of observations and the spread of the data and the amount of empty space there would be are all considered. Fortunately, it is possible and easy to ask R to use more or fewer categories/bars with the breaks parameter, like this:

```
hist(USregionPops$april10census, breaks=20)
```

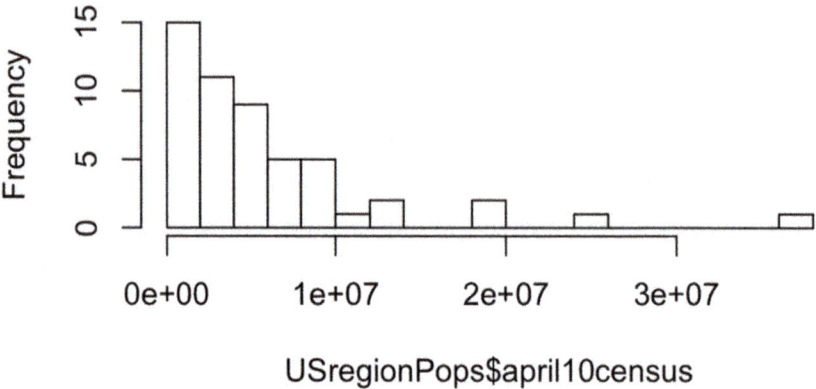

This gives us five bars per tick mark, or about 2 million for each bar. The new histogram above provides finer detail but essentially shows very much the same pattern as before: 15 states with populations under 2 million. The pattern that you see here is referred to as a distribution. This is a distribution that starts off tall on the left and swoops downward quickly as it moves to the right. You might call this a reverse-J distribution because it looks a little like the shape a J makes, although flipped around vertically. More technically, this could be referred to as a Pareto distribution (named after the economist Vilfredo Pareto). We don't have to worry about why it might be a Pareto distribution at this stage, but we can speculate on why the distribution looks the way it does.

First, you can't have a state with zero people in it. This would not make any sense, nor would a negative number for population. A state has to have at least a few people in it, and if you look through U.S. history every state began as a colony or a territory that had at least a few people in it. On the other hand, what does it take for a state or region to grow really large in population? You need a lot of land, first, and then a good reason for lots of people to move there or for lots of people to be born there. In other words, there are many limits to growth: Rhode Island is too small to have a bazillion people in it and Alaska, although it has massive amounts of land, is too cold in the winter for lots of people to want to move there. So while all areas probably started small and grew, it is very difficult for any area to grow really huge. As a result, we have a distribution where most of the cases are clustered near the bottom of the scale and just a few move higher and higher. As you go higher, there are fewer and fewer states that can get that big, and by the time you are out at the end, just shy of 40 million people, there's only one state that has managed to get that big. By the way, do you know or can you guess what that humongous state is? Can you write a line of R code that will reveal that state's name?

## NORMAL DISTRIBUTIONS

There are lots of other distribution shapes. A common one that almost everyone has heard of is sometimes called the bell curve because it is shaped like a bell. The technical name for the bell curve is the normal distribution. The term "normal" was first introduced by Carl Friedrich Gauss (1777–1855), who supposedly named it in a belief that it was the most typical distribution of data that one might find in natural phenomena. The following histogram depicts n=52 random numbers drawn from a normal distribution:

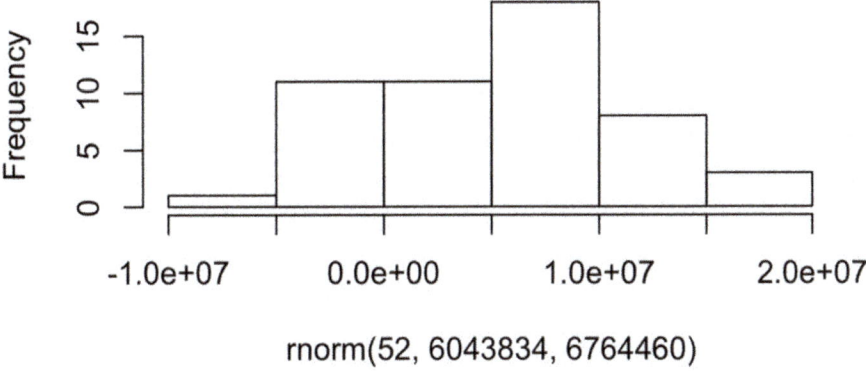

**Histogram of rnorm(52, 6043834, 6764460)**

If you are curious, you might be wondering how R generated the histogram above. You might notice that the histogram that appears above has the label "rnorm" in a couple of places. Here's another of the cool features in R: it is incredibly easy to generate random data to work with when solving problems or giving demonstrations. The data in this histogram were generated by R's rnorm() function, which generates a random dataset that fits the normal distribution (more closely if you generate a lot of data, less closely if you generate only a little). Some further explanation of the rnorm() command will make sense if you remember that the state population data we were using had a mean of 6,053,834 and a standard deviation of 6,823,984. The command used to generate this histogram was:

```
hist(rnorm(52, 6043834, 6764460))
```

The data shown in the histogram above approximate what the distribution of populations might look like if, instead of being a Pareto distribution, they were normally distributed. Note that we used a nested function call: the hist() function that generates the graph surrounds the rnorm() function that generates the new random data. (Pay close attention to the parentheses!) The inside function, rnorm(), is run by R first, with the results of that sent directly and immediately into the hist() function.

The normal distribution is used extensively through applied statistics as a tool for making comparisons. For example, look at the rightmost bar in the previous histogram. The label just to the right of that bar is 3e+07, or 30,000,000. We already know from our real state population data that there is only one actual state with a population in excess of 30 million (if you didn't look it up, it is California). So, if all of a sudden, someone mentioned to you that he or she lived in a state, *other than California*, that had 30 million people, you would automatically think to yourself, "Wow, that's unusual and I'm not sure I believe it." And the reason that you found it hard to believe was that you had a distribution to compare it to. Not only did that distribution have a characteristic shape, it also had a center point, which was the mean, and a spread, which in this case was the standard deviation. Armed with those three pieces of information—the type/shape of distribution, an anchoring point such as the mean, and a spread (also known as the amount of variability)—you have a powerful tool for making comparisons.

In Chapter 6, we will conduct some of these comparisons to see what we can infer about the ways things are in general, based on just a subset of available data, or what statisticians call a sample.

## CASE STUDY: EXPLORING LTR DISTRIBUTIONS

```
Case Key Points:
-  Use histograms to visually explore the distribution of
   LTR, grouped by Type of Travel
```

Rather than just calculating NPS as we did earlier in the book, let's dig into the LTR values in a bit more depth. In particular, let's look at the distribution of LTR values across two key groups—business and personal travel.

```r
library(tidyverse)

#load in the dataset
smallSurvey <- read_csv("smallSurvey.csv")

#remove the NAs from the LTR column
smallSurvey <- filter(smallSurvey, !is.na(LTR))

#get the LTR for all business travels, using core R
bTrue <- smallSurvey$Type.of.Travel=="Business travel"
busTravel <- smallSurvey$LTR[bTrue]

#get the LTR for all personal travel, using tidyverse
perTravel <- smallSurvey %>%
  filter(Type.of.Travel=="Personal Travel") %>%
  pull(LTR)

#define two colors, including transparency (alpha)
myBlue <- rgb(red=0, green=0, blue=0.75, alpha=.75)
myGreen <- rgb(red=0, green=0.75, blue=0, alpha=.75)

#generate two histograms,
# adding the second histogram to the first
hist(busTravel, col=myBlue)
hist(perTravel, col=myGreen, add=TRUE)

#add a legend
legend("topleft", c("Business", "Personal"),
       fill=c(myBlue,myGreen))
```

We used three features to get this done. First, when we defined the color (the fill color), we specified alpha (which controls transparency). When using the rgb function, by default, all the colors, including transparency, range from 0 to 1. A 0 value for alpha makes the color fully transparent, and a value of 1 makes the color opaque (not transparent). Try to experiment with different colors. Another feature we used was that, for the second histogram, we used the add=TRUE parameter, which tells R to add the second histogram to the first histogram. Finally, we created a legend in the top-left part of the histogram visualization.

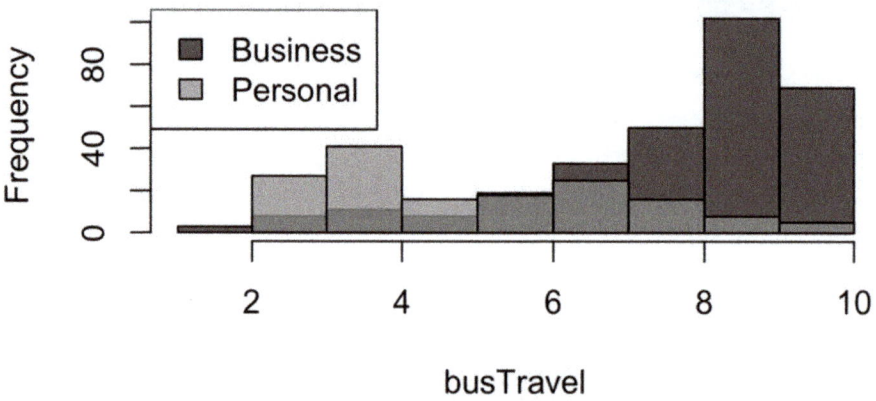

This is a unique way to compare the distributions. In exploring the overlay histograms, we can see that there are many more business travels who were promoters (specifically 9s), and many more personal travelers who were detractors (specifically 3, 4, and 5s). Based on the NPS values, this isn't surprising, but it was possible that the difference in NPS was due to more personal travelers being passive—but this is not the case. There are many more personal travelers who are detractors, which suggests they are unhappy about something about the flight. This needs to be identified and fixed if we want to improve our overall NPS value.

## Chapter Challenges

1. Create a small vector of data called myData that contains the values 1, 1, 1, 2, 2, and 5. Before you calculate the mean, using the mean() function, can you guess what the mean will be?

2. Calculate the variance and the standard deviation of your myData vector using the appropriate R functions.

3. Calculate the mean and standard deviation of the built-in Nile dataset using the appropriate R functions.

4. Using the smallSurvey dataset, create overlaid histograms of LTR, grouped by Gender.

5. In this chapter, we used rnorm() to generate random numbers that closely fit a normal distribution. We also learned that the state population data was a Pareto distribution. Do some research to find an R package that can generate random numbers using the Pareto distribution. Install and library that R package using the appropriate R commands.

6. There are two key parameters for the Pareto function—location and dispersion. The location helps define the numbers along the X-axis. In other words, the shape doesn't change, but changing the location changes the scale of the X-axis. Choose values for location and dispersion that allow you to create a distribution of 52 random numbers that are similar to the distribution of april10census.

7. Create a histogram of the random numbers from the previous exercise and then overlay a histogram of april10census.

8. Make a copy of the readCensus() function and the Numberize() function from this chapter. Test these functions on a different CSV file from the census. You can find a listing of other similar files at this URL: https://www2.census.gov/programs-surveys/popest/tables/2010-2011/state/totals/. If either of your functions causes an error or warning, modify the code to take care of the problem.

## Sources

http://en.wikipedia.org/wiki/Carl_Friedrich_Gauss
http://en.wikipedia.org/wiki/Francis_Galton
https://en.wikipedia.org/wiki/Pareto_distribution
http://en.wikipedia.org/wiki/Karl_Pearson
http://en.wikipedia.org/wiki/Ronald_Fisher
http://en.wikipedia.org/wiki/William_Sealy_Gosset
http://en.wikipedia.org/wiki/Normal_distribution
http://www2.census.gov/programs-surveys/popest
http://www.r-tutor.com/elementary-statistics/numerical-measures/standard-deviation

## R Functions Used in This Chapter

| | |
|---|---|
| filter() | Tidyverse function for subsetting. |
| legend() | Adds a legend to a graphic. |
| library() | Loads a package into memory. |
| mean() | Calculates arithmetic mean. |
| median() | Locates the median. |
| mode() | Tells the data type/mode of a data object. Note: This is *not* the statistical mode. |
| mutate() | Tidyverse function to create, modify, or delete columns. |
| pull() | Tidyverse function to extract a column. |
| var() | Calculates the sample variance. |
| read_csv() | Import a comma separated data file. |
| rgb() | Define a color to use on a graph. |
| sd() | Calculates the sample standard deviation. |
| select() | Tidyverse function to subset columns. |
| slice() | Tidyverse function to subset rows. |
| str_replace_all() | Match and replace one or more instances of a string. |
| hist() | Produces a histogram graphic. |

This text includes access to datasets and select student resources. To learn more, visit sagepub.com

# SAMPLE IN A JAR

## LEARNING OBJECTIVES

Create and interpret sampling distributions.

Use R to sample repetitively.

Understand the effects of randomness when using samples.

Demonstrate the law of large numbers and the central limit theorem.

Gain experience using the following R functions: quantile, replicate, sample, sd, and summary.

Let's be practical: in many situations we cannot get access to all of the data we would like to have. If we are examining the quality of products coming off a production line or the success of a marketing campaign, in most cases we consider ourselves lucky to get even a small percentage of all of the relevant data that might exist. Fortunately, statisticians have worked for a long time on mathematical tools that allow us to make good decisions based on a limited amount of data. The technical term for this is *sampling*. We can use data from a *sample*—a limited subset of all the data that may exist—to reason about a *population*, which is defined as the entirety of the data that are theoretically available. Competent data scientists need to understand the basic concepts of sampling, particularly because they will often use *inferential statistics* to assist with decision-making tasks.

We can make the concept of sampling clearer with a physical example. Imagine a jar full of gumballs of two different colors, red and blue. The jar was filled from a source that provided 100 red gumballs and 100 blue gumballs, but when they were all poured into the jar they got mixed together. If you drew eight gumballs from the jar at random, what colors would you get? If things worked out perfectly, which they rarely do, you would get four red and four blue. This is half and half, the same ratio of red and blue that is in the jar as a whole. Of course, it rarely works out this way, does it? Instead of getting four red and four blue, you might get three red and five blue, or any other mix you can think of. In fact, it would be possible, though perhaps not likely, to get eight red gumballs. The basic situation, though, is that we really don't know what mix of red and blue we will get with one draw of eight gumballs. That's uncertainty for you, the forces of randomness affecting our sample of eight gumballs in unpredictable ways.

Here's an interesting idea, though, that is no help at all in predicting what will happen in any one sample, but is great at showing what will occur *in the long run*. Pull eight gumballs from the jar, count the number of red ones and then throw them back. We do not have to count the number of blue because we can subtract the number of red gumballs from the total (eight gumballs) to know the number of blue gumballs. Mix up the jar again and then draw eight more gumballs and count the number of red. Repeat this process many times. Here's an example of what you might get:

| Draw | # red |
|------|-------|
| 1 | 5 |
| 2 | 3 |
| 3 | 6 |
| 4 | 2 |

Notice that the left-hand column is just counting the number of times we drew a sample. The right-hand column is the interesting one because it is the count of the number of red gumballs in each particular sample draw. In this example, results are all over the place. In sample draw 4, we only have two red gumballs, but in sample draw 3 we have six red gumballs. But the most interesting part of this example is that if you *average* the number of red gumballs over all of the draws, the average comes out to *four red gumballs* per draw, which is exactly what we would expect in a jar that is half red and half blue. Of course, this is a contrived example and we won't always get such a perfect result so quickly, but if you did 4,000 draws instead of four, you would get pretty close to four red gumballs per draw.

This process of repeatedly drawing a subset from a population is called sampling. Note that we are using the word "population" in the previous sentence in its statistical sense to refer to the totality of units from which a sample can be drawn. The population in this example is the whole jar of gumballs. If we do a lot of sampling and record the results each time, the end result is called a sampling distribution.

Next, let's have R help us draw lots of samples from our U.S. state dataset. As a reminder, you can take a quick look at the start of Chapter 5 to see how we read in the U.S. population and created the USstatePops dataframe. Also, it is just a coincidence that our data set includes a variable for the number of people in each state and that this value is referred to as "population." The term population, when used in the statistical sense, does not have to be about people, it is just the complete set of things (e.g., people, cars, bank loans) from which samples can be drawn.

## SAMPLING IN R

Conveniently, R has a function called sample(), that will draw a random sample from a data set with just a single call. We can try it now with our state data:

```
# From Chapter 5 code we need the readCensus()
# function and the Numberize() function to create
# USregionPops.
set.seed(1) # Control randomization to get same result
sample(USregionPops$april10census, size=8,
       replace=TRUE)
[1] 12830632 1328361 1316470 6724540 9687653
[6] 8001024  5686986  672591
```

Note that we are building on code that appeared in Chapters 3 and 4 to read in the Census data and get it ready to sample. We've also introduced a new command here, called set.seed(). This command controls the random number generation process in R so that you can obtain the same results as we did. Code containing functions like sample() that use random numbers can be hard to debug without a way to make the results more predictable. As a matter of good practice, note that we called the sample() function with three arguments. The first argument was the data source. For the second and third arguments, rather than rely on the order in which we specify the arguments, we have used named arguments to make sure that R does what we want it to. The size=8 controls the number of observations we want R to sample. The replace=TRUE argument specifies a style of sampling—called *sampling with replacement*—that statisticians use often to simplify their proofs. For us, sampling with or without replacement does not usually have any practical effects, so we will just go with what the statisticians typically do.

When we're working with variables like april10census, instead of counting gumballs of a specific color we're interested in finding out the average. As you remember from earlier chapters, we call this the mean. So we could also ask R to calculate a mean() of a sample for us:

```
mean(sample(USregionPops$april10census,size=8,
    replace=TRUE))
[1] 9282767
```

There's a nested function call again. The output no longer shows the eight values that R sampled from the complete list. Instead it used those eight values to calculate the mean and display that for us. If you have a good memory, you may remember that the actual mean of our observations is 6,009,064. That's interesting: the mean that we got from this one sample of eight states is really not even close to the true mean value of our complete set of observations. Are we worried? Definitely not! We know that when we draw a sample, whether it is gumballs or states, we will rarely hit the true population mean right on the head, unless we have a very large sample.

## REPEATING OUR SAMPLING

When we are trying to understand what happens in the long run, we're not really interested in any one sample or sample mean, but rather in what happens when we replicate the process of sampling many times. So now we've got to get R to repeat this process for us, not once, not four times, but 400 or 4,000 times. Like most programming languages, R has a variety of ways of repeating an activity. One of the easiest ones to use is the replicate() function. To start, let's just try four replications:

```
replicate(4, mean(sample(USregionPops$april10census,
    size=8,replace=TRUE)),simplify=TRUE)
[1] 3729183 4715687 8353808 3690694
```

Couldn't be any easier! We took the exact same command as before, which was a nested function to calculate the mean() of a random sample of states. This time, we put that command inside the replicate() function so we could run it over and over again. The simplify=TRUE argument asks R to return the results as a simple vector of means, perfect for what we are trying to do. We ran it only four times so that we would not have a big screen full of numbers. From here, though, it is easy to ramp up to repeating the process 400 times. You can try that and see the output, but for here in the book we will encapsulate the whole replicate function inside another call to mean(), so that we can get the average of all 400 of the sample means. Here we go:

```
mean(replicate(400, mean(
    sample(USregionPops$april10census, size=8,
    replace = TRUE)), simplify=TRUE))
[1] 6025845
```

In the command above, the outermost mean() command is what is different from the previous command. So, put into words, this deeply nested command accomplishes the following: (a) Draws 400 samples of size n=8 from our full data set of 51 states. (b) Calculates the mean from each sample and keeps it in a list. (c) When finished with the list of 400 of these means, calculates the mean of that list of means. The resulting value is still not the exact value of the mean of the whole data set, but it is getting much closer. We're off by about 16,781, which is roughly an error of about 0.3% (more precisely, 16,781/ 6,009,064 = 0.28%). Let's push it further and see if we can get closer to the true mean for all of our data:

```
mean(replicate(4000, mean(
    sample(USregionPops$april10census, size=8,
    replace = TRUE)), simplify=TRUE))
[1] 6013936
```

Now we are even closer! If we went up to 40,000 replications we could get even closer. If you run this same code, starting with the set.seed() command from a few pages ago, you should get exactly the same results (note, however, that the folks that maintain R do occasionally change the random number code). If you don't get exactly the same results, you should still be getting closer and closer to the actual mean of april10census.

Now we're ready to take the next step. Instead of summarizing our whole sampling distribution into a single average, let's look at a distribution of means using a histogram. We'll crank up the number of replications to get an even better result. The histogram below

## Sampling Distribution: 40,000 Means

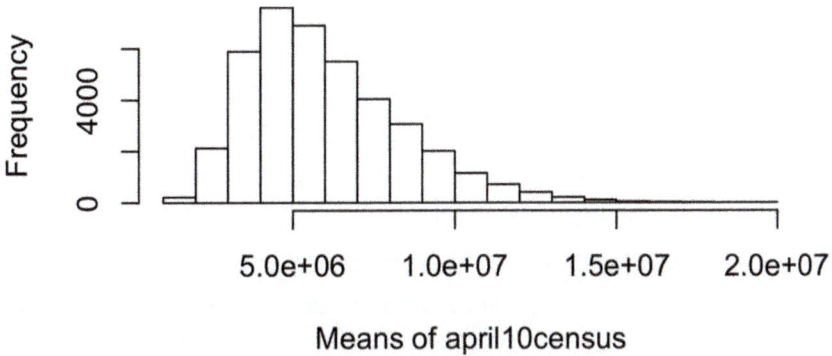

Means of april10census

displays a list of 40,000 means as frequencies. Take a close look so that you can get more practice reading frequency histograms.

The histogram shows a very typical configuration that is almost bell-shaped, although it has a bit of skewness off to the right. The skewness is caused by having either or both the two very large states (California and Texas) in some of the samples. The tallest, and therefore the most frequent, range of values is right near the true mean of 6,009,064. By the way, were you able to figure out the command to generate this histogram on your own? All you had to do was substitute hist() for the outermost mean() in the previous command, and increase the replication from 4,000 to 40,000. Here's the code, including some nice labeling for the histogram:

```
hist(replicate(40000, mean(
    sample(USregionPops$april10census, size=8,
        replace = TRUE)), simplify=TRUE),
        main="Sampling Distribution: 40,000 Means",
        xlab="Means of april10census")
```

# LAW OF LARGE NUMBERS AND THE CENTRAL LIMIT THEOREM

This is a great moment to take a deep breath. We've just covered a couple hundred years of statistical thinking in just a few pages and a few lines of code. In fact, there are two big ideas here, the law of large numbers and the central limit theorem, that we have just par-tially demonstrated. These two ideas took mathematicians including Girolamo Cardano (1501–1576) and Jacob Bernoulli (1654–1705) a long time to figure out. If you look these ideas up, you might find a lot of complex mathematical details, but for our purposes, there are two really important takeaway messages. First, if you run a statistical process a large number of times, it will tend to converge on a stable result (the law of large numbers). For us, we knew what the average population was of our whole dataset. These observations were our population, and we wanted to know how many smaller subsets, or samples, of size n=8 we would have to draw before we could get a good approximation of that true value. We learned that drawing one sample provided a poor result. Drawing 400 samples gave us a mean that was off by 0.3%. Drawing 4,000 samples and then 40,000 gave us means that were off by even less than that. If we had kept going to 400,000 repetitions of our sampling process, we would have come extremely close to the actual average of 6,009,064.

Second, when we are looking at sample means, and we take the law of large numbers into account, we find that the distribution of sampling means starts to create a bell-shaped or normal distribution, and the center of that distribution—the mean of all of those sample means—gets really close to the actual population mean. It gets closer faster for larger samples; in contrast, for smaller samples you have to draw lots and lots of them to get really close. Just for fun, let's illustrate this with a sample size that is larger than 16. Here's a run that repeats only 100 times, but each time draws a sample of n=52 (equal in size to the population):

```
mean(replicate(100, mean(
    sample(USregionPops$april10census,size = 52,
        replace = TRUE)), simplify=TRUE))
[1] 6030024
```

Now, we're off from the true value of the population mean by only about 0.3% again. You might be scratching your head now, saying, "Wait a minute. Isn't a sample of 52 the same thing as the whole list of 52 observations?" This does seem confusing, but it goes back to the question of sampling with replacement that we examined a few pages ago (and that appears in the command above as replace=TRUE). Sampling with replacement means that as you draw out one value to include in your random sample, you immedi-ately chuck it back into the list so that, potentially, it could get drawn again either imme-diately or later. As mentioned before, this practice simplifies the underlying proofs, and it does not cause any practical problems, other than head scratching. In fact, we could go even higher in our sample size with no trouble:

```
mean(replicate(100, mean(
     sample(USregionPops$april10census, size=5200,
            replace=TRUE)), simplify=TRUE))
[1]  5994203
```

That command runs 100 replications using samples of size n=5200. Look how close the mean of the sampling distribution is to the population mean now! Remember that this result will change a little every time you run the procedure, because different random samples are being drawn for each run. But the rule of thumb is that the bigger your sample size, what we're calling "n," the closer your estimate will be to the true value. Likewise, the more trials you run, the closer your population estimate will be.

So, if you've had a chance to catch your breath, let's move on to making use of the sampling distribution. First, let's save one distribution of sample means so that we have a fixed set of numbers to work with. Let's begin by resetting the randomization:

```
set.seed(1)
SampleMeans <- replicate(10000,
                mean(sample(USregionPops$april10census,
                size = 8, replace = TRUE)),
                simplify=TRUE)
```

We're saving a distribution of sample means to a new vector called SampleMeans. We should have 10,000 of them:

```
length(SampleMeans)
[1]  10000
```

And the mean of all of these means should be pretty close to our population mean of 6,009,064:

```
mean(SampleMeans)
[1]  6027481
```

You might also want to run a histogram on SampleMeans and see what the frequency distribution looks like. Right now, all we need to look at is a summary of the list of sample means:

```
summary(SampleMeans)
   Min. 1st Qu.  Median    Mean 3rd Qu.      Max.
1175714  4248342 5587151 6027481 7396833 20320303
```

As a reminder, the 1st Qu. (first quartile) is the value that divides the first quarter of the cases from the other three quarters. Median refers to the value of the case that splits the whole group in half, with half of the cases having higher values and half having lower values. The median is also the dividing line that separates the second quartile from the third quartile. If you need a refresher on the median and quartiles, take a look back at Chapter 2, "Rows and Columns."

This summary is full of useful information. First, take a look at the max and the min. The minimum sample mean in the list was 1,175,714. Think about that for a moment. How could a sample have a mean that small when we know that the true mean is much higher? Rhode Island must have been drawn several times in that sample! The answer comes from the randomness involved in sampling. If you run a process 10,000 times you are definitely going to end up with a few weird examples. It's almost like buying a lottery ticket. The vast majority of tickets are the usual—not a winner. Once in a great while, though, there is a very unusual ticket—a winner. Sampling is the same: the extreme events are unusual, but they do happen if you run the process enough times. The same goes for the maximum: at 20,320,303 the maximum sample mean is much higher than the true mean.

At 5,587,151 the median is quite close to the mean, but not exactly the same because we still have a little rightward skew. The median is very useful because it divides the sample exactly in half: 50%, or exactly 5,000 of the sample means are larger than 5,370,000 and the other 50% are lower. So if we were to draw one more sample from the population it would have a fifty-fifty chance of being above the median. The quartiles help us to cut things up even more finely. The third quartile divides up the bottom 75% from the top 25%. So only 25% of the sample means are higher than 7,396,833. That means if we drew a new sample from the population that there is only a 25% chance that it will be larger than that. Likewise, in the other direction, the first quartile tells us that there is only a 25% chance that a new sample would be less than 4,248,342.

There is a slightly different way of getting the same information from R that will prove more flexible for us in the long run. The quantile() function can show us the same information as the median and the quartiles, like this:

```
quantile(SampleMeans, probs=c(0.25,0.50,0.75))
    25%      50%      75%
4248342 5587151 7396833
```

One reason to use quantile() is that it lets us control exactly where we make the cuts. To get quartiles, we cut at 25% (0.25 in the command just above), at 50%, and at 75%. But what if we wanted instead to cut at the more extreme levels of 2.5% and 97.5%? Easy to do with quantile():

```
quantile(SampleMeans, probs=c(0.025,0.975))
    2.5%     97.5%
2578646 11688932
```

So, this result shows that, if we drew a new sample, there is only a 2.5% chance that the mean would be lower than 2,578,646. Likewise, there is only a 2.5% chance that the new sample mean would be higher than 11,688,932 (because 97.5% of the means in the sampling distribution are lower than that value). Considered from another angle, about 95% of all of the samples we drew fell in the range of 2,578,646 up to 11,688,932. Only about 5% of all sample means in our sampling distribution are more extreme (i.e., outside of that range).

## COMPARING TWO SAMPLES

Now we're getting somewhere: let's put this knowledge to work. Here is a sample showing the number of people in eight different areas, where each of these areas is some kind of a unit associated with a country (e.g., a province, district, or region):

```
2238603 2662480 1632934 822441 1955577 1084979 637026 3388768
```

We can easily get these into R and calculate the sample mean:

```
MysterySample <- c(2238603,2662480,1632934,822441,
                   1955577,1084979,637026,3388768)
mean(MysterySample)
[1] 1802851
```

The mean of our mystery sample is 1,802,851. Here's the question: is this a sample of U.S. regions or is it something else? Looking at it all by itself it would be hard to tell. Some of these observations have larger values than some U.S. states and some do not. Thanks to the work we've done earlier in this chapter, however, we have an excellent basis for comparison. We have the sampling distribution of means, and it is fair to say that if we get a new mean to look at, and the new mean is way out in the extreme areas of the sample distribution, say, below the 2.5% mark or above the 97.5% mark, then it seems much less likely that our MysterySample is a sample of U.S. regions.

In this case, we can see quite clearly that 1,802,851 is on the extreme low end of the sampling distribution. Recall that when we ran the quantile() command we found that only 2.5% of the sample means in the distribution were smaller than 2,578,646.

In fact, we could even play around with a more stringent criterion:

```
quantile(SampleMeans, probs=c(0.005,0.995))
    0.5%     99.5%
1967733 14065397
```

This quantile() command shows that only 0.5% of all the sample means are lower than 1,967,733. So our MysterySample mean of 1,802,851 would definitely be a very rare event, if it were truly a sample of U.S. regions. From this we can infer, tentatively but based on good statistical evidence, that our MysterySample is *not* a sample of U.S. regions. The mean of MysterySample is just too small to be a likely member of our sampling distribution.

And this is in fact correct: MysterySample contains the number of people in a sample of states from Mexico (using 2010 population values). The important thing to take away is that the characteristics of this other group of data points, notably the mean of this sample, was sufficiently different from a known distribution of means that we could make an inference that the sample *was not drawn from the original population of data*. This method of reasoning is the basis for one of the most common methods of statistical inference. You construct a comparison distribution based on some statistical values, you mark off a zone of extreme values, and you compare any new sample of data you get to the comparison distribution to see if it falls in the extreme zone. If it does, you tentatively conclude that the new sample was obtained from some source other than what you used to create the original comparison distribution. Statisticians use some special distributions—for example the "t" distribution—when constructing their tests, so our informal demonstration here does not paint the whole picture. As long as you have understood the essential strategy we have shown here, however, then you are well on your way toward grasping the logic of statistical inference.

On the other hand, if you still feel confused, take heart. There're 400 to 500 years of mathematical developments represented in this chapter. Also, before we had cool programs like R that could be used to create and analyze actual sampling distributions, most of the material above was taught as a set of formulas and proofs. Later in the book we will come back to specific statistical procedures that use the reasoning described above. For now, we just need to take note of three additional pieces of information.

First, we looked at the mean of the sampling distribution with mean() and we looked at its shape with hist(), but we never quantified the spread of the distribution:

```
sd(SampleMeans)
[1] 2406800
```

This shows us the standard deviation of the distribution of sampling means. Statisticians call this the standard error of the mean. This chewy phrase would have been clearer, although longer, if it had been something like this: "the standard deviation of the distribution of sample means for samples (all of the same size) drawn from a population." Unfortunately, statisticians are not known for giving things long, helpful explanatory labels. Suffice to say that when we are looking at a distribution and each data point in that distribution is itself a representation of a sample (e.g., a mean), then the standard deviation is referred to as the standard error.

Second, there is a shortcut to finding out the standard error that does not require actually constructing an empirical distribution of 10,000 (or any other number) of sampling means. It turns out that the standard deviation of the original raw data and the standard error are closely related by some simple algebra:

```
sd(USregionPops$april10census)/sqrt(8)
[1] 2391598
```

The formula in this command takes the standard deviation of the original state data and divides it by the square root of the sample size. Remember three or four pages ago, when we created the SampleMeans vector by using the replicate() and sample() commands, we used a sample size of n=8. That's what you see in the formula above, inside of the sqrt() function. In R and other software, sqrt() is the abbreviation for square root and not for squirt as you might think. So if you have a set of observations and you calculate their standard deviation, you can also calculate the standard error for a distribution of means (each of which has the same sample size), just by dividing by the square root of the sample size. You might notice that the number we got with the shortcut was slightly different than the number that came from the distribution itself, but the difference is not meaningful (and only arises because of randomness in the sampling distribution). Another thing you might have noticed is that the larger the sample size, the smaller the standard error. This leads to an important rule for working with samples: the bigger, the better!

One last thing to learn is another shortcut. We found out the 97.5% cut point by constructing the sampling distribution and then using quantile to tell us the actual cuts. You can also calculate cut points just using the mean and the standard error. Roughly speaking, two standard errors down from the mean is the 2.5% cut point, and two standard errors up from the mean is the 97.5% cut point.

```
StdError <- sd(USregionPops$april10census)/sqrt(8)
CutPoint975 <- mean(USregionPops$april10census) +
                  (2 * StdError)
CutPoint975
[1] 10792259
```

You will notice again that this value is different from what we calculated with the quantile() function using the empirical distribution. The differences arise because of the randomness in the distribution that we constructed. The value above is an estimate that is based on statistical proofs, whereas the empirical SampleMeans vector that we constructed is just one of an infinite set of such vectors that we could create. We could easily reduce the discrepancy between the two methods by using a larger sample size and by having more replications included in the sampling distribution.

To summarize, with a dataset that includes 52 data points with the numbers of people in U.S. regions, and some work using R to construct a distribution of sampling means, we have learned the following:

- Run a statistical process a large number of times and you get a consistent pattern of results.

- Taking the means of a large number of samples and plotting them on a histogram shows that the sample means are fairly well normally distributed and that the center of the distribution is very, very close to the mean of the original raw data.

- This resulting distribution of sample means can be used as a basis for comparisons. By making cut points at the extreme low and high ends of the distribution, for example 2.5% and 97.5%, we have a way of comparing any new information we get.

- If we get a new sample mean, and we find that it is in the extreme zone defined by our cut points, we can tentatively conclude that the sample that made that mean is a different kind of thing from the samples that made the sampling distribution.

- A different way of figuring the cut points involves calculating the standard error based on the standard deviation of the original raw data. This is the method that is used in statistical formulas when we do not have access to a whole population of data and therefore cannot construct our own sampling distribution.

We're not statisticians at this point, but the process of reasoning based on sampling distributions is at the heart of inferential statistics, so if you have followed the logic presented in this chapter, you have made excellent progress toward being a competent user of inferential statistics. You now have the basic knowledge necessary to understand the concept of *statistical significance*. Data scientists need to have this knowledge so that they can correctly apply the statistical tests that decision makers need in order to make good, data-driven choices.

# CASE STUDY: ANALYZING THE IMPACT OF A NEW TREATMENT

> **Case Key Points:**
> - **Did a change in treatment to passengers improve Southeast's NPS?**
> - **We need to ensure our analysis accounts for expected randomness in the results.**
> - **We can use sampling, replication, and quantile to understand if the treatment is better.**

To help improve Southeast's NPS value, at select airports, prior to boarding the flight, free drinks were provided to passengers. These customers were then surveyed at the end of their flight. We have access to these surveys and need to figure out if this change improved Southeast's NPS. Note that while we could just compare the NPS values of the old survey with the new survey after the treatment, even if the NPS value is higher after the treatment, we need to make sure it was not due to sampling error. We can answer this question by comparing the LTR values after the treatment with a comparison distribution. We can build a comparison distribution based on the data we considered in previous chapters from smallSurvey.csv. It is important to note that this is only an informal method of accomplishing this kind of comparison. A formal statistical approach to making this comparison would require some additional decisions about our data as well and a corresponding choice of a statistical procedure.[1] With that in mind, let's read in the new survey.

```
library(tidyverse)

smallSurvey <- read_csv("smallSurvey.csv")

#remove the NAs from the LTR column
smallSurvey <- filter(smallSurvey, !is.na(LTR))
```

---

1  For the statistically minded, NPS is a characteristic of a whole sample rather than an individual observation. Technically the new treatment only gives us a single observation of NPS to compare to a baseline. We can overcome this by comparing LTR scores between the original survey and the new treatment survey using a t-test. Alternatively, we could characterize each participant in our surveys as a promoter or detractor (and optionally include a third category of neutral for those scoring between 7 and 8). Then we could use a chi-square test of independence on the resulting count data.

```
#read in the new survey results after the treatment
newTreatmentDF <- read_csv("newTreatmentSurvey.csv")

# Check the number of rows
nrow(newTreatmentDF)
[1] 120
```

After reading in the new survey results (into newTreatmentDF), let's look at the NPS values, using the CalcNPS function that we created in a previous chapter:

```
CalcNPS(smallSurvey$LTR)
[1] 9.018036

CalcNPS(newTreatmentDF$LTR)
[1] 15.83333
```

So, we can see that NPS was higher among the participants of the survey after the treatment. Maybe this was just due to sampling error or it may have been due to the impact of the treatment on Southeast's customers? Let's explore, using the replication of samples approach we discussed in this chapter:

```
set.seed(100)
# We sample many times from smallSurvey
# using n=120 to match the number of
# observations in the treatment survey.
replicatedNPS <- replicate(1000,
                 CalcNPS(sample(smallSurvey$LTR,
                                size=120,
                                replace=TRUE)))

#Calculate the 2.5% and 97.5% quantiles
thresholdValues <- quantile(replicatedNPS,
                        probs=c(0.025,0.975))

#Generate a histogram of NPS values
hist(replicatedNPS)
```

```
# Mark the 95% central region
abline(v=min(thresholdValues))
abline(v=max(thresholdValues))

#show the new NPS value (linetype is a dashed line)
newTreatmentNPS <- CalcNPS(newTreatmentDF$LTR)
abline(v=newTreatmentNPS, lty="dashed")
```

Examine the histogram below, looking carefully at the two solid lines, which mark the 2.5% and 97.5% quantiles, and the dashed line, which marks the position of newTreatmentNPS.

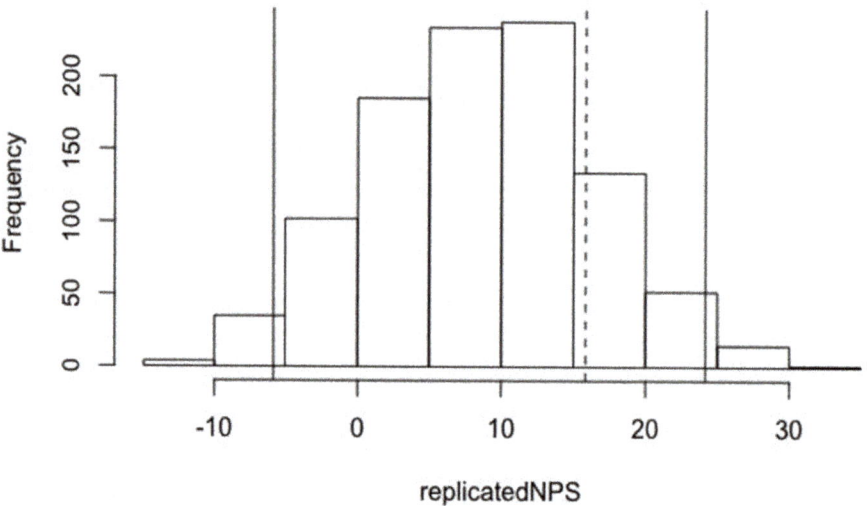

**Histogram of replicatedNPS**

Note where the dashed line falls on the histogram. Even though 15.83 (the NPS for the new treatment) is larger than 9.01 (the NPS for the original survey), when we compare to a lot of replications of samples from the original survey, we see that 15.83 falls within the "central region" of the histogram. The solid vertical lines mark off the central region: 95% of the replications of NPS from the original survey fell into this range. This example shows how important statistical inference is. Even though our result of 15.83 looked promising, the randomness that we have to deal with when working with samples shows that this is probably not a credible level of improvement. If we continued to collect data samples of n=120, we would need to get the NPS for the treatment group up above 25 in order to get a credible difference.

In conclusion, don't forget that this is an informal demonstration that shows the essential logic of how statistical inference works. Statisticians who worked on the same problem would use a formal procedure to perform the comparison. Our demonstration clearly showed the importance, however, of understanding the uncertainty involved in working with samples with data. The smaller the sample, the greater our uncertainty!

## Chapter Challenges

1. Run the following line of code: *sample(c("blue","red"), size=8, replace=T)*. Describe the output that this line of code creates. How many times did your output say blue and how many times did it say red? Create a fraction with the count of blue on top and the total number of reds and blues on the bottom. What would you expect this fraction to be?

2. Run the following line of code: *sample(c("blue","red"),size=8, replace=T) == "blue"*. Examine the output and describe what is different about the output of this line of code when compared to the results of the previous question. R represents values of true as one and false as zero. Enclose that complete line of code with a call to the sum() function. Explain the results.

3. Create a custom function using the code you created for the previous problem. Test the function: when you call it, the function should return the number of blues. Use replicate() to call your function 1000 times. Store the result, which should be a vector of integers between 0 and 8 in a new variable. Create a histogram of the new variable. Describe the shape of the histogram.

4. Use rnorm() to create a vector of 1000 random numbers and store those numbers in a new variable. Create a histogram of the new variable. Describe the shape of the histogram.

5. Using the vector of random numbers from the previous problem, use the quantile() function to find the value for the 2.5% (0.025) quantile and the 97.5% (0.975) quantile. What percentage of your vector of observations falls in between these two numbers?

6. Display the vector of random numbers from the previous problem on a histogram. Use the abline() function to draw vertical lines on the histogram at the 2.5% and 97.5% quantiles. If you observed a new value that was equal to 3.0, would it fall in the central region of this distribution or in one of the tails?

7. Use the mean() function to calculate the average of the replicatedNPS variable that we created in the final block of code in this chapter. Then rerun this piece of code: *CalcNPS(smallSurvey$LTR)*. Explain why the two values are so similar. Also explain why they are not identical.

8. Collect a sample consisting of at least 20 data points and construct a sampling distribution. Calculate the standard error and use this to calculate the 2.5% and 97.5% distribution cut points. The data points you collect should represent instances of the same phenomenon. For instance, you could collect the prices of 20 textbooks, or count the number of words in each of 20 paragraphs.

## Sources

http://en.wikipedia.org/wiki/Central_limit_theorem
http://en.wikipedia.org/wiki/Gerolamo_Cardano
http://en.wikipedia.org/wiki/Jacob_Bernoulli
http://en.wikipedia.org/wiki/Law_of_large_numbers
http://en.wikipedia.org/wiki/List_of_U.S._states_and_territories_by_population
http://www.khanacademy.org/math/statistics/v/central-limit-theorem

## R Functions Used in This Chapter

| | |
|---|---|
| filter() | Tidyverse function to subset rows. |
| length() | The number of elements in a vector. |
| mean() | The arithmetic mean or average of a set of values. |
| nrow() | Number of rows in a data structure. |
| quantile() | Calculates cut points based on percentages/proportions. |
| replicate() | Runs an expression/calculation many times. |
| sample() | Chooses elements at random from a vector. |
| sd() | Calculates standard deviation. |
| sqrt() | Calculates square root. |
| summary() | Summarizes contents of a vector. |

This text includes access to datasets and select student resources. To learn more, visit sagepub.com

# 7

# STORAGE WARS

## LEARNING OBJECTIVES

Recognize the different data sources that are available for R analysis.

Explain the reasons for using file-based data or database data.

Build R code to access data that are available in Excel, JSON, and an SQL database.

Use the sqldf package to access a dataframe as if it was a database.

Use the R filter, summarize(), and group_by() tidyverse functions to do summary analysis on a dataframe.

Gain experience using the following additional R functions: getURL(), fromJSON(), read_excel(), str_replace_all(), dbConnect(), dbGetQuery(), dbListTables(), dbWriteTable(), unlist(), matrix().

Most people who have watched the evolution of technology over recent decades remember a time when storage was expensive and had to be hoarded like gold. Over the past few years, however, the accelerating trend of Moore's Law has made data storage almost "too cheap to meter" (as they used to predict about nuclear power). Although this opens many opportunities, it also means that people keep data around for a long time, since it doesn't make sense to delete anything, and they might keep data around in many different formats. As a result, the world is full of different data formats, some of which are proprietary—designed and owned by a single company such as SAS—and some of which are open, such as the lowly but useful comma-separated variable (CSV) format.

In fact, one of the basic dividing lines in data formats is whether data are human readable or not. Formats that are not human readable, often called binary formats, are efficient in terms of how much information they can pack in per kilobyte, but are also squirrelly in the sense that it is hard to see what is going on inside the file. As you might expect, human-readable formats are inefficient from a storage standpoint, but easy to diagnose when something goes wrong. For high-volume applications, such as credit card processing, the data that are exchanged between systems are almost universally in binary formats. When datasets are archived for later reuse, for example, in the case of government datasets available to the public, they are usually available in multiple formats, at least one of which is a human-readable format.

Another dividing line, as mentioned above, is between proprietary and open formats. One of the most common ways of storing and sharing small datasets is as Microsoft Excel spreadsheets. Although this is a proprietary format, owned by Microsoft, it has also become an informal standard. Dozens of different software applications can read Excel formats (there are different formats from different versions of Excel). In contrast, the OpenDocument format is an open format, managed by a standards consortium, that anyone can use. OpenDocument format is based on XML, which stands for extensible markup language. XML is a whole topic in and of itself, but in brief it is a data exchange format designed specifically to work on the Internet and is both human and machine readable. XML is managed by the W3C consortium, which is responsible for developing and maintaining the many standards and protocols that support the web.

As an open source program with many contributors, R offers a wide variety of methods of connecting with external data sources. This is both a blessing and a curse. There is a solution to almost any data access problem you can imagine with R, but there is also a dizzying array of options available such that it is not always obvious which option to choose. We'll tackle this problem in two different ways.

In the first half of this chapter, we will build on our readCensus() function from earlier in the book and look at methods for importing existing datasets. These might exist on a local computer or on the Internet, but the characteristic they have in common is that they are contained (usually) within one single file. The main trick here is to choose the right command to import those data into R. In the second half of the chapter, we will consider a different strategy, namely extracting data from a source that is not a file. Many data sources, particularly databases, exist not as one single discrete file, but rather as an entry point into a database system. The database system provides methods or calls to query data records from the system, but from the perspective of the user (and of R) the data never really take the form of a file.

# IMPORTING DATA USING RSTUDIO

The first and easiest strategy for getting data into R is to use the data import dialog in RStudio. In the upper-right-hand pane of RStudio, the Workspace tab gives views of currently available data objects, but also has a set of buttons at the top for managing the work space. One of the choices there is the Import Dataset button: this enables a drop-down menu where one choice is to import "From Text (readr). . ." If you click this option and choose an appropriate file, you will get a screen like this:

If you notice the box on the lower right, you will see that as you set up the file name and adjust the options to control the importing process, RStudio shows you what the resulting R code looks like. The first line of the R code is always the same—library(readr)—and it shows you that you are using the read_csv() function from the readr package (which is part of the Tidyverse).

The very first thing to do with this large dialog box is to click on the "Browse" button on the upper right. This will bring up a standard file selection dialog for your operating system and allow you to point and click your way to the correct file. If you want to access a text file from the web, you can also paste in the full URL of the web page that contains the text data. After RStudio has located the file and scanned it, you will see the "Data Preview" window in the middle of the screen fill up with the first few rows of data, the variable names (if your file has them), and the data type for each variable. You can scroll down to look at as many as 50 records and you can scroll sideways (revealing more variables to the right) if your file contains more than about 10 variables.

Let's talk about some of the options that are shown in the box on the bottom left. One important thing to know is that RStudio will try to guess the best defaults for all of these choices, so most of the time you will not need to make any adjustments. "First Row as Names" controls whether or not the first line of the text file is treated as a list of variable names. The "Delimiter" drop-down gives a choice of different characters that can separate the fields/columns in the data. Tab-delimited and comma-delimited are the two most common formats used for interchange between data programs. Clicking on the box next to "Locale" allows several formatting conventions based on where the data were prepared. For example, a dot is used as a decimal point in the United States, whereas a comma is sometimes used for the decimal point in Europe and elsewhere. The Quote drop-down controls which character is used to contain quoted string/text data. The most common method is double quotes. There are several other options that you can control from this dialog and if you are confused about any of them, you can click on the help button at the bottom left, and a web page will load with detailed information.

Of course, we skipped ahead here because we assumed that an appropriate file of data was available for you to import. It might be useful to see some examples of human-readable data:

Name, Age, Gender

"Fred",22,"M"

"Ginger",21,"F"

The above is a very simple example of a comma-delimited file where the first row contains a header, meaning the information about the names of variables. The second and third rows contain actual data. Each field is separated by a comma, and the text strings are enclosed in double quotes. The same file tab-delimited might look like this:

| Name | Age | Gender |
| --- | --- | --- |
| "Fred" | 22 | "M" |
| "Ginger" | 21 | "F" |

Of course, you can't see the tab characters on the screen, but there is a tab character in between each pair of values. In each case, for both comma- and tab-delimited files, one line equals one row of data. The end of a line is marked, invisibly, with a "newline" character. On occasion, you might run into differences between different operating systems on how this end-of-line designation is encoded.

Files containing comma- or tab-delimited data are very common across the Internet, but sometimes we would like to gain direct access to binary files in other formats. There are a variety of packages that one might use to access binary data. A comprehensive access list appears here:

http://cran.r-project.org/doc/manuals/R-data.html

This page shows a range of methods for obtaining data from a variety of programs and formats. In this chapter, we will explore how to read in a dataset using three very common methods. First, we will read in an Excel file. As you will see, this will be very similar to how we read in the CSV format. We will also read a dataset that is available via a database using an industry standard known as structured query language (SQL). Finally, we will access data via java script object notation (JSON), which is a structured, but human readable, way of sharing data. JSON is an increasingly common way of sharing data on the web, particularly from web-based "APIs" (which we discuss in detail later in this chapter).

## ACCESSING EXCEL DATA

Because Excel is such a widely used program for small, informal datasets, we will start with an example here to illustrate both the power and the pitfalls of accessing binary data with R. There are certainly many packages available to help us read in an Excel file, but we will again rely on the Tidyverse family of packages to provide us with a method for importing spreadsheet files. In the example that follows, we will use a function from the readxl package to read Excel data directly from a website. The readxl package is part of the Tidyverse.

Begin by using the library() function to prepare the readxl package. We need to load readxl as a separate step because it is not a core Tidyverse package loaded via library(tidyverse) command:

```
> library("readxl")
```

Now that readxl is installed, we can use the read_excel() function. The documentation for the function is available from RStudio using the help("read_excel") command or at the web page located here:

https://readxl.tidyverse.org/

A review of the documentation reveals that the only required argument to this function is the location of the XLS file, and that this location can be a pathname. Unfortunately, at the current time, the file needs to be a file on the local computer, not a URL for a web location.

If you think back to an early chapter in this book, you may remember that we accessed some census data that had population counts for all the different U.S. states. Previously, we read the data in a CSV format. For this example, we are going to read the Excel file containing that data directly into a dataframe using the read_excel() function by first downloading the file and then reading the file:

```
#define the URL across multiple lines
# (just to make it easier to cut and paste code)

part1 <-"http://www2.census.gov/programs-surveys/"
part2 <- "popest/tables/2010-2011/state/totals/"
part3 <- "nst-est2011-01.xls"
dataFile <- paste0(part1,part2,part3)

#download the file from the web, into tmpExcelFile

download.file(dataFile, "tmpExcelFile.xls")

trying URL 'http://www2.census.gov/programs-surveys/popest/
    tables/2010-2011/state/totals/nst-est2011-01.xls'
Content type 'application/vnd.ms-excel' length 31232 bytes
    (30 KB)
==================================================
downloaded 30 KB
```

The first four lines create the URL of the Excel file we want to download. We split the URL across three separate strings just to make it easier for you to cut and paste the code. Normally, you could just type out the whole URL on one line in your code window. After pasting the URL together, we download from that URL into a temporary local file. The download.file() command reports that 30 kilobytes of data were downloaded into the temporary file. Next, we will import the file with the read_excel() function. Note that read_excel() is a wrapper that tries to guess the format of the Excel file and then dispatch the job of importing it to either read_xls() or read_xlsx(). The former reads older, binary-formatted spreadsheet files, whereas the latter reads in the more modern format that is based on XML. In this case, our census data is in the older format. We could also have called read_xls() directly, rather than having read_excel() make its guess.

```
#now read the excel file into R
testFrame <- read_excel("tmpExcelFile.xls")
New names:
* `` -> `..2`
* `` -> `..3`
* `` -> `..4`
* `` -> `..5`
```

The import succeeded, although it looks like we have some weird variable names to deal with. Next, let's take a look at what we got back by using the glimpse function to summarize the structure of testFrame:

```
glimpse(testFrame)
Observations: 66
Variables: 5
$ `table with row headers in column A and column headers
    in rows 3 through 4. (leading dots indicate sub-parts)`
    <chr> …
$ `..2` <chr> …
$ `..3` <chr> …
$ `..4` <chr> …
$ `..5` <dbl>
```

This is somewhat similar to the results we obtained when we read the comma-separated file in Chapter 3. It's still messy, but in a slightly different way. So now let's clean this datafile. First, the Census Bureau put in header rows that we can eliminate:

```
testFrame <- slice(testFrame, -1:-8)
```

As a reminder, the minus sign refers to the index of rows that should be eliminated from the dataframe. So the notation -1:-8 gets rid of the first eight rows. We assign the result back to the same data object, thereby replacing the original with our new, smaller, cleaner version.

Next, by using the tail() function, we see that the last few rows just contained some Census Bureau notes and that row 52 was blank. So we can safely eliminate those rows like this:

```
testFrame <- slice(testFrame, -54:-58)
testFrame <- slice(testFrame, -52)
```

Now we are ready to perform a couple of data transformations. Before we start these, let's give our first column a more reasonable name by pulling the first column and storing it in a new column called stateName.

```
testFrame$stateName <- pull(testFrame, 1)
```

We've used a little hack here to avoid typing out the ridiculously long name of that first variable/column. We've used the column number notation on the right-hand side of the expression to refer to the first column (the one with the ridiculous name) and simply copied the data into a new column entitled stateName. Let's also remove the offending column with the stupid name so that it does not cause us problems later on:

```
testFrame <- testFrame[,-1]
```

Note that we could have also used the Tidyverse function select(-1) to remove the first column. Next, we can change formats and data types as needed. We can remove the dots from in front of the state names very easily with str_replace():

```
testFrame$stateName <-
    str_replace_all(testFrame$stateName,"\\.","")
```

The function str_replace_all() is included within the Tidyverse set of packages. We previously used gsub(), which is a similar function. The two backslashes in the string expression above are called escape characters and they force the dot that follows to be treated as a literal dot rather than as a wildcard character. The dot on its own is a wildcard that matches one instance of any character.

Next, we need to rename the different columns and turn the text strings into numbers:

```
testFrame <- testFrame %>% rename(april10census = '..2')
testFrame <- testFrame %>% rename(april10base = '..3')
testFrame <- testFrame %>% rename(july10pop = '..4')
testFrame <- testFrame %>% rename(july11pop = '..5')

testFrame <- testFrame %>% mutate_at(
    vars(april10census,april10base,july10pop,july11pop),
                                     as.numeric)
```

Now we are ready to analyze our data or do whatever tasks our project requires. Note that the census files are particularly difficult to work with because of the notes and the unusual column naming. In many cases if you receive a spreadsheet used in a business context, it will often already contain sensible column names and data formats that will make the importing process easier. On a related note, we often get the question of whether it is better to manually edit an Excel file to "fix it up" before trying to import it. The answer to this question depends on the data management processes you are using: if the Excel file was automatically generated by some other business process and will be regenerated week after week or month after month, then you should automate all the necessary transformations in R. On the other hand, if someone hands you a spreadsheet for a one-time analysis activity, and the spreadsheet isn't too large, then feel free to do whatever will produce the best result in the shortest amount of time—even if that includes a little manual editing in the spreadsheet.

## WORKING WITH DATA FROM EXTERNAL DATABASES

Now we are ready to consider another strategy for getting access to data: querying it from external databases. Depending on your familiarity with computer programming and databases, you might notice that the method of obtaining the data is quite different here. In the example above, we had a file (sometimes rather messy) that contained a complete copy of the data that we wanted, and we read that file into R and stored it in our local computer's memory. We also have the option, which the example above did not show, of saving a copy of our R data object on our local file storage. This is a good and reasonable strategy for small- to medium-sized datasets, which we'll define just for the sake of argument as anything up to 100 megabytes.

But what if the data you want to work with is really large—too large to represent in your computer's memory all at once and too large to store on your own hard drive? This situation could occur even with smaller datasets if the data owner did not want people making complete copies of their data, but rather wanted everyone who was using it to work from one official version of the data. In a similar vein, there are many situations where multiple users need to share access to data: it is much better to have them work with a database that was designed for this purpose. Without some special additions, R is not an ideal choice for maintaining data that must be used simultaneously by more than one user. For these reasons, it becomes necessary to do one or both of the following things:

Allow R to send messages to the large, remote database, perhaps via the web, asking for summaries, subsets, or samples of the data.

Allow R to send computation requests to a distributed data processing system asking for the results of calculations performed on the large remote database, perhaps via a web service.

Like most contemporary programming languages, R provides several methods for performing these two tasks. We will explore two basic ways to access these remote data services.

# ACCESSING A DATABASE

The first strategy we will explore to access remote systems or data involves using a package that provides a client that can connect up to the database server. The R client supports sending commands—mostly in SQL —to a database server. The database server returns a result to the R client, which places it in an R data object (typically a dataframe) for use in further processing or visualization.

The R community has developed a range of client software to enable R to connect up with other databases. Here are the major databases for which R has client software:

RMySQL: Connects to MySQL, perhaps the most popular open source database in the world. MySQL is the M in LAMP, which is the acronym for Linux, Apache, MySQL, and PHP. Together, these four software systems provide a complete solution for data-driven web applications.

ROracle: Connects with the widely used Oracle commercial database package. Oracle is a widely deployed commercial database system. Interestingly, Oracle acquired Sun Microsystems in 2010 and thereby gained control of the open source MySQL system.

RPostgreSQL: Connects with the well-developed, full-featured PostgreSQL (sometimes just called Postgres) database system. PostgreSQL is a much older system than MySQL and has a much larger developer community. Unlike MySQL, which is effectively now controlled by Oracle, PostgreSQL has a developer community that is independent of any company and a licensing scheme that allows anybody to modify and reuse the code.

RSQlite: Connects with SQlite, another open source, independently developed database system. As the name suggests, SQlite has a very light code footprint, meaning that it is fast and compact.

RMongo: Connects with the MongoDB system, which is the only system here that does not use SQL. Instead, MongoDB uses JavaScript to access data. As such it is well suited for web development applications.

RODBC: Connects with ODBC compliant databases, which include Microsoft's SQLserver, Microsoft Access, and Microsoft Excel, among others. Note that these applications are native to Windows and Windows Server, and as such the support for

Mac OS and Linux is limited. On the other hand, if you are just using R/RStudio as a "client" to access data over the Internet, it doesn't matter so much whether the data are stored on a Windows system.

For demonstration purposes, we will create a local installation of RMySQL and connect to it from R/RStudio. This requires installing a copy of MySQL on your computer. Use your web browser to go to this page:

http://dev.mysql.com/downloads/

Then look for the MySQL Community Server. The term "community" in this context refers to the free, open source developer community version of MySQL. We used version 8 of MySQL for this demonstration. Note that there are also commercial versions of SQL developed and marketed by various companies. Download the version of MySQL Community Server that is most appropriate for your computer's operating system and install it. At this writing, the R packages we are using did not support the more advanced password facility that MySQL offers, so we are using the standard password facility from version 5 of MySQL (an option that you can control in later versions of MySQL). Note that unlike user applications, such as a word processor, there is not much of a user interface for this kind of server software. Instead, this software mostly runs quietly in the background, providing services that other programs can use. This is the essence of the client–server idea. In most cases, the server will be on some remote computer to which we do not have physical access. As noted above, for this demonstration you will run the server on your own computer.

On the Mac installation used in preparation of this chapter, the installer included the MySQL Preference Pane, which allows for turning the server on and off. Because we are just doing a demonstration here, and we want to avoid future security problems, it is sensible to turn the MySQL server off after completing the demonstration. In Windows, you can use the MySQL Workbench to control the server settings on your local computer. On either Windows or Mac, you will need to create an initial database in the system. We will call our database "test." On Windows, using the MySQL Workbench, you can use the "Create Schema" dialog to establish a new database. On the Mac, you can use the terminal application and type a command line like this:

```
mysql --user=root --password=MyPW --execute="CREATE DATABASE test"
```

You will need to substitute into that command line the password that you established when you installed MySQL. You may also need to run this command from within the "bin" folder where the MySQL programs are stored. The MySQL Preference Pane shows the location of this folder.

Returning to R, use install.packages() and library() to prepare the RMySQL package for use. If everything is working the way it should, you should be able to run the following command from the command line:

```
library("RMySQL)
con <- dbConnect(dbDriver("MySQL"), username="root", pass-
    word="MyPW", dbname="test")
```

As noted above, you will need to substitute into that command line the password that you established when you installed MySQL. The dbConnect() function establishes a linkage or connection between R and the database we want to use. Using dbConnect() as the starting point for our database access underscores the point that we are connecting to an external resource and we must therefore manage the connection.

The dbDriver() function provided as an argument to dbConnect specifies that we want to use a MySQL client. The database name—specified as dbname = "test"—refers to the database that we created after installing MySQL. A database is like a big container that can hold many different tables, where each table is like a dataframe. We can use the dbListTables() function to see what tables are available to us:

```
dbListTables(con)
character(0)
```

The response character(0) means that this is an empty list, so no tables have been established within our database. This is not surprising, because we just installed MySQL and created "test" as an empty database. We can use the census data we obtained earlier in the chapter to create our first table within the "test" database:

```
dbWriteTable(con, name="census", value=testFrame,
    overwrite=TRUE)
[1] TRUE
```

Take note of the arguments supplied to the dbWriteTable() function. The first argument provides the database connection to the test database that we established with the dbConnect() function. The census argument gives our new table in MySQL a name. We use testFrame as the source of data—as noted above a dataframe and a relational database table are very similar in structure. Finally, we provide the argument overwrite=TRUE, which was not really needed in this case—because we know that there were no existing tables—but could be important in other operations where we need to make sure to replace any old table that might have been left around from previous work. The function returns the logical value TRUE to signal that it was able to finish the request that we made. This is important in programming new functions because we can use the signal of success or failure to guide subsequent steps and provide error or success messages. Note that on some installations of MySQL starting with Version 8, it may be necessary to control a global security configuration variable called "local_infile" in order to allow R to upload a data table from R into MySQL. From either the MySQL Workbench or the terminal command line, issue this SQL command to allow the system to load local tables:

```
"SET GLOBAL local_infile = true"
```

Now if we run dbListTables() we should see our new table:

```
dbListTables(con)
[1] "census"
```

Now we can run an SQL query on our table:

```
dbGetQuery(con, "SELECT stateName, july11pop FROM
                 census WHERE july11pop<1000000")
              stateName    july11pop
1                Alaska      722718
2              Delaware      907135
3   District of Columbia     617996
4               Montana      998199
5          North Dakota      683932
6          South Dakota      824082
7               Vermont      626431
8               Wyoming      568158
```

Note that the dbGetQuery() call shown above breaks into two lines, but the string starting with SELECT has to be typed all on one line. The capitalized words in that string are the SQL commands. SELECT in combination with WHERE chooses a subset of the table that meets the condition we specified, namely that the value of july11pop needed to be less than 1,000,000 for that row to be included. The fields named after SELECT are the ones that will appear in the result. The FROM command chooses the table from which to extract the data. SQL is a very powerful and flexible language and although we present a few more examples of SQL below, it is beyond the scope of this chapter to give a more complete SQL tutorial.

In this case we did not assign the results of dbGetQuery() to another data object, so the results were just echoed to the R console. But it would be easy to assign the results to a dataframe and then use that dataframe for subsequent calculations or visualizations. Before we finish with MySQL, let's disconnect R from the database system, so that we don't leave any loose ends lying around. After running this command, you can also shut off the MySQL server on your computer's operating system.

```
dbDisconnect(con)
[1] TRUE
```

To emphasize a point made above, the typical motivation for accessing data through MySQL or another database system is that a large database exists on a remote server. Rather than having our own complete copy of those data, we can use dbConnect(), dbGetQuery(), and other database functions to access the remote data through SQL. We can also use SQL to specify subsets of the data, to preprocess the data with sorting and other operations, and to create summaries of the data. SQL is also particularly well suited to joining data from multiple tables to make new combinations. In the present example, we used only one table, it was a very small table, and we had created it ourselves in R from an Excel source, so none of these were very good motivations for storing our data in MySQL, but this was only a demonstration.

# COMPARING SQL AND R/TIDYVERSE FOR ACCESSING A DATASET

In R, there is a library sqldf, that enables us to treat a dataframe as a database. So, for example, we can do the same SQL query using sqldf on a dataframe, that we previously did using SQL on a database. As a first example, as shown below, we can use SQL to compute the average of a column within testFrame, and compare the results with computing the mean directly in R. Note that the code below assumes that we have already installed the sqldf package and run library("sqldf"). The options() command below might also be needed if you have been using MySQL, and it directs sqldf to use dataframes for its databases—otherwise sqldf would try to connect to MySQL or another external database.

```
library("sqldf")
options(sqldf.driver = "SQLite")
sqldf("select avg(april10base) From testFrame")
avg(april10base)
1 6009064

mean(testFrame$april10base)
[1] 6009064
```

As you can see, we can do SQL commands using the dataframe as the database. The actual SQL is the same as normal SQL. So, we can also do some more advanced SQL commands, and compare that code to similar functionality available via Tidyverse. For example, we can select the state names that meet the condition where the july11pop is greater than a certain value:

```
sqldf("select stateName From testFrame
                Where july11pop<1000000")
            stateName
1              Alaska
2            Delaware
3 District of Columbia
4             Montana
5        North Dakota
```

```
6              South Dakota
7                 Vermont
8                 Wyoming
```

Using tidyverse, we can do something similar with the filter command to remove all the rows that do not meet the specified condition (july11pop is less than the 1,000,000) and the select command to select the column of interest (the state name):

```
testFrame %>%
    filter(july11pop<1000000) %>%
    select(stateName)
# A tibble: 7 x 1
  stateName
  <chr>
1 Alaska
2 Delaware
3 Montana
4 North Dakota
5 South Dakota
6 Vermont
7 Wyoming
```

Let's also explore the ability to group subsets of our data to calculate the average population by region of the country. To accomplish this, we need to add a region for each state in the country. R has some built-in datasets of state data, so we can make a temporary dataframe containing the state name and the region.

```
sregions <- data.frame(stateName=state.name, region=state.
    region)
head(sregions)
      stateName region
1       Alabama  South
2        Alaska   West
3       Arizona   West
4      Arkansas  South
5    California   West
6      Colorado   West
```

Now we have a list of state names and their corresponding regions. Let's match that up with our existing data.

```
newFrame <- sqldf("select testFrame.stateName,
    july11pop, region from testFrame join sregions on
    testFrame.stateName=sregions.stateName")
```

This is our best SQL statement yet! It selects the three columns that we want to retrieve: the stateName, july11pop, and region columns. It also "joins" testFrame and sregions by matching them up based on the values of stateName. A join is a very powerful SQL statement that creates linkages between two database tables using a "key" field that exists in both tables. We've saved the result in a new dataframe called newFrame. With this new dataframe, we can use the Group by SQL function to determine the average population for each region, based on the states in a specific region.

```
sqldf("select AVG(july11pop) From newFrame
                              Group by region")
    AVG(july11pop)
1         5596570
2         6169066
3         7214296
4         5604981
```

In R, we can do something very similar using the group_by function for the region column, and then summarizing those values by computing the mean of the july11pop values for the grouped states. Seeing these functions in action might make this easier to understand:

```
newFrame %>%
      group_by(region) %>%
      summarize(regionMean=mean(july11pop))
region          regionMean
 <fct>              <dbl>
1 Northeast      6169066.
2 South          7214296.
```

```
3 North Central 5596570.
4 West          5604981.
```

As you can see, this result provides the same data as the Group by SQL command. Let's use these region means to do more with R. Specifically, let's store the region mean for each state. This is more complicated than many other tasks we have done: we have four regions, but many states. We need to figure out which region mean should be associated with each state.

To do this, we first calculate the region means in a regionMean column within our testFrame via the use of the group_by function that we previously used and the mutate function that added a column, based on the grouped by means.

```
newFrame %<>%
    group_by(region) %>%
    mutate(regionMean = mean(july11pop))
```

The Tidyverse mutate() command used the groupings to calculate the mean within each region. You can also see the use of a new symbol "%<>%," which works like the pipe symbol ("%>%"), but then stores the result back into the dataframe (in this case, into newFrame).

We can look at some of the results by selecting the columns of interest and slicing the dataset (getting one row). Note that the Tidyverse slice(1) function gives us the first row for each of the different groups!

```
newFrame %>%
    select(stateName, region, regionMean) %>%
    slice(1)
# A tibble: 4 x 3
# Groups: region [4]
  stateName     region        regionMean
  <chr>         <fct>              <dbl>
1 Connecticut   Northeast        6146360.
2 Alabama       South            7122127.
3 Illinois      North Central    5577249.
4 Alaska        West             5534273.
```

Those examples were a lot to take in because we showed off one of the key maxims of working in R (as well as many other languages): there are usually several different ways of accomplishing any given task. You may become involved in projects that involve SQL coding and you may have to reuse SQL code that others have produced. In those cases, using sqldf() or another database access package to run SQL commands within R can give you all of the flexibility and power that SQL offers. On the other hand, if you are writing new R code, you can accomplish just about anything that SQL can do by using the appropriate Tidyverse commands. So many choices!

## ACCESSING JSON DATA

The next strategy we will explore involves the use of an application programming interface (API) to communicate with another application or database system. We will explore JSON, an increasingly common way to share data on the web. JSON is a structured, but human readable way of sending back some data from an application or a website. Sometimes those data are static, but other times a website will use JSON to supply up-to-the-minute information. JSON was created by Douglas Crockford in the early 2000s, while he was working at a start-up funded by Tesla Ventures. Although originally derived from the JavaScript scripting language, JSON is a language-independent data format and code for creating and parsing. JSON is available for many programming languages, including R!

We will start by exploring how to get recent exchange rate information. Because this information changes frequently, using an excel spreadsheet of exchange rates can cause problems, because the rates stored in a spreadsheet go quickly out of date. We might also want the exchange rate for a specific day in the past. Let's use a website that offers a JSON interface to exchange rate data. There are many websites that offer this capability (you can google "foreign exchange rates json" to see many possible websites that also provide this data). We will use openexchangerates.org within our code. Like most of the websites, openexchangerates requires that we have an app ID key to do a JSON query. Websites use this strategy so that, if a person or business wanted to make many, many queries, the website could track and charge for that service. We will not be using that many JSON requests and so can easily register at their website to get a free app ID key. It is a simple process: first you create an account (the free level), which, as of this writing, can be found at https://openexchangerates.org/signup/free. After you get an account, the next step is to get an "app ID," which we will use on our JSON requests. Note that the free level provides up to 1,000 JSON queries per month.

The open exchange rates API allows a user (program or person) to supply a request. The site will return a list of exchange rates. A different request can be used to get the exchange rates for a specific day in the past. The API can be accessed over the web, using what is called an HTTP GET request. HTTP is the hypertext transfer protocol, and it is the standard method for requesting and receiving web page data. A GET request consists of information that is included in the URL string to specify some details about the information we are hoping to get back from the request. Here is an example GET request to the open exchange rates API:

https://openexchangerates.org/api/latest.json?app_id=yourKeyGoesHere

This request can be typed into a web browser as a web address, however, you need to update the "yourKeyGoesHere" with the key you got from open exchange rates. The first part of the web address should look familiar: the http://openexchangerates.org part of the URL specifies the domain name just like a regular web page. The next part of the URL, api/latest.json?app_id=, tells openexchangerates which API we want to use, and the json indicates that we would like to receive our result in JSON. Finally, the last part specifies the our app_id.

As previously mentioned, you can type that whole URL into the address field of any web browser and you should get a sensible result back. The JSON notation is not beautiful, but you will see that it makes sense and provides the names of individual data items along with their values. Here's a small excerpt that shows the key parts of the data object that we are trying to get our hands on:

```
{
    "disclaimer": "Usage subject to terms…
    "license": "https://openexchangerates.org/license",
    "timestamp": 1563548400,
    "base": "USD",
    "rates": {
      "AED": 3.673158,
```

```
"AFN": 80.051007,
"ALL": 109,
"AMD": 476.417628,
```

There's much more data in the JSON object that was returned, and we can use the R jsonlite package to extract the data we need from the structure without having to parse it ourselves.

To have R send the HTTP GET requests to openexchangerates, we will also use the RCurl package. This will give us a single command to send the request and receive the result back—essentially doing all of the quirky steps that a web browser takes care of automatically for us. To get started, install.packages() and library() the two packages we will need—RCurl and jsonlite. If you are working on a Windows machine, you might need to jump through a hoop or two to get RCurl, but it is available for Windows even if it is not in the standard CRAN repository. Search for RCurl Windows if you run into trouble.

Let's create a new helper function to take the address field and turn it into the URL that we need:

```
# Load the necessary libraries before getting started
library("RCurl")
library("jsonlite")

#Format a URL to get a JSON exchange rate
getRateURL <- function(YOUR_APP_ID) {
    rURL <- "https://openexchangerates.org/api/latest"
    secondPart <- ".json?app_id="
    url <- paste0(rURL,secondPart,YOUR_APP_ID)
    return(url)
}
```

There are three simple steps here. The first line initializes the beginning part of the URL into a string called root. We next initialize the second part of the URL and then use paste0() to glue together the separate parts as well as the app ID. This creates a string that looks like the one in the example above. The final step converts the string to a legal URL using a utility function called URLencode() that RCurl provides. Let's test it with a fake app_id:

```
getRateURL("abc123")
[1] "https://openexchangerates.org/api/latest.
   json?app_id=abc123"
```

Looks good! Remember that you can type this function at the command line or you can create it in the script editing window in the upper-left-hand pane of RStudio. The latter is the better way to go; if you click the Source on Save checkmark, RStudio will make sure to update R's stored version of your function every time you save the script file. Now we can use our new function, getRateURL() to actually request the data:

```
# Replace with your app_id from the site
appID <- "abc123"

#get the URL
url <- getRateURL(appID)

#get the data from the web
apiResult <- getURL(url)

#parse the JSON data into a dataframe
fxStruct <- fromJSON(apiResult)
fxStructDF <- data.frame(fxStruct)

#look at the Euro conversion rate (for USD)
fxStructDF$rates.EUR
[1] 0.891107
```

Before you run this code, make sure to go to the website and get your own free app_id. Use that value in place of abc123 in the code above. The first thing this code does is to pass our app id string to getRateURL() to develop the formatted URL. Then the code passes the URL to getURL(), which actually does the work of sending the request out onto the Internet. The getURL() function is part of the RCurl package. This step is just like typing a URL into the address box of your browser.

We capture the result in an object called apiResult. If we were to stop and look inside this, we would find the JSON structure that appeared above. We can pass this structure to the function fromJSON(), and finally, we convert the list from JSON into a dataframe. This is a regular R dataframe such that we can access any individual element using regular $ notation. The fromJSON() function has done all the heavy lifting of breaking the JSON structure into its component pieces. With just a few lines of R code we have harnessed the power of the web to convert an exchange rate.

Now let's try to read a large JSON dataset. Our example that we will parse is a dataset about the Citi Bike program in New York City. There are similar programs in many cities. The basic idea is that a person can rent a bike from one bike location and ride it to another location in the city. The person can leave it there. So, for example, maybe you take a bike to work, lock it at a location near work, but in the evening, if it's raining, you can take the train home. The next day, you can ride a different bike to work. Of course, if it rained every afternoon for a week, and everyone acted the same way, eventually, there would be no bikes in some locations (and no empty spaces in other Citi Bike locations). Hence, Citi Bike makes data available about how many bikes and spaces are available at each of its locations. One of the ways Citi Bike make these data available is via JSON. To start, after loading the jsonlite and RCurl libraries, we load the JSON dataset with the following code:

```
bikeURL <- paste0('https://gbfs.citibikenyc.com/',
                  'gbfs/en/station_status.json')
apiResult <- getURL(bikeURL)
results <- fromJSON(apiResult)
```

First, we captured the result in an object called apiResult. Note that, as was previously mentioned, just as for a CSV file, JSON is human readable. So, if we type the url into a browser, we can see the results on a web page, just as we did for the exchange rate API. If we were to stop and look inside the apiResult, we would find the JSON structure. We then pass this structure to the function fromJSON()—and put the result in an object called results. Just as before, this is a regular R dataframe such that we can access any individual element using regular $ notation. Using this notation, we get the stations dataframe from the results, as shown below:

```
stations <- results$data$stations
```

The next we simplify the stations dataframe, by just keeping the attributes of interest:

```
cols <- c('num_bikes_disabled','num_docks_disabled',
    'station_id', 'num_ebikes_available',
    'num_bikes_available', 'num_docks_available')

stations = stations[,cols]
nrow(stations)
[1] 1050
```

Although this was a bit of a hassle, we are starting to see some real data—specifically, that there are 1,050 places where someone can grab or return a bike. Let's look at one station to see the type of information available for each station:

```
 str(stations)
'data.frame': 1050 obs. of 6 variables:
 $ num_bikes_disabled  : int 1 0 1 0 1 1 3 0 2 1 ...
 $ num_docks_disabled  : int 0 0 0 0 0 0 0 0 0 ...
 $ station_id          : chr "72" "79" "82" "83" ...
 $ num_ebikes_available: int 0 0 0 0 0 0 0 0 0 ...
 $ num_bikes_available : int 4 5 10 45 4 9 4 31 25 1 ...
 $ num_docks_available : int 50 28 16 17 45 9 12 0 3 ...
```

Now we finally have interesting data! We can see there are 50 docks (the places to park a bike) available at the first station, and that there are four bikes available, which you can see is another data element in the list. There are other interesting pieces of information, such as the number of disables (not working) bikes at the station.

We are done reading in a JSON dataset! However, just for fun, before we move on let's take a look at some of the data. Of course, if we rerun the code, we might get different results since these data update throughout the day, every day.

```
mean(stations$num_docks_available)
[1] 17.69238


mean(stations$num_bikes_available)
[1] 11.73429
```

```
bikesAvailDF <-
        stations[stations$num_bikes_available >0,]
nrow(bikesAvailDF)
[1] 944
```

We can see that there is an average of roughly 18 docks available at each station, and there is an average of roughly 12 bikes available at each station. However, there are 944 stations with at least one bike available (and remember, there are a total of 1,050 stations).

We have covered a lot in the chapter and an important takeaway point is that there are many ways to store and access data. One of our jobs, as data scientists, is to be able to read the data from any available source and put it into a usable format within R for further processing.

# CASE STUDY: READING, CLEANING, AND EXPLORING A SURVEY DATASET

```
Case Key Points:
-  Read a JSON file that has more complete survey data.
-  Clean the dataset (survey) by removing NAs and determine
   the percentage of the datafile was removed via cleaning.
-  Create an attribute that will have a true/false based
   on if the arrival time was delayed by more than five
   minutes.
-  Create a different attribute that will have a true/false
   based on if that person was a detractor.
```

Let's explore a more complete airline survey dataset, that is available via JSON. First, we can read in the new JSON datafile.

```
#Read in the JSON datafile
library(jsonlite)
mydata.list <- fromJSON("completeSurvey.json" )
surveyWithNA <- data.frame(mydata.list)

#Look at the datafile (don't use View - it's too big)
glimpse(surveyWithNA)
```

Depending on the speed of your computer, this might take a couple of minutes. When it is done and you look at the output of glimpse, you will see 32 variables (attributes). Here's a description of these attributes:

1. **Likelihood to Recommend**—the airline is rated on a scale of 1 to 10, which shows how likely the customer is to recommend the airline to their friends (10 is very likely, and 1 is not very likely).

2. **Airline Status**—each customer has a different type of airline status or package, which are platinum, gold, silver, and blue.

3. **Age**—the specific customer's age. That is starting from 15 to 85 years old.

4. **Gender**—male or female.

5. **Price Sensitivity**—the grade to which the price affects customers purchasing. The price sensitivity has a range from 0 to 5.

6. **Year of First Flight**—the first flight of each single customer. The range of year of the first flight for each customer has been started in 2003 until 2012.

7. **Flights Per Year**—the number of flights that each customer has taken in the most recent 12 months. The range starting from 0 to 100.

8. **Loyalty**—an index of loyalty ranging from -1 to 1 that reflects the proportion of flights taken on other airlines versus flights taken on this airline. A higher index means more loyalty.

9. **Type of Travel**—is to provide three traveling purposes for each consumer, which are business travel, mileage tickets based on loyalty card, and personal travel such as to see the family or go on vacation.

10. **Total Frequent Flyer Accounts**—how many frequent flyer accounts the customer has.

11. **Shopping Amount at Airport**—the spending in dollars on non-food/drink goods and services at the airport(s) where the customer was before, between, or after flights.

12. **Eating and Drinking at Airport**—the spending in dollars on food/drink goods and services at the airport(s) where the customer was before, between, or after flights.

13. **Class**—it consisted of three different kinds of service levels such as, business, economy plus, and economy. Moreover, customers have the option to choose their seat.

14. **Day of Month**—it means the traveling day of each customer. This attribute shows a total of 31 days of the month.

15. **Flight Date**—all of these data abbreviate the passenger's flight date travel, which were since 2014 and only in January, February, and March.

16. **Partner Code**—this airline works with wholly and partially owned subsidiary companies to deliver regional flights. For example, AA, AS, B6, and DL.

17. **Partner Name**—these are the full names of the subsidiary airline companies. Pseudonyms have been substituted in place of the real names.

18. **Origin City**—refers to actual city that customers have departed from. For example, Yuma, Arizona; Waco, Texas; and Toledo, Ohio.

19. **Origin State**—same thing as origin city except it's what state customers have departed from. For example, Texas, Ohio, Alaska, and Utah.

20. **Destination City**—the place to which passenger travels to. For example, Akron, Ohio; Alpena, Michigan; Austin, Texas; and Boston Massachusetts.

21. **Destination State**—the state to which the passenger travels to. Some examples of destination states include Alaska, Kentucky, Iowa, and Florida.

22. **Scheduled Departure Hour**—the specific time at which passengers are scheduled to depart. In this data, the scheduled departure hour is starting at 1 a.m. until 23 p.m.

23. **Departure Delay in Minutes**—which are minutes of departure delayed for each passenger, when compared to schedule. In this data, the range is starting from 0 until 1,128 minutes.

24. **Arrival Delay in Minutes**—how many minutes of arrival delayed of each passenger. Range of delayed minutes in this data is starting from 0 until 1,115 minutes.

25. **Flight Cancelled**—occurs when the airline does not operates the flight at all, and that is for a certain reason.

26. **Flight Time in Minutes**—indicates time period to the destination.

27. **Flight Distance**—the extent of space between two places. Also, this means how many minutes passengers are traveling between two different places. Range in this data starts from 31 until 4,983 minutes.

28. **olong**—the longitude of the origin city.

29. **olat**—the latitude of the origin city.

30. **dlong**—the longitude of the destination city.

31. **dlat**—the latitude of the destination city.

32. **freeText**—free form text response provided by the customer.

First, let's remove any NAs from the dataset:

```
#Remove rows with the 'Likelihood.to.recommend' == NA
survey <- surveyWithNA %>%
       filter(!is.na(Likelihood.to.recommend))

#What percentage was removed via the cleaning?
(1 - nrow(survey)/nrow(surveyWithNA) ) * 100
[1] 0.004540295

#Remove any row with an NA
survey <- na.omit(surveyWithNA)

#What percentage was removed via this cleaning?
(1 - nrow(survey)/nrow(surveyWithNA) ) * 100
[1] 99.71623
```

Wow! If we remove all the rows with any NA, we will remove over 99% of the dataset. So, for now, let's just remove the surveys with NA in the Likelihood.to.recommend column.

```
#Remove rows with the 'Likelihood.to.recommend' == NA
survey <- surveyWithNA %>%
       filter(!is.na(Likelihood.to.recommend))
```

Finally, let's create two new attributes

```
#Was the arrival delayed by more than 5 minutes.
survey$Big.Arrival.Delay <-
        survey$Arrival.Delay.in.Minutes > 5
#Was the person a detractor.
survey$Detractor <- survey$Likelihood.to.recommend < 7
```

We will hold off doing extensive analysis until future chapters, but for now, let's explore the impact of a big arrival delay on the percentage of people that are detractors.

```
survey %>%
    group_by(Big.Arrival.Delay) %>%
    summarize(percentDetractor = mean(Detractor) )
#    A tibble: 3 x 2
    Big.Arrival.Delay percentDetractor
    <lgl>             <dbl>
1   FALSE             0.261
2   TRUE              0.616
```

So, we can see that approximately 62% of the people who had a large delay were detractors, but only 26% of the people who did not have a large delay were detractors. This should, of course, not be shocking—people do not like when their flight is delayed!

## Chapter Challenges

1.  Create an Excel file on your local computer that contains at least two columns and a minimum of three rows. Make sure that the first row contains variable names. Read the Excel file into R using the readxl package and the read_excel() command. Use the glimpse() command (from the Tidyverse) to provide an overview of your data once it has been imported into R.

2.  Copy the mtcars built-in dataset into a new dataframe called myCars. Use the slice() command (from the Tidyverse) to remove the first 16 rows of your new dataframe. How many rows are left?

3.  Use sqldf() and the appropriate SQL command to retrieve the rows from mtcars that have mpg greater than 20. How many records (rows) were returned?

4.  Use pipes and the filter() command (from the Tidyverse) to get the rows from mtcars that have mpg greater than 20.

5.  Use sqldf() and the appropriate SQL command to calculate the average of the hp variable in the mtcars dataset. Compare that value to the result of using the mean() command on the same column of data.

6.  Use the summary() command to explore the large case dataset that we imported from JSON at the beginning of the chapter. Find the two numeric columns that have many NAs (say, more than 1,000). Use the is.na() command on each of those columns to create lists of which observations are missing. Store the resulting lists in new variables.

7.  Run table() on the two new variables from Exercise 6. Write a comment describing what you see. If you wanted to eliminate rows that had missing data on both of those variables, how many rows would be lost?

8.  Explore the web for other JSON datasets. Find one that is interesting and read the JSON dataset into R. Work with the JSON dataset to make sure it can be easily used by creating a dataframe with the key information that was read using JSON.

## Sources

http://cran.r-project.org/doc/manuals/R-data.html

www.json.org

http://dev.mysql.com/downloads/

http://en.wikipedia.org/wiki/Comparison_of_relational_database_management_systems

## R Functions Used in This Chapter

getURL() Gets the results of a web page.

fromJSON() Converts a JSON data source to R.

library() Makes an R package available for use.

read.xls() Imports data from a binary R file; part of the gdata package.

str_replace() Replaces one character string with another.

str_replace_all() Replaces multiple instances of a character string with another.

dbConnect() Connects to an SQL database.

dbGetQuery() Runs an SQL query and return the results.

dbListTables() Shows the tables available in a connection.

dbWriteTable() Sends a data table to an SQL system.

install.packages() Gets the code for an R package.

sqldf() Treats a dataframe as a database for SQL commands.

This text includes access to datasets and select student resources. To learn more, visit sagepub.com

# 8

# PICTURES VERSUS NUMBERS

# LEARNING OBJECTIVES

Understand what visualization is, and how it compares with statistical analysis.

Describe the key characteristics in an effective visualization.

Effectively use the ggplot2 package, including understanding the three key components (data, aesthetics, geometry).

Construct histograms, boxplots, line charts, bar charts, scatter charts, and heatmaps in R, using ggplot2.

Gain experience using the following R functions: ggplot (and building layers in ggplot via ggtitle, geom_histogram, geom_boxlot, geom_line, geom_col, geom_point, geom_text, coord_flip, theme, format, scale_color_continuous).

Sometimes it is really helpful to "see" your data. Seeing the data is typically known as visualization. We can think of visualization as turning data into pictures. More formally, in the book *Interactive Data Visualization* (2015, Boca Raton, FL: CRC Press), Matthew Ward, Georges Grinstein, and Daniel Keim define visualization as "the communication of information using graphical representations." Information visualization is the use of visual representations of abstract data. In other words, information visualization is used when there is no well-defined two-dimensional or three-dimensional representation of the data. In this chapter, we will explore information visualization. In Chapter 9, we will explore data that have a geometric component, just as our Citi Bike data had a geometric component of stations (that had a physical address).

Visualization is often useful since human vision has the highest bandwidth of all our senses, in that human vision is fast and can process information in parallel. In addition, the brain is tuned for rapid visual pattern recognition—we can scan an image, quickly recognize anomalies, and remember that image. For example, quickly reviewing a grid of numbers (perhaps an Excel spreadsheet) and finding the large and small numbers can be difficult. However, if the grid cells are color coded based on the numeric values, it is much easier to identify the largest and smallest numbers.

# A VISUALIZATION OVERVIEW

There are six key components one can use to create a visualization. To help think about these components, let's imagine a simple scatterplot with dots (or other symbols) arrayed on a flat surface (like a computer screen) with an X-axis along the bottom and a Y-axis along the side. Here are the six components:

Proximity/location: The position of the symbol relative to the X- and Y-axes.

Color: The color of each symbol. Beyond proximity (location), color is the most common component of a data visualization. Note that 7–10% of men have red-green color blindness, so the use of color needs to take this into account.

Size: The size of each symbol in the scatterplot.

Texture: The shape of the symbol and whether the symbol is a solid color or a pattern.

Annotation: Labels and legends that we use on our scatterplots.

Interactivity: The capability to select one or more symbols and get information about it, as well as zooming, animation, and other features.

Before we start exploring how to create visualizations, one last point to remember is that often, in a visualization, we must focus on making sure that the picture is easy to understand. A common mistake is to create a visualization that contains a lot of information but that is difficult to understand. For example, it is easy to create a visualization that has so much information that there is information overload, and it would be more effective to actually show less data! To address this concern, we describe 10 principles that should be useful to think about as you create a visualization.

1. Simplicity. The statistician and information designer Edward Tufte is famous for suggesting that you should create the simplest graph that conveys the information you want to convey. This is a good rule to remember!

2. Encoding. Consider the type of encoding used to connect a numeric value to a graphical feature, and try to make the encoding intuitive. For example, a larger numeric value should be represented by a larger dot and a smaller value by a smaller dot.

3. Patterns versus details. Make a choice whether to highlight big picture patterns or fine-level details. It is very hard to do both in the same graphic.

4. Ranges. Select meaningful ranges for the axes.

5. Transformations. Transforming data can be useful, particularly when a set of numeric values cover a very large range. For example, a natural log transformation can compress the range 1–1,000 into a seven-point scale.

6. Density. Use transparency to represent data where many points are plotted near to or on top of one another. Another useful strategy to avoid the problem of "overplotting" is to use jitter—a technique that moves points very slightly and randomly.

7. Connections. Use lines to connect sequential data. This is particularly important when showing a time series.

8. Aggregates. Combine data by creating meaningful groups.

9. Comparison. Keep axis ranges as similar as possible when comparing multiple graphs.

10. Color. Select an appropriate color scheme, based on the meaning of the data. For example, gradations of heat might be represented with shades of blue and red, whereas the density of plant life might be shown with yellow and green.

Now we are set to begin creating visualizations! In fact, before this chapter we have used some of the R base graphics during our initial exploration of datasets. For example, when we wanted to understand the distribution of a vector (such as population of states within the United States), we computed the mean, range, quantiles, and other attributes such as skewness, but often it is much easier to understand information presented in a picture. In this case, to understand the distribution of a set of numbers (or a column in a dataset), we used a histogram. This visualization provided a view of the data that complemented our descriptive statistics that we generated in Chapters 5 and 6.

# BASIC PLOTS IN R

So, let's continue to explore the states population dataset that we introduced in Chapter 3:

```
dfStates <- readCensus("nst-est2011-01.csv")
```

We can start by reviewing the R base graphics that we have previously used. For example, if we want to understand the distribution of the state populations, we can show the histogram:

```
hist(dfStates$july11pop)
```

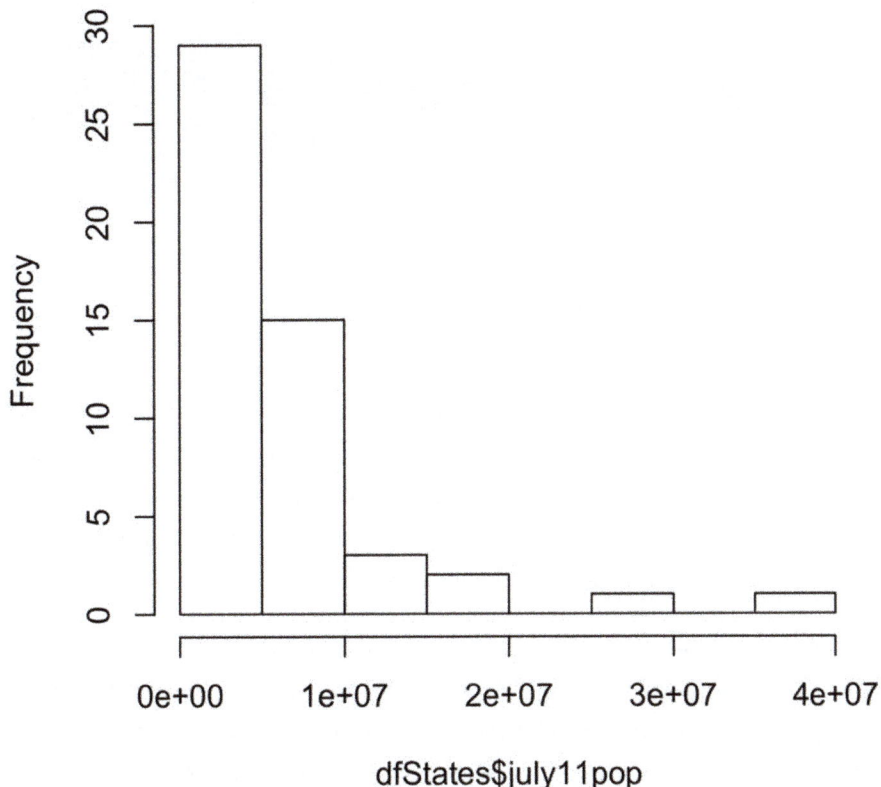

Using R base graphics, we can also show a bar plot (a bar chart):

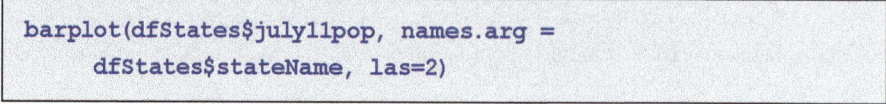

```
barplot(dfStates$july11pop, names.arg =
    dfStates$stateName, las=2)
```

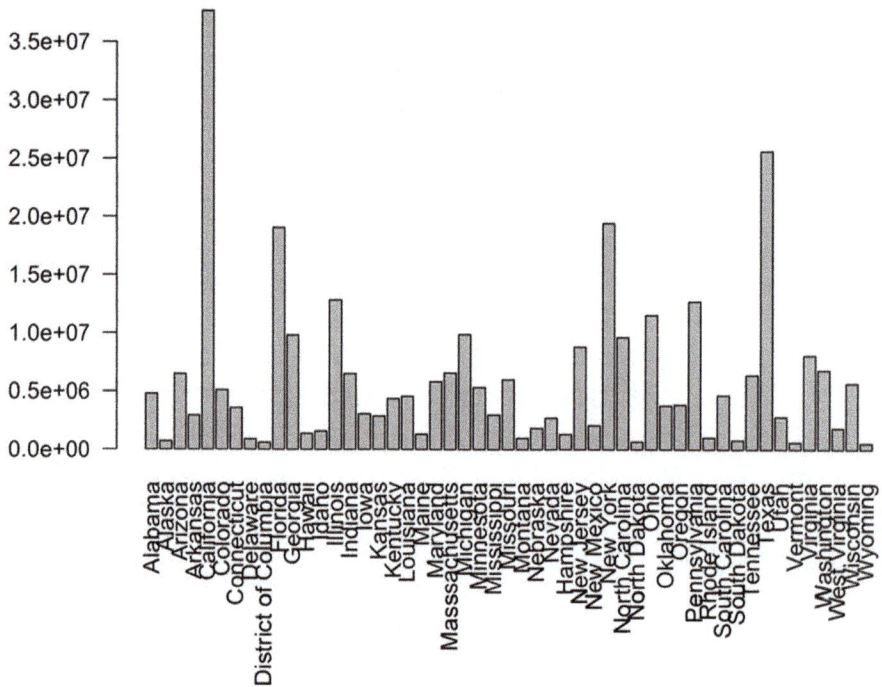

# USING THE GGPLOT2 PACKAGE

Although doing these simple charts in R's base graphics is very easy, if we want to create more-advanced visualizations, we need to explore an advanced visualization package, known as ggplot2, which is part of the tidyverse set of packages. As we will see, doing simple things in ggplot2 is a bit more complicated, but that extra work makes it much easier to build advanced and more useful visualizations.

According to ggplot2's own website (http://ggplot2.org/), "ggplot2 is a plotting system for R, based on the *grammar of graphics*, which tries to keep the good parts of base and lattice graphics and discard the bad parts. It takes care of many of the fiddly details that make plotting a hassle (like drawing legends) as well as providing a powerful model of graphics that makes it easy to produce complex multi-layered graphics." The "gg" stands for grammar of graphics. The package was created by Hadley Wickham in 2005 and is now the most commonly used visualization tool within the R ecosystem.

The concept behind ggplot2 is that it divides the definition of a plot into three different fundamental parts: Plot = data + Aesthetics + Geometry. The components of every plot can be defined as follows:

**Data**, which needs to be a dataframe.

**Aesthetics**, which is used to indicate x and y variables. It can also be used to control the color, the size, or the shape of points, the height of bars, and so on.

**Geometry**, which defines the type of graphics (histogram, box plot, line plot, density plot, dot plot, . . . .).

Before we get started using ggplot, we need to ensure that ggplot2 has been installed and libraried. Rather than doing this manually, let's create a function that will assist us and make the activity more repeatable. The function will take as input the name of a package. It then tests whether the package has been downloaded—installed—from the R code repository. If it has not yet been downloaded/installed, the function takes care of this. Then we use a new function, called require() to prepare the package for further use. Let's call our function EnsurePackage, because it ensures that a package is ready for us to use. It might make sense to create this function in a new R source file. If so, you should click the File menu and then click New to create a new file of R script. Then, type or copy/paste the following code:

```
EnsurePackage<-function(x) {
  x <- as.character(x)

  if (!require(x,character.only=TRUE)) {
    install.packages(pkgs=x, repos="http://cran.r-
    project.org")
    require(x,character.only=TRUE)
  }
}
```

On Windows machines, the folder where new R packages are stored has to be configured to allow R to put new files there ("write" permissions). In Windows Explorer, you may need to right click on the folder and choose Properties->Security, then choose your username and user group, click Edit, enable all permissions, and click OK. If you run into trouble, check out the Windows FAQ at CRAN by searching or using this web address: http://cran.r-project.org/bin/windows/base/rw-FAQ.html.

The require() function does the same thing as library(), which we have used throughout the book, but it also returns the value FALSE if the package you requested in the argument x has not yet been downloaded. That same line of code also contains another new feature, the "if" statement. This is what computer scientists call a conditional. It tests the stuff inside the parentheses to see if it evaluates to TRUE or FALSE. If TRUE, the program continues to run the script in between the inner pair of curly braces (lines 4 and 8). If FALSE, all the stuff in the curly braces is skipped. Also, in the third line, in case you are curious, the arguments to the require() function include x, which is the name of the package that was passed into the function, and character.only=TRUE, which tells the require() function to expect x to be a character string. Last thing to notice about this third line: there is an exclamation mark (!) character that reverses the results of the logical test. Technically, it is the Boolean function NOT. It requires some mental gyration that when require() returns FALSE, the ! inverts it to TRUE, and that is when the code inside the inner curly braces runs.

Once you have this code in a script window, as with other functions you define, make sure to select the whole function and click Run in the toolbar to make R aware of the function. There is also a checkbox on that same toolbar called Source on Save that will keep us from having to click on the Run button all the time. If you click the checkmark, then every time you save the source code file, RStudio will rerun the code. If you get in the habit of saving after every code change, you will always be running the latest version of your function.

Now we are ready to put EnsurePackage() to work:

```
EnsurePackage("tidyverse")
```

Note that we could have ensured that just ggplot2 was installed and libraried, but we will use other aspects of tidyverse later in this chapter, so we ensured all of tidyverse. Now that we can use ggplot2, let's explore one key aspect of the ggplot() function—the fact that we build up the plot with layers. The code below shows a histogram being built.

```r
#The data
g <- ggplot(dfStates)

#Add the aesthetic to the plot variable
g <- g + aes(x=july11pop)

#add the geometry
g <- g + geom_histogram(binwidth=5000000,
                        color="black", fill="white")

#add the title
g <- g + ggtitle("states population histogram")
g
```

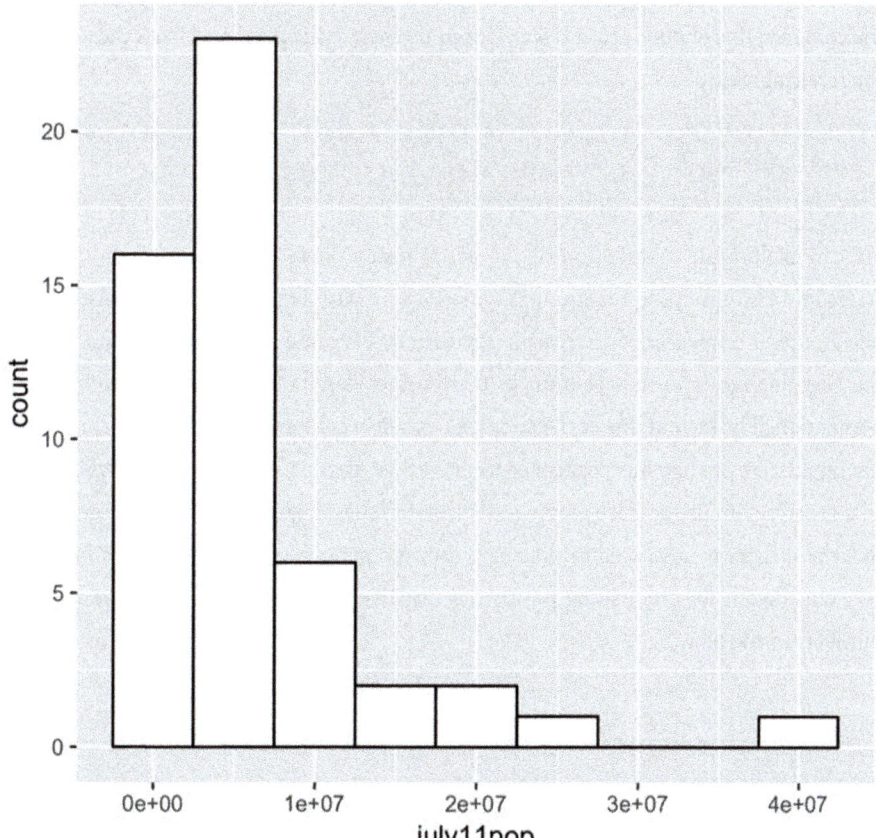

To review the code, the first line creates a ggplot, where the dataframe to be used is dfStates. Note that once we specify the dataframe (dfStates), ggplot looks at the columns within the dataset (such as july11pop). The next line of code defines the aesthetics, specifically, that the X-axis will be the july11pop population. On the following line, the geometry is defined, by stating that we want to use a histogram with the bars being white with a black outline; finally, we add a title.

Another way to examine the distribution of a set of numbers is to create a boxplot. A boxplot consists of a box, whiskers, and outliers. The box contains the middle 50% of the data, whereas the whiskers cover about 99% of the data, not counting outliers. The boxplot procedure has an algorithm to decide on what data points get shown as an outlier—often this contains any point that is farther away from the box than 1.5 times the width of the box. Note that the code below takes a different strategy from the previous code example by putting the data, aesthetic, and geometry all on one line. We also did not store the resulting visualization in a variable. For simple graphics that render quickly, there's no need to store the ggplot specification in a variable because we can simply run the complete line of code again if we want to regenerate the graphic. Here's the code and the resulting plot:

```
ggplot(dfStates) + aes(y=july11pop) + geom_boxplot()
```

We can explore the distribution of the population a bit more in depth by putting the states into two groups—one group for those states with an increase in population and one group for states with a decrease in population. We can use the following code, where the first line creates a new column in the dfStates dataframe, based on the change in population. The second line of the code creates a new column in the dataframe, noting if the population change was positive or negative. We use this as a grouping variable: states that grew go into the positive group and states that shrank go in the negative group. Note that the variable we are actually plotting is the total population of the state as of July 2011. So even though we grouped by positive or negative change, we won't see any negative numbers in the plot.

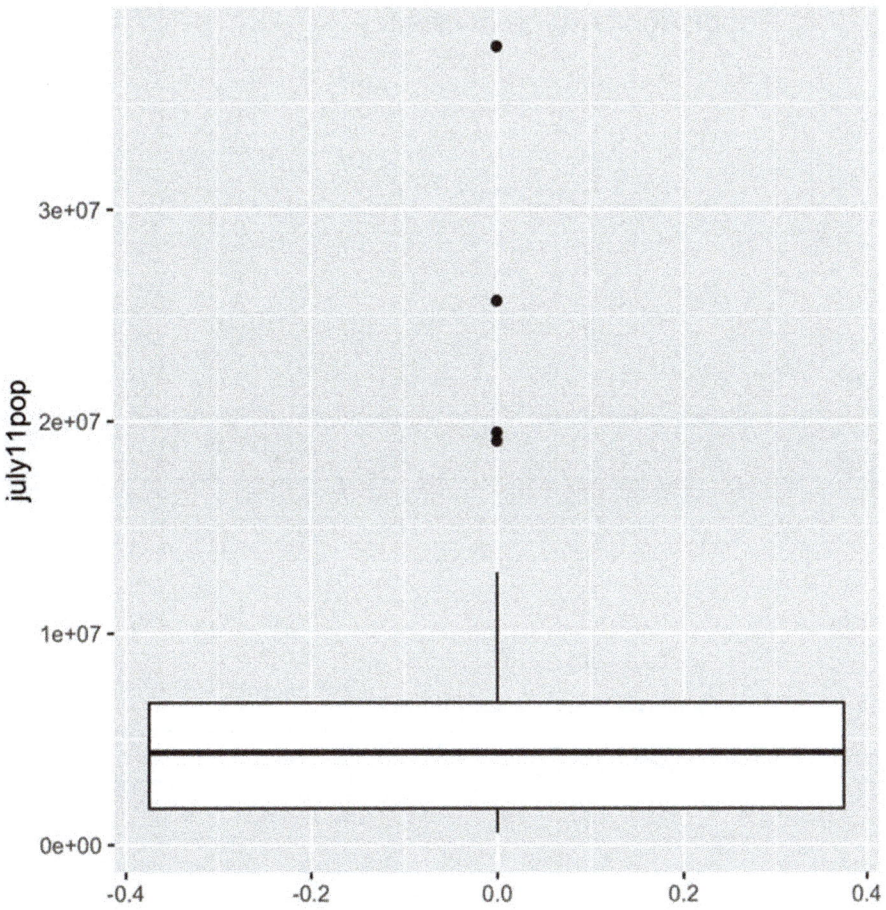

```
#create the two new attributes
dfStates$popChange <- dfStates$july11pop -
                               dfStates$july10pop

dfStates$increasePop <-
    ifelse(dfStates$popChange > 0,
                          "positive", "negative")

#now generate / display the boxplot
ggplot(dfStates) +
  aes(x=increasePop, y=july11pop) +
  geom_boxplot() +
  ggtitle('Population by type of change')
```

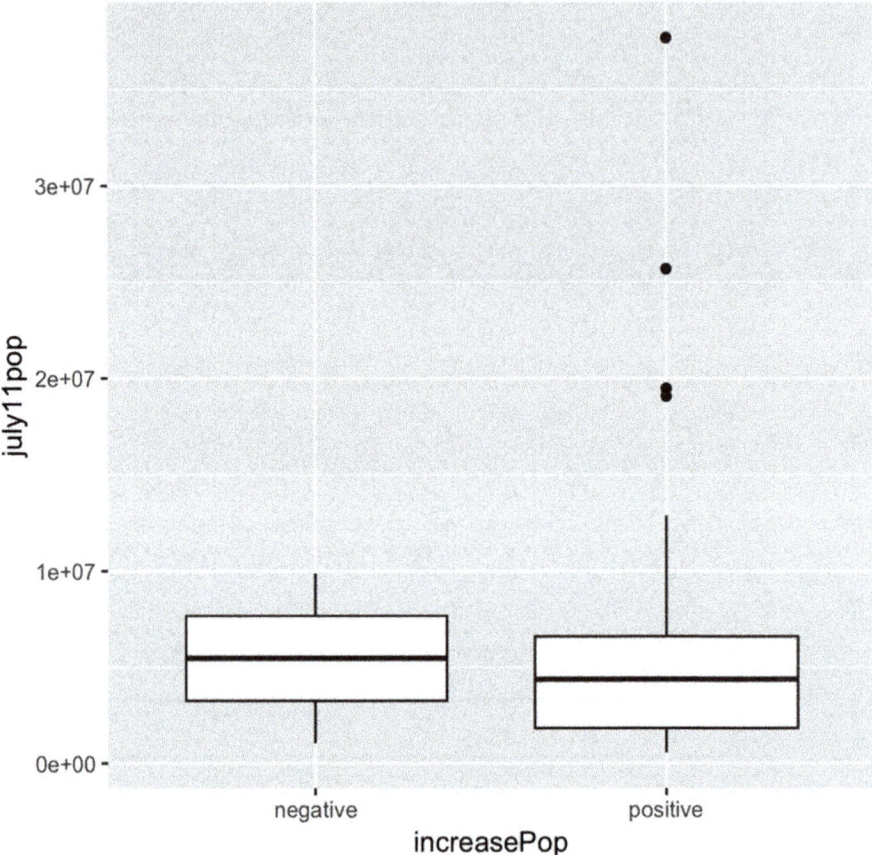

**Population by type of change**

In addition to histograms and boxplots, we can also use ggplot2 to create line and bar charts. To create a line chart, we use the geom_line() function; to create a bar chart, we use the geom_col() function. You can see in the code below that we rotate the x labels (the state names), so that we can easily read the state name. Finally, note that the height of the bar (or line) represents the value in a column of our dataframe (the July 2011 population).

```
ggplot(dfStates) +
    aes(x=reorder(stateName, july11pop),
        y=july11pop, group=1) +
    geom_line() +
    theme(axis.text.x = element_text(angle = 90,
                hjust = 1))
```

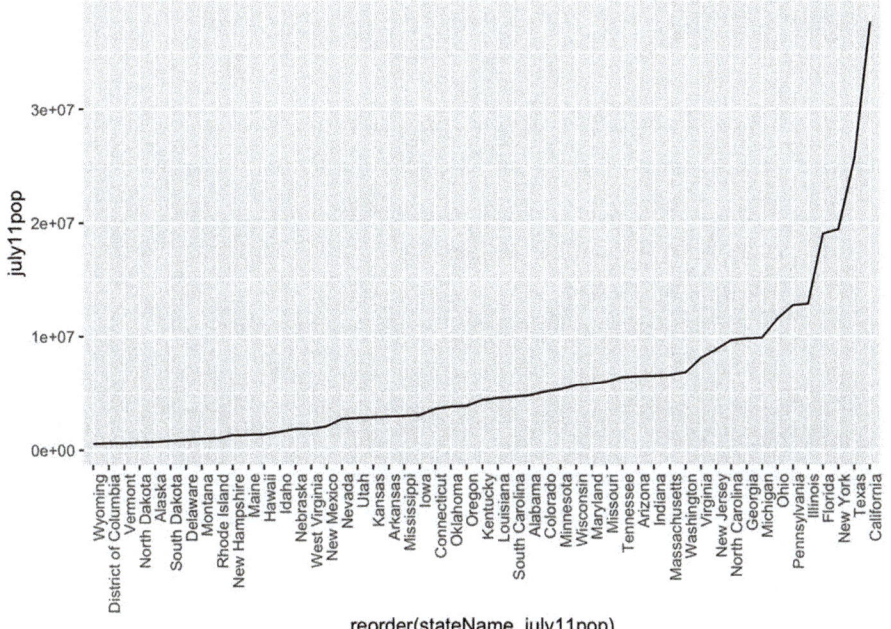

```
ggplot(dfStates) +
    aes(x=reorder(stateName, july11pop),
        y=july11pop) +
    geom_col() +
    theme(axis.text.x = element_text(angle = 90,
            hjust = 1))
```

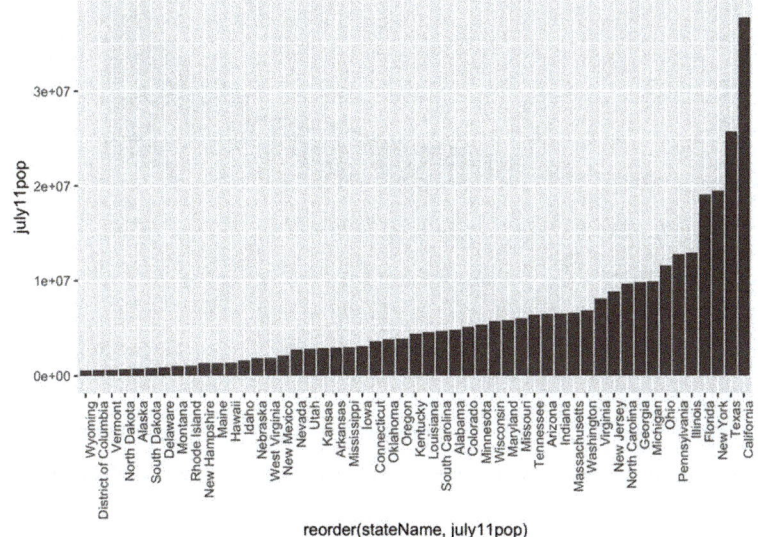

# MORE-ADVANCED VISUALIZATIONS

We can refine the bar chart by having the color of the bars represent another variable. So, let's create a visualization where the bar color represents the percent change in population.

```
#visualize the % change attribute
dfStates$percentChange <-
        dfStates$popChange/dfStates$july10pop * 100

#make the % change
ggplot(dfStates) +
    aes(x=reorder(stateName, july11pop),
        y=july11pop, group=1, fill=percentChange) +
    geom_col() +
    theme(axis.text.x = element_text(angle = 90,
                hjust = 1))
```

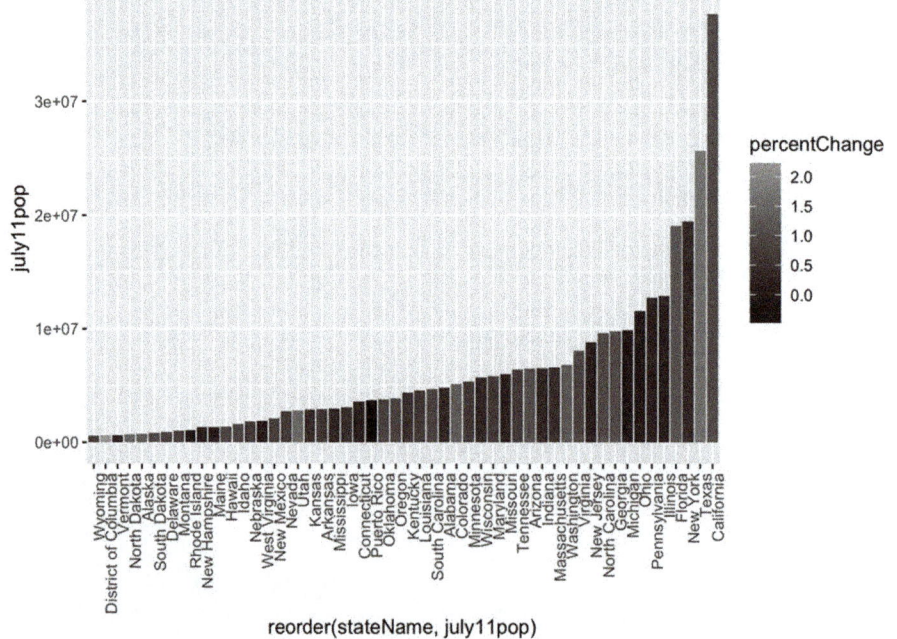

The last type of visualization we will explore is a scatterplot, which provides a way to look at the data across two dimensions. Let's create a scatterplot where each point represents a state. We can place the point on the two-dimensional grid based on the population change (the X-axis) and the percent change (the Y-axis). In addition, we color the points based on the July 2011 population. Just to demonstrate the capability, we use that population for the size of the point as well. Typically, a data scientist would not encode a value into more than one feature of a graph.

```
g <- ggplot(dfStates)+
        aes(x=popChange, y=percentChange,
            size=july11pop, color=july11pop) +
        geom_point()

g
```

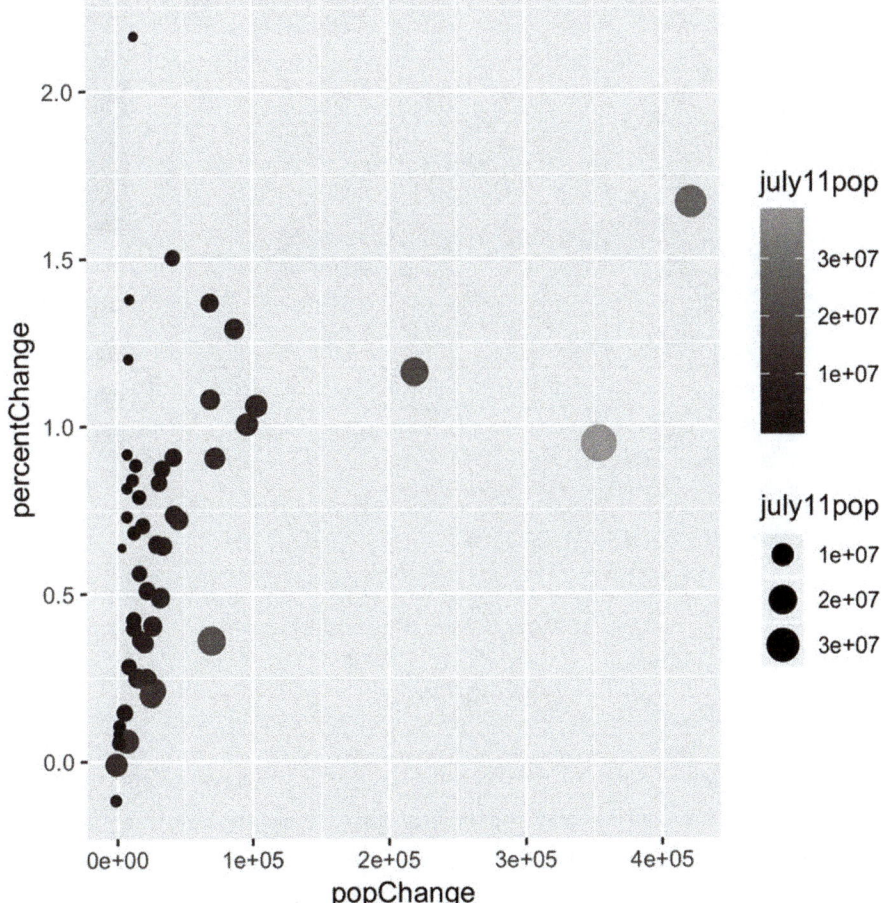

You can see we saved the visualization in a variable ("g"), so we can add another layer. Let's use that stored visualization variable and add some labeling to show the name of each state. Note that we defined some additional aesthetics for the text (the size, and the vertical adjustment of where to place the text).

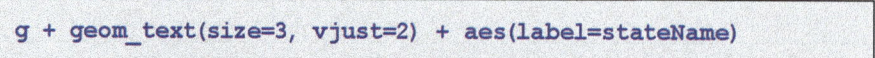

```
g + geom_text(size=3, vjust=2) + aes(label=stateName)
```

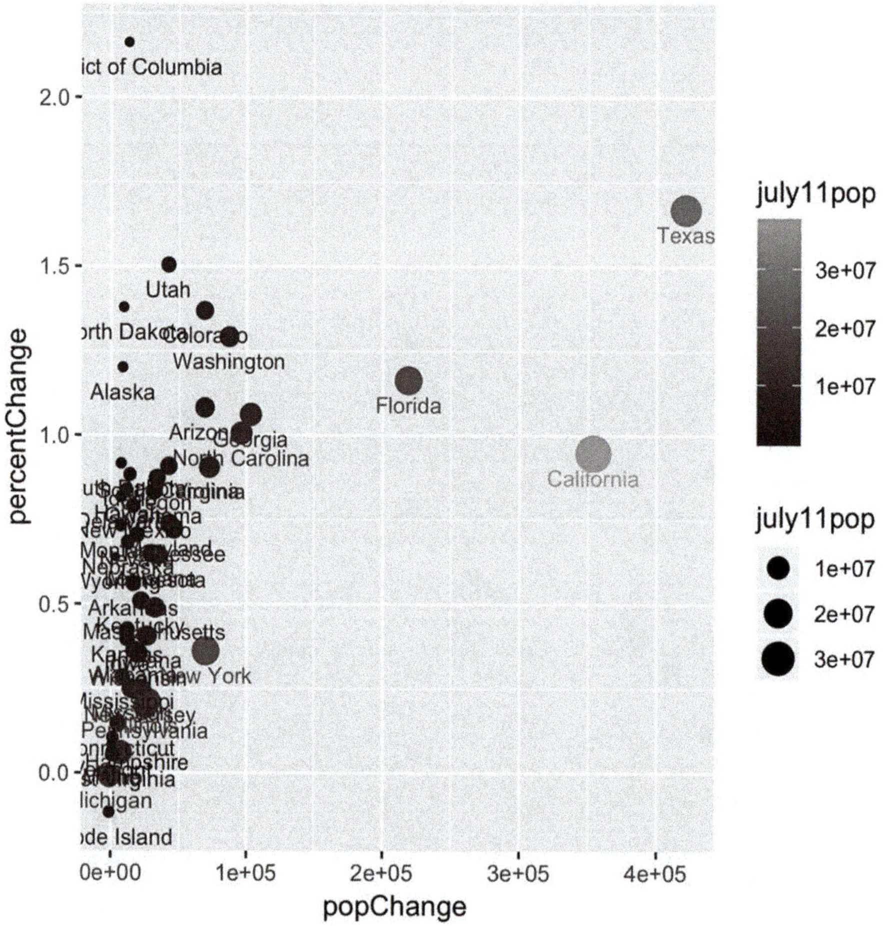

By examining this scatterplot, we see that some states are outliers (some have large populations and some have much smaller populations). For example, the District of Columbia has a very small population and a small absolute population change, but has the largest percent increase in population. Texas is a very large state and has both a high absolute and high percentage increase in population.

This chart has now become very cluttered. Let's clean it up by doing several actions. First, let's define a set of key (or important) states. These are the states that have a percentage change of at least 1% and a population change of at least 100,000 people. With these criteria, we define a new column in the dfStates dataframe, keyState, to be true if that state fits our defined criteria of percentage and population change. In the scatter chart, we show the key states by defining the shape of the symbol within the scatterplot to dependent on the keyState column. We also only show the text for the key states. Next, we clean up the format of the color key, defining the three values to be shown in the key as well as formatting the numbers to include commas, so the numbers are easier to see. Finally, we change the color scale to range from white to black.

```r
#define the criteria to show the text for the state
  minPerChange <- 1
minPopChange <- 100000

#determine the key states
dfStates$keyState <- dfStates$popChange>minPopChange &
            dfStates$percentChange > minPerChange

#create a new dataframe of just the key states
keyStatesDF <- dfStates[dfStates$keyState,]

#define labels showing min, max and median
minLabel <- format(min(dfStates$july11pop),
            big.mark=",", trim=TRUE)
maxLabel <- format(max(dfStates$july11pop),
            big.mark=",", trim=TRUE)
medianLabel <- format(median(dfStates$july11pop),
            big.mark=",", trim=TRUE)

#now generate the plot
g <- ggplot(dfStates) +
    aes(x=popChange,y=percentChange,
            size=july11pop, color=july11pop,
            shape=keyState) +
    geom_point() +
    geom_text(data=keyStatesDF,
            aes(label=stateName, hjust=1, vjust=-1))
```

```
#add the color scale
g + scale_color_continuous(name="Pop",
          low = "white",high = "black",
          breaks = with(dfStates,
                    c(min(july11pop), median(july11pop),
                                      max(july11pop))),
          labels = c(minLabel, medianLabel, maxLabel))
```

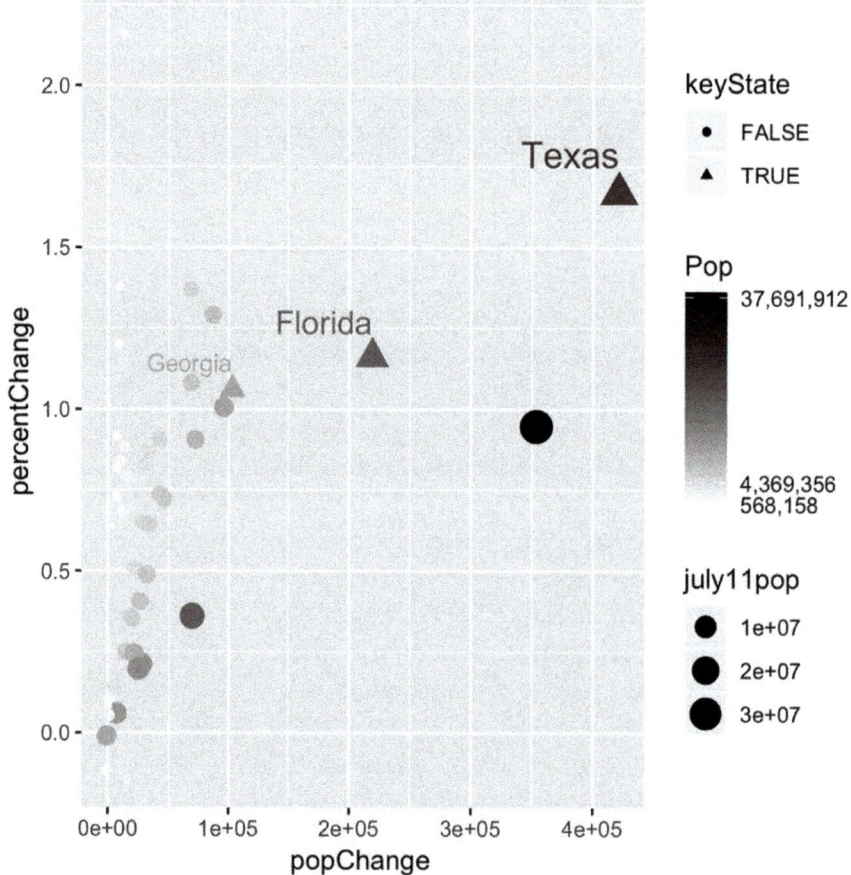

In this visualization it is now easy to see the three states of greatest interest because of their population growth—Georgia, Florida, and Texas. By using scale_color_continuous() with a black-and-white coloring scheme, we have effectively put many of the states with low growth into the background. Our labeling is also much less cluttered because we have only labeled the high growth states. To make sure that you understand all the codes in that display, copy it into your RStudio and make some adjustments to see what happens. For example, change the value of minPerChange to 0.5 or less and the value of minPopChange to 50,000 or less. In Chapter 9, we will continue to explore visualizations with the ggplot2 package, but will expand our focus to visualize data that can be shown on a map.

# CASE STUDY: VISUALIZING KEY ATTRIBUTES RELATED TO NPS

```
Case Key Points:
- Create a function to read our survey dataset
- Visualize some different combinations of attributes  and
  see how those attributes might impact net promoter score
  (NPS)
- See how to integrate tidyverse pipes with GGPLOT layers
```

Since we will continue to use the new survey dataset, let's create a function to read it into a dataframe and remove any NAs (just for the likelihood to recommend column). At the same time, we will also add the delayed and detractor columns to the dataset:

```r
#Read in the JSON datafile
library(jsonlite)
readSurveyData <- function(fileName) {
    mydata.list <- fromJSON(fileName)
    surveyWithNA <- data.frame(mydata.list)

    #Remove rows with'Likelihood.to.recommend' == NA
    survey <- surveyWithNA %>%
            filter(!is.na(Likelihood.to.recommend))

    #Was the arrival delayed a lot
    survey$Big.Arrival.Delay <-
        survey$Arrival.Delay.in.Minutes > 5

    #Was the person a detractor.
    survey$Detractor <-
        survey$Likelihood.to.recommend < 7
    return(survey)

}
```

Now that we have the function, let's use the function to read in the dataset. Don't forget that you may need to use the setwd() function or the Session menu in RStudio to make sure that R is looking in the right folder to find your JSON file.

```r
survey <- readSurveyData("completeSurvey.json")
```

We can first look at histograms, similar to what we did in Chapter 5, for example, by exploring the overall distribution of the Likelihood.to.recommend attribute. Notice that because ggplot2 is part of tidyverse, we can pass (pipe) the dataframe to ggplot (rather than having the survey dataframe as a parameter to ggplot).

```r
survey %>%
    ggplot() +
        geom_histogram(binwidth=1,
                          fill="black", color="white",
                aes(x= Likelihood.to.recommend))
```

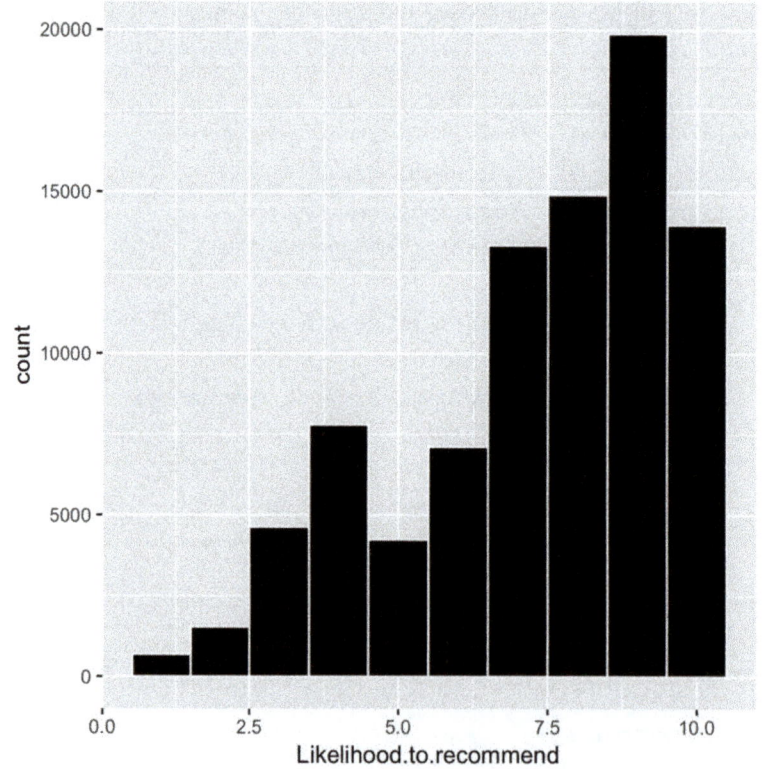

Next, we can explore the distribution across the different types of travel, using the "facet_wrap" function within ggplot.

```
survey %>%
    ggplot() +
        geom_histogram(binwidth=1,
                aes(x= Likelihood.to.recommend)) +
        facet_wrap(~Type.of.Travel)
```

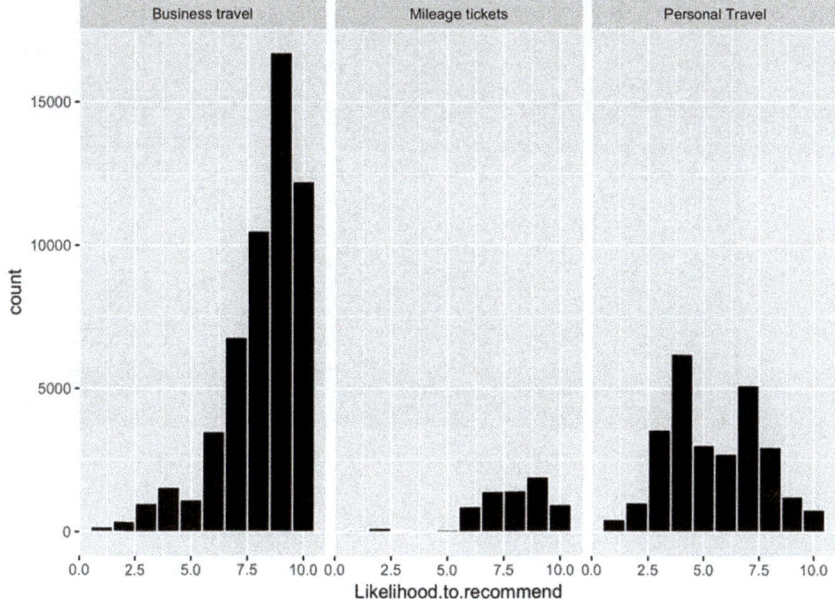

We can also use a barchart to do the same analysis we did in Chapter 7 by exploring whether Big.Arrival.Delay impacts the number of detractors.

```
#create a simple dataframe to visualize
summaryDF <- survey %>%
    group_by(Big.Arrival.Delay) %>%
    summarize( percentDetractor = mean(Detractor) )

#generate the barchart
ggplot(summaryDF) +
    aes(x=Big.Arrival.Delay, y=percentDetractor) +
    geom_col()
```

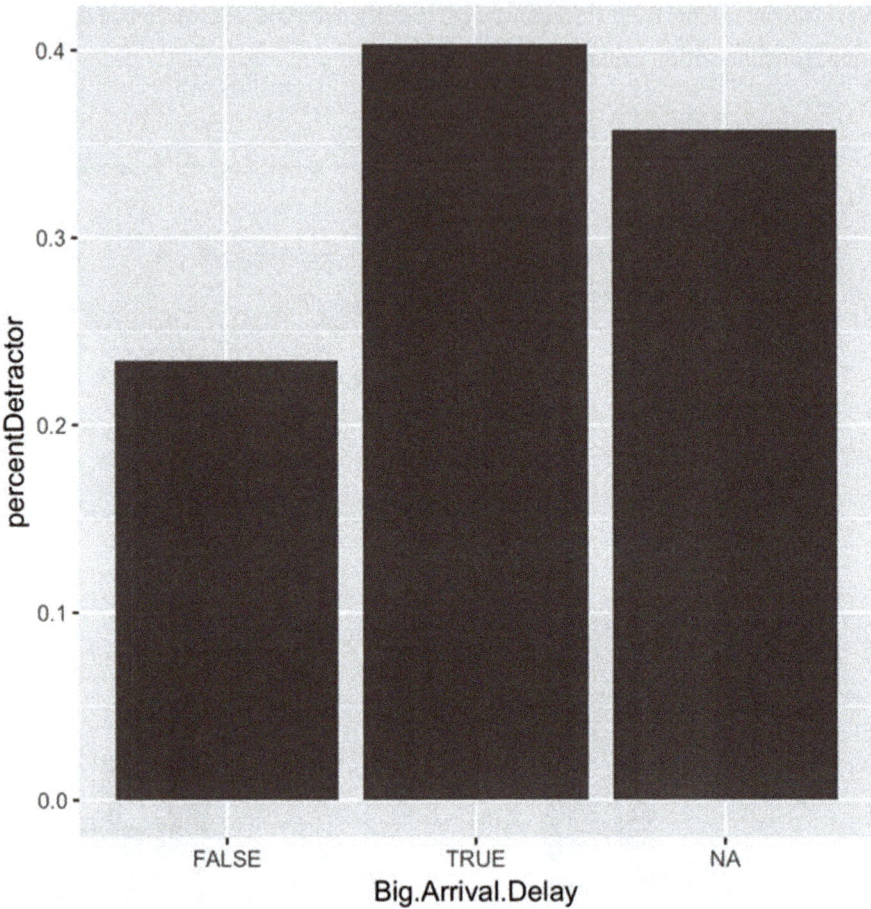

We can also combine these last two steps: some people think this makes the code easier to read, whereas others think it makes the code more difficult to read. You'll have to decide for yourself. This code generates the same visualization.

```
survey %>%
    group_by(Big.Arrival.Delay) %>%
    summarize(percentDetractor = mean(Detractor) ) %>%
    ggplot() +
        aes(x=Big.Arrival.Delay, y=percentDetractor) +
        geom_col()
```

Let's now look at a different attribute, age. Note that to explore age, it can be helpful to put age into groups. So, we will create age groups (by creating a rounded age attribute).

Note that when we use the "-1" within the round function, R will round to the nearest 10, thus creating our age by decades grouping. With this rounded age attribute, we can explore each age group via a boxplot:

```
#round age - and make it a factor
survey$roundAge <-
        as.factor(round(survey$Age, digits=-1))
#generate the box plot
ggplot(survey)+
    aes(x=roundAge, y=Likelihood.to.recommend) +
    geom_boxplot()
```

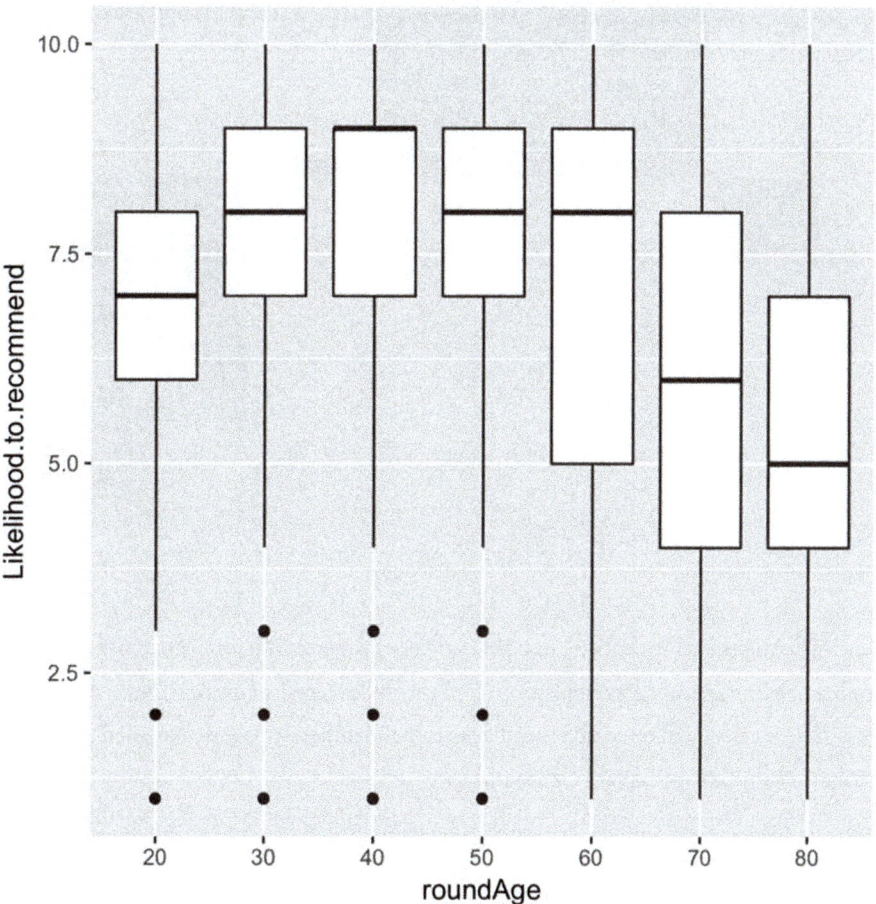

Now instead of examining the distribution of likelihood to recommend, let's explore the NPS values (since this is the focus of our overall analysis). We can start by generating a bar chart of NPS values by the rounded age attribute.

```
survey %>%
  group_by(roundAge) %>%
  summarize(nps = CalcNPS(Likelihood.to.recommend))%>%
  ggplot() +
    aes(x=roundAge, y=nps) +
    geom_col()
```

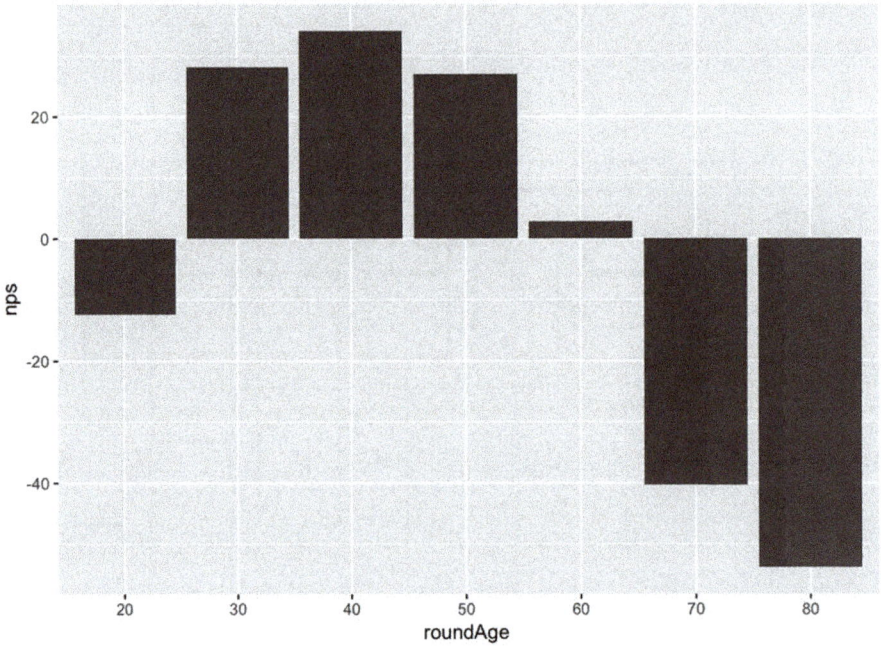

Wow! The difference in NPS across different age groups really jumps out! We can also explore how the arrival delay impacts NPS in the following visualization. Note that to get the different arrival delays to be columns next to each other, we use the position = "dodge" attribute within the geom_col command.

```
survey %>%
  group_by(Big.Arrival.Delay, roundAge) %>%
  summarize(nps=CalcNPS(Likelihood.to.recommend)) %>%
```

```
ggplot() +
   aes(x= roundAge, y=nps,
      fill= Big.Arrival.Delay) +
   geom_col(position = "dodge")
```

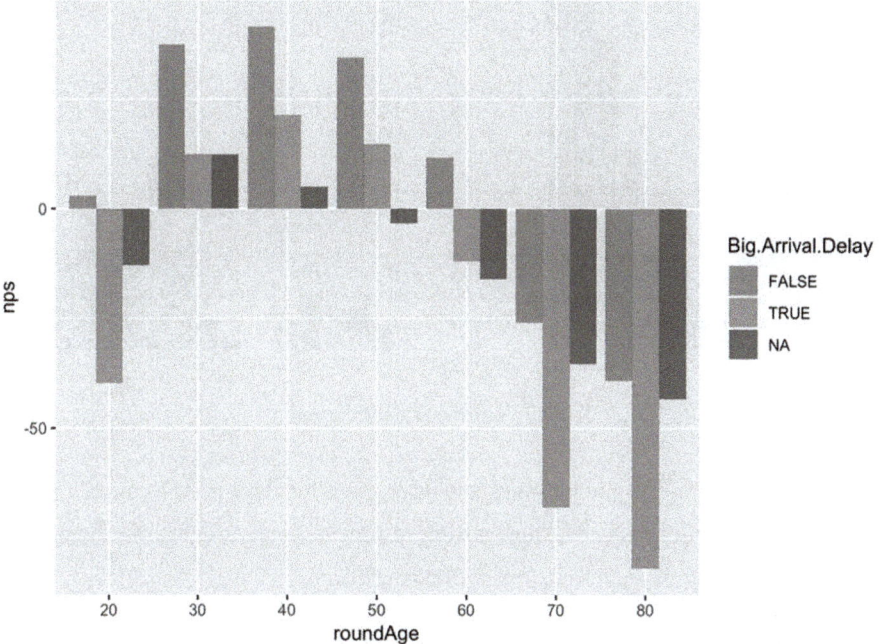

Finally, let's explore the Likelihood to recommend, similar to how we analyzed it in Chapter 5, where we generate a histogram for the different travel types. Note that our use of facet_wrap creates different histograms for each type of travel.

```
survey %>%
  ggplot() +
      geom_histogram(binwidth=1,
                          fill="black", color="white",
                  aes(x=Likelihood.to.recommend)) +
      facet_wrap(~Type.of.Travel)
```

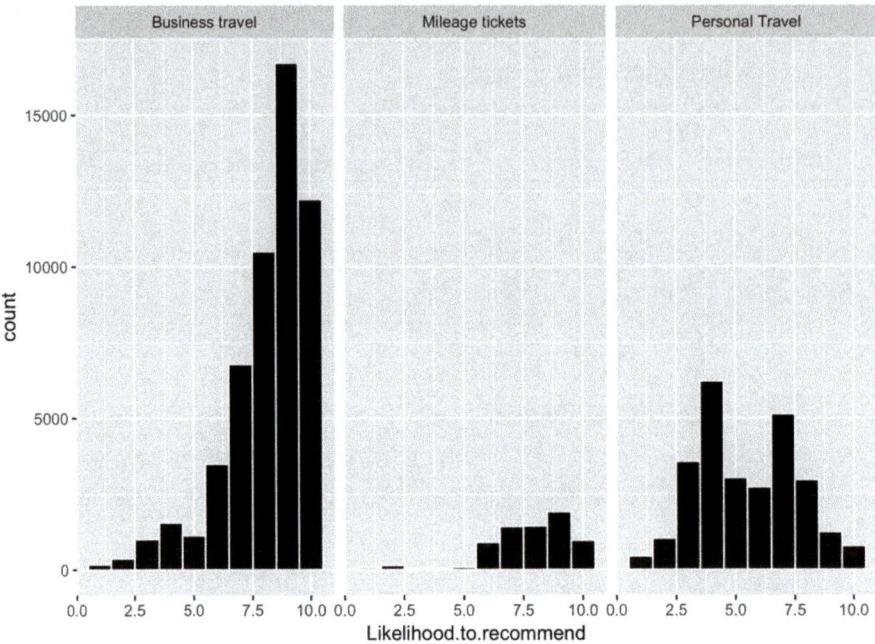

This is also a very striking result—see how helpful it is for there to be a common Y-axis across the three histograms. We are starting to provide some insight into the possible drivers for the positive and negative experiences of fliers!

## Chapter Challenges
(Note that problems 1–6 below require the use of the complete dataset. Refer to the code at the beginning of the case study in this chapter for reading in the data from the JSON file.)

1. Write a paragraph that describes the last graph in this chapter (histogram of Likelihood. to.recommend, grouped by Type.of.Travel). What could airline managers do about the data you described?

2. Create a bar chart of NPS by type of Type.of.Travel and Class. Which attribute do you think is more important in determining a person's likelihood to recommend?

3. Create a bar chart of NPS value by Origin.State. Which state has the lowest NPS value?

4. Create a bar chart of NPS value by Destination.State. Which state has the lowest NPS value? In a sentence or two, compare these results to the results from Problem 3.

5. Create a scatterplot with Shopping.Amount.at.Airport on the X-axis and Eating.and.Drinking. at.Airport on the Y-axis. Describe in a sentence or two what the graph tells you about most people's spending behavior at the airport.

6. Create a new dataframe that only contains rows where the person spent more than $400 on shopping at the airport. Redo the scatterplot from Problem 5, but this time set the color of the dot based on Likelihood.to.recommend. In a brief paragraph, describe what you see. Make sure to mention the number of rows.

7. Create a bar chart, showing the average population in each region of the United States. To do this, you will need to add the region to each state (as was done in Chapter 3). You will need to do something similar here, adding the region to the dfStates dataframe, and then figuring out how to calculate and display the mean for each region.

## Sources

https://www.rstudio.com/wp-content/uploads/2015/04/ggplot2-cheatsheet.pdf
http://ggplot2.org

## R Functions Used in This Chapter

round() Rounds a number (or vector of numbers).

hist() Generates a histogram using R's base graphics.

barplot() Generates a bar chart using R's base graphics.

data.frame() Organize variables into a rectangular data structure.

filter() Tidyverse function to subset rows of data.

format() Format an R object for printing.

fromJSON() Extract data from JSON-formatted input.

function() Define a function for later reuse.

ggplot() Starts the creation of a ggplot, defining the dataframe to be used.

group_by() Tidyverse function to organize data into groups.

summarize() Tidyverse function to create a data summary.

### Functions to Add Layers to a ggplot

| | |
|---|---|
| ggtitle() | Adds a title to the plot. |
| geom_histogram() | Creates a histogram. |
| geom_boxplot() | Creates a boxplot. |
| geom_line() | Creates a line chart. |
| geom_col() | Creates a bar chart. |
| geom_point() | Adds points to your plot. |
| geom_text() | Adds text to your plot. |
| coord_flip() | Rotates the chart by 90 degrees. |
| theme() | Refines the visual look of the chart (e.g., text). |
| format() | Enables a number to be printed in a pretty, easy-to-read format. |
| scale_color_continuous() | Defines a color range for mapping data to a color. |

This text includes access to datasets and select student resources. To learn more, visit sagepub.com

# 9

## MAP MASHUP

## LEARNING OBJECTIVES

Demonstrate the integration of disparate data sources and formats producing a representative information model for decision-making.

Utilize ggplot() for geographic map representation.

Plot geographic and numerical data within one visualization.

Gain experience using the following R functions: paste, as.character, geocode, gsub, ggplot() (and building layers in ggplot() via ggmap, geom_point, coord_map).

In this chapter, we continue our exploration of visually displaying information, and tackle a mashup challenge. "Mashup" is a term that originated in the music business decades ago related to the practice of overlaying one music recording on top of another one. The term has entered general usage to mean anything that brings together disparate influences or elements. In the application development area, mashup often refers to bringing together various sources of data to create a new product with unique value.

One of the first examples of a map mashup was HousingMaps (http://www.housingmaps. com), a web application that grabbed apartment rental listings from the classified advertising service Craigslist and plotted them on an interactive map that shows the location of each listing. This app helped to popularize the idea that it might be useful to show real estate availability on a map. Although it's hard to imagine now, previously, real estate showed properties via lists and images and then people would have to manually look up the location on a different map! HousingMaps worked so well that Craigslist built its own map interface for finding rental properties.

Showing a dot where each house is located is far more intuitive than just showing a list of addresses: this example shows the power of using maps to display information in an effective and helpful way. As data scientists, we need to not only be able to calculate and analyze data, but also to display the results in an intuitive manner. One could also encode more meaning in such a map. For example, rather than just a dot for each rental available, we could color-code the symbol and have different types of symbols. We could have apartments be one shape and single-family houses be another shape. We could color-code based on price. As you can see, map visualizations are similar in concept to the visualizations we previously discussed, but with the added geographical component of the displayed information.

As we just mentioned color-coding, now would be a good time to explain how to use color and still accommodate the many people who have one or another form of color blindness. One approach is to use a gray scale (a range from white to black), which we did at the end of Chapter 8. Another approach is to pick a color range that varies intensity from light to dark (such as ranging from white to light blue to dark blue).

# CREATING MAP VISUALIZATIONS WITH GGPLOT2

Let's start with generating a simple map using the ggplot2 package. We do this in a similar fashion to other ggplot() charts. Before we get started, we need to review a little geography—specifically the meaning of longitude and latitude. As shown in the diagram below on the right, latitude lines are horizontal and parallel full circles, where 0 is the equator; +90 degrees is the North Pole, and -90 degrees is the South Pole (latitude lines are full circles). As shown on the left side of the diagram, longitude lines are vertical arcs: they are not parallel and 0 represents the prime meridian in Greenwich, UK; +60 degrees is east and splits Europe from Asia; -60 degrees is west and passes through middle

of South America; ±180 is in the middle of the Pacific Ocean. Longitude lines are half circles and that is why the overall range is ±180.

We created the graphic above with the help of the maps package and the mapproj package and have included the code for this on the companion website. Although you can make simple maps with these packages, we really need the ggplot2 package to make more sophisticated, data-based maps. Luckily, there is a companion package that helps ggplot() with mapping, known as ggmap. Once that is installed, we can get the map of the United States with the following line of code:

```
us <- map_data("state")
```

If you use the glimpse (or use the str) command, you can see that there are 7,243 observations (rows) with six variables (long, lat, group, order, region, and subregion) in the us dataframe. The attribute long specifies the longitude (x location) and lat specifies latitude (y location).

Taken together, we can see that us is a dataframe of points, and we can visualize the points with the following ggplot() code:

```
ggplot(us) +
  geom_point(aes(x=long,y=lat))
```

Yup, it is a map of the United States, but it is pretty weird looking, for two reasons. First, all of those dots are obviously defining the borders of the states: we would much rather have thin, continuous lines instead of those big dots. Second, the map looks squashed because R has adjusted the calibration of the axes to make the result a square. The X-axis has two tick marks covering 20 degrees between each axis label, whereas the Y-axis has two tick marks covering just 5 degrees between labels. In addition, the graphic above does not account for the curvature of the earth.

At small scales, for example, the area of a town or small city, longitude, and latitude work like a regular Cartesian grid. At larger scales, however, the spherical shape of the earth interferes with plotting the latitude and longitude on a flat surface. We use a technique called a *map projection* to render a spherical area onto a flat surface. All map projections create some kind of visual distortion, because a spherical object just does not want to be flat! Generally, though, we are used to seeing global maps with these distortions, so we don't normally even think about it. For example, in the next two figures you can see two different map projections for rendering the whole globe on a rectangular grid. The first map shows a Mercator projection: this was developed in the 1500s as an aid to ocean navigation. Using a map with this projection, ship captains can set one compass direction and reliably get to their destinations. The Mercator projection is extremely common and is the one you have most likely seen on global maps.

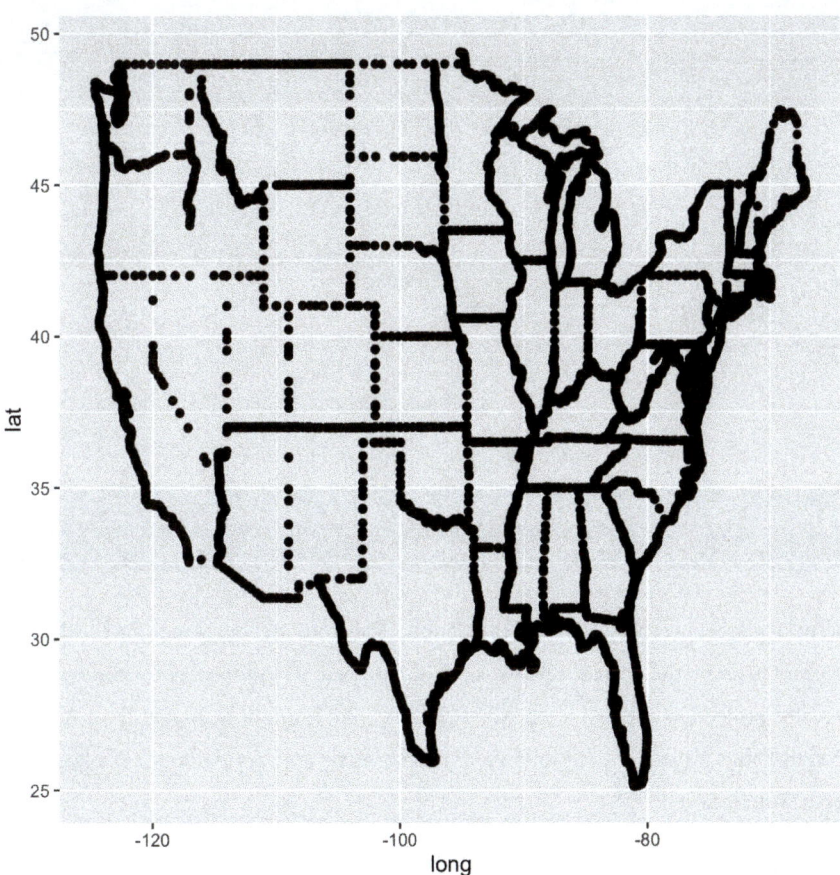

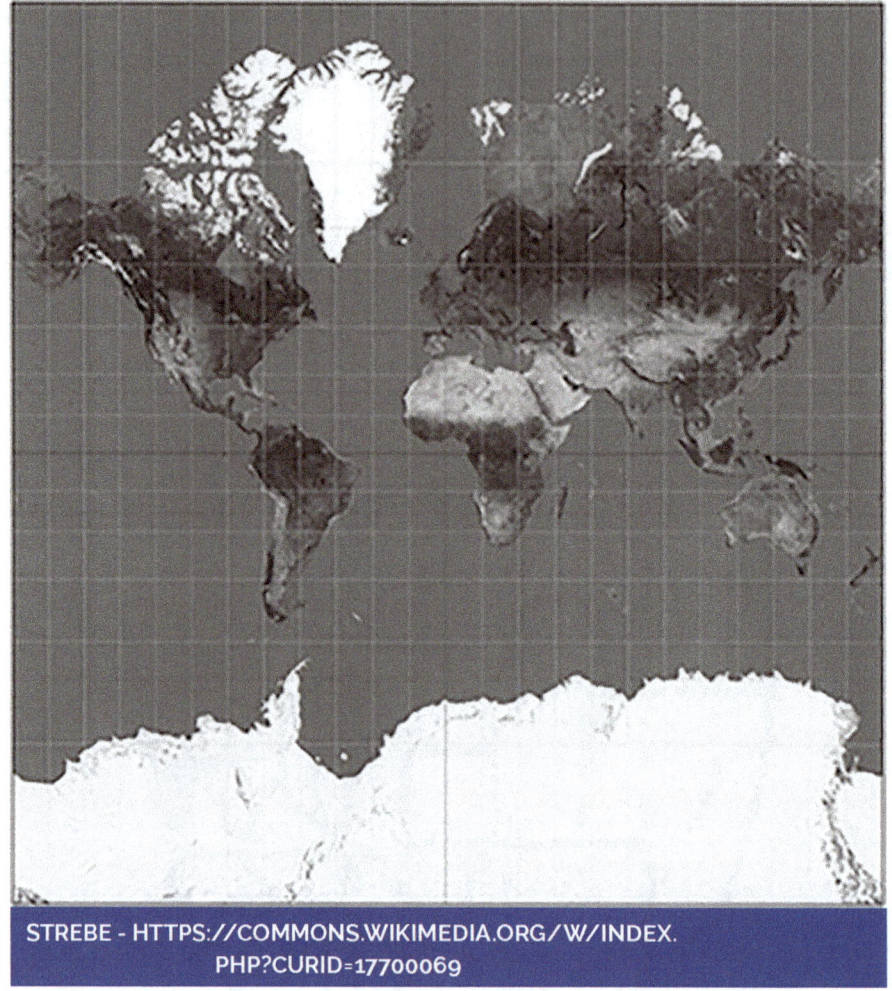

STREBE - HTTPS://COMMONS.WIKIMEDIA.ORG/W/INDEX.
PHP?CURID=17700069

The next map shows a Gall-Peters projection. This one was developed in the 1800s in an effort to show the correct relative sizes of the earth's land masses. Note how, in the Mercator projection above, North America looks like it might be bigger than Africa. In the Gall-Peters projection that follows, Africa correctly appears as about 20% larger than North America.

So, whenever we use ggplot() to render a map where the curvature of the earth is large enough to matter, we need to choose a map projection based on the intended purpose of the map. We can choose the appropriate projection by using the coord_map function, which makes sure to project the map in the way we would like. For example, we can specify coord_map(projection = "mercator"), to use the Mercator projection. Note that

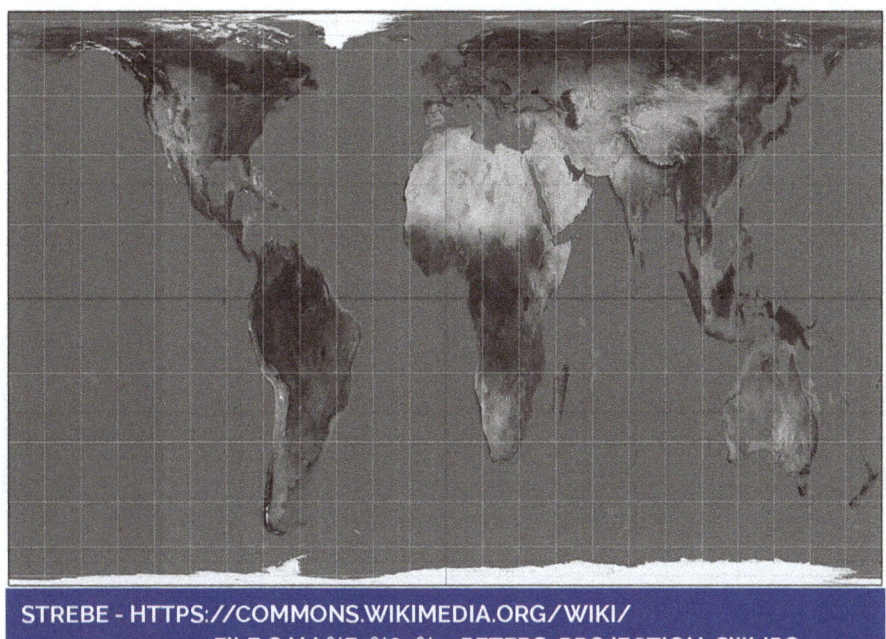

STREBE - HTTPS://COMMONS.WIKIMEDIA.ORG/WIKI/
FILE:GALL%E2%80%93PETERS_PROJECTION_SW.JPG

Mercator is the default choice for the coord_map function, so we can simply use the following code to generate a map with a suitable projection:

```
ggplot(us) +
  geom_point(aes(x=long,y=lat)) + coord_map()
```

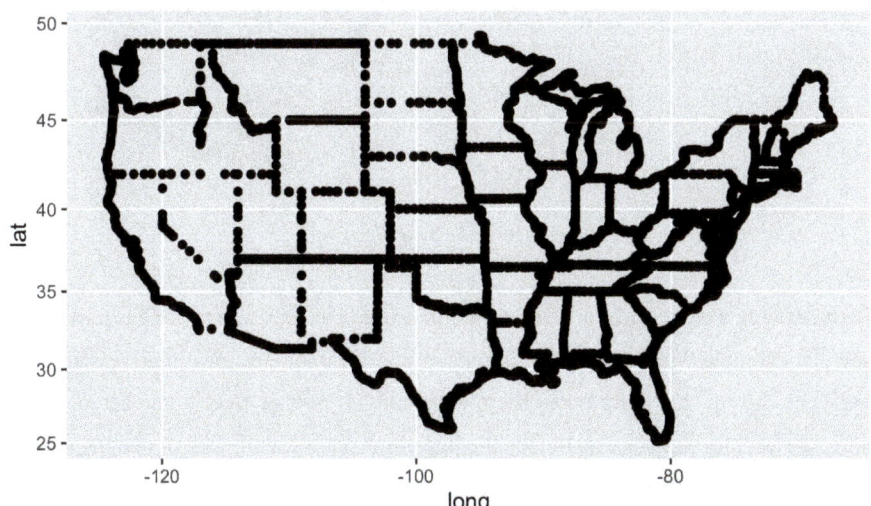

That U.S. map looks a lot better than before, although we still have thick dots instead of thin lines. We will fix that a little later, but for now, let's look at the other fields in the us dataframe. The region variable defines all of the points that belong with a given state. Let's break out one state to show how this works: in the code below, we filter the us data to create a subset of the data where the region value is equal to New York. We will store this in a new dataframe called NYData. Then in the subsequent ggplot, we show off the points in the NYData dataframe.

```
#zoom into NY
NYData <- us %>% filter(region=="new york")

ggplot(NYData) +
  geom_point(aes(x=long,y=lat)) + coord_map()
```

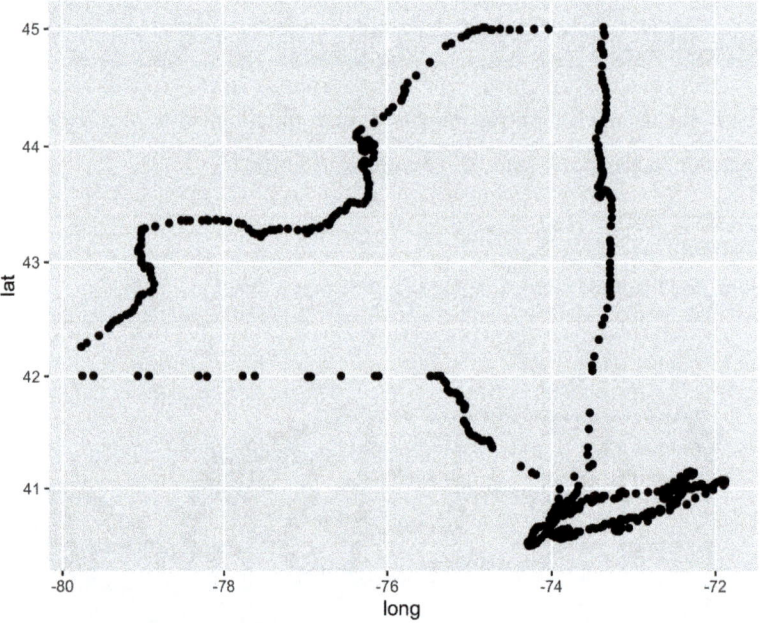

When drawing a map, there is often more than one "chunk of land" that is part of the state. For example, Manhattan is an island, so it is different landmass than upstate New York. The "group" attribute notes these different "chunks of land." The actual group names are not meaningful, and in fact, are just numbers. But with a bit of playing around, we can look at one of the groups in New York.

```
NYGroupLevelData <- us %>% filter(group==35)

ggplot(NYGroupLevelData) +
  geom_point(aes(x=long,y=lat)) +
  coord_map()
```

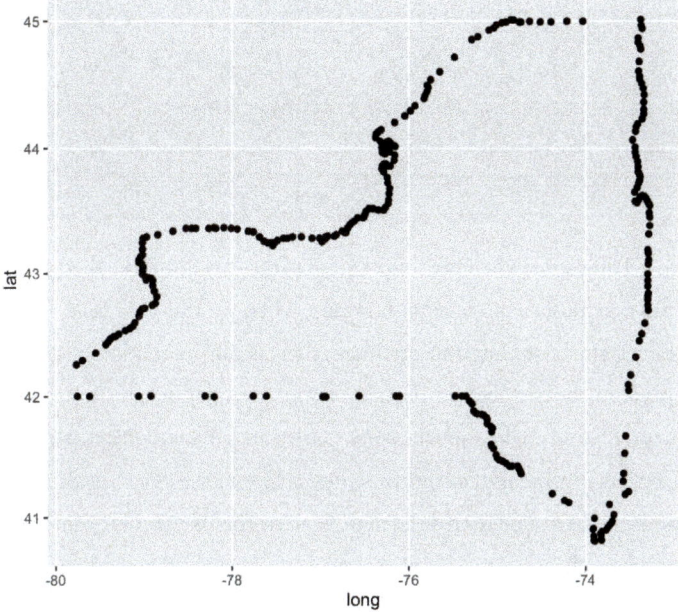

Now we are ready to improve the look of our map by plotting lines instead of dots. For this task, we will use the geom_polygon() command. Remember that a polygon is any closed shape like a circle or square, but also including more complex shapes like the outline of a state or country. The geom_polygon() command takes a list of dots and connects them together in the proper sequence to make a closed shape.

```
#generate the map using lines
ggplot(us) +
  geom_polygon(color="black", fill="white",
            aes(x=long,y=lat, group=group)) +
  coord_map()
```

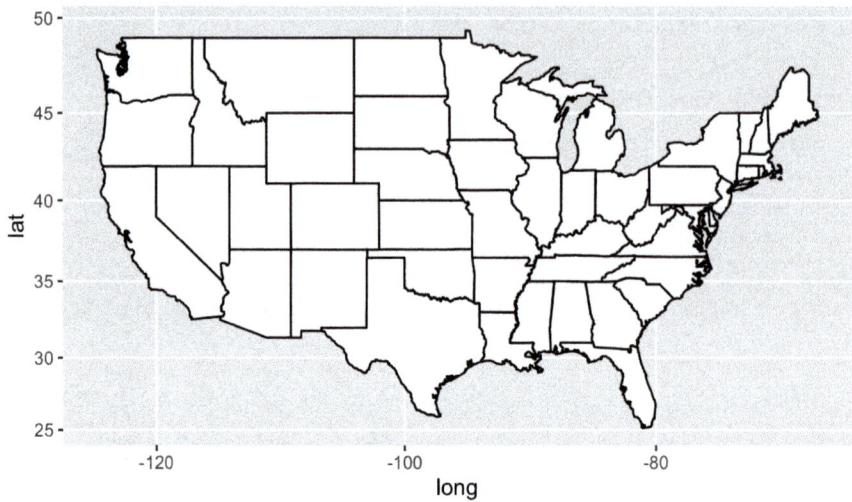

Now we are getting somewhere! A simple figure like this is often called a *base map*. The map becomes much more interesting, however, when we add data to it. For example, we can shade each state, based on some attribute, such as the population of the state. In order to do this mashup, we can read in the state population dataset in the same way we have done in Chapter 5 and make sure the state names are all lowercase to be consistent with the region attribute in the us dataframe, which is lower case. After reading in the dataset, we then combine the population information with the us geometry information, using the merge command:

```
#Use the readCensus function defined in Chapter 5
url <- "http://www2.census.gov/programs-surveys/popest/
        tables/2010-2011/state/totals/nst-est2011-01.csv"
dfStates <- readCensus(url)

#make sure everything is lowercase
dfStates$state <- tolower(dfStates$stateName)

#combine dataframes, using state and region to merge
dfStatesWithGeom<- merge(dfStates, us,
                         by.x="state",by.y="region")

#restore the order for the points in the polygon
dfStatesWithGeom <-dfStatesWithGeom %>% arrange(order)
```

The last line uses the order attribute, which is from the "us" dataframe, that has not yet been discussed. It defines the order of the points to draw a polygon. Sometimes, when doing a merge, the order of the rows gets lost. However, for our geom_polygon() command, we need to make sure the points are in the order specified by the order attribute.

Having done all this work, now we are finally able to create a map, with the fill color representing the population of each state. We do this by telling ggplot() to fill each state based on the july11pop column of data. Everything else is the same as the simple map we previously created. The technical name for this type of visualization is a choropleth map, but many people call it a "heat map," since this type of visualization can be used to show temperature forecasts on a weather map.

```
myMap <- ggplot(dfStatesWithGeom) +
  geom_polygon(color="black",
      aes(x=long,y=lat, group=group, fill=july11pop)) +
      coord_map()
myMap
```

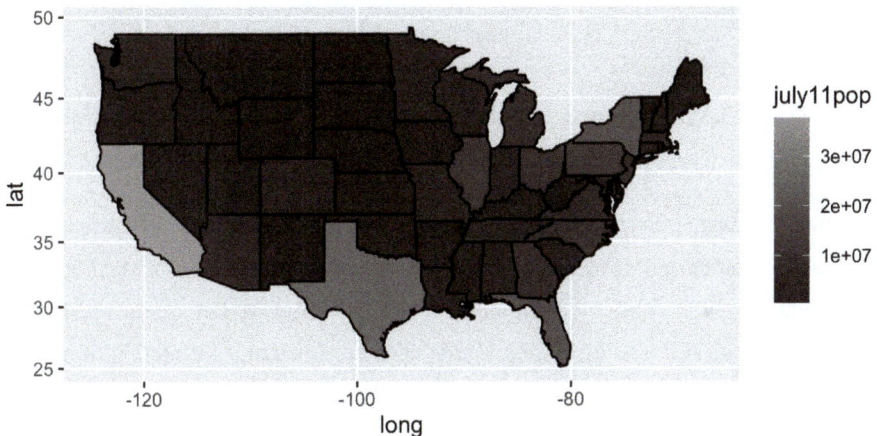

In looking at the map, we can see the states with the highest population are California, Texas, and New York. Note that we created a variable to store the map visualization ("myMap"). This R object is stored and ready to use for future visualizations.

# SHOWING POINTS ON A MAP

Let's now add some points to the map. We can start by just hard coding the latitude and longitude of a specific location. For example, we can create a made-up point somewhere in Texas:

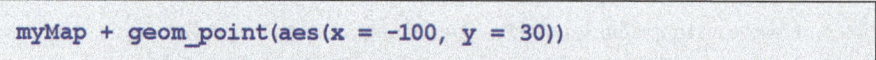

```
myMap + geom_point(aes(x = -100, y = 30))
```

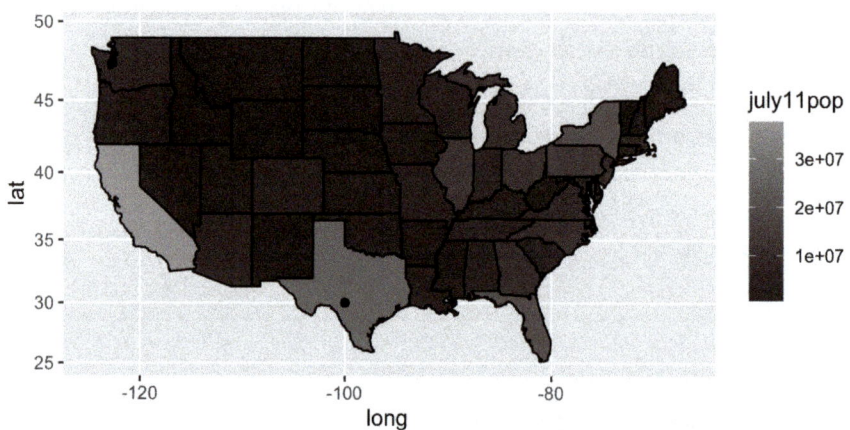

Now southern Texas contains a little black dot. We used geom_point() to create that single point, specified by x (longitude) and y (latitude) within the geom_point() function.

We can also show a point on the map using a logical location. A logical location is the address of a location, as opposed to specific latitude and longitude coordinates. Let's find where Syracuse, New York, is located on the map. To do this, we can use the open street map's free web service (see https://nominatim.openstreetmap.org/ for more information on the service), which for a given address, returns the latitude, longitude, as well as other information, such as the bounding box for the city.

```
#use two libraries
library(jsonlite)
library(stringr)

#address to be geocoded
address <- "syracuse, NY"
```

```
#replace spaces with '%20' (web standard for a space)
address <- str_replace_all(address, " ", "%20")

#define the url to get the geocode
urlofGEOCode <- paste0(
    'https://nominatim.openstreetmap.org/search/',
    address,'?format=json&addressdetails=0&limit=1')

#get the location data, in JSON format
df <- jsonlite::fromJSON(urlofGEOCode)

#get the longitude and latitude from the dataframe
longitude = as.numeric(df$lon)
latitude = as.numeric(df$lat)

#show as a white point (the longitude and latitude)
myMap + geom_point(aes(x = longitude, y = latitude),
                                         color="white")
```

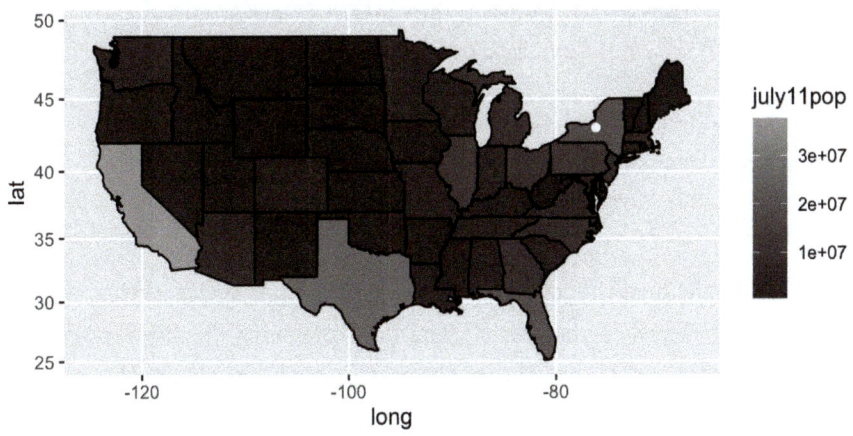

We can see the white point in the middle of New York state. We should mention that the URL returns the information via Java Script Object Notation (JSON) (the web data format we previously explored in Chapter 7). Note that this interface is pretty easy to use, does not require an account or application ID, but has a rate restriction that only allows one address conversion per second. Note that the terms of service for online geocoding services are usually quite specific about how their interfaces can be used, so make sure you read the terms of service before you create any software applications that use a geocoding service. The U.S. Geological Service (USGS) website has a searchable database for finding open sources of map data and some of these sources can be used commercially.

Next, let's show data as points on the map! For example, we can put a point at the center of each state, and have the color (or size) represent the population. To do this, we note that ggmap provides the list of state names available as a variable (state.names), as well as the centers of each state (state.center). So, we create a simple little stateCenter dataframe, and then merge that with our existing larger dataframe. Note that, as before, the states should be in lower case, just to be consistent across dataframes (when we try to merge), which is why we used the tolower command.

```
#create a dataframe with state centers and population
stateCenter <- data.frame(
          state=tolower(state.name),
          x=state.center$x,
          y=state.center$y)


#merge with the dataframe we have been using
dfStatesWithCenter <- merge(dfStatesWithGeom,
                     stateCenter, by="state")

#don't forget to sort on the order attribute
dfStatesWithCenter <- dfStatesWithCenter %>%
                                arrange(order)
```

As you can see, the merge function creates a new dataframe by identifying common columns (via the named column "state"), and then combining the different attributes (columns). Now that we have our desired dataframe, creating the visualization is similar to what we have previously done but this time showing the center of each state.

```
#add a points layer with color=population
ggplot(dfStatesWithCenter) +
  geom_polygon(color="black", fill="white",
          aes(x=long,y=lat, group=group)) +
  geom_point(aes(x=x,y=y, color=july11pop)) +
  coord_map()
```

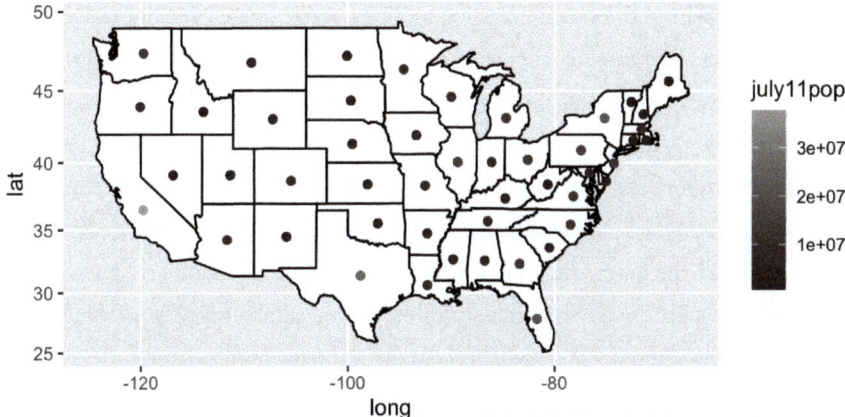

We can make the map more interesting by putting an image of a map "behind" our points and outline of states. Up until this point, all our visualizations have been with *vector graphics*, which works by drawing lines between points (or drawing markers at a point). However, as shown in the figure below, *raster graphics* treats every image as a grid of pixels rather than a set of smooth lines. In the figure below, the diagonal line that goes from the top left to the bottom right is a raster drawing, whereas the one that goes from lower left to upper right is a vector drawing. Notice that the raster line has "jaggies" because each individual dot is visible.

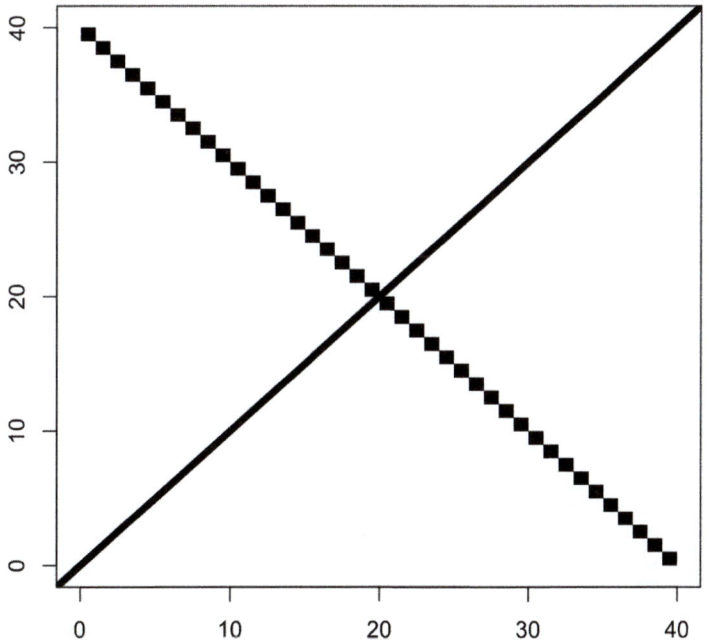

Our new map, behind the vector graphics, will be a raster image, which can include terrain information. To create a background raster image map for our visualization, we can use the get_stamenmap(), which is another function in the ggmap package. Stamenmaps are "tiled" images of varying levels of detail (the higher the zoom number, the more detail). In addition to the level of zoom (detail), we also need to provide the range of longitude and latitude (i.e., the bounding box of the map image, in longitude and latitude). Below we use all the longitude and latitude points in our dataframe to determine the bounding box for our image. For more information on stamen maps, you can check out the website of the company that created them (http://maps.stamen.com).

```r
#put a map image behind the visualizaiton
bb <- c(left = min(dfStatesWithCenter$long),
        bottom = min(dfStatesWithCenter$lat),
        right = max(dfStatesWithCenter$long),
        top = max(dfStatesWithCenter$lat))


#actually get the map
# note if the zoom is too large, it will take a long
# time to load the maps across the internet
map <- get_stamenmap(bbox = bb, zoom=4)


#show the map using the ggmap command
ggmap(map)
```

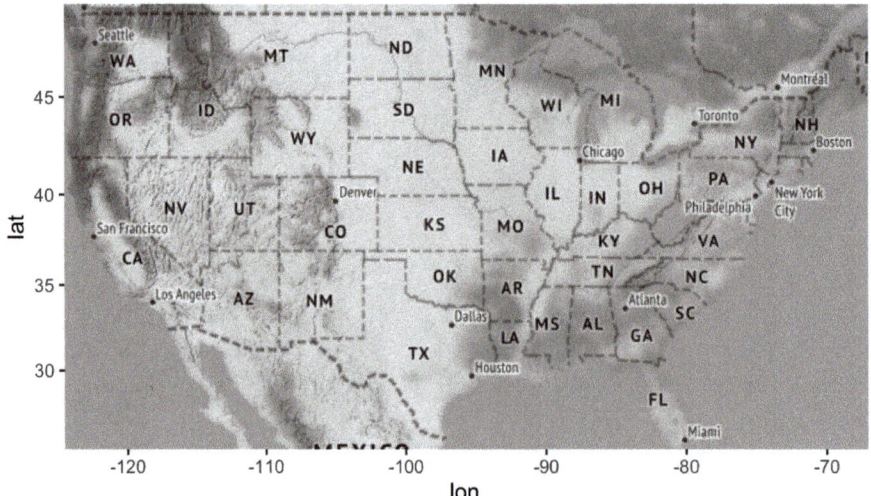

Cool! This shows a map as an image—and now we need to put data (via points) onto the map, which we can do via the geom_point command, which can be a layer within the ggmap, just like geom_point can be a layer when using the ggplot() command.

```
#add a points layer with color=population
ggmap(map) +
  geom_polygon(data= dfStatesWithCenter,
                              color="black", fill="NA",
            aes(x=long,y=lat, group=group)) +
  geom_point(data= dfStatesWithCenter, size=4,
            aes(x=x,y=y, color=july11pop))
```

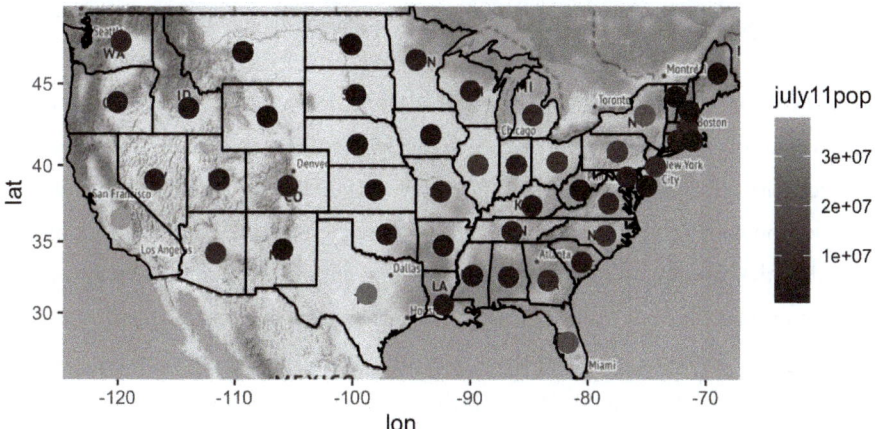

Rather than showing the population as points, we can go back to color-coding the states to be based on population, but make each state somewhat transparent, so we can see the map background as well as the color. Within the geom_polygon command, we can specify alpha, which ranges from 0 (fully transparent) to 1 (fully opaque). The code for generating this visualization is shown below:

```
ggmap(map) +
  geom_polygon(data=dfStatesWithGeom,
            color="black", alpha=0.8,
        aes(x=long,y=lat, group=group, fill=july11pop))
```

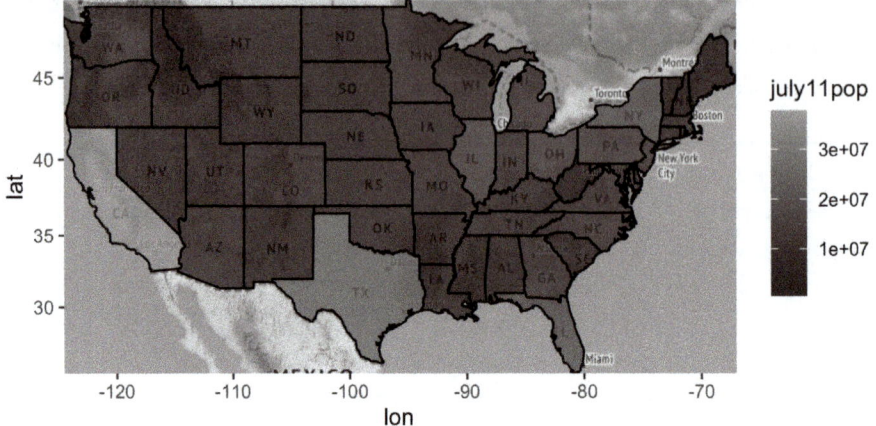

# ZOOMING INTO A SUBSET OF A MAP

Now, let's use our new knowledge to do a more advanced mashup. There are certainly many sources of location data (home prices, colleges, locations of restaurants, etc.). However, we will stick with a JSON dataset that we have previously used: the Citibike data. Our goal is to show on a map the number of available bikes at each bike station. Since Citibike is focused on the New York City area, we need to zoom our map to focus on that area (if we didn't zoom into the New York area, all the bike stations would roughly be in the same location, since the map is currently the map of the entire United States). First, as a quick review, let's read in the Citibike dataset. If this seems confusing, it probably makes sense to go back and reread Chapter 7, where we discussed importing data from various sources.

```
library(RCurl)
library(jsonlite)

bikeURL <-
"https://feeds.citibikenyc.com/stations/stations.json"
apiResult <- getURL(bikeURL)
results <- fromJSON(apiResult)
stations <- results[[2]]
allBikeData <- data.frame(stations)
```

OK. Now that we have the bike data, we can review the attributes in allBikeData and notice that each station has the longitude and latitude already defined. So, we can use those values to generate the points on the map. We then can use the availableBikes attributes to define the size of each of the points. However, before we generate the map, we need to calculate the bounding box around New York City, and then get the stamen map for that region (with a bit more detail, as noted by the higher zoom level). Although this all sounds very messy, the actual code, shown below, is hopefully, not that complicated:

```
#get the bounding box for the map
bb <- c(left = min(allBikeData$longitude),
        bottom = min(allBikeData$latitude),
        right = max(allBikeData$longitude),
        top = max(allBikeData$latitude))


#get the new background map
mapNY <- get_stamenmap(bbox = bb, zoom=12)


# visualize the points & map, scaling the points
ggmap(mapNY) +
  geom_point(data=allBikeData,
             alpha=0.5, color="black",
             aes( x=longitude,
                  y=latitude,
                  size=availableBikes)) +
  scale_size(range=c(0, 2))
```

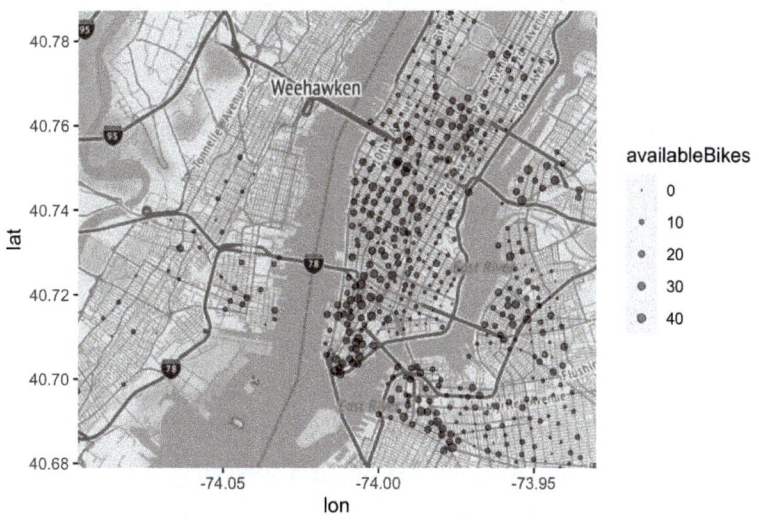

That map really looks nice and gives us, at a glance, a clear view of where a rider could most easily find a bike. This completes our focus on visualizations, until much later, when we explore interactive applications via the use of Shiny Apps. In Chapter 10, we turn to linear modeling, which is our first exploration of predictive models.

# CASE STUDY: EXPLORE NPS BY STATE AND CITY

```
Case Key Points:
-  Generate dataframes that have net promoter score (NPS) by
   state and by city
-  Visualize the NPS values on a map
```

To start, we will review getting the map data from ggmap, as well as calculating the bounding box for all the points.

```
#get the US map
us <- map_data("state")


#Calculate the bounding box
bb <- c(left = min(us$long), bottom = min(us$lat),
        right = max(us$long), top = max(us$lat))
```

With that information, we can get the raster image map, to use as our background map.

```
map <- get_stamenmap(bbox = bb, zoom=5)
```

OK. Now that we have our map, let's create a dataframe, that has the NPS value for each origin city of the flights. The code below might look a bit tricky, but we have covered all the concepts used to create the NPSbyCity dataframe. In short, starting with the survey dataframe we used in Chapter 8, we use the group_by() function to tell tidyverse how we want to group the data. Then we summarize the data, generating (for each origin.city) a cityNPS value (via our CalcNPS function that we defined in our functions chapter, and have used in Chapters 4, 6, and 8). We also have the number of flights from that city (via the "n()" function). Finally, we want to have the longitude and latitude for each city. Each row of our survey has that information, so a simple way to generate that data for the new dataframe is to calculate the mean of the longitude (olong) and latitude (olat). Note that since, for each group, the olong and olat are the same (since each group contains the rows for a specific city), we could have also calculated the min or the max of olong and olat and generated the same results.

```
#generate a dataframe with NPS values per city
NPSbyCity <- survey %>%
  group_by(Origin.City) %>%
  summarize(cityNPS=CalcNPS(Likelihood.to.recommend),
            num=n(), olong=mean(olong), olat=mean(olat))
```

Now that we have our NPS by city dataframe, we can create a visualization, where we show the NPS value for each city.

```
ggmap(map) +
  geom_point(data=NPSbyCity,
      aes(x=olong, y=olat, size=num, color=cityNPS))
```

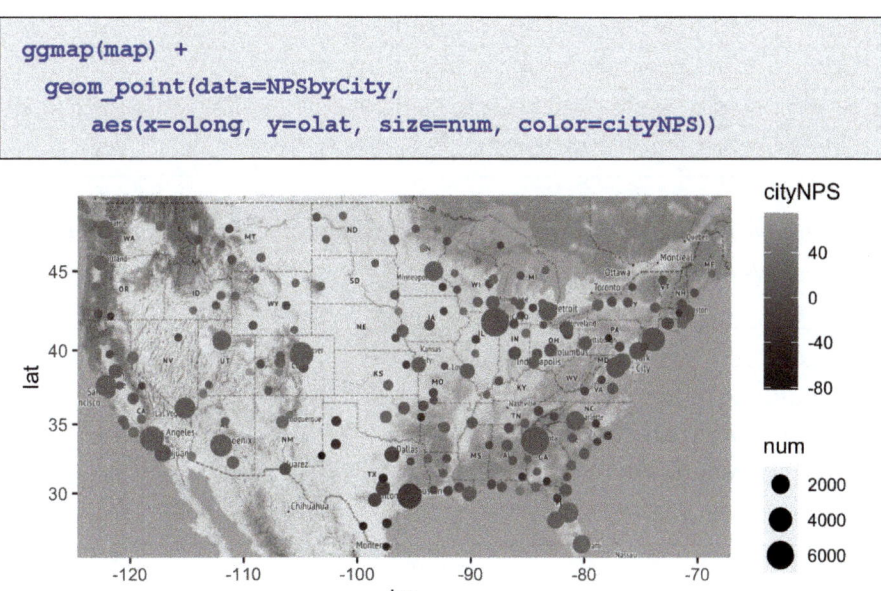

Although this has promise for becoming an interesting visualization, it seems a bit cluttered and difficult to interpret. Let's simplify the visualization by showing an NPS value per state, using a choropleth with color-coding (i.e., a heatmap). To do this, we need NPS values for each state. The code to generate this information is similar to our NPS by city analysis. However, note that for this visualization, we removed flights from Puerto Rico, since that is not included in the "us" geometry dataframe.

```
#explore per state NPS
npsByStateDF <- survey %>%
  filter(Origin.State != "Puerto Rico") %>%
  mutate(state=tolower(Origin.State)) %>%
  group_by(state) %>%
  summarize(stateNPS =
            CalcNPS(Likelihood.to.recommend))
```

Once we have the NPS by state, we need to combine that information with the geometry information within the us dataframe, using the merge function.

```
#merge the geom state info with the data
NPSwithGeom <- merge(us, npsByStateDF,
          by.y="state", by.x="region")

#make sure the points are in the correct order
NPSwithGeom <- NPSwithGeom %>% arrange(order)
```

Now that we have all the information in one dataframe, the visualization is similar to what we have previously done:

```
#visualize the "heatmap"
ggmap(map) +
  geom_polygon(data= NPSwithGeom,
      color="black", alpha=0.9,
      aes(x=long,y=lat, group=group, fill=stateNPS))
```

Note that with this visualization, we can easily see that departures from Texas have a much lower NPS than other states, which might be important for the airline to understand. We can drill a bit deeper, by combining our previous two visualizations (i.e., let's put the NPS values for each city on our NPS heatmap). The only addition is the "scale_color_gradient" function, which defines the range for colors for the points (note that we could have used scale_fill_gradient to define the range of colors for the heatmap).

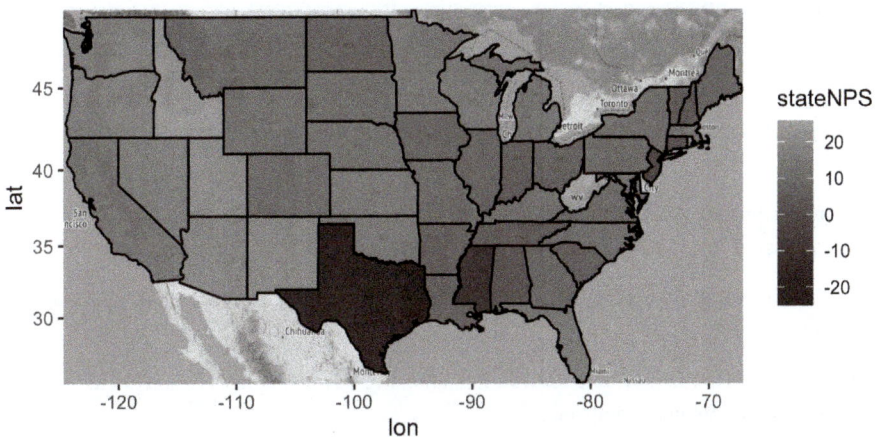

```
ggmap(map) +
  geom_polygon(data= NPSwithGeom,
     color="black", alpha=0.9,
     aes(x=long,y=lat, group=group, fill=stateNPS)) +
  geom_point(data=NPSbyCity,
     aes(x=olong, y=olat, color=cityNPS)) +
  scale_color_gradient(low="black", high="white")
```

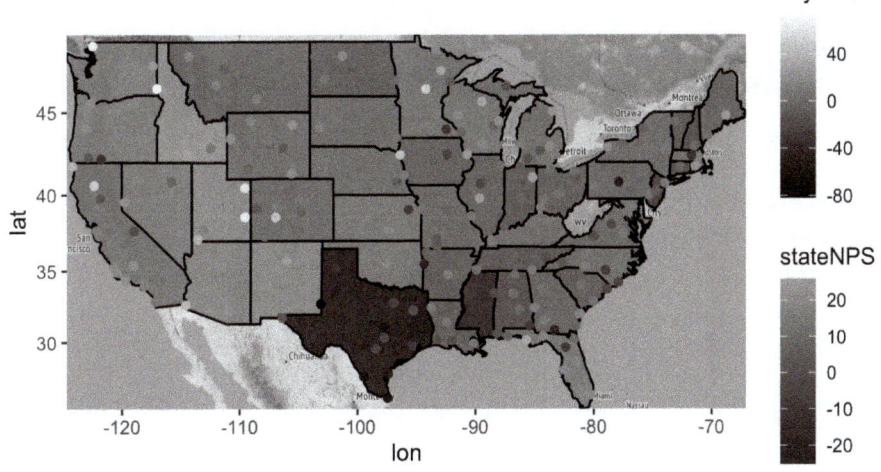

## Chapter Challenge

1. Go to syracuse.craiglist.org and click on the apts/housing for rent link. Switch to the map view and search for "Syracuse University." Review the map and report how many listings there are near the university.

2. Install the ggmap package if you have not done so already and run library(ggmap). Then run help("map_data") and report a list of maps that are built into the package.

3. Using the code in this chapter as an example, use the geom_point() function from ggplot() to make a map of New Zealand.

4. Count the number of regions in the map data for New Zealand. One way to do this is to use the table() command on the region variable in the map data.

5. Improve your map from Problem 4 by using a Mercator projection.

6. Improve your map of New Zealand again by switching from geom_point() to geom_polygon().

7. Generate a map, showing the number of available bike slots in New York City.

8. Using the case study data, generate a heatmap of NPS values for the *destination* states.

9. Find a census dataset with additional information (https://www2.census.gov/programs-surveys/popest/datasets/2010-2016/national/totals/nst-est2016-alldata.csv). Parse the dataset and then display the data in a useful manner, using the different visualization techniques we have covered in Chapter 8 and this chapter.

## Sources

http://blog.programmableweb.com/2012/06/21/7-free-geocoding-apis-google-bing-yahoo-and-mapquest/
https://developers.google.com/maps/terms
http://en.wikipedia.org/wiki/Open_Mashup_Alliance
http://www.housingmaps.com/

## R Functions Used in This Chapter

| | |
|---|---|
| c() | Combine elements to make a vector. |
| coord_map() | Makes sure the map does not show up stretched or distorted. |
| data.frame() | Creates a dataframe. |
| filter() | Tidyverse function to select rows. |
| fromJSON() | Convert from JSON format into a data structure. |
| geom_point() | Adds point(s) to a visualization. |
| geom_polygon() | Adds filled polygons to a visualization. |
| get_stamenmap() | Gets a raster image map |
| ggmap() | Creates a map visualization. |
| ggplot() | Creates a ggplot. |
| ggtitle() | Adds a title to a visualization. |
| group_by() | Tidyverse function to organize data into groups. |
| map_data() | Finds a map to be used by ggplot. |
| max() | Returns the maximum value from a vector. |
| merge() | Joins two data sets according to a matching key. |
| mutate() | Tidyverse function to modify columns. |
| str_replace_all() | Multiple string substitution. |
| summarize() | Tidyverse function to create column summaries. |
| tolower() | Changes all uppercase letters to lowercase. |

This text includes access to datasets and select student resources. To learn more, visit sagepub.com

# 10

## LINING UP OUR MODELS

## LEARNING OBJECTIVES

Understand the difference between supervised and unsupervised learning.

Understand the difference between regression and classification.

Explain and be able to use cross validation techniques.

Build models and use models to interpret and understand the data.

Utilize the lm package to create and interpret linear models.

Use the Caret package to build linear models.

## WHAT IS A MODEL?

In order to build a model, we first need to understand what a model is. People use the word "model" in many ways. Some have nothing to do with data, such as using the term to connote a person who might appear in a magazine wearing a certain sweater, shirt, or watch. Another use of the word describes a small representation of a larger set of objects (such as a model railroad). In this chapter, we won't discuss either fashion models or miniature trains. Instead, we will use data to develop an understanding of how a predictor variable connects with an outcome variable. We will discuss predictive models that are calculated by software programs (in our case, R libraries).

## SUPERVISED AND UNSUPERVISED MACHINE LEARNING

Machine learning, which is a term that refers to a variety of computer algorithms that process data and find patterns, is used to create predictive models. Machine learning techniques fall into two broad categories: supervised learning techniques and unsupervised learning techniques. Supervised learning is when we use an algorithm on an initial set of data (the supervised phase) to create a model, and then use the resulting trained model to make predictions on new data. The algorithm is simply a set of processing instructions—think of it as a recipe—for taking in some data and creating a predicted result.

Unsupervised learning is when we use an algorithm to group, or otherwise understand the data. In this approach, the algorithm must discover insights on its own with no prior knowledge of categories (i.e., unsupervised learning is a self-learning technique). To reinforce the difference between supervised and unsupervised learning: if we were to get an algorithm to cluster or group together similar days based on weather, this would be an example of unsupervised learning (there might be a cluster of days that are rainy, windy, and cold, and a different cluster that is warm, sunny, and no wind). Another unsupervised learning technique could be used to generate rules, such as if it's sunny and mild, it will (likely) not rain. We will discuss unsupervised learning in Chapter 12.

An important supervised prediction technique is called *regression*, which is when we try to use some input variables to predict a continuous quantity output variable. A very simple algorithm for prediction is linear regression. A relatively straightforward application of mathematics allows linear regression to transform a dataset into a linear equation (a sets of slopes and an intercept). The linear equation allows us to make predictions for "metric" outcome variables. For example, we could use the number of oil changes for a vehicle to predict the repair costs for that vehicle. All we would need is some previous data on some vehicles' oil changes and repair costs. Linear regression would use these data to calculate a slope to go with the number of oil changes and an intercept. Then we could plug in a new value for the number of oil changes to learn the predicted cost of repairs. Another important prediction technique is called *classification*, which is when we try to use some input variables to predict a categorical outcome. For example, we could use atmospheric measurements such as air pressure to predict whether there will be rain or no rain tomorrow.

Let's clarify the difference between these two kinds of supervised prediction problems (regression versus classification). Regression is the term used when we are trying to predict a metric variable—that is, a variable like temperature or repair costs that can have an ordered set of values on some measurement scale. Classification is a term we use when we are trying to predict a set of distinct possibilities, such as between one of two choices (e.g., on or off, true or false). Take the weather as a simple example. Some days are cloudy, some are sunny. The barometer rises some days and falls others. The wind might be strong or weak and it might come from various directions. If we collect data on a bunch of days and use those data to build a machine learning model, the model might predict that cloudy days with a falling barometer and with the wind from the east indicate that it is likely to rain. We could use a machine learning model to predict the weather in future days—if we were predicting rain/no rain, which would be a classifier and if we were predicting the amount of rain that would be regression.

In this chapter, we will examine linear regression, which as previously noted, can be considered as a simple supervised machine learning technique. In Chapter 11, we will examine supervised learning techniques for classification. Two chapters ahead from here, we will explore unsupervised learning.

# LINEAR MODELING

Finding relationships between variables is one of the basic aims of data science. The question, "Does X influence Y?" is of prime concern for data analysts from every sector: Are house prices influenced by incomes? Is the growth rate of crops improved by fertilizer? Do taller sprinters run faster? We can answer these kinds of questions by building predictive models. One of the simplest forms of predictive model is called a linear model because it uses the slope and the intercept of a line to represent the relationship between an X (predictor) variable and a Y (outcome) variable. This method is often used by statisticians and is known as linear modeling. The term linear model actually covers a wide variety of methods, from the relatively simple to the very sophisticated, but all these methods create models that can be used for prediction. You can get an idea of how many different methods statisticians have developed by looking at the regression analysis page in Wikipedia and checking out the number of models listed on the right-hand sidebar (and, by the way, that list is not exhaustive).

The original ideas behind linear regression (which is a synonym for linear model) were developed by some of the usual statistical suspects behind many of the ideas we've seen already, such as Gauss, Galton, and Pearson. The biggest individual contribution was probably by Gauss, who used the procedure to predict movements of other planets in the solar system when they were hidden from view and to correctly predict when and where they would appear again.

The basis of all these methods is the idea that it is possible to fit a line to a set of data points that represents the effect an independent variable (AKA predictor) is having on a dependent variable (AKA outcome). It is easy to visualize how this works with one variable changing in step with another variable. The following chart shows a line fitted to a series of points, using the so-called least squares method (a relatively simple method of finding a best-fitting line). The chart shows how the relationship between an input (independent) variable—on the horizontal X-axis—relates to the output (dependent) values on the Y-axis. In other words, the output variable is dependent (is a function) of the independent variable.

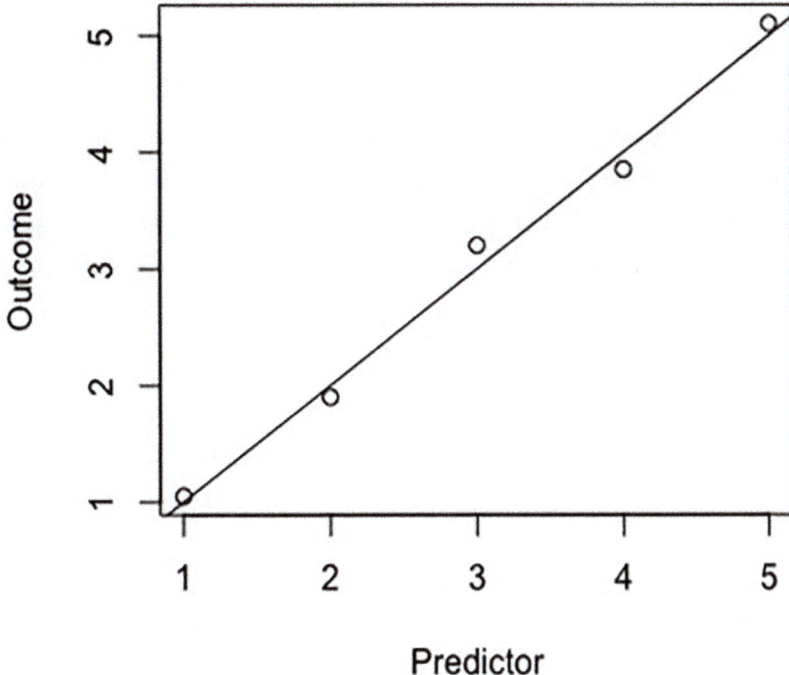

Note that although the line fits the points fairly well, with an even split (as even as it can be for five points!) of points above and below the line, none of the points are precisely on the line—the training data do not fit the line precisely. As we discuss the concepts in regression analysis further, we will see that understanding these discrepancies is just as important as understanding the line itself.

The mathematical idea that allows us to create lines of best fit for a set of data points like this is that we can find a line that will minimize the squared distances between the line and each of the points. Once the model calculates the line that minimizes the squared distance for all the points, the model represents the line with an equation you might remember from algebra:

$$Y=bX+a.$$

Do not worry if you have never taken an algebra course: all you need to understand is that the equation has two values that describe the line (b and a). The letter "b" denotes the slope of the line and the letter "a" describes where the line crosses the Y-axis, also known as the Y-intercept. These values are calculated by applying some math to the training data. Note that a linear model requires a minimum of two observations (in the simplest case, two X,Y pairs). In practice, most datasets used for training a linear model have dozens, hundreds, or thousands of observations. Once b and a have been calculated, the equation can then be used to predict the Y value that might result from any given X value.

Although the mathematics behind these techniques can be managed by anyone with a little knowledge of matrix algebra, the reality is that even with only a few data points, the process of fitting a line with manual calculations becomes very tedious, very quickly. This is why software programs, from spreadsheets to R, all include prepackaged methods for conducting linear modeling. Because these tools are so widely available and so easy to use, we will not discuss the specifics of how the calculations are done, but will move quickly to an example of how we use R to do it.

To generate a linear model in R, we can use the lm function, which given a list of points, generating what it thinks is the best-fitted line for the data points. In other words, lm will calculate the appropriate b and a, based on the input data. After that we can use the predict function: When the model is given a new X value, it will use the equation of a line ($Y = bX + a$), to calculate a predicted Y value. We can now explore how to use linear model in an example.

## AN EXAMPLE—CAR MAINTENANCE

Is changing the oil of a car more frequently a good thing? Does it save money in the long run? Let's use linear regression to address this question. Let's say that we were just put in charge of maintaining a fleet of company cars. We know that the company replaces the cars every three years, and in fact the company just replaced the cars (i.e., bought a new fleet of cars). The person who was previously in charge of the car maintenance didn't have a schedule for when to change the oil, but rather changed the oil whenever the car happened to be available. Luckily, good maintenance records were kept, and now we want to try and figure out, in a data-driven approach, if changing the oil frequently is a good idea. The following R code defines our dataset:

```
oilChanges <- c(3,5,2,3,1,4,6,4,3,2,0,10,7,8)
repairs <- c(300, 300, 500, 400, 700, 420, 100, 290,
        475, 620, 600, 0, 200, 50)
miles <- c(20100, 23200, 19200, 22100, 18400, 23400,
        17900, 19900, 20100, 24100, 18200, 19600, 20800,
        19700)
oil <- data.frame(oilChanges, repairs, miles)
View(oil)
```

|    | oilChanges | repairs | miles |
|----|-----------|---------|-------|
| 1  | 3         | 300     | 20100 |
| 2  | 5         | 300     | 23200 |
| 3  | 2         | 500     | 19200 |
| 4  | 3         | 400     | 22100 |
| 5  | 1         | 700     | 18400 |
| 6  | 4         | 420     | 23400 |
| 7  | 6         | 100     | 17900 |
| 8  | 4         | 290     | 19900 |
| 9  | 3         | 475     | 20100 |
| 10 | 2         | 620     | 24100 |
| 11 | 0         | 600     | 18200 |
| 12 | 10        | 0       | 19600 |
| 13 | 7         | 200     | 20800 |
| 14 | 8         | 50      | 19700 |

Let's look at the data for the cars that were just replaced. The dataset provides three columns of information. First, there is the number of oil changes that each car had during the past three years. The next column shows the total amount of repairs (in dollars). Finally, we have the miles driven by each car.

Given these data, can we determine whether changing the oil frequently is a good thing. Our independent variables are oilChanges and miles. The dependent variable (the one we are trying to predict) is repair costs. Before building a model, we should do some exploratory analysis, which professional data scientists always do prior to building a model. In this case, we can display (plot) the points with the following R command:

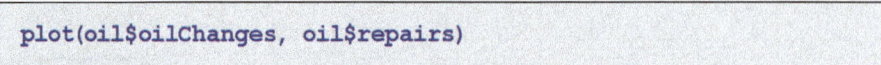

```
plot(oil$oilChanges, oil$repairs)
```

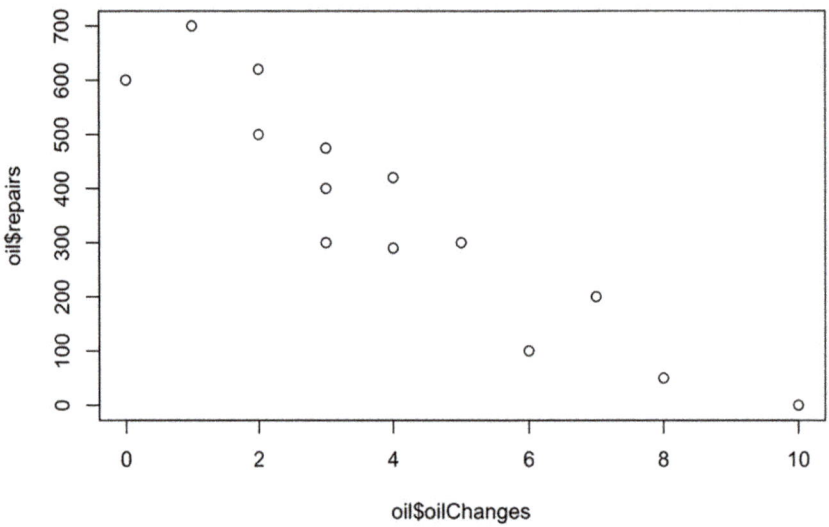

We can see a general trend: the repairs are high when the number of oil changes is low, and the repairs are low when the number of oil changes is high. That's a very clear pattern! Now let's explore the other predictor—miles driven—in relation to repair costs. This time we will create the display with ggplot:

```
library(ggplot2)
ggplot(oil, aes(x=miles, y=repairs)) + geom_point()
```

Although this visualization looks great in ggplot, we don't see as clear a pattern as we did with oil changes. So just to start simple, let's build our first model with only oilChanges as the independent variable. Here is the code for building a linear model:

```
model1 <- lm(formula=repairs ~ oilChanges, data=oil)
```

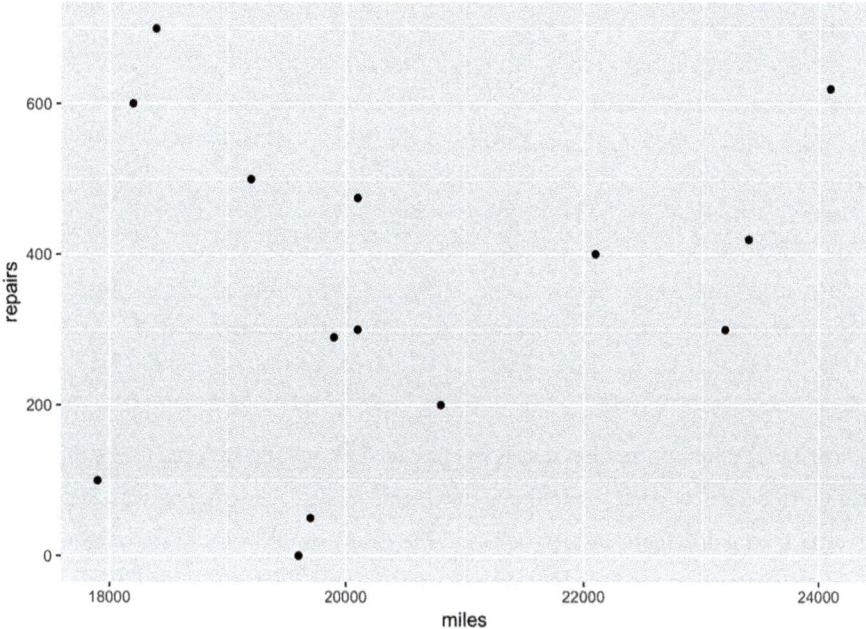

The lm command creates a data structure that contains everything we need to know about the results. We want to hang on to all of that information, so we store the output of lm in an object called model1. Note that the lm command takes two parameters: the first tells lm to use oilChanges to predict repairs. The squiggly line [~], which is called a tilde character, tells lm which independent and dependent variables are to be modeled, with the entry on the left being the dependent variable and everything on the right being the predictors. The other parameter tells lm the name of the dataframe where we have stored the training data. Note that because we supplied the name of the dataframe, we do not need to use the $ notation with the predictors (i.e., no need for oil$repairs or oil$oil-Changes). In the next command, we request an overview of the contents of our model.

```
summary(model1)

Call:
lm(formula = repairs ~ oilChanges, data = oil)

Residuals:
    Min      1Q   Median      3Q      Max
-136.208 -48.195  -0.211  54.782  119.803
```

```
Coefficients:
            Estimate Std. Error t value Pr(>|t|)
(Intercept) 652.191      40.537  16.089  1.74e-09 ***
oilChanges -71.994        8.202  -8.778  1.44e-06 ***
---
Signif. codes: 0 '***' 0.001 '**' 0.01 '*' 0.05 '.'


Residual standard error: 82.72 on 12 degrees of freedom
Multiple R-squared: 0.8653, Adjusted R-squared: 0.854
F-statistic: 77.05 on 1 and 12 DF, p-value: 1.436e-06
```

Whoa! That's a lot information that R has provided for us, and we need to use this information to decide whether we are happy with this model. Being happy with the model involves several different considerations and there is no simple rule. To start, we will look at the R-squared value, also known as the coefficient of determination. Note that there is no connection between the term R-squared, which is a commonly used statistical quantity, and the name of our statistics package.

The R-squared value can be interpreted as the proportion of the variation in the dependent variable that is accounted for by the whole set of independent variables (in this case just one independent variable). An R-squared value of 1.0 would mean that the X variable(s) made perfect predictions of the Y variable—every point in the training data fell right on the line. An R-squared value of zero would indicate that the X variable(s) did not predict the Y variable at all. R-squared cannot be negative. In the output, you can actually see two different R-squared values. You are always safe if you focus on the *adjusted* R-squared value. The adjusted R-squared value takes into account the number of predictors and the sample size. With a small sample and many predictors, adjusted R-squared will be much smaller (and more correct!) than plain R-squared. With a larger sample and not too many predictors, adjusted R-squared and plain R-squared will be about the same.

In this example, there was an adjusted R-squared of 0.854, which means that the oilChanges variable accounts for about 85.4% of the repair costs (stated another way, oilChanges can explain 85.4% of the variation in repair costs). Note that there is no absolute rule for what makes an R-squared good. Much depends on the purpose of the analysis. In the analysis of human behavior, which is notoriously unpredictable, an R-squared of 0.20 or 0.30 might be considered quite good. In this case, because we are working with a mechanical device whose operation depends on basic concepts of materials engineering and physics, the adjusted R-squared of 0.854 looks like a solid result that can provide actionable insight for the fleet manager.

Although the adjusted R-squared is perhaps the most important output to evaluate from the model, let's explore some of the other outputs. First, at the top of the output we can see the actual call used to create the model. This is helpful if we are exploring a model, but couldn't review the actual R code used to create the model. Next, we can see the residuals, which are the differences between the actual observed values and the predicted values. These residuals are also known as the errors of prediction. We see five summary numbers concerning residuals. One way to explore how well the model fits the data is to see whether the error (residual) is symmetrically distributed across these five summary points and for the median to be close to zero.

The next section in the output describes the coefficients of the model. The coefficients are two constants that represent the intercept and slope terms in the linear model (remember the equation $Y = bX + a$: the slope is b and the intercept is a). In this example, the coefficient estimate contains two rows: the first row is the intercept. The intercept, in our example, is essentially the expected value of the repairs when there were zero oil changes. The second row in the coefficients is the slope, or in our example, the effect that oil changes have on vehicle repairs. The slope in our model is saying that for every additional oil change, the expected repairs go down by $71.99. It might help if you ask yourself, "A one unit change in X leads to how much change in Y?" In this case an increase in X of 1 leads to a change in Y of -71.99.

Finally, one other output to explore is the p-value. The $Pr(>|t|)$ abbreviation, which is typically known as a p-value, describes the probability of observing any value equal or larger than the absolute value of a t-statistic under the assumption that the X and the Y are unrelated. A small p-value is preferred: it indicates that it is unlikely to have observed a slope value this large due to the effects of sampling error. We have discussed sampling error earlier in the book as the distortions that occur in statistical values (like the mean/ average) when we don't have access to a complete population (and therefore must work with a sample). In most statistical analyses, a p-value under 0.05 is considered a good cutoff point. In our model example, the p-values are very close to zero. Note the "signif." codes associated to each estimate. The asterisks are a shorthand for different cutoffs for p-values. As long as we see at least one asterisk, we can conclude that a systematic relationship probably exists between oil changes and repairs.

Next, we can show the line of best fit (based on the model) to the X-Y plot of repair costs against oil changes with a call to abline (pronounced A-B-line) that includes the output of the lm command as its only argument:

```
plot(oil$oilChanges, oil$repairs)
abline(model1)
```

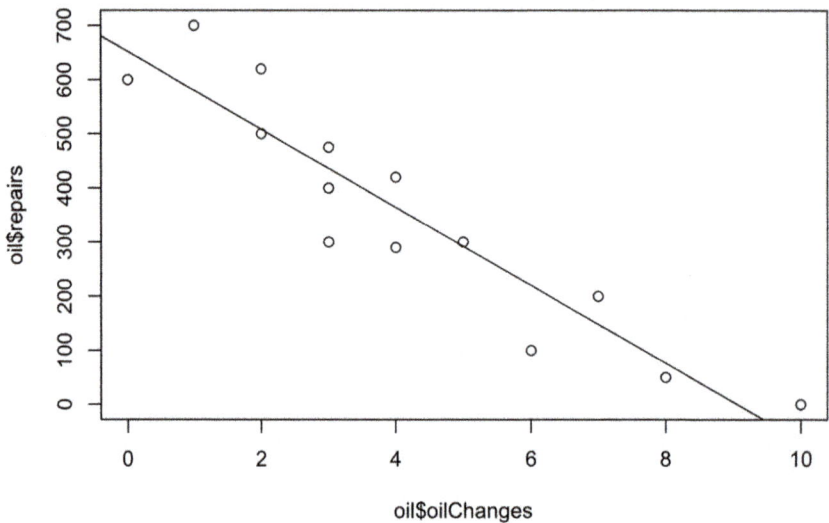

The previous model suggests that we should do as many oil changes as possible. For example, the line predicts very low (almost zero) repairs if we do nine or more oil changes, but about $680 if we do no oil changes.

Next, let's try using both oilChanges and miles to create a new linear model. Perhaps both variables could do a better job predicting repair costs (as opposed to just using oil-Changes). We can do this with the following R code, which includes the two predictors by putting a plus sign between them:

```
m <- lm(formula=repairs ~ oilChanges + miles,
        data=oil)
summary(m)

Call:
lm(formula = repairs ~ oilChanges + miles, data = oil)
```

```
Residuals:
    Min      1Q   Median    3Q      Max
-130.488  -53.810  -1.712  46.301  151.182


Coefficients:
                Estimate Std. Error t value Pr(>|t|)
   (Intercept) 343.26567 231.42285    1.483    0.166
   oilChanges  -71.98591   7.93052   -9.077 1.93e-06 ***
   miles         0.01508   0.01114    1.354    0.203
   ---
   Signif. codes:  0 '***' 0.001 '**'  0.01 '*' 0.05 '.'


Residual standard error: 79.98 on 11 degrees of freedom
Multiple R-squared: 0.8845, Adjusted R-squared: 0.8635
F-statistic: 42.12 on 2 and 11 DF, p-value: 6.982e-06
```

We can see that the new model is slightly better (a slightly higher adjusted R-squared value of 0.8635 compared to the previous model's 0.854). You can also see that oil-Changes has *** but miles does not. This is because the model calculated that only the slope on oilChanges was statistically significant. This result is not surprising, because our initial X-Y plot suggested that miles did not show an obvious pattern in relation to repair costs. So, in this case, we could stick with our original model where we predict repair costs as a function of the number of oil changes.

In the work we have done so far, we've ignored one important element of the situation: we did not factor the cost of an oil change into our analysis. Let's assume that oil changes are very expensive. After all, when the car is having its oil changed, the driver cannot use the car for company business. We also have to pay the mechanic and buy the oil and the filter. Putting that all together, let's model the cost of the oil change as $350 per oil change. The following code creates additional columns in our dataset to compute and show the total cost for each car (which is the cost of the repairs plus the cost of doing the oil changes). The code then plots the results (this time using ggplot):

```
oil$oilChangeCost <- oil$oilChanges * 350
oil$totalCost <- oil$oilChangeCost + oil$repairs
```

```
ggplot(oil, aes(x=oilChanges, y=totalCost)) + geom_point() +
    geom_smooth(method="lm")
```

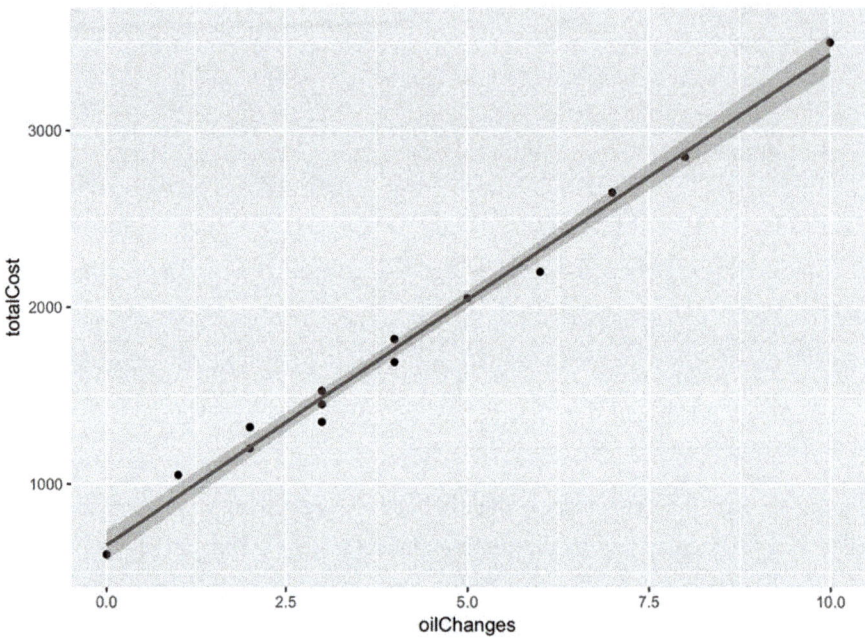

Wow—now the analysis shows that we shouldn't do any oil changes at all because the lowest total cost appears at zero oil changes! Notice that when using ggplot, we use the "geom_smooth" command, which is similar to the abline() function in the core R package. The gray area around the blue line indicates uncertainty around the prediction at any given level of X. We can see that the model has less uncertainty around five oil changes, as compared to zero or 10 oil changes. This makes sense, because there were more data points in and around those middle values. Let's double-check our results by having R predict the total repair costs for a given number of oil changes with the following R code:

```
m <- lm(formula=totalCost ~ oilChanges, data=oil)

test = data.frame(oilChanges=0)
predict(m, test, type="response")
652.191
```

```
test = data.frame(oilChanges=5)
predict(m, test, type="response")
2042.219

test = data.frame(oilChanges=10)
predict(m, test, type="response")
3432.247
```

Note that we did not review any summary statistics for this model such as R-squared. That's because our calculation of totalCost mathematically contains a direct influence from oilChanges. This artificially inflates the R-squared and the p-values.

We can see that as the number of oil changes increases, so does the predicted total cost of maintenance. Of course, we still may not have all the important information that should be modeled. For example, perhaps the resale value of each car (after it has completed its three years of service) was also affected by maintenance. This represents a situation that often arises when doing data science. That is, we have some data to create a model, but we are not sure whether the model covers all the circumstances that could possibly impact the results of our analysis. We may be missing certain variables that we need to do a better job of modeling, or some of the data we have might be contaminated by influences that we cannot see. That's why it is important, when reporting the results of a predictive model, to be cautious about claiming that x causes y or that increasing x is guaranteed to decrease y or the other way around. The statistics can provide helpful guidance, but accurately predicting the future is always quite tricky.

## USING THE CARET PACKAGE

In addition to using the lm function directly, we can load and use the Caret package, which is an R package that supports many machine learning techniques. The Caret package (short for Classification And REgression Training) contains functions to simplify the model training process for both regression and classification. Caret does not actually do the modeling, it just provides a consistent interface for accessing a large number of individual specialized R packages. For example, when you build a linear model using Caret, Caret calls the lm function, just as we did earlier in this chapter. This is important because when you try to run the R code, Caret might note additional packages that need to be installed.

Keeping this in mind, you can see below that we can use Caret to create a linear model, just as we used lm directly to generate a linear model earlier in the book. Note that the trControl argument refers to how we should control the training of the model, but we do not have to worry about that just yet, which is why we use method of "none."

```
#install and library the caret package as needed
install.packages("caret")
library(caret)

#create the model, letting caret's train function
#call the 'lm' function
model1 <- train(repairs ~ oilChanges, data = oil,
            trControl=trainControl(method = "none"),
            method = "lm")
summary(model1)

Call:
lm(formula = .outcome ~ ., data = dat)

Residuals:
   Min      1Q Median    3Q     Max
-136.208 -48.195 -0.211 54.782 119.803

Coefficients:
            Estimate Std. Error t value Pr(>|t|)
(Intercept) 652.191      40.537  16.089 1.74e-09 ***
oilChanges   -71.994       8.202  -8.778 1.44e-06 ***
---
Signif. codes: 0 '***' 0.001 '**' 0.01 '*' 0.05 '.'

Residual standard error: 82.72 on 12 degrees of freedom
Multiple R-squared: 0.8653, Adjusted R-squared: 0.854
F-statistic: 77.05 on 1 and 12 DF, p-value: 1.436e-06
```

As you can see, a summary of model1 shows that it is the same as the model that was generated when directly using the lm function (i.e., in this situation, using train() or lm() directly will result in the same model).

# PARTITIONING INTO TRAINING AND CROSS VALIDATION DATASETS

There is one last important concept that we have not yet covered with respect to supervised learning (i.e., working on a classification or regression problem). Specifically, our predictive model, created from our machine learning algorithm, will inevitably make mistakes. For example, the model might predict rain for Thursday but it turns out that Thursday is sunny. When predicting repair costs of $2,000, we might actually have repair costs of $2,350. When using regression, a summary of the error could be calculated as 1 – the adjusted R-squared value. So, if we had an R-squared value of 0.86, the corresponding model error would be 1 – 0.86 = 0.14. Mathematicians refer to this error value as the coefficient of alienation. For any prediction problem, we want our error value to be as small as possible.

Improving prediction accuracy (i.e., reducing the error rate) is the basic goal of supervised machine learning: we use a substantial number of training cases to help the algorithm discover the underlying pattern. Once the algorithm has detected the pattern from the training data, it stores a set of numbers and other information that describe the trained machine learning model. We can then apply the model to some new X data (i.e., new values of our predictors).

Here's a new trick: after we find out what really happens with that new data, we can see how well our model performed on new data by checking the predicted values against the actual events—for example, we can use our new model to suggest the number of oil changes (or to predict whether tomorrow will be sunny).

Rather than waiting for these future events to happen (and then seeing the accuracy of the model), we can just divide the data that we already have into two chunks, a training dataset and a test dataset (which is also sometimes called a holdout sample or a cross validation sample). For example, if we do not want to wait a couple of years to see the accuracy of our maintenance model, we might randomly sample two-thirds of that data that we already have to train our model and save the rest of the data to use in *testing* our trained model. Using the weather example, if we had historical weather data from the past three years (1,095 days in total), we might randomly sample two years of that data to train our model (730 days of training data) and then save the rest of the sample (365 days of test data) to use in *testing* our trained model.

You might be thinking "why can't we just calculate the accuracy for the data that was used to generate the model?" A test dataset helps us to detect and possibly avoid the problem of *overfitting*. In theory, many of the more-advanced machine learning algorithms, such as the techniques we will use in Chapters 11, 12, and 15, are sufficiently powerful that they can be pushed to the point of memorizing the input data, and so, can perfectly predict the outcome data in the training dataset. The big problem with this, though, is that this overfitted model won't generalize to a new dataset. In effect, if we push the algorithm too hard, it will become too specialized on the training data and won't work anywhere else. In most cases, the whole point of creating a model is to use it to predict values on future data that the model has never seen. In short, we want to make sure our model generalizes from our training data to new, unseen data (overfitting is not usually a big issue with linear regression, but overfitting will be an issue with the techniques we describe in Chapter 11).

With this in mind, let's redo our car maintenance example, but this time, have a dataset to train (i.e., build) the model and a different dataset to test (i.e., evaluate) the model. There is no universal approach on how much of the data should be set aside for training, and how much for testing, but as a rule of thumb, when using this partitioning approach, you can use somewhere between two-thirds to three-quarters of the dataset to train and the remainder to test. Furthermore, when using the partitioning approach, it is important to randomize the selection of cases for the training and test sets to ensure that there is no systematic bias in the selection of cases. In other words, we need to randomize the cases because we have no way of knowing how the original dataset was sorted. In case it was sorted on some variable of interest, we do not just want to take the first two-thirds of the cases as the training set.

Fortunately, the Caret package contains the createDataPartition command, which randomly samples without replacement from a list of numbers ranging from one to the final element index of the dataset to be partitioned, which we can use to create our train and test datasets. One important aspect of the createDataPartition command is that the command uses the dependent variable (the outcome that we hope to predict) as an input. This input variable helps the function to ensure that the differing values of Y are equally well represented in both the training and test sets. Let's think through an example with a small number of cases: February weather in Syracuse, New York. Our overall dataset contains 28 days, of which it was sunny on 16 days and cloudy (and snowed) on 12 days—that's about 57% sunny days. We tell createDataPartition() that we want half of our data (14 days) for training and the remainder (14 days) as a hold out for testing. The createDataPartition() command will randomly sample to make sure that both datasets contain a random selection of eight sunny days and six snowy days—again about 57% sunny days in each dataset. Let's try it with some R code to see what happens:

```
#use the 'set.seed' to enable repeatable results
set.seed(10)

# Make sure caret is loaded and ready
library(caret)

# Create our weather outcome variable
sunnyDays.percentCloudy <-
                sample(1:10, 16, replace=TRUE)
cloudyDays.percentCloudy <-
                sample(90:100, 12, replace=TRUE)
percentCloudyAllDays <- c(sunnyDays.percentCloudy,
                          cloudyDays.percentCloudy)

# The p=0.5 splits the dataset in half
trainList <- createDataPartition(percentCloudyAllDays,
                                 p=0.5, list=FALSE)

# Show the results
data.frame( trainList,
        cloudPercent=percentCloudyAllDays[trainList] )

Resample1 cloudPercent
1      2             10
2      3              7
3      4              8
4      5              6
5      8              8
6      9             10
7     12              2
8     16              6
9     17             96
10    18            100
11    21             94
12    22             98
13    23             91
14    27             90
15    28             96
```

The middle column of output above, under the heading "Resample1," shows the row indices (from the original data) that createDataPartition() randomly sampled. You can count the values in the right-hand column to see that we have eight sunny days and six snowy days (57% sunny), the same as the full dataset. Also remember by putting a minus sign in front of trainIndex, you can get all of the rows that belong in the test dataset instead. Try it! Because this is a random set of indices, if the code ran again, without using the set.seed(10), we would get different index numbers in the trainList.

```
#create train and test datasets
trainData <- percentCloudyAllDays[trainList,]
testData <- percentCloudyAllDays[-trainList,]
```

Now we are ready to partition our oil dataframe dataset, remembering that the repairs attribute is our dependent variable, and so, we supply that attribute to the createData-Partition function.

```
# makes the sampling predictable
set.seed(123)


# Randomly sample for training dataset elements
trainList <- createDataPartition(
     y=oil$repairs, p=.66, list=FALSE)
```

Note that we first use the set.seed() function, so that when we rerun the code, we get the same results, and also so that you can reproduce the same results as us as long as you use the set.seed() function with the same value of 111. If you provide a different number, R will generate a different set of random samples.

We can confirm that the indices are a random subset of all the indices by looking at the first few cases:

```
head(trainList[,1])
[1] 2 3 4 5 6 7
```

Now we are ready to generate our training and testing datasets from the original oil dataset by using the randomized set of indices that we created in the trainList. As previously mentioned, because the test dataset is composed of all the data points that were not in the train dataset, we can use the negative sign with the trainList to create the testData variable:

```
#create train and test datasets
trainData <- oil[trainList,]
testData <- oil[-trainList,]
```

We now have two separate datasets, representing the training and test breakdown of the original data, and can use our training dataset to build our linear model. The following command generates a model based on the training dataset:

```
lm.model <- train(repairs ~ oilChanges+miles,
                  data = trainData,
                  trControl=trainControl(method = "none"),
                  method = "lm")

summary(lm.model)

Call:
lm(formula = .outcome ~ ., data = dat)

Residuals:
    Min      1Q Median    3Q     Max
-105.634 -44.656 -7.598 38.243 139.677

Coefficients:
              Estimate Std. Error t value Pr(>|t|)
(Intercept) 481.929815 270.636209   1.781 0.118169
oilChanges  -70.130613   9.227283  -7.600 0.000126 ***
miles         0.008072   0.013508   0.598 0.568957
---
Signif. codes: 0 '***' 0.001 '**' 0.01 '*' 0.05 '.' 0.1 ' ' 1

Residual standard error: 80.93 on 7 degrees of freedom
Multiple R-squared: 0.893, Adjusted R-squared: 0.8624
F-statistic: 29.21 on 2 and 7 DF, p-value: 0.0004008
```

This code is similar to the code we ran previously, where we used both oil changes and miles to predict repairs. We can see that the adjusted R-squared is about the same as before. This won't always be the case: with a different random sample of observations in our training data, we might get a value of adjusted R-squared that came out slightly lower or slightly higher. Additionally, we should not be surprised to see that oilChanges is an important predictor, but that the miles attribute was not.

To understand the quality of our model in predicted novel data, we first use the predict function to generate the predicted values. Then, we can look at the squared correlation between the predicted values of Y and the original values for the Y variable (repairs) in the test dataset. This shows a value roughly the same as the R-squared value from the training data. Again here, we might see a somewhat lower or high value if the random sampling that partitioned the training and test datasets turned out differently.

```
predictValues <- predict(lm.model, newdata=testData)
cor(predictValues, testData$repairs)^2
[1] 0.8625948
```

## USING K-FOLD CROSS VALIDATION

Partitioning your data into train and test datasets can work reasonably well if you have a lot of data, let's say more than 1,000 observations/rows (such as our weather example). However, if you do not have a lot of data (like our car maintenance example), or if your data are very complex, then partitioning your data might not be the best strategy. In fact, in 1995 a researcher named Ron Kohavi published a study that compared the partitioning strategy to a few other methods. After looking over the results, Kohavi recommended a different approach, known by the gooey phrase *stratified k-fold cross validation*. With the stratified k-fold strategy, you tell your training algorithm to follow these four steps: (a) randomly divide up *all* your available data into k-separate chunks (it turns out that k = 10 is often the best choice), where each chunk has roughly the same balance of outcomes (i.e., if it rains on average on two of every 10 days, then every chunk of training data must contain 20% rainy days); (b) let the algorithm train a model where one of the k-separate chunks is kept out of the training data, and is rather used as the test dataset for the model built with the other k-1 chunks; (c) combine the results of the k separate models into one overall model; and (d) report the error rate and accuracy of the overall model.

Luckily, it is easy to use k-fold cross validation using the Caret package. So, let's try it using the same train and test dataset from our car maintenance example. As you can see in the following code, to use k-fold cross validation within the Caret package, we first call the trainControl function, stating that we want to use repeated cross validation "repeatedcv," and defining k (the number of folds). The "repeated" part of the cross validation is important in that doing k-fold cross validation typically generates different results that depend on how we split the data. So, to account for this variation, one typically repeats the whole k-fold cross validation multiple times, which are then averaged together. We then pass the results of that train control function to the train function.

```
trctrl <- trainControl(method="repeatedcv",
                        number=10, repeats=3)
lm.model1 <- train(repairs ~ oilChanges + miles,
                   data = trainData,
                   method = "lm",
                   trControl=trctrl)
Warning message:
In nominalTrainWorkflow(x = x, y = y, wts = weights,
info = trainInfo): there were missing values in
resampled performance measures.
```

One of the things that you may notice from the code is that the train function does most of the work of k-fold cross validation for you. You can just specify the number of folds that you want—again 10 is often a good choice, and the number of times the cross validation should be repeated, and then let the algorithm do its thing.

So now, with our specified parameters, the lm algorithm will run 30 times! That is, R will do 10-fold cross validations three times (with each 10-fold cross validation having 10 iterations being repeated three times). Note that each fold (iteration) will be done with 90% of the training data, and each fold will be evaluated (validated) with 10% of the training data. Don't worry if you get a warning when running this code. The warning is due to the fact that we are working with such a small dataset. Let's look at the model generated:

```
summary(lm.model1)
Call:
lm(formula = .outcome ~ ., data = dat)
```

```
Residuals:
    Min      1Q Median     3Q      Max
-105.634 -44.656 -7.598 38.243 139.677


Coefficients:
              Estimate Std. Error t value Pr(>|t|)
(Intercept) 481.929815 270.636209    1.781  0.118169
oilChanges  -70.130613   9.227283   -7.600  0.000126 ***
miles         0.008072   0.013508    0.598  0.568957
---
Signif. codes: 0 '***' 0.001 '**' 0.01 '*' 0.05


Residual standard error: 80.93 on 7 degrees of freedom
Multiple R-squared: 0.893, Adjusted R-squared: 0.8624
F-statistic: 29.21 on 2 and 7 DF, p-value: 0.0004008
```

You can see that the adjusted R-squared was the same as when using the full dataset. Just as before, we can predict unknown (i.e., testData) values and calculate the squared correlation between those predictions and the true values from testData.

```
predictValues <- predict(lm.model1, newdata=testData)
cor(predictValues, testData$repairs)^2
[1] 0.8625948
```

You might wonder why using the k-fold repeated cross validation didn't improve our results. This is because a linear model is a simple model, not prone to overfitting, and hence, using k-fold cross validation did not improve our resulting model. However, as we move to more advanced models, overfitting becomes an increasing concern and k-fold cross validation becomes increasingly useful.

A related question you might have is that since there is some validation data for each iteration when using k-fold cross validation, which can provide an accuracy/error estimate, why can't we use all the data for the creation of the model (rather than holding out some test data). That is an excellent point, and one addressed by Ron Kohavi. The answer is that it is generally best to use all our data for training—assuming we are using k-fold cross validation—and just forget about having a test set at all. The k-fold cross validation process helps us avoid overfitting and we can feel assured that the resulting model quality will hold up in future samples. Note, however, that professional data scientists often work with clients who demand a demonstration of cross validation in a holdout sample. If you have lots of data for training (e.g., thousands of observations), just go along with what the client wants. There's no harm in holding out some test data if you have a lot of training data and your results when testing predictions in the test data should come out very close to what your k-fold cross validation process produced when training the model in the first place.

To summarize, in this chapter, we explored how to model relationships among variables by using a simple linear model. We looked at best-fitting lines, the meaning of R-squared, and how to interpret the slope, also known as b value in a linear model. We also used the Caret package to partition data intro training and tests sets. We demonstrated k-fold cross validation as a valuable method for overfitting, even though we don't need to worry about that much with simple linear models. To emphasize the point: we discussed how to do the manual partitioning strategy not because it is better but, because certain audiences for data science results may insist that you show them how your trained model performs on a holdout sample. We should also note that there are other training strategies besides k-fold cross validation and partitioning (e.g., bootstrapping), which may also sometimes be requested by clients. In Chapter 11, we will use the Caret package to explore two classification machine learning algorithms: Support Vector Machines and Classification and Regression Trees.

# CASE STUDY: BUILDING A LINEAR MODEL USING SURVEY DATA

> **Case Key Points:**
> - **Build a linear model to predict Likelihood.to.recommend**
> - **Explore variables that might have a non-linear relationship**

Let's read in the survey dataset and try to build a linear model predicting Likelihood.
to.recommend from Type.of.Travel, Airline.Status and Age.

```
#load survey
library(tidyverse)
library(jsonlite)
mydata.list <- fromJSON("completeSurvey.json" )
surveyWithNA <- data.frame(mydata.list)

#Remove rows with'Likelihood.to.recommend' == NA
survey <- surveyWithNA %>%
    filter(!is.na(Likelihood.to.recommend))

#build a model
    trctrl <- trainControl(method="repeatedcv",
        number=10, repeats=3)
lmOut <- train(Likelihood.to.recommend ~ Type.of.Travel +
    Airline.Status + Age,
    data=survey,
    trControl= trctrl,
    method = "lm")

summary(lmOut)
Call:
    lm(formula = .outcome ~ ., data = dat)

Residuals:
  Min     1Q Median   3Q    Max
-7.5509 -1.1301 0.2311 1.2753 4.8945

Coefficients:
            Estimate Std. Error t-value Pr(>|t|)
(Intercept) 7.9605333   0.0179446  443.618 < 2e-16 ***

Type.of.TravelMileage tickets
            -0.2165703   0.0227131  -9.535 < 2e-16 ***
```

```
Type.of.TravelPersonal Travel
          -2.4914030    0.0142455    -174.891 < 2e-16 ***


Airline.StatusGold
           0.7819691    0.0221014      35.381 < 2e-16 ***


Airline.StatusPlatinum
           0.2165740    0.0338719       6.394 1.62e-10 ***


Airline.StatusSilver
           1.4348614    0.0153865      93.254 < 2e-16 ***


Age        -0.0049138    0.0003716     -13.222 < 2e-16 ***
---
Signif. codes: 0 '***' 0.001 '**' 0.01 '*' 0.05 '.' 0.1 ' ' 1


Residual standard error: 1.782 on 88089 degrees of freedom
Multiple R-squared: 0.3692, Adjusted R-squared: 0.3692
F-statistic: 8593 on 6 and 88089 DF, p-value: < 2.2e-16
```

We can see that the model has an adjusted R-squared of 0.3692. Given that we are predicting a human behavior —namely a flier's response on the survey to the question about Likelihood.to.recommend—this represents a very promising model.

As all of the predictors are statistically significant, we should make sure to provide an interpretation for each one. As an example, let's explore Age. We can see that the coefficient is negative, so Likelihood.to.recommend decreases as Age increases. We should first examine a bivariate scatterplot.

```
# Downsample to make the graph easier to read
survey %>% sample_n(size=300,replace=T) %>%
ggplot() + aes(x=Age, y=Likelihood.to.recommend) +
   geom_point() +
geom_smooth(method="lm")
```

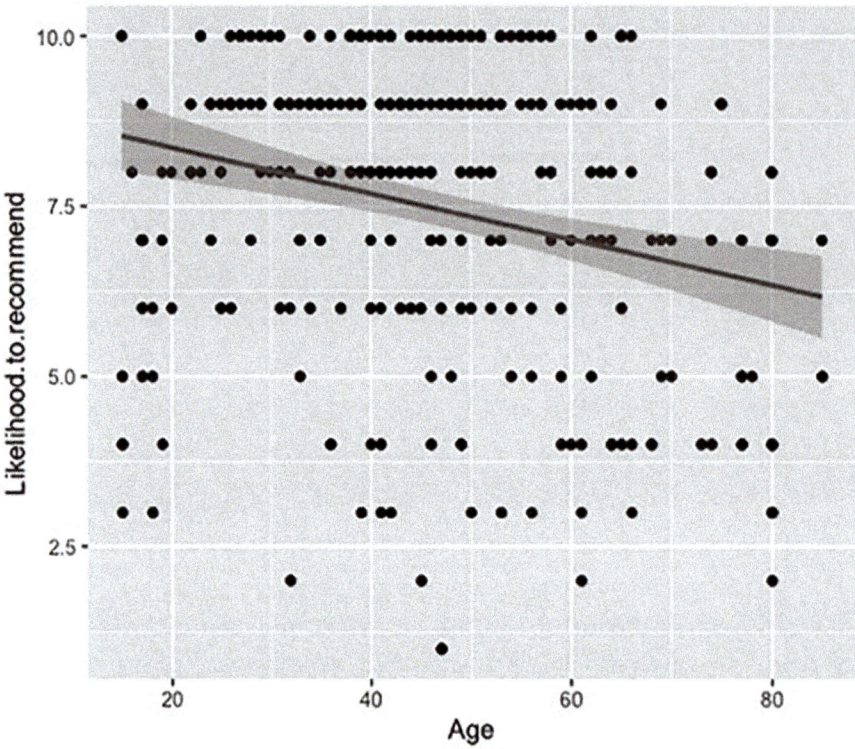

That scatterplot is hard to read, mainly because the Likelihood.to.recommend variable has discrete integer values (which makes the points look like they are in rows). The fitted line certainly shows a negative relationship that corresponds to the output of lm. But maybe connection is not linear, as can be seen by the following visualization:

```
# First, recode Age to represent each decade
survey$roundedAge <- as.factor(round(survey$Age,-1))

# Now make a bar plot by decade group
survey %>%
  group_by(roundedAge) %>%
  summarize(ltr=mean(Likelihood.to.recommend)) %>%
  ggplot() + aes(x=roundedAge, y=ltr) + geom_col()
```

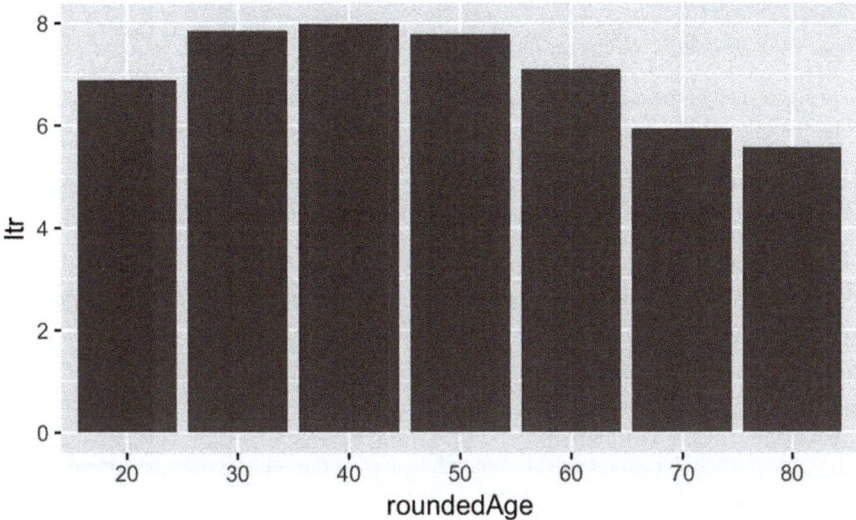

This bar graph shows that Likelihood.to.recommend is lower for 20-year-olds as well as for people who are 60 and older. So, the relationship between Age and Likelihood.to.recommend is not exactly linear. If we wanted to get more precision in our prediction, we might have to model a curved relationship between these two variables. One simple way to do that would be to square the values of Age. Try it and see whether you can improve the prediction of Likelihood.to.recommend.

## Chapter Challenges

1.  Create a bivariate scatterplot of the mpg and hp variables from the mtcars dataset that is built into R. Report whether the relationship between the two variables looks linear or something else.

2.  Create an lm() model to predict mpg from hp using the mtcars dataset that is built into R. Report the R-squared value and indicate whether the slope (b) value for hp is statistically significant.

3.  Create a bivariate scatterplot of the mpg and hp variables as before, but this time add the best-fitting line using abline(). You could also use ggplot() instead of plot(), in which case you would need to include geom_smooth(method="lm") to add the best-fitting line to the scatterplot.

4.  Add the variable wt to your prediction model for the mtcars dataset. Make sure to report and interpret the R-squared value and say which predictors are statistically significant.

5.  Use the predict() command and the output object from lm() to predict the value of mpg, assuming the wt equals 3.2 and hp equals 146.7.

6.  Use lm() to create a linear model of the dataset airquality, which is built into R. Which variable should be the dependent variable? What is the best model you can create? What is the R-squared for that model? Which predictors are significant?

7.  Using the case study dataset, add a new variable into the mix for predicting Likelihood. to.recommend. As a reminder, the predictors that we have already included are Type.of.Travel, Airline.Status, and Age. Can you find another predictor variable that is also statistically significant?

8.  You might find it interesting to explore a write-up of some actual work done on predictive car maintenance. The following blog post includes many techniques beyond linear modeling and also demonstrates the challenge of collecting useful and actionable data. https://blog.pivotal.io/data-science-pivotal/products/the-data-science-behind-predictive-maintenance-for-connected-cars

## Sources

http://stat.ethz.ch/R-manual/R-patched/library/stats/html/lm.html
http://www.ddiez.com/teac/r/linear_models.php

## R Functions Used in This Chapter

| | |
|---|---|
| abline() | Plots a best-fitting line on the top of a scatterplot. |
| cor() | Pearson's correlations among variables. |
| createDataPartition() | Chooses elements at random from a vector. |
| filter() | Tidyverse function to select a subset of rows. |
| ggplot() | Uses geom_point and stat_smooth. |
| lm() | Stands for linear models and, for this chapter, multiple regression. |
| plot() | Is a general purpose graphing function that has many uses in R. |
| predict() | Uses a model to predict a variable (output). |
| sample() | Chooses a sample of elements from an object. |
| sample_n() | Tidyverse function to sample a set of rows from a table. |
| ste.seed() | Controls randomization for tasks like sampling. |
| summary() | Provides a statistical summary of numeric data. |
| train() | Uses the caret package to train a model. |
| trainControl() | Uses the caret to set up control parameters for training a model. |
| View() | Shows a dataframe in an easy-to-read format. |

This text includes access to datasets and select student resources. To learn more, visit sagepub.com

# 11

# WHAT'S YOUR VECTOR, VICTOR?

## LEARNING OBJECTIVES

Understand support vector machine (SVM) machine learning.

Understand partition and classification (rpart) machine learning.

Develop SVM and rpart R code using the Caret package.

## MORE SUPERVISED LEARNING

In Chapter 10, we introduced the idea of machine learning as an algorithmic method of processing data. We differentiated between supervised learning—which emphasizes making predictions—and unsupervised learning, a set of techniques for finding patterns in unlabeled data. We also introduced linear regression, a simple prediction technique that has been around for a long time. Linear regression works with metric outcome variables—outcomes that can be measured on an ordered scale (e.g., temperature, weight, mpg). In this chapter, we introduce classification techniques. Classifiers, as data scientists call them, make predictions about discrete outcomes: Yes/No, True/False, Sunny/Cloudy/Rainy, Dog/Cat/Goat/Horse, and so on. Similar to linear regression, our goal is to develop a model using some training data and then use that model to make predictions with some novel input data.

## A CLASSIFICATION EXAMPLE

Let's create a supervised learning model to classify whether a person's income exceeds $50,000 a year. This is a classification problem, because we are restricting the outcome to two discrete choices (≤$50,000 or >$50,000). You might be thinking, why don't we just predict the actual value for income? First, that would be a regression problem (which we discussed in Chapter 10), rather than a classification problem, but more importantly, the dataset we have available only has a binary (also known as dichotomous) variable for income: a factor variable indicating income either ≤$50,000 or >$50,000. We extracted this dataset from the UCI (University of California, Irvine) Machine Learning repository. This repository is a collection of almost 500 datasets that are freely available as a service to the machine learning community. This specific dataset was donated by Barry Becker from an analysis of the 1994 census, and is typically called the "Adult" dataset. You can explore the information about the dataset for yourself from the UCI website: http://archive.ics.uci.edu/ml/datasets/Adult. As shown in the table below, there are 15 columns (14 attributes, and the known target variable "income").

| Column Name | Possible Values |
| --- | --- |
| income | <50K, >50K |
| age | Continuous |
| workclass | Private, Self-emp-not-inc, Self-emp-inc, Federal-gov, Local-gov, State-gov, Without-pay, Never-worked |
| fnlwgt | Continuous |
| education | Bachelors, Some-college, 11th, HS-grad, Prof-school, Assoc-acdm, Assoc-voc, 9th, 7th-8th, 12th, Masters, 1st-4th, 10th, Doctorate, 5th-6th, Preschool |
| education-num | Continuous |
| marital-status | Married-civ-spouse, Divorced, Never-married, Separated, Widowed, Married-spouse-absent, Married-AF-spouse |
| occupation | Tech-support, Craft-repair, Other-service, Sales, Exec-managerial, Prof-specialty, Handlers-cleaners, Machine-op-inspct, Adm-clerical, Farming-fishing, Transport-moving, Priv-house-serv, Protective-serv, Armed-Forces. |
| relationship | Wife, Own-child, Husband, Not-in-family, Other-relative, Unmarried. |
| race | White, Asian-Pac-Islander, Amer-Indian-Eskimo, Other, Black. |
| sex (gender) | Female, Male |
| capital-gain | Continuous |
| capital-loss | Continuous |
| hours-per-week | Continuous |
| native-country | United-States, Cambodia, England, Puerto-Rico, Canada, Germany, Outlying-US(Guam-USVI-etc), India, Japan, Greece, South Korea, China, Cuba, Iran, Honduras, Philippines, Italy, Poland, Jamaica, Vietnam, Mexico, Portugal, Ireland, France, Dominican-Republic, Laos, Ecuador, Taiwan, Haiti, Colombia, Hungary, Guatemala, Nicaragua, Scotland, Thailand, Yugoslavia, El-Salvador, Trinidad&Tobago, Peru, Hong-Kong, Holland-Netherlands |

While many of the variables are self-explanatory, some are trickier to understand. The attribute fnlwgt represents final weight, which is the number of units in the target population that the responding row represents. While these weights are important for obtaining accurate estimates of population values, we will ignore them for this analysis just to keep things simple. The attribute education_num stands for the number of years of education in total, which is a continuous representation of the education categorical variable. The attribute relationship represents the responding person's role in the family. Finally, the capital_gain and capital_loss attributes are income from investment sources other than wages or salary.

Keeping all that in mind, we can now load the data with the following command by first reading the dataset from the UCI website. Specifically, the dataset is at:

http://archive.ics.uci.edu/ml/machine-learning-databases/adult/adult.data

```
webSite <- "http://archive.ics.uci.edu/ml/"
dataLocation <- "machine-learning-databases"
adultData <- "/adult/adult.data"
theUrl <- paste0(webSite, dataLocation, adultData)
incomeDF <- read_csv(theUrl, col_names=FALSE)
```

Because the UCI dataset does not have metadata within the datafile, let's assign column names to the dataframe.

```
col_names <- c("age", "workclass", "fnlwgt",
               "education", "education_num",
               "marital_status", "occupation",
               "relationship"", "race", "sex",
               "capital_gain", "capital_loss",
               "hours_per_week", "native_country",
               "income")
colnames(incomeDF) <- col_names
```

We can now inspect the dataset:

```
glimpse(incomeDF)
    Observations: 32,561
    Variables: 15
    $ age <dbl> 39, 50, 38, …
    $ workclass <chr> "State-gov", "Self-emp-not-…
    $ fnlwgt <dbl> 77516, 83311, 215646, 234721, …
    $ education <chr> "Bachelors", "Bachelors", …
    $ education_num <dbl> 13, 13, 9, 7, 13, 14, 5, …
    $ marital_status <chr> "Never-married", "Married-civ…
    $ occupation <chr> "Adm-clerical", "Exec-…
    $ relationship <chr> "Not-in-family", "Husband", …
    $ race <chr> "White", "White", "White", …
    $ sex <chr> "Male", "Male", "Male",…
    $ capital_gain <dbl> 2174, 0, 0, 0, 0, 0, …
    $ capital_loss <dbl> 0, 0, 0, 0, 0, 0, 0, …
    $ hours_per_week <dbl> 40, 13, 40, 40, 40, …
    $ native_country <chr> "United-States", "United…
    $ income <chr> "<=50K", "<=50K", "<50K"…
```

Some of the lines of output have been removed from the material above to save space. The output shows that the data structure has 32,561 rows and 15 columns. If you inspect a few of the column names that emerged from the glimpse() command, you will see that each value for income is coded (as character data) to be either ≤50K or <50K. Let's explore this variable some more:

```
table(incomeDF$income)
<=50K <50K
24720 7841
```

We used the table() function to summarize the income variable: table() is helpful for summarizing discrete variables. Remember that we refer to a variable like this as a binary or dichotomous variable. The output shows us that there are 24,720 people that were classified as having an income of less than 50K, and 7,841 people that had an income of more than 50K.

We need to clean the data to get it ready for analysis. First, as previously noted, we will ignore the fnlwgt attribute, which we can do by removing it from the dataframe with the select() command from the dplyr package. Note that we use the dplyr prefix on the call to select() because this is a function name used in several packages. Depending on which packages you have loaded, R might get confused about which select() function we want to use. In this situation, we want the tidyverse version of select(), which comes from the dplyr package:

```
library(dplyr)
incomeDF <- dplyr::select(incomeDF, -fnlwgt)
```

Note that if you ran library(tidyverse) instead of library(dplyr), you would still see dplyr as one of the loaded packages and could still use dplyr::select().

Next, we can create better predictor variables by creating more general groupings for categorical variables such as education. This is known as *feature engineering*, which is the process of applying human knowledge to the data to create better predictor variables that can help the machine learning algorithms create more accurate results and/or work faster. We can also use feature engineering to help handle missing data.

As part of the feature engineering process, we also decide what to do with missing elements. In this dataset, missing elements are noted with a "?." We could try to replace those unknown values via a process of *imputing* those missing values. Imputing is a fancy word for using statistics to make an educated guess. For example, a simple approach could be to calculate the mean of the known values or the most commonly occurring value and use that value for all instances that are missing. One could also use more advanced techniques to impute missing values, but for the sake of simplicity, we will just define a unique category for the missing data. In this way, we help ensure that we are not introducing bias into our model. If we removed rows that contained the missing data, we might be losing important aspects of the data. For example, education might be missing primarily for those without a high school diploma. Leaving them out of the analysis could create bias in the resulting model by ignoring this important group.

The code below does our feature engineering by first changing the strings into factors (categorical variables) to make our fixes easier.

```
# Update each column to be a factor - if it's a string
incomeDF <- mutate_if(incomeDF,is.character, factor)
```

Now, we can define new levels for the factors for some of the attributes. We will make some repairs to the workclass, education, marital_status, occupation, and native_country variables. In each case we will recode the original set of seven or more different options into a much smaller set of four to six options using the levels() command. For several variables, we will also grab the "?," which was the indicator for missing data, and recode that into a level called unknown:

```
levels(incomeDF$workclass) <- list(
      public=c("Federal-gov","State-gov","Local-gov"),
      private=c("Private","Self-emp-not-inc",
              "Self-emp-inc"),
      other= c("Never-worked","Without-pay", "?"))
levels(incomeDF$education)<- list(
      noCollege=c("Preschool", "1st-4th",
              "5th-6th","7th-8th", "9th",
              Assoc-acdm","Assoc-voc","10th",
              "11th","12th", "HS-grad"),
      graduate=c("Bachelors","Some-college"),
      master=c("Masters", "Prof-school"),
      phd=c("Doctorate"))
levels(incomeDF$marital_status)<- list(
       divorce=c("Divorced","Separated"),
       married=c("Married-AF-spouse",
           "Married-civ-spouse",
           "Married-spouse-absent"),
      notmarried=c("Never-married"),
      widowed=c("Widowed"))
levels(incomeDF$occupation)<- list(
      clerical=c("Adm-clerical"),
      tradeskill=c("Craft-repair",
           "Machine-op-inspct","Other-service"),
```

```
        physical = c("Transport-moving",
            "Priv-house-serv","Protective-serv",
            "Handlers-cleaners"),
        highskill=c("Sales","Tech-support","Armed-Forces",
            "Prof-specialty","Exec-managerial"),
        agricultr=c("Farming-fishing"),
        unknown = c("?"))
levels(incomeDF$native_country)<- list(
        Asia=c("Vietnam","Laos","Cambodia","Thailand",
            "Japan", "South", "China","India","Hong-Kong",
            "Iran", "Philippines", "Taiwan"),
        NorthAmerica=c("Canada","Cuba",
            "Dominican-Republic","Guatemala","Haiti",
            "Honduras","Jamaica","Mexico","Nicaragua",
            "Puerto-Rico","El-Salvador","United-States",
            "Outlying-US(Guam-USVI-etc)"),
        SouthAmerica=c("Ecuador","Peru","Colombia",
            "Trinadad&Tobago"),
        Europe=c("England","France","Germany","Greece",
            "Holland-Netherlands","Italy","Hungary",
            "Ireland", "Poland","Portugal","Scotland",
            "Yugoslavia"),
        unknown = c("?"))
```

You might be wondering how we decided on the new set of options for each variable. For example, we recoded the 10 original options for workclass into public, private, and other. It is possible to use statistical analyses as a guide to useful choices. For instance, we could have compared instances where workclass was coded as Federal-gov to see if they were similar to those coded as State-gov. In this case, we used knowledge from previous projects suggesting that public sector workers share many similarities but are meaningfully different from private sector workers in several respects. There is no one correct way to do this kind of recoding—you can use your knowledge of the problem domain as a starting point and also be ready to revise your choices if analytic results suggest that you should.

# SUPERVISED LEARNING VIA SUPPORT VECTOR MACHINES

Using this dataset, let's now create a model to classify people into low or high income. The algorithm needs to use the predictors (i.e., the attributes we just cleaned/engineered) to divide the data into two classes (i.e., ≤50K and >50K). We will first use a technique called "support vector machines" to perform the classification. This technique, sometimes referred to as SVM, is a widely used  machine learning approach. An SVM uses the input data to develop a geometric boundary that separates the data by class. Let's pretend for a moment that we are using just two predictors, X and Y, to divide data into two classes: income  ≤50K and income >50K. The algorithm tries to find the position of a line on the plot of X and Y that separates the ≤50K and >50K cases. In the graph below, you can think of the solid dots as being low income and the open dots as being high income. We have a perfect result here, as we have drawn a line that puts all of the solid dots (income ≤50K) to the left of the line and all of the open dots (income >50K) to the right of the line.

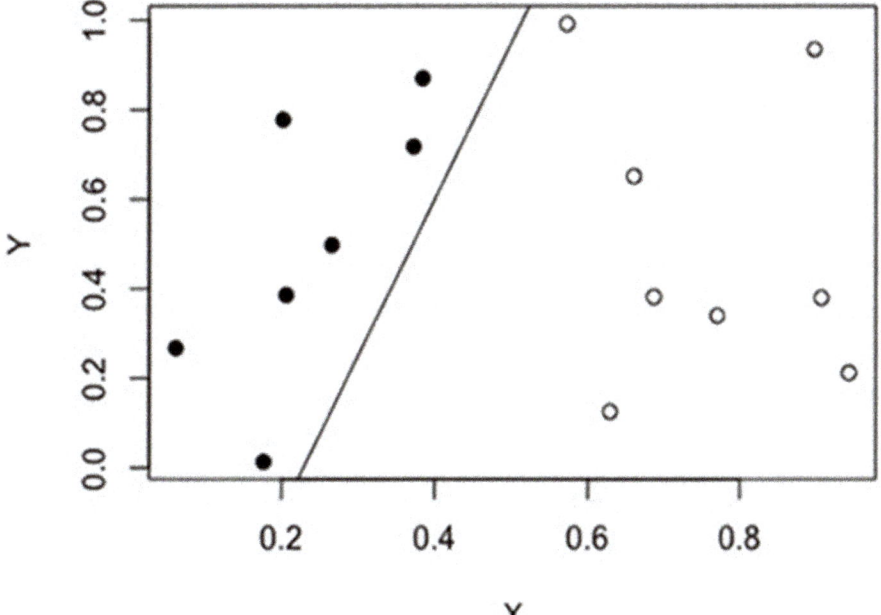

It is more typical, however, that the data are not this cleanly divided. In another dataset shown on the graph below, we have one solid dot that ends up on the wrong side of the line. The algorithm could try to adjust the position of the line to get a clean separation between the solid and open dots, but real data are usually way too messy to achieve a perfect result.

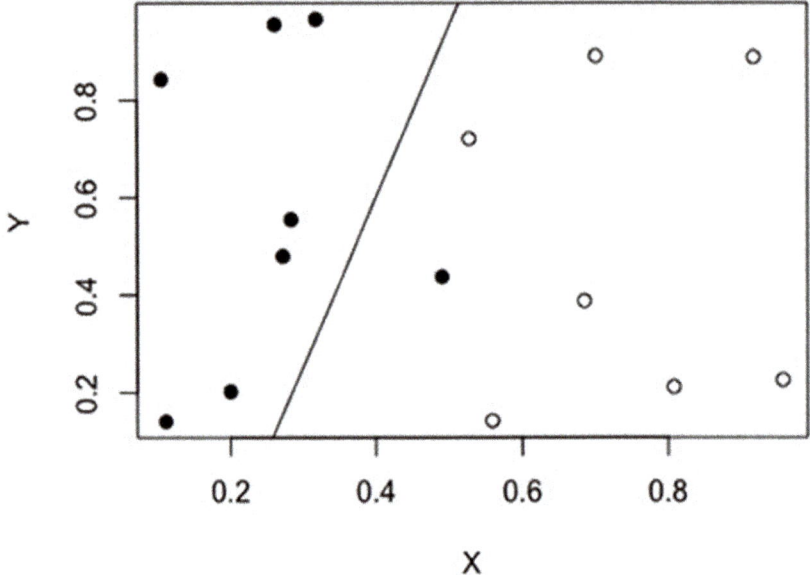

So, how does an SVM solve this challenge? An SVM maps a set of inputs into a new space with the goal of being able to describe geometric boundaries separating different regions. The input data (the independent variables) from a given observation are processed through a mapping algorithm called a kernel (the kernel is simply a formula that processes each case's vector of input data), and the resulting kernel output determines the position of that case in space. A support vector is one particular observation/row of that dataset that happens to fall close to the geometric boundary—its nearness to the boundary makes it influential in determining exactly where the boundary falls.

A simple three-dimensional mapping example illustrates how this works. We can take a messy two-dimensional set of dots from an X-Y plot, and include a third dimension, Z, making it much easier to separate the two cases. Visually, you can see how this might be done. The previous two-dimensional plot above appears again on the left-hand side of the figure below. On the right-hand side, we lay the 2D plot flat on the ground and then add a third dimension, Z. With this third dimension we can now draw a plane that perfectly separates the solid dots from the open dots. Our kernel in this case would turn the X and Y inputs into Z and each dot's position on Z puts it above or below the separator plane.

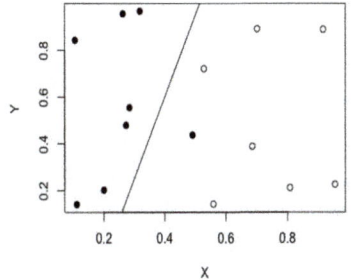 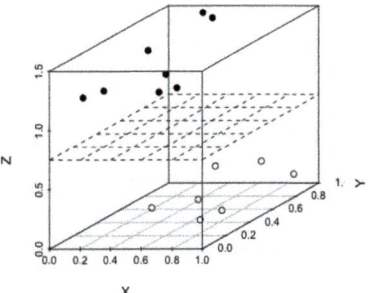

Here's another example to illustrate the idea: imagine looking at a picture of a snow-capped mountain photographed from high above the earth, such that the mountain looks like a small, white circle completely surrounded by a region of green trees. Using a pair of scissors, there is no way of cutting the photo on a straight line so that all of the white snow is on one side of the cut and all of the green trees are on the other. In other words, there is no simple linear separator that could correctly separate or classify the white and green areas given their positions on the two-dimensional photograph.

However, instead of a piece of paper, think about a realistic three-dimensional clay mold of the mountain. Now all the white points occupy a cone at the peak of the mountain and all of the green points lie at the base of the mountain. Imagine inserting a sheet of cardboard through the clay model in a way that divides the snow-capped peak from the green-tree-covered base. It is much easier to do now because the white points are sticking up into the high altitude and the green points are all at a lower altitude on the base of the mountain.

The altitude of that piece of cardboard defines the planar separator that divides the snow from the trees. An SVM analysis of this scenario would take the original two-dimensional data and find a projection into a new dimension that would optimize the division between green points and white points. We could mathematically describe the position of the cardboard that achieves the best separation. Given future inputs describing a previously unknown data point, the SVM kernel could then map the data into the three-dimensional space and then report whether the point was above the cardboard (a white point) or below the cardboard (a green point).

# SUPPORT VECTOR MACHINES IN R

Just as we did in Chapter 10 for linear models, before building an SVM model, we need to create test and training datasets. Review Chapter 10 if you need additional hints for understanding this code.

```
# makes the sampling predictable
set.seed(111)
# Randomly sample for training dataset elements
trainList <- createDataPartition(
                    y=incomeDF$income, p=.70, list=FALSE)
# Create train and test datasets
trainData <- incomeDF [trainList,]
testData <- incomeDF [-trainList,]
```

So now we have two separate datasets, representing the training and test breakdown of the original data. Remember, because this is a random set of indices, if the code were to run again without using set.seed(111), we would get different train and test datasets.

We are now ready to train our support vector model. First, we will build the model using the simple partitioning approach, with separate datasets for training and testing. The following command generates a model based on the training dataset:

```
svm.model <- train(income ~ ., data = trainData,
              method = "svmRadial",
              trControl=trainControl(method = "none"),
              preProcess = c("center", "scale"))
```

Let's examine this command in some detail. The first argument, income ~ ., specifies the model we want to test using R's formula language. Using the word "income" as the first element in this expression means that we want to use the binary income variable (i.e., whether the person earns more or less than 50K) as the outcome variable that our model predicts. As was mentioned in Chapter 10, the tilde character (~) is an R expression that separates the left-hand side of the formula (output) from the right-hand side (inputs/ predictors). Finally, the dot character (.) is a shorthand that tells R to use all of the other variables in the dataframe as the predictors. We can avoid a lot of typing by using the dot, as long as our dataset only includes variables that can be used in the analysis. The data parameter lets us specify which dataframe to use in the analysis. In this case, we have specified that the procedure should use the trainData training set that we developed.

The next parameter is an interesting one: method = "svmRadial." You will remember from the earlier discussion that the kernel is a customizable part of the SVM algorithm that lets us transform the problem into multidimensional space. In this case, the svm-Radial designation refers to the radial basis function. One simple way of thinking about the radial basis function is this: imagine a circle with the origin (0,0) at the center. Now choose any point (X, Y) that falls on the circle. Finally, draw a straight line from the origin (0,0) to (X, Y). That line is a radius and its length would be the output of the radial basis function when X and Y are the input. In simplified terms, the radial basis function kernel takes the set of inputs from each row in a dataset and calculates a distance value based on the combination of the many variables in the row. The weighting of each data point is adjusted by the algorithm in order to get the maximum separation of distance between the income ≤50K cases and the income >50K cases.

The trControl argument refers to how we should control the training of the model, but since we are using a simple partitioning (train and test) approach, we do not have to worry about that just yet, which is why we use the method of "none."

The final parameter states that there should be some pre-processing of the data. Specifically, for some machine learning algorithms, including SVM, the results may improve when each variable is adjusted to have a mean of zero and a standard deviation of one. So, we center and scale the data before the SVM algorithm starts. The "center" transformation calculates the mean for an attribute and subtracts it from each value. The "scale" transformation calculates the standard deviation for an attribute and divides each value by that standard deviation.

Note that if you try to run this code on your machine, it might take anywhere from a few seconds to a few minutes to complete. This is because we have a fair amount of data, and the SVM algorithm is computationally intensive. Let's have a look at what our output structure contains:

```
svm.model
Support Vector Machines with Radial Basis Function Kernel
22793 samples
  13 predictor
   2 classes: '<=50K', '<50K'
Pre-processing: centered (32), scaled (32)
Resampling: None
```

While this doesn't show much, we can see that there were 22,793 samples, which is the number of rows (observations) in the trainData object. We can also see that the data were centered and scaled, with 13 attributes used for prediction (the 14th was our target variable—income). Finally, we can see that there was no resampling (so no cross validation).

The real test for our SVM is to use the model we generated through this training process to predict the outcomes in a novel dataset. Fortunately, because we prepared ourselves, we have testData ready to go. The following commands use testData to evaluate our model using a confusion matrix:

```
predictValues <- predict(svm.model, newdata=testData)
confusionMatrix(predictValues, testData$income)
Confusion Matrix and Statistics
          Reference
Prediction <=50K <50K
    <=50K 6969 1100
    <50K 447 1252

             Accuracy : 0.8416
               95% CI : (0.8342, 0.8488)
  No Information Rate : 0.7592
  P-Value [Acc < NIR] : < 2.2e-16
                Kappa : 0.5215
```

```
Mcnemar's Test P-Value : < 2.2e-16
           Sensitivity : 0.9397
           Specificity : 0.5323
        Pos Pred Value : 0.8637
        Neg Pred Value : 0.7369
            Prevalence : 0.7592
        Detection Rate : 0.7135
  Detection Prevalence : 0.8261
     Balanced Accuracy : 0.7360
       'Positive' Class : <=50K
```

The first command in the block above uses our model output from before, namely svm. model, as the parameters for prediction. It uses testData, which the support vectors have never seen before, to generate predictions. The output from the predict() command is a vector of factors, with two levels "<=50K" and "<50K."

In the second command above, we output the confusion matrix (and many additional statistics) about our prediction. As you can see in the output, the confusion matrix contains four values: the top-left value shows the number of correct predictions for "<=50K," the diagonal down from that value (the lower-right value in the matrix) shows the number of correct predictions for ">50K," the top-right value shows the number of predictions of "<=50K" that were not correct (i.e., the SVM model predicted "<=50K" but the actual value was ">50K"), and finally, the lower-left value shows the number of incorrect predictions for ">50K". So, in looking at the confusion matrix, along the off-diagonal of the confusion matrix, we see the incorrect classifications: 447 cases that were ≤50K, but were classified as >50K by the SVM and 1,100 cases that were >50K, but were classified as ≤50K by the SVM. On the main diagonal, we see 6,969 cases correctly classified as ≤50K and 1,252 cases correctly classified as >50K.

Overall, it looks like the model is OK, but far from perfect. The simplest way of judging model quality is to look at the accuracy of the model. In our case, the model was 84.16% accurate. You can calculate this overall accuracy measure by hand like this: (6,969 + 1,252) / (6,969 + 1,252 + 447 + 1100). However, we need to keep in mind the "No Information Rate," which shows what our accuracy would be if the model just designated everyone as ≤50K (i.e., the simplest model would always pick the most prevalent class). This "No Information Rate," where income ≤50K, comprised 75.92% of the cases in the test data. With this in mind, the simplest approach, which is to always guess ≤50K, would be correct 75.92% of the time. Putting the "No Information Rate" together with our accuracy means that our model is only 8% better than simply classifying everyone as ≤50K! But 8% improvement over chance is better than nothing. We know that by looking at the "P-Value [Acc < NIR]" (is the Accuracy better than the No Information Rate). This value shows the probability of observing at least this much improvement if, in fact, the accuracy was no better than the No Information Rate. If this probability value is less than 0.05, which it is in our case (the value was less than 2.2e-16, a really small number), we have evidence that the SVM predictions represent an improvement over guessing. The Kappa statistic, showing as 52.15%, also takes into account the possibility of correct classifications just by chance, so some people prefer quoting it instead of overall accuracy.

Sometimes we are more interested in certain kinds of errors. For example, consider which is worse: a person who gets mistakenly classified as having income >50K or a person that gets mistakenly classified as having income ≤50? Perhaps these two types of errors are equivalent, but in some situations, one is worse than the other. For example, if we are trying to identify potential students for need-based financial aid, so that we could give those students information on financial aid, and income ≤50K is a key threshold in being able to get aid, we would be more concerned about being mistakenly classifying someone as having income >50K, because in this situation, someone who needs information on how to apply for need-based financial aid would not get the information (the other error, where someone who does not qualify gets information on how to apply for need-based financial aid would not be so bad since they could just ignore the information).

With this in mind, let's consider two additional measures of error. First, *sensitivity* was calculated as 6969/(6969 + 447) = 0.9397. You can see that this is the number of correct classifications of ≤50K divided by the total number of classifications of ≤50K. On the other hand, *specificity* was calculated as 1252/(1252 + 1100) = 0.5323129, which is the number of correct classifications of >50K divided by the total number of classifications of >50K. These two metrics, sensitivity and specificity, show that the model performed much better at predicting the more prevalent class.

Note that running this SVM model took roughly a minute on the computer we used. Soon we will use k-fold cross validation, where the algorithm will be building at least 10 models. This could easily take half an hour (or maybe more, depending on the computer running the R code). So maybe we're actually trying to use too much data? In machine learning, as we add more data, the model tends to get more accurate. That's great! However, we rarely ask if we *need* to use all of those data. We might be able to achieve a "good enough" result with a smaller, more manageable dataset. Generally, the strongest predictors in a model will be easy for the algorithm to identify with even a relatively small number of observations. Of course, using more data might allow the model to capture unusual patterns, but these patterns might not generalize to new unknown data.

So, before building a model from our large dataset, let's try a smaller training set. Building a training pipeline using a randomly subsampled dataset will certainly let us work faster. Of course, we can always go back later, and build models on the complete dataset. In this next example, we will use just 5% of the data for our training to see whether there is a difference in model performance.

```
# Set up the same data as for the 1st example
set.seed(111)
# Create the test and train dataset
subsetList <- createDataPartition(
                y= incomeDF$income,p=.05, list=FALSE)
trainData <- incomeDF[subsetList,]
testData <- incomeDF[-subsetList,]
# Generate the SVM model
svm.model <- train(income ~ ., data = trainData,
            method = "svmRadial",
            trControl=trainControl(method = "none"),
            preProcess = c("center", "scale"))
```

Since we have randomly sampled 5% of the data for training, 95% is left for the test dataset—more than 30,000 observations in all. Remember that we are doing this not because it is an especially good idea, but just to see how much the model's performance is impaired by using a much smaller training dataset. Let's look at the calculated confusion matrix:

```
predictValues <- predict(svm.model,
                    newdata = testData)
confusionMatrix(predictValues, testData$income)
Confusion Matrix and Statistics
          Reference
Prediction <=50K <50K
```

```
        <=50K 21784 3739
        <50K 1700 3709
                  Accuracy : 0.8242
                    95% CI : (0.8199, 0.8284)
      No Information Rate : 0.7592
      P-Value [Acc < NIR] : < 2.2e-16
                     Kappa : 0.4695
   Mcnemar's Test P-Value : < 2.2e-16
               Sensitivity : 0.9276
               Specificity : 0.4980
            Pos Pred Value : 0.8535
            Neg Pred Value : 0.6857
                Prevalence : 0.7592
            Detection Rate : 0.7043
      Detection Prevalence : 0.8251
         Balanced Accuracy : 0.7128
          'Positive' Class : <=50K
```

We can see that we have many more predicted values (because we used 95% of the dataset for testing). We can also note that the accuracy was 82.42%, which is about 2% less accurate than when we built the model with 70% of the data (i.e., 84.16% versus 82.42%). In some situations, that could be considered a meaningful loss of performance, so we may have cut down our training data a little too much.

So now let's try k-fold cross validation with a larger chunk of data used for training. For this dataset, which is quite large, we can use 70% of the data for training and holdout 30%.

```r
# Set up the same data as for the 1st example
set.seed(111)
# Create the test and train dataset
trainList <- createDataPartition(
              y=incomeDF$income,p=.70, list=FALSE)
trainData <- incomeDF [trainList,]
testData <- incomeDF [-trainList,]
# Generate the SVM model
```

```
trctrl <- trainControl(method="repeatedcv", number=10)
svm.model.kfold <- train(income ~ .,
                         data = trainData,
                         method = "svmRadial",
                         trControl=trctrl,
                         preProcess = c("center", "scale"))
```

First, we can see the training method is now repeated cross validation ("repeatedcv"). In the object that we use to control the training process, we defined k (the number of folds) to be 10. The algorithm will also use a process of model tuning (three different values of C: more on this later), so in reality, the SVM algorithm will run 30 repetitions (10 folds times three values of C). Depending upon your computer, this could take a while. Go grab some coffee while you're waiting!

```
svm.model.kfold
Support Vector Machines with Radial Basis Function Kernel
22793 samples
   13 predictor
    2 classes: '<=50K', '<50K'
Pre-processing: centered (32), scaled (32)
Resampling: Cross-Validated (10 fold)
Summary of sample sizes: 20514, 20515, 20513, ...
Resampling results across tuning parameters:
   C    Accuracy   Kappa
   0.25 0.8465737  0.5363002
   0.50 0.8486358  0.5451597
   1.00 0.8490745  0.5484574
Tuning parameter "sigma" was held constant at a value of
0.02903579. Accuracy was used to select the optimal model
using the largest value. The final values used for the model
were sigma = 0.02903579 and C = 1.
```

The accuracy for the final training model was 84.9%, slightly better than either of the other models we have tried. If you are confused about how R calculated the accuracy (since the predictions with the test data have yet to be done), remember that when doing k-fold cross validation, for each repetition of the model, R holds out 1/k amount of data.

It is that hold out data that is used to calculate the accuracy for each of the iterations in the k-fold cross validation process. The final accuracy is the average of each of the iteration's validation accuracy calculations.

Because we still do have a holdout sample, testData, we can also test the model on novel data and see if there is any shrinkage in model quality. Using the testData to produce a new set of predictions, here's a look at the confusion matrix:

```
predictValues <- predict(svm.model.kfold,
                              newdata = testData)
confusionMatrix(predictValues, testData$income)
Confusion Matrix and Statistics
          Reference
Prediction <=50K <50K
    <=50K 6947 1028
     <50K 469 1324

               Accuracy : 0.8467
                 95% CI : (0.8394, 0.8538)
    No Information Rate : 0.7592
    P-Value [Acc < NIR] : < 2.2e-16
                  Kappa : 0.5438
 Mcnemar's Test P-Value : < 2.2e-16
            Sensitivity : 0.9368
            Specificity : 0.5629
         Pos Pred Value : 0.8711
         Neg Pred Value : 0.7384
             Prevalence : 0.7592
         Detection Rate : 0.7112
   Detection Prevalence : 0.8164
      Balanced Accuracy : 0.7498
       'Positive' Class : <=50K
```

The overall prediction accuracy in testData was 84.67%, essentially identical to accuracy from the k-fold cross-validated original model. When using k-fold cross validation for the training process we should not generally see much shrinkage when the model is applied to novel data. We've also shown meaningful improvement in specificity over either of the previous models, showing that we have gotten a little better at predicting the non-prevalent class.

Remember that the final piece of output from training was, "The final values used for the model were sigma = 0.02903579 and C = 1." The C = 1 refers to the so-called "cost of constraints." Remember back to our example of the white top on the green mountain? When we put the piece of cardboard (the planar separation function) through the mountain, what if we happen to get one green point on the white side or one white point on the green side? This is the kind of mistake that influences how the algorithm places the piece of cardboard. We can force these mistakes to be more or less costly, and thus, to have more influence on the position of our piece of cardboard and the margin of separation that it defines. If we specify a large value of C we will likely get fewer mistakes, but at the cost of having the cardboard cut a very close margin between the green and white points. On the other hand, if we have a low value of C we will get a more generalizable model, but one that makes more classification mistakes when we are building the model.

But wait, how and why did the train command know the accuracy of the model for three different values of C? Well, it turns out, when using k-fold cross validation, that a process known as *model tuning* is also performed. This model tuning is a process of identifying the best parameters for the machine learning algorithm. For SVM, model tuning is focused on identifying the best value of the cost parameter, C. When using the simple partitioning (train and test) approach, this model tuning needs to be done explicitly by the data scientist. When using k-fold (and other resampling techniques, like bootstrapping), the training function does the tuning for you. By default, tuning is done three times, and that is why we see the accuracy of the model with three different values of C. So, when using k-fold with 10 folds, we actually ran the SVM machine learning algorithm 30 times (10 times for each of the C values evaluated), to create 30 models. That's why it took so long to run. Note that we can also see that the sigma parameter—a value that controls overfitting—was automatically selected for us. Thank goodness for that, because it would have taken a lot of experimentation to choose a reasonable value without the help of the tuning process.

To finish this section on SVMs, let's take a peek at what these "support vectors" actually are. Remember that the idea of a support vector is that it is an observation from the dataset that is close to the separator line or plane (or hyperplane) and therefore influential on the specific position of the line or plane. For each support vector, there is a weight, called alpha, that determines its "strength" in influencing the position of the line or plane. Most of these alphas are zero, because generally speaking many of the points in the dataset are pretty far from the separator. We will look inside the training output object to find these alpha values. Because we are working with an advanced R object, we will use the "@" to access elements of the object. First, let's see the number of support vectors ("nSV"):

```
svm.model.kfold$finalModel@nSV
8055
```

So, in our training data with n = 22,793 observations, 8,055 of the observations are close to the separator (about 35% of them). That also means that alpha is zero for the other 14,738 observations, indicating that those observations were far enough away from the separator that they didn't have any influence on its position. Now we can review the list of alpha values for the actual support vectors. Let's make a histogram of the nonzero alphas with the following command:

```
hist(svm.model.boot$finalModel@alpha[[1]],
                        main="Histogram of Alpha")
```

Note that these are stored in a nested list, hence the need for the 1 expression to access the first list in the list of lists. Because the particular dataset we are using only has two classes (≤50K or >50K), we need only one set of support vectors. If the outcome variable had more than two levels (e.g., low income, not sure, and high income), we would see additional support vectors to be able to classify the cases into more than two groups. The histogram output on the next page reveals the range of the support vectors from 0 to 1.

The maximum value of alpha is equal to the cost parameter that we discussed earlier. We can see that many of the support vectors are at this maximum alpha value. The support vectors at the maximum represent the observations that were right up against the separator. With respect to our mountain metaphor, these are the white points and green points that are right up against the cardboard. We could also write some code to reveal which specific observations these were, and this could give us further insight into what combinations of input attributes are most important in the classification process. Unfortunately, using this strategy to get a handle on exactly how the SVM model works is tricky and does not provide full insight into how the prediction is actually made, which has led some data scientists to call SVM a "black box" whose inner workings are

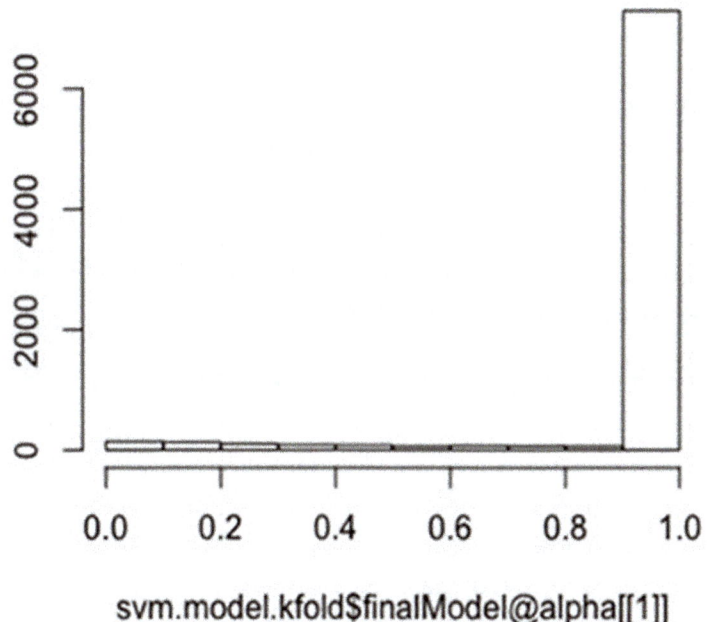

**Histogram of Alpha**

svm.model.kfold$finalModel@alpha[[1]]

inscrutable. In the next section we will examine Classification and Regression Trees, a different approach to classification that provides more transparency on how the classification actually gets done.

## SUPERVISED LEARNING VIA CLASSIFICATION AND REGRESSION TREES

As we just mentioned, while SVM can be very powerful, there is a fundamental challenge when using it: the algorithm is not transparent in terms of its internal workings. Thinking about all of the code we ran earlier in the chapter, we still don't know which attributes are important in the SVM model. Using a black-box algorithm can be problematic because we may need to provide a clear explanation of how a prediction or classification process works for some audiences. This explanation might be needed for legal reasons (e.g., why did you decline a customer) or to help managers understand how the machine learning algorithm is doing the classification (e.g., how is this model working). In the examples below, we will explore a different machine learning approach that can provide a more intuitive explanation of how the model works. Of course, sometimes these easier-to-understand models do not perform as well as the black-box methods. So, when building machine learning models, you need to think about whether model transparency is important for your project and whether you can or should tolerate somewhat lower accuracy in exchange for greater transparency.

Our new approach, Classification and Regression Trees, can be imagined as a procedure similar to the game "20 questions." We ask a series of questions, and the answer to each subsequent question helps further reduce the uncertainty about which classification is most likely correct. Specifically, we will use the rpart algorithm (Recursive Partitioning And Regression Trees). In our example, we will define a decision tree of rules that defines whether we think a person has income ≤50K or >50K.

As can be seen below, the code for using rpart is very similar to the code we used to create an SVM model except the method is now "rpart" (rather than "svmRadial"). Notice that we are using the same training control as before (k-fold cross validation with k = 10). However, we did define one additional parameter. The tuneLength parameter tells the algorithm how many different default values to try for the main tuning parameter of the algorithm. So, rather than the default of three for the tuning length, we will have 50 (so, for each cross validation, we will try 50 different values for tuning).

```
model.rpart <- train(income ~ ., method = "rpart",
                     data = trainData,
                     trControl=trctrl,
                     tuneLength = 50)
```

And the output is:

```
model.rpart
    CART
    22793 samples
       13 predictor
        2 classes: '<=50K', '<50K'
    No pre-processing
    Resampling: Cross-Validated (10 fold)
    Summary of sample sizes: 20513, 20514, 20514, ...
    Resampling results across tuning parameters:
      cp             Accuracy Kappa
```

```
    0.000000000   0.8453914    0.5589241
    0.002524530   0.8558336    0.5677266
    0.005049059   0.8444260    0.5338438
    0.007573589   0.8414870    0.5198794

         .
         .
         .


Accuracy was used to select the optimal model using
the largest value. The final value used for the model was
cp = 0.00252453.
```

There are 50 lines of resampling results, but they are all worse than the second one in the list above, so we left them out. For each line, we can see that Caret was tuning "cp," which is the complexity parameter. The complexity parameter is an important tuning parameter for the rpart algorithm. The complexity parameter is used to control the number of trees in the final solution. If the cost of adding another branch to the decision tree from the current node is above the value of cp, then building that additional subtree does not continue. Of course, just like for the cost parameter "C" in SVM, having more trees will create a more accurate model for the training data, but might not be generalizable to other (i.e., new) data.

We can see that the accuracy we obtained (as part of the k-fold validation) was actually better than our SVM models with accuracy of 85.58% and Kappa of 56.77%, but let's see how this model does with our test data.

```
predictValues <- predict(model.rpart,
                                 newdata=testData)
confusionMatrix(predictValues, testData$income)
Confusion Matrix and Statistics
          Reference
Prediction <=50K <50K
     <=50K 7027 1010
     <50K 389 1342

               Accuracy : 0.8568
                 95% CI : (0.8497, 0.8637)
   No Information Rate : 0.7592
   P-Value [Acc < NIR] : < 2.2e-16

                  Kappa : 0.5695
```

```
Mcnemar's Test P-Value : < 2.2e-16
            Sensitivity : 0.9475
            Specificity : 0.5706
         Pos Pred Value : 0.8743
         Neg Pred Value : 0.7753
             Prevalence : 0.7592
         Detection Rate : 0.7194
   Detection Prevalence : 0.8228
      Balanced Accuracy : 0.7591
        'Positive' Class : <=50K
```

Our accuracy with the test data was slightly better than the accuracy with the training data! Importantly, the rpart algorithm even slightly outperformed our best SVM model. Because we are creating decision trees, we can visualize the trees directly:

```
library(rpart.plot)
rpart.plot(model.rpart$finalModel)
```

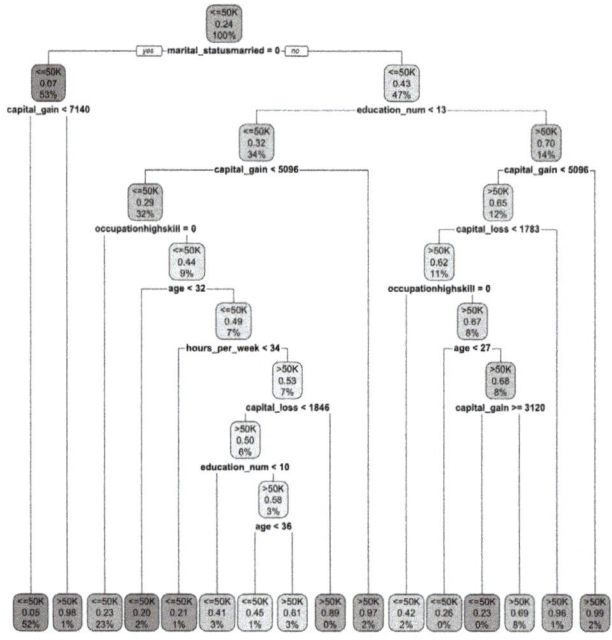

That's really hard to read without being able to zoom in, but the overall shape gives a flavor of how the model works. The top-level split is on marital status and the second-level splits include whether someone had capital gains (which would mean that they had investments that generated income) and education level. By the time we get to the bottom, we have lots of "leaf" nodes that show whether someone should be classified as income ≤50K or >50K. When you run this code in R-Studio, use the Zoom button in the Plots window to explore the tree in greater detail.

Equally interesting, we can also explore which attributes were most important:

```
varImp(model.rpart)
     rpart variable importance

       only 20 most important variables shown (out of 35)
                                           Overall
     capital_gain                          100.00000
     education_num                          81.18847
     occupationhighskill                    76.57482
     marital_statusmarried                  62.91087
     marital_statusnotmarried               33.00638
     capital_loss                           21.02974
     age                                    16.64804
     educationmaster                        12.50413
     hours_per_week                         12.25226
     occupationtradeskill                   11.27548
     educationgraduate                       4.48821
     relationshipNot-in-family               0.74911
     relationshipWife                        0.23291
     raceWhite                               0.20507
     educationphd                            0.16772
     raceAsian-Pac-Islander                  0.08788
```

We've left out four predictors with a variable importance of 0. We can see that capital gains/losses, education level, marital status, and occupation are among the most important predictors.

We could stop here, except for one important issue: is it appropriate to use all of these attributes? Because this model could be used within the banking industry to decide which people should get more credit, it would be highly inappropriate (and in some places, illegal) to use the sex, age, and race attributes within our model. So, let's remove those attributes from our dataset and then rerun the analysis.

```
trainData <- dplyr::select(trainData, -sex, -age, -race)
rpart.model.new <- train(income ~ .,
                         method = "rpart",
                         trControl=trctrl,
                         data = trainData, tuneLength = 50)
predictValues <- predict(rpart.model.new,
                                 newdata = testData)
cm <-confusionMatrix(predictValues, testData$income)
cm$overall[1]
     Accuracy
   0.8511466
```

This time, we explicitly just looked at the accuracy of the model, within the confusion matrix information. We can see that the accuracy went down just a tiny amount. If you take the time to plot the new decision tree, you will see that it is somewhat simpler and even easier to interpret. So, using rpart and trimming out variables that would not be ethical to use in loan or credit decisions, we have a model that is explainable and nearly as accurate as the best model we produced.

This completes our focus on predictive modeling. In Chapter 10 we used linear regression for predictive modeling of metric variables. In this chapter, you've seen two supervised predictive classification algorithms, SVM and rpart, and we've experimented with various training strategies. There are many other algorithms to explore, as well as a whole world of tuning parameters and resampling methods. The Caret package provides access to a host of these options. Alas, the exploration of these other possibilities is beyond our scope—but feel free to explore!

## CASE STUDY: BUILDING SUPERVISED MODELS FROM THE SURVEY

```
Case Key Points:
- Use SVM and rpart ML techniques to predict detractors
- Explore how these results could improve
  likelihood to recommend
```

Let's read in our survey dataset and generate some machine learning models that can predict whether a customer will be a detractor. If we could do this prediction before the flight took off, we might be able to get the airline to proactively reach out to those customers to try to improve their likelihood to recommend the airline. So, let's start by reading in the survey dataset and doing some basic data cleaning.

```
#load survey
library(jsonlite)
mydata.list <- fromJSON("completeSurvey.json" )
surveyWithNA <- data.frame(mydata.list)
#Remove rows with'Likelihood.to.recommend' == NA
survey <- surveyWithNA %<%
    filter(!is.na(Likelihood.to.recommend))
#predict who will be a detractor
survey$Detractor <-
        as.factor(survey$Likelihood.to.recommend < 7)
```

Now, we can create our train and test datasets, using the set.seed() to make sure we can reproduce our results. Note that we only use 5% of the dataset for training, mainly due to the fact that with a larger dataset, the computation would take too long on most laptop computers.

```
#make sure we can reproduce our results
set.seed(123)
# create train and test dataset
trainList <- createDataPartition(y=survey$Detractor,
                                 p=.05,list=FALSE)
trainSet <- survey[trainList,]
testSet <- survey[-trainList,]
```

Next, we can build our SVM model.

```
#Build an SVM model, predicting who will be a detractor
trctrl <- trainControl(method = "cv", number = 10)
svmModel <- train(Detractor ~
                    Eating.and.Drinking.at.Airport +
```

```
                        Age +
                        Airline.Status +
                        Type.of.Travel,
                  data=trainSet,
                  method="svmRadial",
                  preProc=c("center","scale"),
                  trControl=trctrl)
svmModel
Support Vector Machines with Radial Basis Function Kernel
4406 samples
  4 predictor
  2 classes: 'FALSE', 'TRUE'
Pre-processing: centered (7), scaled (7)
Resampling: Cross-Validated (10 fold)
Summary of sample sizes: 3965, 3965, 3966, 3965, 3965, 3965,
   ...
Resampling results across tuning parameters:
  C    Accuracy Kappa
  0.25 0.8054958 0.5155570
  0.50 0.8064028 0.5186005
  1.00 0.8061755 0.5185955
The tuning parameter "sigma" was held constant at a value
of 0.3172824. Accuracy was used to select the optimal model
using the largest value. The final values used for the model
were sigma = 0.3172824 and C = 0.5.
```

The results look promising, in that for training, the accuracy was around 80%. Of course, we now need to evaluate our SVM model on our test dataset.

```
predOut <- predict(svmModel,newdata=testSet)
confusionMatrix(predOut, testSet$Detractor)
Confusion Matrix and Statistics
            Reference
Prediction FALSE  TRUE
     FALSE 52635  9143
     TRUE   6346 15566
                Accuracy : 0.8149
                  95% CI : (0.8123, 0.8176)
     No Information Rate : 0.7048
```

```
      P-Value [Acc < NIR]  :  < 2.2e-16
                   Kappa   :  0.5401
  Mcnemar's Test P-Value   :  < 2.2e-16
             Sensitivity   :  0.8924
             Specificity   :  0.6300
          Pos Pred Value   :  0.8520
          Neg Pred Value   :  0.7104
              Prevalence   :  0.7048
          Detection Rate   :  0.6289
    Detection Prevalence   :  0.7382
       Balanced Accuracy   :  0.7612
         'Positive' Class  :  FALSE
```

The accuracy is a little more than 81%, showing no shrinkage as compared with the training results and above the 70% "no information rate." The Kappa value of 0.54 shows the level of performance over chance and is consistent with the income prediction models that we were testing earlier in the chapter. Let's now try a model with fewer attributes— sticking with those that should be easy to know prior to the flight, specifically the type of travel and the airline status.

```
svmModel1 <-train(Detractor~
                    Airline.Status + Type.of.Travel,
                  data=trainSet,
                  method="svmRadial",
                  preProc=c("center","scale"),
                  trControl=trctrl)
#Assess Fit with new data
predOut <- predict(svmModel1,newdata=testSet)
confusionMatrix(predOut, testSet$Detractor)
Confusion Matrix and Statistics
          Reference
Prediction FALSE  TRUE
     FALSE 52641  9137
     TRUE   6340 15572

                Accuracy  :  0.8151
                  95% CI  :  (0.8124, 0.8177)
     No Information Rate  :  0.7048
     P-Value [Acc < NIR]  :  < 2.2e-16
```

```
                      Kappa : 0.5405
      Mcnemar's Test P-Value : < 2.2e-16
                Sensitivity : 0.8925
                Specificity : 0.6302
              Pos Pred Value : 0.8521
              Neg Pred Value : 0.7107
                 Prevalence : 0.7048
             Detection Rate : 0.6290
       Detection Prevalence : 0.7382
           Balanced Accuracy : 0.7614
            'Positive' Class : FALSE
```

Well, it looks like using only these two attributes, we have the same accuracy (roughly 81%). This model is better, because it provides the same accuracy, but uses fewer attributes. As a result, it will be easier for the airline to know which customers will likely be detractors (and then do something proactively with those customers). Now let's try decision trees, to see if we find similar or different results. As you can see below, the rpart model, using all the same attributes, has a similar accuracy.

```
library(rpart)
cartTree.model <- train(Detractor ~
                        Eating.and.Drinking.at.Airport+
                        Age+
                        Airline.Status+
                        Type.of.Travel,
                   data=trainSet,
                   method="rpart",
                   tuneLength=10,
                   trControl=trctrl)
predOut <- predict(cartTree.model,newdata=testSet)
confusionMatrix(predOut, testSet$Detractor)
Confusion Matrix and Statistics
          Reference
Prediction FALSE  TRUE
     FALSE 52162  8540
     TRUE   6819 16169
              Accuracy : 0.8165
```

```
                   95% CI : (0.8138, 0.8191)
     No Information Rate : 0.7048
     P-Value [Acc < NIR] : < 2.2e-16
                   Kappa : 0.5499
 Mcnemar's Test P-Value : < 2.2e-16
             Sensitivity : 0.8844
             Specificity : 0.6544
          Pos Pred Value : 0.8593
          Neg Pred Value : 0.7034
              Prevalence : 0.7048
          Detection Rate : 0.6233
    Detection Prevalence : 0.7253
       Balanced Accuracy : 0.7694
        'Positive' Class : FALSE
```

Finally, let's review variable importance, to see what might be done to simplify our model (rather than just guessing, which is what we did with the SVM learning effort above).

```
varImp(cartTree.model)
rpart variable importance

                                     Overall
Type.of.TravelPersonal Travel        100.000
Airline.StatusSilver                  55.760
Age                                   33.608
Eating.and.Drinking.at.Airport        32.523
Airline.StatusGold                     5.602
Type.of.TravelMileage tickets          1.780
Airline.StatusPlatinum                 1.218
`Type.of.TravelPersonal Travel`        0.000
`Type.of.TravelMileage tickets`        0.000
```

We can now see why our simplified SVM model was just as effective—the two most important attributes are type of travel and airline status. For completeness' sake, we can also build a simplified rpart model.

```
cartTree.model1 <- train(Detractor ~
                         Airline.Status+Type.of.Travel,
                     data=trainSet,
                     method="rpart",
                tuneLength=10,
                trControl=trctrl)
predOut <- predict(cartTree.model,newdata=testSet)
confusionMatrix(predOut, testSet$Detractor)
Confusion Matrix and Statistics
          Reference
Prediction FALSE TRUE
     FALSE 52162  8540
     TRUE   6819 16169

               Accuracy : 0.8165
                 95% CI : (0.8138, 0.8191)
    No Information Rate : 0.7048
    P-Value [Acc < NIR] : < 2.2e-16
                  Kappa : 0.5499
 Mcnemar's Test P-Value : < 2.2e-16
            Sensitivity : 0.8844
            Specificity : 0.6544
         Pos Pred Value : 0.8593
         Neg Pred Value : 0.7034
             Prevalence : 0.7048
         Detection Rate : 0.6233
   Detection Prevalence : 0.7253
      Balanced Accuracy : 0.7694
       'Positive' Class : FALSE
```

Not surprisingly, just as with our SVM model, our accuracy is the same, roughly 81%. However, with this model, we can explain how the model works to the managers at Southeast airlines, using the tree visualization.

```
library(rpart.plot)
rpart.plot(cartTree.model1$finalModel)
```

As a deep dive into how to interpret this visualization (also see the table that follows), we note that if the type of travel is not personal (i.e., personal travel = 0), we move left and

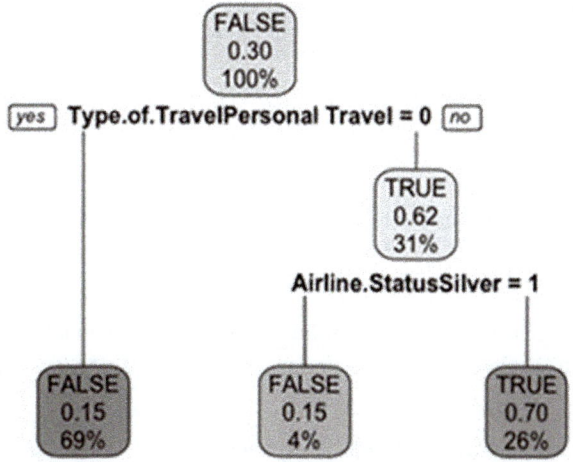

the algorithm predicts that Detractor=FALSE. This will occur in 69% of all surveys, and the error rate will be 0.15 (15%). On the other hand, if the travel is personal we move right in the tree and then consider whether the person's airline status is silver. If the personal traveler has an airline status of silver, then we move right again and this person will be Detractor=TRUE. This will occur in 26% of all surveys, but we will have a high error rate of 0.70 (70%) for this prediction. Finally, looking at the middle leaf (airline status is not silver), the person will be Detractor=FALSE, which will occur in 4% of surveys and will have a low error rate of 0.15 (15%). Having said all of that, you might still be wondering what the topmost node means. The topmost node shows what would happen if we had no information from any predictors. In this case, the best guess would be Detractor=FALSE, and that would have an error rate of 0.30 (30%). Look back at the confusion matrix and you will see that this is consistent with the No Information Rate of 0.7048. Phew! That was pretty complicated but it helps to demonstrate the value of a machine learning model that provides algorithm transparency. Here's the table that summarizes the results shown in the leaf nodes of the tree:

| Condition/Situation | How often the condition occurs: | Accuracy of the prediction: | Implying an error rate of: |
|---|---|---|---|
| Type of travel is not personal | 69% | 85% | 15% |
| Type of travel is personal and airline status is sliver | 26% | 70% | 30% |
| Type of travel is personal and airline status is not sliver | 4% | 85% | 15% |

## Chapter Challenges

1. Load and pre-process the income dataset as shown in this chapter. Split the data into training and test sets with 50% for each. Run an SVM model without k-fold cross validation. Compare the results to the first run in this chapter.

2. Load and pre-process the income dataset as shown in this chapter. Split the data into training and test sets with 50% for each. Run an rpart model without k-fold cross validation. Compare the results to the first run in this chapter.

3. Remove the variables capital_gain and capital_loss from the income dataset. Run SVM and rpart models on these, without k-fold cross validation, and compare the results to the first run in this chapter.

4. Load and pre-process the survey dataset as shown in this chapter. Create a new binary outcome variable called Promoter, like this:survey$Promoter <- as.factor(survey$Likelihood.to. recommend < 8). Then run a classification model, using the same four predictors as shown in this chapter, using SVM, using k-fold cross validation with k = 10. Compare the results to those shown in this chapter.

5. Repeat the previous exercise, using rpart instead of SVM.

6. Using the survey dataset, calculate a new variable showing whether or not the flight was delayed by more than five minutes, like this: survey$Delayed <- as.factor(survey$Departure.Delay.In. Minutes < 5). Then add this as a predictor to the classification model that you ran in the previous exercise.

7. Look up the term "confusion matrix" and then follow up on some other terms such as Type I error, Type II error, sensitivity, and specificity. Describe how an SVM model could be modified to do better at either sensitivity or specificity (by exploring metric='Sensitivity' parameter within the train command).

## Sources

https://cran.r-project.org/web/packages/caret/vignettes/caret.html
http://en.wikipedia.org/wiki/Confusion_matrix
http://cran.r-project.org/web/packages/kernlab/kernlab.pdf
http://stackoverflow.com/questions/9480605/what-is-the-relation-between-the-number-of-support-vectors-and-training-data-and
http://www.louisaslett.com/Courses/Data_Mining/ST4003-Lab7-Introduction_to_Support_Vector_Machines.pdf
http://www.jstatsoft.org/v11/i09/paper

## R Functions Used in this Chapter

| | |
|---|---|
| as.factor() | Coerce an object, particularly a string, to a factor variable. |
| c() | Combine elements into a vector. |
| confusionMatrix() | Generates a confusion matrix for predicted and actual values. |
| createDataPartition() | Chooses elements at random from a vector. |
| filter() | Tidyverse function to subset rows using columns values. |
| glimpse() | Tidyverse function to provide a summary of a data object. |
| hist() | Creates a histogram for a given vector. |
| list() | Create an R list object. |
| mutate_if() | Tidyverse function to change a column for some cases. |
| predict() | Uses a model to predict an outcome. |
| select() | Tidyverse function to choose a subset of rows. |
| set.seed() | Control randomization in procedures like createDataPartition(). |
| table() | Creates tabular results for a given list of categorical (factor) variables. |
| train() | Generic caret function to run training procedure. |

This text includes access to datasets and select student resources. To learn more, visit sagepub.com

# 12

# HI HO, HI HO—DATA MINING WE GO

## LEARNING OBJECTIVES

Describe the difference between unsupervised data mining and supervised data mining.

Apply the four data mining processes (data preparation, exploratory data analysis, model development, and interpretation of results).

Use the association rules mining algorithm to uncover patterns.

Develop data mining R code using the arules package.

In Chapters 10 and 11, we examined predictive techniques—situations where we have an outcome variable that we want to predict. We used regression to predict a metric variable and classification to predict a categorical variable. In the realm of data mining and machine learning, these are known as supervised techniques because the outcome variable "supervises" the process of training the algorithm. In this chapter, we examine a family of data mining techniques where the algorithm has to figure out patterns in the data without having an outcome variable. We call these unsupervised data mining or unsupervised machine learning techniques.

One funny story about unsupervised data mining that gets mentioned quite frequently is the legendary supermarket manager who analyzed patterns of purchasing behavior and found that diapers and beer were often purchased together. The story tells that the manager then decided to put a beer display close to the diaper aisle and supposedly sold more of both products as a result. Another familiar example that online vendors use every day appears when the website says, "People who bought this book were also interested in these other books." This example is often referred to as a recommender system and is an example of an unsupervised data mining technique that we will examine in this chapter. Keep in mind that machine learning is not exactly the same thing as data mining and vice versa. Not all data mining techniques rely on what researchers would consider machine learning. In fact, the association rules mining technique we will explore below predates the development of many modern machine learning algorithms.

# DATA MINING PROCESSES

Data mining typically consists of four processes: (a) data preparation, (b) exploratory data analysis, (c) model development, and (d) interpretation of results. Although this sounds like a neat, linear set of steps, there is often a lot of back and forth through these processes, and especially among the first three. The other point that is interesting about these four steps is that Steps 3 and 4 seem like the most fun, but Step 1 usually takes the most time. Step 1 involves making sure that the data are organized in the right way, that missing data fields are filled in, that inaccurate data are located and repaired or deleted, and that data are recoded as necessary to make them amenable to the kind of analysis we have in mind.

Step 2 is very similar to activities we have done earlier in this book: getting to know the data using histograms and other visualization tools, and looking for preliminary hints that will guide our model choice. The exploration process also involves figuring out the right values for key parameters. We will see some of that activity in this chapter.

Step 3—choosing and developing a model—is by far the most complex and most interesting of the activities of a data miner. It is here where you test out a selection of the most appropriate data mining techniques. Depending on the structure of a dataset, there could be dozens of options, and choosing the most promising one has as much art in it as science. We had some practice performing model development in Chapter 10, where we developed linear models.

For this chapter, we have decided to only explore association rules mining. So, we will not really have to do Step 3 here, because we will not have two or more different mining techniques to compare. Remember that in Chapter 11, we did consider two different machine learning approaches to classification.

Step 4—the interpretation of results—focuses on making sense out of what the data mining algorithm has produced. This is the most important step from the perspective of the data user, because this is where an actionable conclusion is formed. When we discussed the story of beer and diapers, the interpretation of the association rules derived from grocery purchasing data how the beer–diapers rule was supposedly discovered. Translating that rule into a new configuration of store displays demonstrates the idea that useful analytic output can lead to a practical action on the part of the data user.

# ASSOCIATION RULES DATA

Let's begin by talking a little about association rules. Take a look at the following figure with all the boxes and arrows:

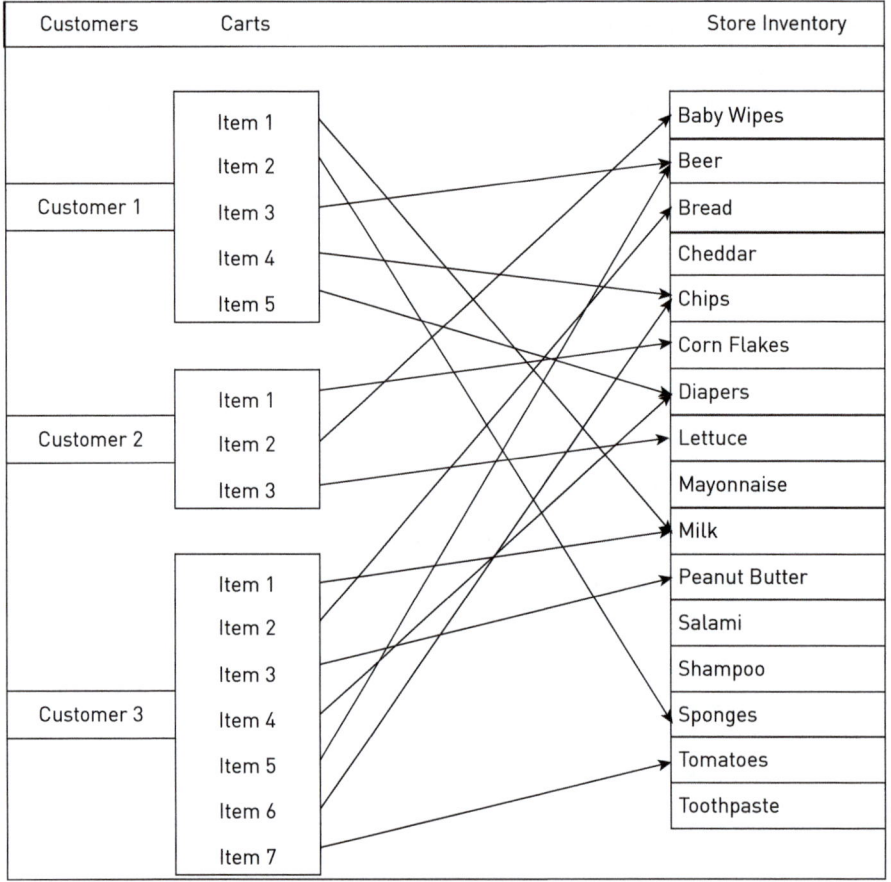

From the figure, you can see that each supermarket customer has a grocery cart that contains several items from the larger set of items that the grocery store stocks. The association rules algorithm (also sometimes called affinity analysis or market basket analysis) tries out many if-then propositions, such as, "If diapers are purchased, then beer is also purchased." The algorithm uses a dataset of transactions (in the previous example, these are the individual shopping carts) to evaluate a long list of these rules for a value known as *support*. Support is the proportion of times that a particular combination occurs across all shopping carts. The algorithm also evaluates another quantity called *confidence*, which is how frequently a particular if-then rule occurs among all the times when the "if" item is present. In the output from R's association rule algorithm, the "if" side of the rule is referred to as the "left-hand side" (LHS) and the "then" side of the rule is referred to as the "right-hand side" (RHS). The RHS is always just one item, for example, diapers. The LHS, however, can have more than one item in it. In the diapers–beer example, our LHS was just diapers, but we might also find a rule that had additional items on the LHS.

If you look back at the figure, we had support of 0.67 (the diapers–beer association occurred in two out of the three carts) and confidence of 1.0 ("beer" occurred 100% of the time with "diapers"). In practice, both support and confidence are generally much lower than in this example, but even a rule with low support and smallish confidence might reveal purchasing patterns that grocery store managers could use to guide pricing, coupon offers, or advertising strategies.

# ASSOCIATION RULES MINING

We can get started with association rules mining very easily using the R package known as arules. In RStudio, you can get the arules package ready using the following commands:

```
install.packages("arules")
library(arules)
```

We will begin our exploration of association rules mining using a dataset that is built in to the arules package. For the sake of familiarity, we will use the Groceries dataset. Note that by using the built-in Groceries dataset, we have relieved ourselves of the burden of data preparation, because the authors of the arules package have generously made sure that Groceries is ready to be analyzed. So we are skipping right to Step 2 in our four-step process—exploratory data analysis. You can make the Groceries dataset ready with this command:

```
data(Groceries)
```

Next, let's run the summary() function on Groceries so that we can see what is in there:

```
summary(Groceries)
transactions as itemMatrix in sparse format with
9,835 rows (elements/itemsets/transactions) and
169 columns (items) and a density of 0.02609146

most frequent items:
      whole milk        other vegetables          rolls/buns
              2513                    1903                1809
          soda                 yogurt             (Other)
          1715                   1372              34055

element (itemset/transaction) length distribution:
sizes
   1     2     3     4     5     6     7     8     9    10    11
2159  1643  1299  1005   855   645   545   438   350   246   182
  12    13    14    15    16    17    18    19    20    21    22
 117    78    77    55    46    29    14    14     9    11     4
  23    24    26    27    28    29    32
   6     1     1     1     1     3     1

      Min. 1st Qu.    Median      Mean 3rd  Qu.       Max.
     1.000   2.000     3.000     4.409   6.000     32.000

includes extended item information—examples:
        labels       level2              level1
1 frankfurter sausage meat and sausage
2        sausage sausage meat and sausage
3     liver loaf sausage meat and sausage
```

Right after the summary command line, we see that Groceries is an itemMatrix object in sparse format. We have a rectangular data structure with 9,835 rows and 169 columns, where each row is a list of items that might appear in a grocery cart. The columns are the individual items that could be in the cart. A little later in the output, we see that there are 169 columns, which means that there are 169 items. The word "matrix," in this case, is just referring to this rectangular data structure. The reason the matrix is called sparse is that very few of these items exist in any given grocery basket (row). By the way, when an item appears in a basket, its cell contains a one (1), whereas if an item is not in a basket, its cell contains a zero (0). In any given row, most of the cells are zero and very few are one, and this is what is meant by sparse. We can see from the Min, Median, Mean, and Max output that every cart has at least one item, half the carts have more than three items, the average number of items in a cart is 4.4, and the maximum number of items in a cart is 32.

The output also shows us which items occur in grocery baskets most frequently. If you like working with spreadsheets, you could imagine going to the very bottom of the column that is marked "whole milk" and putting in a formula to sum up all the ones in that column. You would come up with 2,513, indicating that there are 2,513 grocery baskets that contain whole milk. Remember that every row/basket that has a one in the whole milk column contains whole milk, whereas every row/basket with a zero does not contain whole milk. You might wonder what the data field would look like whether a grocery cart contained two gallons of whole milk. For the present data mining exercise, we can ignore that problem by assuming that any non-zero amount of whole milk is represented by a one. Other data mining techniques could take advantage of knowing the exact amount of a product, but association rules does not need to know that amount—just whether the product is present or absent.

Another way of inspecting our sparse matrix is with the itemFrequencyPlot() function. This produces a bar graph that is similar in concept to a histogram: it shows the relative frequency of occurrence of different items in the matrix. When using the itemFrequencyPlot() function, you must specify the minimum level of support needed to include an item in the plot. Remember the mention of support earlier in the chapter—in this case, it simply refers to the relative frequency of occurrence of something. We can make a guess as to what level of support to choose based on the results of the summary() function we ran earlier in the chapter. For example, the item "yogurt" appeared in 1,372 out of 9,835 rows, or in about 14% of cases. So we can set the support parameter to somewhere around 10%–15% in order to get a manageable number of items:

```
itemFrequencyPlot(Groceries, support=0.1)
```

This command produces the following plot:

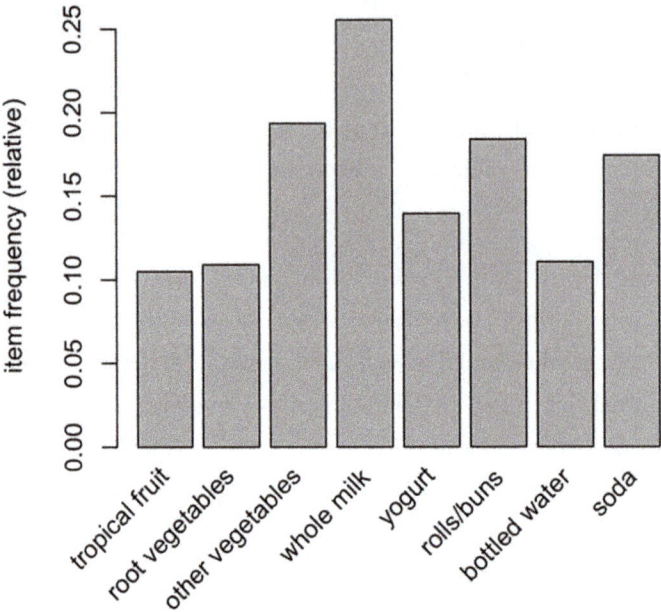

We can see that yogurt is right around 14% as expected and we also see a few other items not mentioned in the summary such as bottled water and tropical fruit.

You should experiment with using different levels of support, just so that you can get a sense of the other common items in the dataset. If you show more than about 10 items, you will find that the labels on the X-axis start to overlap and obscure one another. Use the cex.names parameter to turn down the font size on the labels. This will keep the labels from overlapping at the expense of making the font size much smaller. Here's an example:

```
itemFrequencyPlot(Groceries, support=0.05, cex.names=0.5)
```

As you can see, this command yields about 25 items on the X-axis. Without worrying too much about the labels, you can also experiment with lower values of support, just to get a feel for how many items appear at the lower frequencies. We need to guess at a minimum level of support that will give us quite a substantial number of items that can potentially be part of a rule. Nonetheless, it should also be obvious that an item that occurs only very rarely in the grocery baskets is unlikely to be of much use to us in terms of creating meaningful rules. Let's pretend, for example, that the item "Venezuelan Anteater Cheese" occurred only once in the whole set of 9,835 carts. Even if we did end up with a rule about

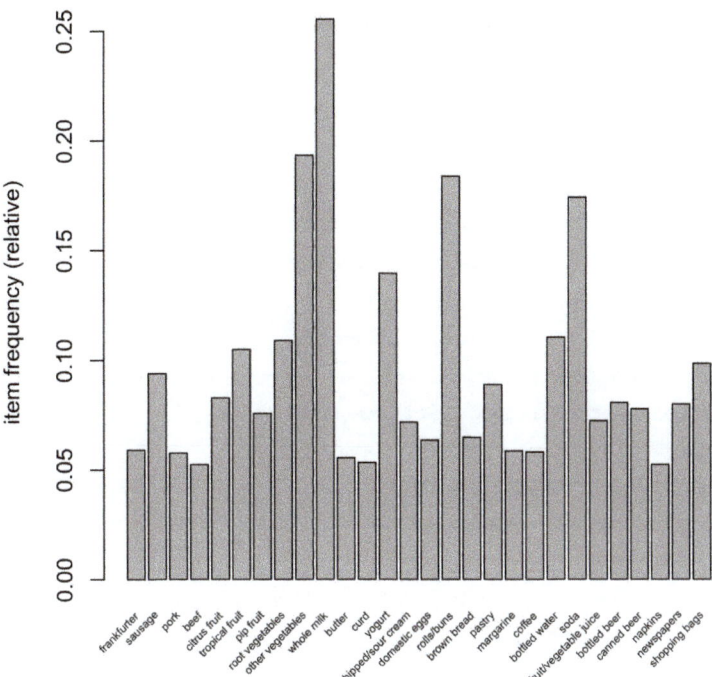

this item, it won't apply very often, and is therefore unlikely to be useful to store managers or others. So, we want to focus our attention on items that occur with some meaningful frequency in the dataset. Whether this is 1% or 0.005%, or something somewhat larger or smaller will depend on the size of the dataset and the intended use of the rules.

Before we generate our first set of rules, let's take a step back and explore the type of data object that itemFrequencyPlot (and the other associated functions with arules) needs. You might have noticed that it is *not* a dataframe (you can see this by doing the str command on the Groceries dataset). In fact, you can see it is a transactions dataset.

But what if we have a dataframe: can we convert it to a transactions dataset? Yes, sometimes this is possible, but it depends on the dataframe. Let's look at a different dataframe and convert it to a transactions dataset. To do this, we will use the AdultUCI dataset that we previously used in Chapter 11, when exploring classification. However, this time, we can load the data directly with the built-in AdultUCI dataset. If you want to explore what the columns in the dataset mean, you can do the help(AdultUCI) command at the R console to get some additional information (or go back and review Chapter 11). In any event, you can see that we first need to convert any numbers or strings into factors. Also note that since some of the column names have a dash (-), we need to quote that column name, so R does not get confused and think, for example, that we want to subtract num from

AdultUCI$education. After doing all this work, we can finally convert the dataframe into a transactions dataset, which we can then use to generate an itemFrequencyPlot.

```
data(AdultUCI)
AdultUCI.t <- AdultUCI
AdultUCI.t$age <- as.factor(AdultUCI.t$age)
AdultUCI.t$fnlwgt <- as.factor(AdultUCI.t$fnlwgt)
AdultUCI.t$'education-num' <-
as.factor(AdultUCI.t$'education-num')
AdultUCI.t$'capital-gain' <-
as.factor(AdultUCI.t$'capital-gain')
AdultUCI.t$'capital-loss' <-
as.factor(AdultUCI.t$'capital-loss')
AdultUCI.t$'hours-per-week' <-
as.factor(AdultUCI.t$'hours-per-week')
AdultUCI.trans <- as(AdultUCI.t, "transactions")
itemFrequencyPlot(AdultUCI.trans, support=0.2,
cex.names=1.1)
```

You can see that we have copied AdultUCI into AdultUCI.t so that we don't disturb the original dataset. Then we do several transformations to make some of the variables, such as age, into factor variables. Every variable that comes from a dataframe and ends up in a transactions database must somehow become a binary attribute. The as() function in the second to last line helps to make those transformations. After converting the dataframe to a transactions dataset, we display the item frequency plot.

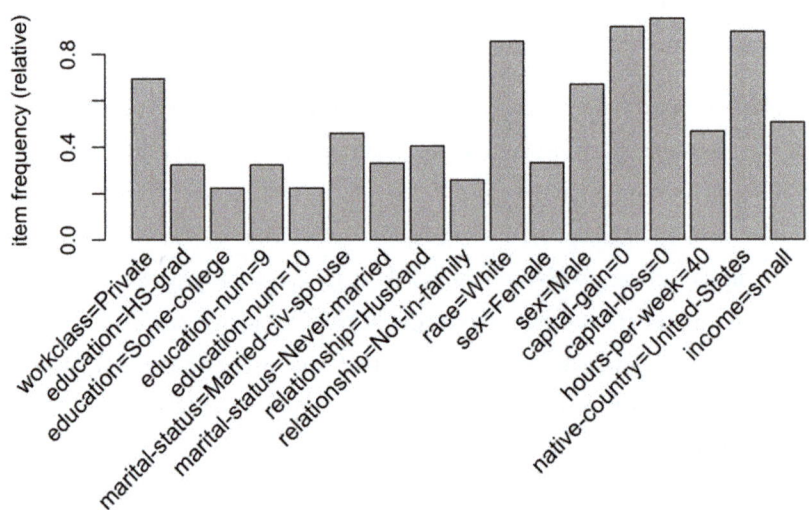

OK, now that we understand a little more about the transactions dataset, we are ready to generate some rules with the apriori() command. The term "apriori" refers to the specific algorithm that R will use to scan the dataset for appropriate rules. Apriori is a very commonly used algorithm and it is quite efficient at finding rules in transaction data.

# EXPLORING HOW THE ASSOCIATION RULES ALGORITHM WORKS

If you are wondering how apriori works, well, as shown in the following figure, apriori uses an iterative approach known as level-wise search. Basically, at the first level, we have individual items such as bread or milk (these are known as one-item sets) that are frequently found (i.e., have sufficient support, as defined in the apriori command). At the next level, the two-item sets we need to consider must have the property that each of their subsets must also have sufficient support. The algorithm keeps going up levels until there are no more combinations to be found. So, for example, as shown in our following example diagram, if we know at Level 2 that the sets {Milk Tea}, {Bread Tea}, {Bread Fish}, and {Tea Fish} are the only sets with sufficient support, then at Level 3 we join these with each other to produce {Milk Tea Bread}, {Milk Tea Fish}, {Milk Bread Fish}, and {Bread Tea Fish}. But we only need to consider {Bread Tea Fish}, since the others each have subsets with insufficient support—such as {Milk Fish} or {Milk Bread}.

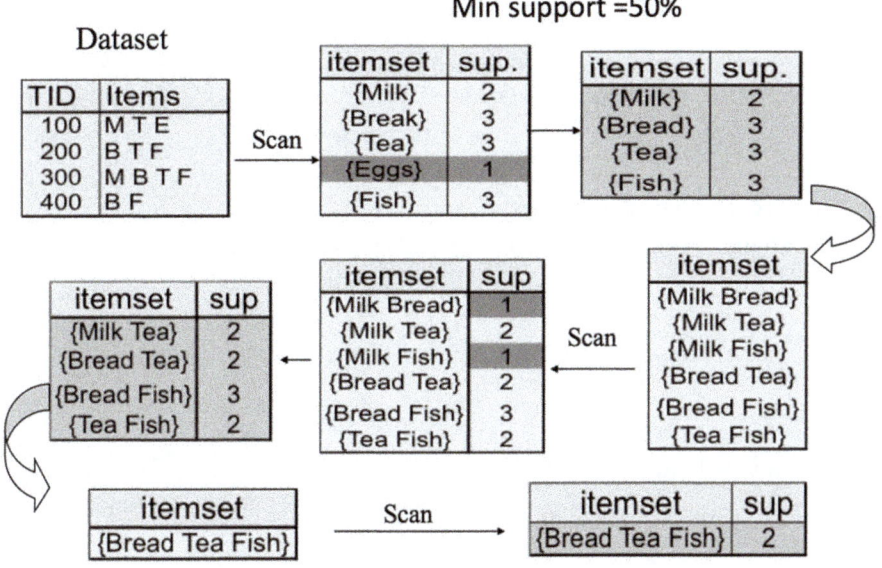

Apriori rules are in the form of "if LHS, then RHS." The abbreviation LHS means "left-hand side" and, naturally, RHS means "right-hand side." So, each rule states that when the thing or things on the LHS of the equation occur(s), the thing on the RHS occurs a certain percentage of the time. To reiterate a definition provided earlier in the chapter, support for a rule refers to the frequency of cooccurrence of both members of the pair, that is, LHS and RHS together. The confidence of a rule refers to the proportion of the time that LHS and RHS occur together versus the total number of appearances of LHS. For example, if Milk and Bread occur together in 10% of the grocery carts (i.e., support), and Milk (by itself, ignoring Bread) occurs in 25% of the carts, then the confidence of the Milk/Bread rule is 0.10/0.25 = 0.40.

There are other measures that can help us zero in on good association rules—such as lift and conviction—but we will put off discussing these until a little later.

One reminder before we start using apriori(). For most of the work that data miners do with association rules, the RHS part of the equation contains just one item, like Bread. On the other hand, the LHS part can and will contain multiple items. A simple rule might just have Milk in LHS and Bread in RHS, but a more complex rule might have Milk and Bread together in LHS with Tea in RHS.

## BUILDING ASSOCIATION RULES IN R

OK, let's give apriori a try:

```
apriori(Groceries,parameter=list(support=0.005,
                                 confidence=0.5))
  Apriori
  parameter specification:
  confidence minval smax arem aval originalSupport
         0.5        0.1     1    none FALSE            TRUE
      support minlen    maxlen        target            ext
      0.005         1        10         rules      FALSE

Algorithmic control:
filter tree heap memopt load sort verbose
     0.1 TRUE TRUE    FALSE TRUE         2        TRUE
Absolute minimum support count: 49
```

```
set item appearances ...[0 item(s)] done [0.00s].
set transactions ...[169 item(s), 9835 transaction(s)]
done [0.00s].
sorting and recoding items ... [120 item(s)] done
[0.00s].
creating transaction tree ... done [0.01s].
checking subsets of size 1 2 3 4 done [0.01s].
writing ... [120 rule(s)] done [0.00s].
creating S4 object ... done [0.00s].
set of 120 rules
```

We set up the apriori() command to use a support of 0.005 (half a percent) and confidence of 0.5 (50%) as the minimums. These values are confirmed in the first few lines of output. Some other confirmations, such as the value of minval and smax, are not relevant to us right now—they have sensible defaults provided by the apriori() implementation. The minlen and maxlen parameters also have sensible defaults: these refer to the minimum and maximum length of an item set that will be considered in generating rules. Obviously, you can't generate a rule unless you have at least one item in an item set, and setting maxlen to 10 ensures that we will not have any rules that contain more than 10 items. If you recall from earlier in the chapter, the average cart only has 4.4 items, so we are not very likely to produce rules involving more than 10 items.

In fact, a little later in the apriori() output above, we see that the apriori() algorithm only had to examine subsets of size one, two, three, and four. Apparently, no rule in this output contains more than four items. At the very end of the output, we see that 120 rules were generated. Later, we will examine ways of making sense out of a large number of rules, but for now let's agree that 120 is too many rules to examine. Let's move our support to 1% and rerun apriori(). This time we will store the resulting rules in a data structure called ruleset:

```
ruleset <- apriori(Groceries, parameter =
    list(support = 0.01,confidence = 0.5))
```

If you examine the output from this command, you should find that we have slimmed down to 15 rules, quite a manageable number to examine one by one. We can get a preliminary look at the rules using the summary function, like this:

```
summary(ruleset)
set of 15 rules

rule length distribution (lhs + rhs):sizes
3
15


      Min.    1st Qu.    Median      Mean    3rd Qu.       Max.
        3          3         3         3          3          3


summary of quality measures:
          support               confidence              lift
Min.       :0.01007   Min.       :0.5000   Min.       :1.984
1st Qu.    :0.01174   1st Qu.    :0.5151   1st Qu.    :2.036
Median     :0.01230   Median     :0.5245   Median     :2.203
Mean       :0.01316   Mean       :0.5411   Mean       :2.299
3rd Qu.    :0.01403   3rd Qu.    :0.5718   3rd Qu.    :2.432
Max.       :0.02227   Max.       :0.5862   Max.       :3.030


mining info:
     data ntransactions support confidence
Groceries               9835    0.01        0.5
```

Looking through this output, we can see that there are 15 rules in total. Rule length distribution shows that all 15 of the rules have exactly three elements (counting both the LHS and the RHS). Then, under summary of quality measures, we have an overview of the distributions of support, confidence, and a value called lift.

Researchers have done a lot of work trying to come up with ways of measuring how interesting a rule is. A more interesting rule could be a more useful rule because it is more novel or unexpected. Lift is one such measure of interestingness. Lift takes into account the support for a rule, but also gives more weight to rules where the LHS and/or the RHS occurs less frequently. In other words, lift favors situations where LHS and RHS are not abundant but where the relatively few occurrences always happen together. The larger the value of lift, the more interesting the rule might be.

Now we are ready to take a closer look at the rules we generated. The inspect() command gives us the detailed contents of the data object generated by apriori():

```
inspect(ruleset)
     lhs
     rhs                   support confidence    lift
1    {curd,yogurt}
=> {whole milk}            0.01006609 0.5823529 2.279125
2     {other vegetables,butter}
=> {whole milk}            0.01148958 0.5736041 2.244885
3 {other vegetables,domestic eggs}
=> {whole milk}            0.01230300 0.5525114 2.162336
4 {yogurt, whipped/sour cream}
=> {whole milk}            0.01087951 0.5245098 2.052747
5 {other vegetables,whipped/sour cream}
=> {whole milk}            0.01464159 0.5070423 1.984385
6 {pip fruit,other vegetables}
=> {whole milk}            0.01352313 0.5175097 2.025351
7 {citrus fruit,root vegetables}
=> {other vegetables}      0.01037112 0.5862069 3.029608
8 {tropical fruit,root vegetables}
=> {other vegetables}      0.01230300 0.5845411 3.020999
9 {tropical fruit, root vegetables}
=> {whole milk}            0.01199797 0.5700483 2.230969
10 {tropical fruit, yogurt}
=> {whole milk}            0.01514997 0.5173611 2.024770
11 {root vegetables, yogurt}
=> {other vegetables}      0.01291307 0.5000000 2.584078
12 {root vegetables, yogurt}
=> {whole milk}            0.01453991 0.5629921 2.203354
13 {root vegetables,rolls/buns}
=> {other vegetables}      0.01220132 0.5020921 2.594890
14 {root vegetables, rolls/buns}
=> {whole milk}            0.01270971 0.5230126 2.046888
15 {other vegetables, yogurt}
=> {whole milk}            0.02226741 0.5128806 2.007235
```

You can see that each of the 15 rules shows the LHS, the RHS, the support, the confidence, and the lift. Rules 7 and 8 have the highest level of lift: the fruits and vegetables involved in these two rules have a relatively low frequency of occurrence, but their support and confidence are both relatively high. Contrast these two rules with Rule 1, which also has high confidence. The reason for this contrast is that milk is a frequently occurring item, so there is not much novelty to that rule. On the other hand, the combination of fruits, root vegetables, and other vegetables suggests a need to find out more about customers whose carts contain only vegetarian or vegan items.

Now it is possible that we have set our parameters for confidence and support too stringently and as a result we have missed some truly novel combinations that might lead us to better insights. We can use a data visualization package to help explore this possibility. The R package called arulesViz has methods of visualizing the rule sets generated by apriori() that can help us examine a larger set of rules. First, install and library the arulesViz package:

```
install.packages("arulesViz")
library(arulesViz)
```

These commands will give the usual raft of status and progress messages. When you run the second command, you might find that three or four data objects are masked. As before, these warnings generally will not compromise the operation of the package.

Now let's return to our apriori() command, but we will be much more lenient this time in our minimum support and confidence parameters:

```
ruleset <- apriori(Groceries,
        parameter=list(support=0.005, confidence=0.35))
```

We brought support back to 0.005 and confidence down to 35%. When you run this command, you should find that you now generate 357 rules. That is way too many rules to examine manually, so let's use the arulesViz package to see what we have. We will use the plot() command that we have also used earlier in the book. You might ask yourself why we needed to library the arulesViz package if we are simply going to use an old command. The answer to this riddle is that arulesViz has put some plumbing into place so that when the plot() command receives a data object of type rules (as generated by apriori), it will use custom code that is built into arulesViz to do the plot. The command is very simple:

```
plot(ruleset)
```

The following figure contains the result:

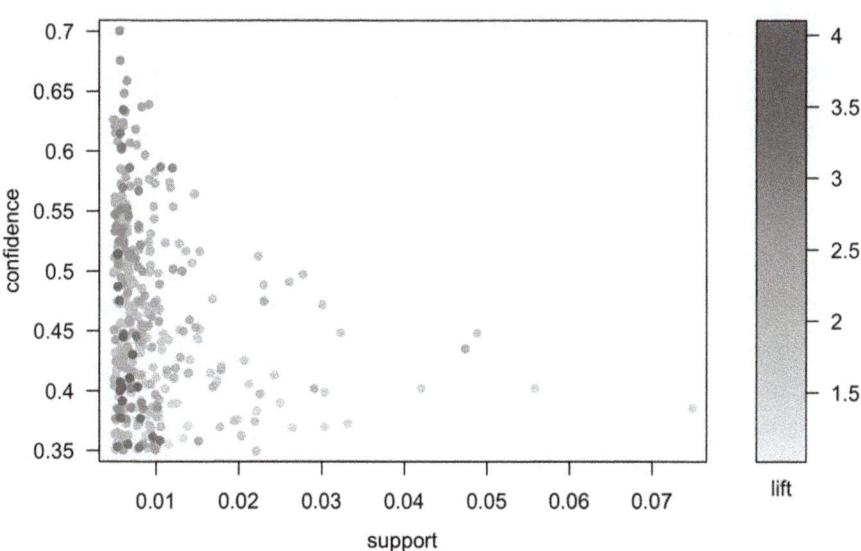

Even though we see a two-dimensional plot, we actually have three variables represented here. Support is on the X-axis and confidence is on the Y-axis. All else being equal, we would like to have rules that have high support and high confidence. We know, however, that lift serves as a measure of interestingness, and we are also interested in the rules with the highest lift. On this plot, the lift is shown by the darkness of a dot that appears on the plot. The darker the dot, the closer the lift of that rule is to 4.0, which appears to be the highest lift value among these 357 rules.

The other thing we can see from this plot is that although the support of rules ranges from somewhere below 1% all the way up above 7%, all the rules with high lift seem to have support below 1%. On the other hand, there are rules with high lift and high confidence, which sounds quite positive.

Based on this evidence, let's focus on a smaller set of rules that have only the very highest levels of lift. The following command makes a subset of the larger set of rules by choosing only those rules that have lift higher than 3.5:

```
goodrules <- ruleset[quality(ruleset)$lift > 3.5]
```

Note that the use of the square brackets with our data structure ruleset allows us to index only those elements of the data object that meet our criteria. In this case, we use the expression quality(ruleset)$lift to tap into the lift parameter for each rule. The inequality test > 3.5 gives us just those rules with the highest lift. When you run this line of code, you should find that goodrules contains just nine rules. Let's inspect those nine rules:

```
inspect(goodrules)
lhs
    rhs                 support     confidence      lift
1 {herbs}
        => {root vegetables} 0.007015760 0.4312500 3.956477
2 {onions, other vegetables}
        => {root vegetables} 0.005693950 0.4000000 3.669776
3 {beef, other vegetables}
        => {root vegetables} 0.007930859 0.4020619 3.688692
4 {tropical fruit, curd}
        => {yogurt}          0.005287239 0.5148515 3.690645
5 {citrus fruit, pip fruit}
        => {tropical fruit} 0.005592272 0.4044118 3.854060
6 {pip fruit, other vegetables, whole milk}
        => {root vegetables} 0.005490595 0.4060150 3.724961
7 {citrus fruit, other vegetables, whole milk}
        => {root vegetables} 0.005795628 0.4453125 4.085493
8 {root vegetables, whole milk, yogurt}
        => {tropical fruit} 0.005693950 0.3916084 3.732043
9 {tropical fruit, other vegetables, whole milk}
        => {root vegetables} 0.007015760 0.4107143 3.768074
```

When you look over these rules, it seems evident that shoppers are purchasing particular combinations of items that go together in recipes. The first three rules really seem like ingredients for soup! Rules 4 and 5 seem like a fruit platter with dip. The other four rules might also connect to a recipe, although it is not quite as obvious what.

The key takeaway point here is that using a good visualization tool to examine the results of a data mining activity can enhance the process of sorting through the evidence and making sense of it. If we were to present these results to a store manager (and we would certainly do a little more digging before formulating our final conclusions), we might recommend that recipes could be published along with coupons and popular recipes, such as for homemade soup, and to have all of the ingredients grouped together in the store along with signs saying, "Mmmm, homemade soup!"

# CASE STUDY: EXPLORING ASSOCIATION RULES WITHIN THE SURVEY

```
Case Key Points:
- Munge our dataset to be able to apply rule mining
- Run arules to predict detractors
- Explore rules generated by apriori
```

Just as with the AdultUCI dataset, in order to use apriori on our customer survey dataset, we need to create a dataset that only has categorical (e.g., true/false) attributes and then convert it to a transactions dataset. Some attributes, such as Airline.Status, are easy to make into a factor, but others, such as Age, require a bit of thought (i.e., feature engineering), as we likely want to treat someone who is 32 with the same rule as someone who is 31. One approach for handling Age is to round the attribute. This would mean for Age, we are looking for rules based on a person's "decade." This approach can also work for other similar attributes such as Shopping.Amount.at.Airport. Of course, there are other ways to group attributes (e.g., Age could be young, midlife, and old). In fact, the arules package has a function called discretize() that could change Age into those three groups. Sticking with our simpler method, the following code creates some attributes from our survey, to which we then can apply rule mining.

```
#load survey
library(jsonlite)
mydata.list <- fromJSON("completeSurvey.json")
surveyWithNA <- data.frame(mydata.list)
```

```
#Remove rows with'Likelihood.to.recommend' == NA
survey <- surveyWithNA %>%
    filter(!is.na(Likelihood.to.recommend))

#look for detractor rules
Detractor <- as.factor(survey$Likelihood.to.recommend <7)

#Define several attributes as factors
Age <- as.factor(round(survey$Age, digits=-1))
Price.Sensitivity <- as.factor(survey$Price.Sensitivity)
Shopping.Amount.at.Airport <-
        as.factor(round(survey$Shopping.Amount.at.Airport,
                digits=-2))
Class <- survey$Class
Type.of.Travel <- survey$Type.of.Travel
Airline.Status <- survey$Airline.Status
Gender <- survey$Gender
Origin.state <- survey$Origin.State

rSurvey <- data.frame(Detractor, Age, Price.Sensitivity,
        Shopping.Amount.at.Airport,
                    Class, Type.of.Travel,
        Airline.Status, Gender, Origin.state)
rSurvey.trans <- as(rSurvey, "transactions")
```

Notice that we also defined our target, Detractor, to be a factor rather than a specific level of likelihood.to.recommend. Let's first view the item frequency:

```
#make sure we have access to the functions
library(arules)
library(arulesViz)

#Explore item frequency
itemFrequencyPlot(rSurvey.trans, support=0.1,
cex.names=0.7)
```

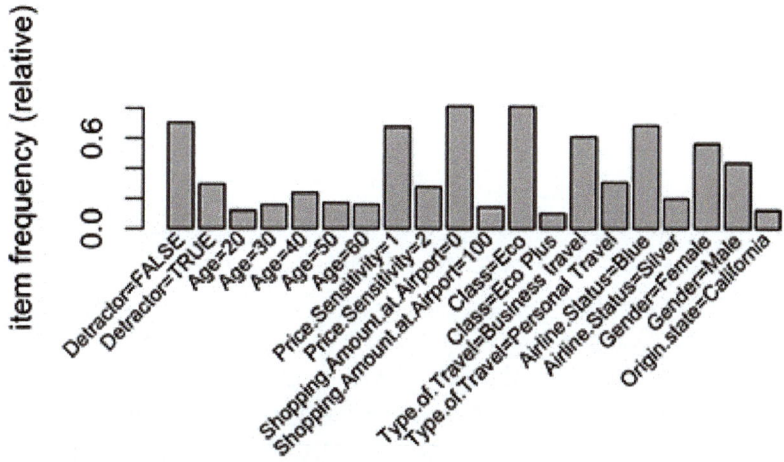

Next, we can try to generate some rules:

```
ruleset <- apriori(rSurvey.trans,
            parameter=list(supp=0.1, conf=0.6),
            appearance =
                  list(default="lhs",
                        rhs=("Detractor=TRUE")))
ruleset
set of 13 rules


inspect(ruleset)
    lhs
    rhs support confidence lift count
[1] {Type.of.Travel=Personal Travel}
    => {Detractor=TRUE} 0.1930533 0.6270924 2.124062 17008
[2] {Type.of.Travel=Personal Travel,
    Gender=Female}
    => {Detractor=TRUE} 0.1285017 0.6316465 2.139487 11321
[3] {Price.Sensitivity=1, Type.of.Travel=Personal Travel}
    => {Detractor=TRUE} 0.1161975 0.6027438 2.041589 10237
[4] {Type.of.Travel=Personal Travel, Airline.Status=Blue}
    => {Detractor=TRUE} 0.1701816 0.7149738 2.421730 14993
[5] {Class=Eco, Type.of.Travel=Personal Travel}
    => {Detractor=TRUE} 0.1584677 0.6259696 2.120258 13961
```

```
[6] {Shopping.Amount.at.Airport=0,
     Type.of.Travel=Personal Travel}
  => {Detractor=TRUE} 0.1582860 0.6329430 2.143878 13945
[7] {Type.of.Travel=Personal Travel,
     Airline.Status=Blue, Gender=Female}
  => {Detractor=TRUE} 0.1141544 0.7237334 2.451400 10057
[8] {Class=Eco, Type.of.Travel=Personal Travel,
     Gender=Female}
  => {Detractor=TRUE} 0.1021566 0.6306054 2.135961 9000
[9] {Shopping.Amount.at.Airport=0,
     Type.of.Travel=Personal Travel, Gender=Female}
  => {Detractor=TRUE} 0.1019296 0.6383735 2.162272 8980
[10] {Class=Eco, Type.of.Travel=Personal Travel,
     Airline.Status=Blue}
  => {Detractor=TRUE} 0.1395687 0.7148422 2.421284 12296
[11] {Shopping.Amount.at.Airport=0,
     Type.of.Travel=Personal Travel, Airline.Status=Blue}
  => {Detractor=TRUE} 0.1401589 0.7150799 2.422089 12348
[12] {Shopping.Amount.at.Airport=0,
     Class=Eco, Type.of.Travel=Personal Travel}
  => {Detractor=TRUE} 0.1303859 0.6312579 2.138171 11487
[13] {Shopping.Amount.at.Airport=0, Class=Eco,
     Type.of.Travel=Personal Travel,Airline.Status=Blue}
  => {Detractor=TRUE} 0.1153916 0.7147075 2.420828 10166
```

In looking at the rules, we can see two main themes in the thirteen rules. All the rules have Type.of.Travel=Personal Travel, and many of the rules have Airline.Status=Blue. We can look at the details of those rules:

```
inspect(ruleset[c(1,4)])
        lhs
        rhs        support      confidence lift        count
[1] {Type.of.Travel=Personal Travel}
=> {Detractor=TRUE} 0.1930533 0.6270924 2.124062 17008

[2] {Type.of.Travel=Personal Travel Airline.Status=Blue}
=> {Detractor=TRUE} 0.1701816 0.7149738 2.421730 14993
```

Note that Rule 4 from the first display was automatically numbered to be Rule 2 in the second display. We can see that without Airline.Status=Blue, there is higher support, but lower confidence. Finally, we can plot the 13 rules, where we can see the rules with Airline.Status (the rules with a higher confidence) and those without Airline.Status (the rules with lower confidence).

```
plot(ruleset)
```

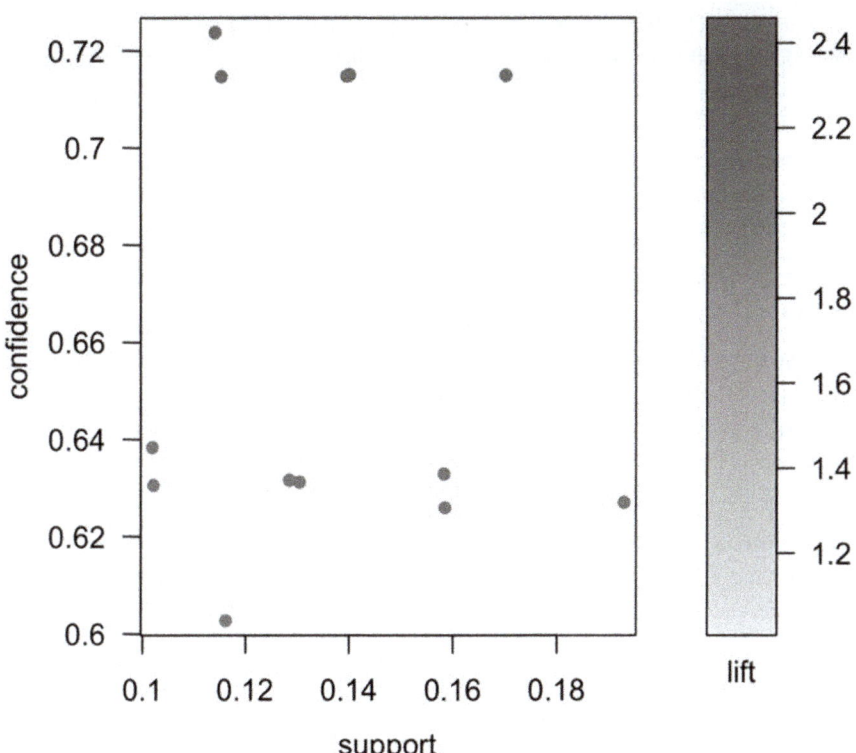

It may have struck you that by setting our RHS to be Detractor=TRUE, we have conducted an unsupervised data mining analysis that shows us some promising predictors. These predictors could be used later in a supervised analysis. This simple example shows that unsupervised and supervised data mining techniques are complementary to one another.

# Chapter Challenges

1. The arules package contains a dataset called Income that has attributes of different households including an indication of whether the annual earnings in the household were greater than $40,000. Prepare the data for analysis and examine the data using these three lines of code:

   library(arules)

   data("Income")

   summary(Income)

   Use a comment to report the number of rows and columns in this dataset. Also report the three most frequently occurring items.

2. Create an item frequency plot for the Income data using a support value of 0.40. Look at the resulting plot and report whether there are more males or more females represented in the dataset.

3. Run an apriori analysis on the Income data, using the following parameters:

   parameter=list(supp=0.4, conf=0.75). Store the result in a new object and report the number of rules that were generated. Look for a rule with {income=$0-$40,000} on the RHS and report that rule. Report the support, confidence, and lift for that rule.

4. Plot the rule set from the previous problem. Don't forget to library(arulesViz) first. Based on the plot, how many rules are there with a lift of 1.6 or higher?

5. Conduct a new analysis of the Income dataset, this time forcing the RHS to be {income=$40,000+} using the minimum support of 0.1, minimum confidence of 0.75, and the following argument to control the RHS:list(default="lhs", rhs=("income=$40,000+"). Report how many rules were generated, create a plot of the rules, and report the maximum lift value shown on the legend of the plot.

6. Filter the rule set created in Problem 5 to focus on the highest lift rules. Look back through the chapter for how to use the quality() function to extract lift values from the rule set. Choose a lift value for filtering based on the maximum lift value shown on the legend of the plot from Problem 5.

7. Based on the smaller "high lift" rule set generated in Problem 6, report the most complex rule (i.e., the one with the most items in the LHS). Make sure to report the support, confidence, and lift for that rule. Describe in your own words what that rule is saying and why it makes sense.

8. Install the DescTools package and library() it. Use the Untable() command to convert the built-in Titanic dataset into a dataframe. Use the as() function shown earlier in the chapter to coerce this dataframe into a transactions database. Report the number of rows and columns and create an item frequency plot.

# Sources

http://en.wikipedia.org/wiki/Association_rule_learning

http://jmlr.csail.mit.edu/papers/volume12/hahsler11a/hahsler11a.pdf

http://journal.r-project.org/archive/2009-2/RJournal_2009-2_Williams.pdf

http://www.r-bloggers.com/examples-and-resources-on-association-rule-mining-with-r/

http://rattle.togaware.com

http://www.statsoft.com/textbook/association-rules/

## Reference

Michael, H., Kurt, H., & Thomas, R. (2006). Implications of probabilistic data modeling for mining association rules. In M. Spiliopoulou, R. Kruse, C. Borgelt, A. Nuernberger & W. Gaul (Eds.), *From data and information analysis to knowledge engineering, studies in classification, data analysis, and knowledge organization* (pp. 598–605). Berlin, Germany: Springer-Verlag.

# R Functions Used in This Chapter

| | |
|---|---|
| apriori() | Uses the algorithm of the same name to analyze a transaction dataset and generate rules. |
| as.factor() | Coerce a variable (usually a string) into a factor. |
| data() | Make a data set from a package available. |
| itemFrequencyPlot() | Shows the relative frequency of commonly occurring items in the spare occurrence matrix. |
| inspect() | Shows the contents of the data object generated by apriori() that generates the association rules. |
| install.packages() | Loads package from the CRAN repository. |
| list() | Create an R list object from a set of data objects. |
| plot() | Generic plotting function that can be customized by packages like arulesViz. |
| summary() | Provides an overview of the contents of a data structure. |

This text includes access to datasets and select student resources. To learn more, visit sagepub.com

# 13

# WORD PERFECT (TEXT MINING)

## LEARNING OBJECTIVES

Access and analyze unstructured data.

Explain the purpose of word clouds.

Apply text mining and word cloud packages to do basic text mining.

Demonstrate accessing and analyzing unstructured data.

Explain sentiment analysis.

Code and use the sentiment analysis text mining technique.

Assess other uses of text mining.

Practice doing R coding using the following R functions: readlines, scan, htmlTreeParse, xpathApply, VectorSource, corpus, tm_map, TermDocumentMatrix, sumRows, scan, names, match.

Chapters 5, 6, and 10 focused on analysis of highly structured data by building on earlier knowledge of samples and distributions. With highly structured datasets, we generally have a list of variables, many of which are numeric or categorical, and a list of observations, where each observation contains values for most or all of the variables. Our diagnostics and visualizations focused on understanding each variable to facilitate analysis and interpretation. This chapter switches gears to focus on manipulating datasets that do not offer such convenient, well-ordered structures. Some data scientists refer to these as "unstructured" datasets, even though the data may nonetheless be quite well organized. For example, digital images are sometimes referred to as unstructured, even though they usually include a rectangular grid of points where each point has three values to represent the three primary colors of red, green, and blue. In this chapter, we will focus on another kind of unstructured data: natural language texts. Text data are everywhere and can include books, news articles, speeches, discussion boards, and web pages. Additional sources of text include Twitter (which companies can mine to understand positive and negative attitudes about their products), product reviews (such as Yelp and TripAdvisor), and free-form answers to surveys.

So, let's begin our exploration of natural language text data. The picture at the start of this chapter shows an example of a diagnostic visualization of a text dataset. The visualization is a word cloud that was generated by summarizing a body of text as input. These word clouds are fun to look at, but they also contain some useful information. The geometric arrangement of words on the figure is partly random and partly designed and organized to please the eye. The font size of each word conveys some measure of its importance in the "corpus" that was presented to the word cloud graphics program. A word corpus, from the Latin word for body, is a word that text analysts use to refer to a body of textual material, usually consisting of multiple documents. When thinking about a corpus of textual data, a set of documents could really be anything: web pages, word processing documents on your computer, a set of tweets, or a set of government reports. In most cases, text analysts think of a collection of documents, each of which contains some natural language text, as a corpus if they plan to analyze all the documents together.

Similar to visualizations like histograms and scatterplots, word clouds are useful when trying to get a quick understanding from free-form text data (such as "please let us know whether you have any additional thoughts about using our product"). A word cloud can give a high-level view of how people have responded. When someone is trying to get a quick overview of a speech or essay, a word cloud could show the most frequently occurring words.

In this chapter, we will use some new R packages to investigate the text from a speech and to create a word cloud like the one shown at the start of this chapter. Before beginning our work with the R packages, we need to read in a text source. As an example, let's explore a famous historical speech by Susan B. Anthony. In the 1800s, women in the United States lacked the right to vote. Famous suffragist Susan B. Anthony spoke publicly after being arrested for voting in the presidential election of 1872, an unlawful act at the time. You can read the speech at http://www.historyplace.com/speeches/anthony. htm. We can use R to read the text directly from the web page.

## READING-IN TEXT FILES

To begin working on our word cloud of the speech, let's create a new RStudio project to hold our text analysis code. A project in RStudio helps to keep all of the different pieces and parts of an activity together, including the datasets and variables that you establish as well as the functions that you write. For professional uses of R and RStudio, it is important to have one project for each major activity: this keeps different datasets and variable names from interfering with one other. Click on the Project menu in RStudio and then click on New Project. You will usually have a choice of three kinds of new projects: a brand-new, or clean, project; an existing directory of files that will get turned into a project folder; or a project that comes out of a version control system. Choose New Directory to start a brand-new project. You can call your project whatever you want, but because this project develops a word cloud, you might want to call the project wordcloud. You also have a choice in the dialog box about where on your computer RStudio will create the new directory. RStudio will respond by showing a blank console screen and an R workspace that does not contain any of the old variables and data that you previously created.

To get started with our new project, the first task we need to do is import the text we want to analyze. As you have learned, there are many different ways to read data into R. Until now, we have used techniques for reading in comma-separated variable (CSV) files and other formats that are good at storing structured data. If we want to read in unstructured (text-based) data, we need some new functions, especially if we are extracting text from a web page.

As shown below, we can read directly from a web page into an R data structure. If you have ever looked at a web page in its most raw form, you know that it is full of special labels, called "tags," which make it possible for your browser to display and format the page properly. These tags are part of a computer language called hyper-text markup language (HTML). We must parse the HTML and convert it into simple text by removing the tags. To do this, we can use the htmlTreeParse function (in the XML package) to read a web page. We then parse the HTML document to look for paragraphs. HTML denotes paragraphs by using <p>, so we look for that tag, starting at the root of the document. Finally, we "unlist" the results to create a vector of character strings.

```r
library("XML")
library("quanteda")

# Note the web location for the speech
sbaLocation <- "URLencode(http://www.historyplace.com/
speeches/anthony.htm")

# Read and parse HTML file
doc.html = htmlTreeParse(sbaLocation, useInternal = TRUE)
```

```
# Extract all paragraphs (HTML tag is p, starting at
# the root of the document). unlist() flattens the list to
# create a character vector.
sba = unlist(xpathApply(doc.html, '//p', xmlValue))


sba <- sba[3:10] # These are the sections of the speech
head(sba, 1) # Review the first paragraph

[1] "Friends and fellow citizens: I stand before you tonight
under indictment\n for the alleged crime of having voted
at the last presidential election,\n without having a law-
ful\n right to vote. It shall be my work this evening to
prove to you that in\n thus voting, I not only committed no
crime, but, instead, simply exercised\n my citizen's rights,
guaranteed to me and all United States citizens by\n the
National Constitution, beyond the power of any state to
deny. "
```

Once we read in the speech (in the code above we stored the results into the variable sba, for Susan B. Anthony), we can see that it is simply a vector. Each element in the vector can contain lots of words, however, as we can see in the output for sba, a given vector might contain several sentences of text.

# CREATING WORD CLOUDS USING THE QUANTEDA PACKAGE

Now that we have the text of the speech, we need to process it to get it ready for presentation as a word cloud. We can use the quanteda package to process our texts. This package was created by Professor Ken Benoit of the London School of Economics to conduct quantitative analysis of textual data, or what some people refer to as text mining. By the way, text mining refers to the practice of extracting useful analytic information from corpora of text (the word "corpora" is the plural of corpus). Although some people use the terms "text mining" and "natural language processing" interchangeably, there are some subtle differences worth considering. First, the "mining" part of text mining refers to an area of practice that looks for notable patterns in large datasets, or what some people refer to as knowledge discovery in databases. In contrast, natural language processing reflects a more general interest in understanding how machines can be programmed (or can learn on their own) how to make sense of human language. Thinking about the difference from another angle, text mining usually focuses on statistical approaches to analyzing text data, using strategies that involve word frequencies and other measures of how words are used in a corpus. In natural language processing, however, one is more likely to focus on linguistics, and therefore to organize text into its component grammatical elements such as nouns and verbs. In the case of the quanteda package, we are firmly in the statistical camp, where the main goal is to subdivide a corpus into lists of words and then to tally up the different words we have found. The following commands get that process started:

```
sbaCorpus <- corpus(sba) # Convert to a corpus
sbaCorpus <- corpus_reshape(sbaCorpus, to="sentences")
sbaCorpus # Reports the number of documents

# Now convert the corpus to a document-feature matrix
sbaDFM <- dfm(sbaCorpus, remove_punct=TRUE,
                         remove=stopwords("english"))

sbaDFM
Document-feature matrix (DFM) of 19 documents, 190 features
(93.3% sparse).
```

In the first step, we convert our text file vector (sba) into a corpus, storing the result in a new data object called sbaCorpus. In the second step, we restructure the corpus to have each sentence become its own "document." Document, in this context, refers to a unit of analysis within a corpus: Every corpus is made up of one or more (usually a lot more) documents. Finally, in the third step we transform the corpus and its documents into a so-called DFM. These data structures contain the information that text miners care about: the documents, their component words, any metadata we may have about the documents (such as document titles), and information about how the corpus was created (such as the fact that we removed punctuation). The corpus provides a simple list of all of this information, whereas the DFM represents it as a matrix with the documents as the rows and the features (in this case just the individual words in the speech) as the columns. Note how the output of the final command reports on the structure of the DFM: a matrix of 19 documents (rows) and 190 features (columns). The 19 documents are the sentences from the original speech, whereas the features are the words from each sentence. With 19 documents and 190 features, our matrix contains 3,610 cells, where each cell contains a number that tells how many times a particular word appeared in a particular document/sentence. According to the quanteda package, the matrix is 93.3% sparse, which implies that more than 3,300 of those cells contain zeroes. In text mining, a sparse matrix like this is very common and is a natural result of the inventiveness of human language: with thousands of words to choose from, no sentence (or larger document) contains more than a handful of all possible words.

The "remove=stopwords("english")" argument in the dfm() command deserves a little explanation. Researchers who developed the early search engines for electronic databases found that words such as "the," "a," and "at" appeared so commonly in so many different parts of the text that they interfered with proper development of the search engine. In contrast, the unique and unusual nouns, verbs, and adjectives that appeared in a document did a much better job of setting a document apart from other documents in a corpus, such that researchers decided that they should filter out all of the short, commonly used words. The term "stop words" seems to have originated in the 1960s to signify words that a computer processing system would stop using because they had little meaning in a data processing task. To simplify the removal of stop words, the quanteda package contains lists of such words for various languages.

At this point, we have processed our corpus into a nice uniform "bag of words" that contains no punctuation or stop words. We are now ready to conduct a statistical analysis of the corpus by working on the DFM. Note that the DFM goes by different names depending on who is talking about it. Other common names are a "term-document matrix" or a "document-term matrix." For the most part, these names are all interchangeable. Before we generate our word cloud, let's review some information on the frequency of various words in the documents. Helpfully, quanteda provides the textstat_frequency() function, which returns a data structure containing term frequency information that can help us make sense of our corpus:

```
textstat_frequency(sbaDFM)[1:10, ]
      feature  frequency  rank  docfreq  group
1     women          7     1         7    all
2     citizens       5     2         4    all
3     states         5     2         4    all
4     people         5     2         4    all
```

| 5 | oligarchy | 5 | 2 | 2 | all |
| 6 | united | 4 | 6 | 3 | all |
| 7 | blessings | 4 | 6 | 4 | all |
| 8 | liberty | 4 | 6 | 4 | all |
| 9 | law | 4 | 6 | 2 | all |
| 10 | every | 4 | 6 | 2 | all |

In the output, we can see the top 10 words in the corpus. For example, the word "women" was used seven times in Anthony's speech. This data structure also provides a rank ordering of the frequency of words. The word "women" is the most frequently used word, so it has frequency rank of one. Note that the next four words, all of which occur five times in the corpus, are all tied for second place in frequency rank. The next column to the right is the document frequency: this shows the number of different documents in which a word appeared. Remember that in our DFM one document equals one sentence from the speech. The rightmost column contains a grouping indicator that we are not using in this analysis.

Now we are ready to create a word cloud. The textplot_wordcloud() function has lots of optional parameters for making the word cloud more colorful, controlling its shape, and controlling how frequently an item must occur to show in the cloud. We have used the default settings for all of these parameters for the sake of simplicity. We pass to the textplot_wordcloud() function DFM we just created and it produces the graphic that you see below.

Word clouds are an important first step when starting to examine a corpus of text data. In more complex data sets, a word cloud will show nuisance words, such as misspellings or acronyms, that you may want to filter out of the DFM or modify. This simple word cloud looks fine, so we will now take the next analytic step by using another technique for textual data known as sentiment analysis.

# EXPLORING THE TEXT VIA SENTIMENT ANALYSIS

Sentiment analysis sounds complex, and in fact, there are many ways to do sentiment analysis, but we will use a simple strategy based on word frequency. Our process will use dictionaries of positive and negative words created by professor Bing Liu, and then count how many positive and negative words there are in our corpus. Given this analysis strategy, we can compute a positive score and a negative score for any text. A common application of sentiment analysis would be in summarizing customer reviews of products or services to improve understanding of the customer experience. So, let's continue to use Susan B. Anthony's speech to conduct our sentiment analysis. Was the speech positive in its tone overall or was it negative? To begin, let's load the positive and negative dictionary files and clean them up to get ready to use. To find a positive and negative word list, we reference Dr. Liu's website on sentiment analysis: https://www.cs.uic.edu/~liub/FBS/sentiment-analysis.html

About halfway down the web page, you can see a section titled "Opinion Lexicon (or Sentiment Lexicon)." The first bullet in this section contains a link to a list of positive- and negative-opinion words or sentiment words for English. When you click on this link, it downloads a compressed file that contains a folder that has both positive and negative words. There will be one text file for the positive words and one file for the negative words. You can search for the same files in uncompressed form at the code repository site known as Github. Once you download those files, save them to a place where R can easily access them. This code reads in the positive words dictionary:

```
posFile <- "positive-words.txt"
posWords <- scan(posFile, character(0),sep = "\n")
Read 2040 items
```

Let's review what we just did. First, we set up a file name for the text file containing the positive words. Note this code assumes the text files are in R's default directory. You can get and set R's working directory with the getwd() and setwd() functions. The positive file contained 2,040 lines of text, but note that the beginning of the file contains 34 lines of header information that we need to remove. Let's take a look at the first few words of the positive word list, after removing the 34 lines of header:

```
posWords <- posWords[-1:-34] # Remove the header
head(posWords,12)

[1] "a+"          "abound"        "abounds"       "abundance"
[5] "abundant"  "accessable"  "accessible"  "acclaim"
[9] "acclaimed" "acclamation" "accolade"    "accolades"
```

We can see that the dictionary intentionally contains common misspellings of words like accessible, as well as plurals of nouns like accolade. Including these variations makes it easier to use the dictionary, because there is less preprocessing that the analyst must do to get matches between the words in the DFM and the words in the dictionary. Running the command length(posWords) shows that there are 2,006 positive words in the list, once we removed the header information. Next, we can use a powerful function from the quanteda package called dfm_match() to create a new DFM that shows where all of the matches occur:

```
posDFM<- dfm_match(sbaDFM, posWords)
posDFM

Document-feature matrix of: 19 documents, 2,006 features
(100.0% sparse).
```

Very interesting! The dfm_match() function has created a brand-new DFM. This new DFM contains the same documents as before—the 19 sentences from the speech—but the number of features has been expanded to cover all the words in the positive word list. By the way, don't worry about the report that the matrix is 100% sparse—there are some non-zero cells in the matrix and the report of 100% sparse is simply due to rounding error. Each cell of our sparse matrix now shows, for each document, how many times each word in the positive word list matched something in one of the sentences of the speech. We can now use textstat_frequency() on this new DFM to examine a list of word frequencies that only includes these positive words:

```
posFreq <- textstat_frequency(posDFM)

# Cut it down to retain words that occur at least once
posFreq <- posFreq[posFreq$frequency>0, ]
posFreq

        feature frequency rank docfreq group
1        liberty         4    1       4   all
2          right         2    2       2   all
3         secure         2    2       2   all
4       educated         1    4       1   all
5      enjoyment         1    4       1   all
6         lawful         1    4       1   all
7        perfect         1    4       1   all
8      precisely         1    4       1   all
9           rich         1    4       1   all
10       supreme         1    4       1   all
11          well         1    4       1   all
12          work         1    4       1   all
```

This data structure is very informative: There were 12 positive words used throughout the speech. Words such as liberty, enjoyment, and perfect have obvious positive connotations, confirming that our matching process worked the way we hoped. If we add up all of the numbers in the frequency column, we find that these 12 words have been used a total of 17 times. The word liberty appeared in four sentences, whereas right and secure appear in two sentences each, and the rest of the positive words each appear in just one document/sentence.

Repeating this analysis to match the negative words is very straightforward and the code for it appears below. As it turns out, the speech contains a total of 11 negative words such as crime and hateful, and these words are used a total of 13 times throughout the speech. Thus, the positive words have a very slight advantage over the negative words in terms of their frequency of occurrence.

```
negFile <- "negative-words.txt"
negWords <- scan(negFile, character(0),sep = "\n")
negWords <- negWords[-1:-34] # Remove the header

negDFM<- dfm_match(sbaDFM, negWords) # Do the matching
negDFM # Report on the size of the sparse matrix
negFreq <- textstat_frequency(negDFM)

# Retain negative words that occur at least once
negFreq <- negFreq[negFreq$frequency>0, ]
dim(negFreq) # How many negative words?
negFreq # Show them
sum(negFreq$frequency) # 13 usages of negative words
```

# TOPIC MODELING

The sentiment analysis we did was fun and easy: we matched words from the DFM with dictionaries of positive and negative words and then counted how often words from those dictionaries occurred in the corpus. Although simple, this approach can help us draw general conclusions about the overall tone of a set of documents. To dig a little deeper, though, we need to use statistical techniques that reveal more details about the individual documents in our corpus.

One family of such techniques is called topic modeling. Topic modeling creates a set of statistical profiles of word frequencies: each profile in the set is called a "topic" and every document in the corpus is represented as a mixture of these topics. Like the dictionary-based sentiment analysis we did above, topic modeling uses the frequencies of words to make sense out of the corpus of documents. Unlike our sentiment analysis, topic modeling allows us to create two or more unique profiles of word frequencies.

To make the statistical processing work properly, every topic actually contains at least a small contribution from every word in the corpus. In a good topic model, however, certain words make a given topic distinctive by contributing strongly to that topic and that topic alone. Every document is considered to be a mixture of all the topics, but in a good model each document is represented strongly by just one topic. Consider the first two lines of the Robert Frost poem *In a Poem* shown in the center of the following figure. If we treat each line as a document, we have a corpus with two documents and eight features (the features are highlighted in each line of the poem). If we create a topic model containing two topics, topic 1 contains the terms sentencing, goes, blithely, and way, with 25% weight for each. Topic 1 also contains the words takes, playfully, objected, and rhyme, but these all have a weight of zero. Topic 2 completely reverses those weights.

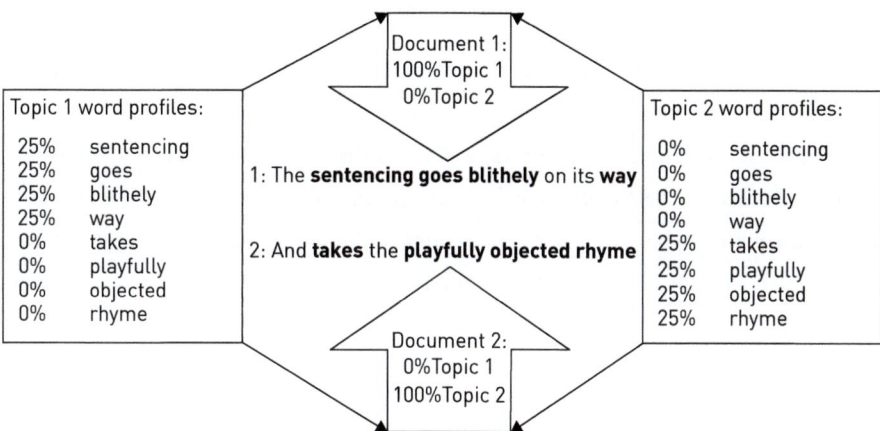

Given these two distinctive profiles of words, we can say that document 1 (the first line of the poem) is composed of 100% topic 1 and 0% topic 2. Document 2 is composed of 0% topic 1 and 100% topic 2. Of course, a more complex set of documents and terms won't ever turn out this cleanly, but creating a topic model can allow us to associate each document with a small set of topics. You could imagine using this method with product reviews, or web pages, or social media postings in order to automatically sort these kinds documents into groups based on whether the customer has a complaint, a compliment, a suggestion, or something else. Let's apply topic modeling to our Susan B. Anthony speech and see what we get.

```
# LDA topic modeling - with four topics
sbaTopics <- convert(sbaDFM, to = "topicmodels")
sbaModel <- LDA(sbaTopics, k=4)
```

In the first line of code, we convert our DFM to a new data object. All of the information is preserved, but the data structure is simplified in preparation for the next line. In the second line of code, the LDA() function performs the actual topic modeling. LDA stands for Latent Dirichlet Allocation. This refers to a statistical analysis process that the function uses to establish a set of topics. The k = 4 argument tells the function that we want to establish four topics. The analyst must specify this number, so it is typical to try out different numbers of topics to find the smallest number of topics that can provide an interpretable result. It is also possible to use a statistical criterion, in this case referred to as "perplexity," to choose an appropriate number of topics. In this case, we experimented with three, four, and five topics and found that four topics provided a useful result.

The topic modeling process produces two matrices of coefficients, called beta and gamma, that together define how words, topics, and documents are connected with one other. The "beta" matrix shows the proportion of times that each word appears in each topic. When we look at the beta matrix for the Susan B. Anthony example, we should expect to find four columns—because that was the number of topics we requested—and 190 rows, one for each word in our DFM. The next block of code shown above plots these values for the top five words in each of the four columns.

```
# Plot beta: The per word per topic probability
par(mfrow=c(2,2)) # Make a four pane plot display
for (i in 1:4) {
    topicWords <- exp(sbaModel@beta[i, ])
    names(topicWords) <- sbaModel@terms
    barplot(sort(topicWords,decreasing=TRUE)[1:5],las=2)
}
par(mfrow=c(1,1)) # Restore a full pane plot display
```

Let's focus on topic four, shown in the lower left pane of the figure. The words united and states each account for about 6% of the words that appear in topic four. Constitution, establish, and blessings each account for about 3%. Taken together, these five words account for more than 20% of all the words that appear in this topic. All 185 of the other words in the corpus also have beta values (though much smaller values than these five words) and together all of the beta values for a topic add up to one. By the way, we use a neat little R trick to create this four-pane plot window: the par() command, used twice in that code with mfrow as an argument, can be used to set the number of rows and columns in the plot window.

Next, let's focus on the gamma matrix. The gamma matrix connects the topics with the documents. In our example, each document has a set of four gamma coefficients, one for each of our four topics. These four coefficients add up to one. Each coefficient shows how

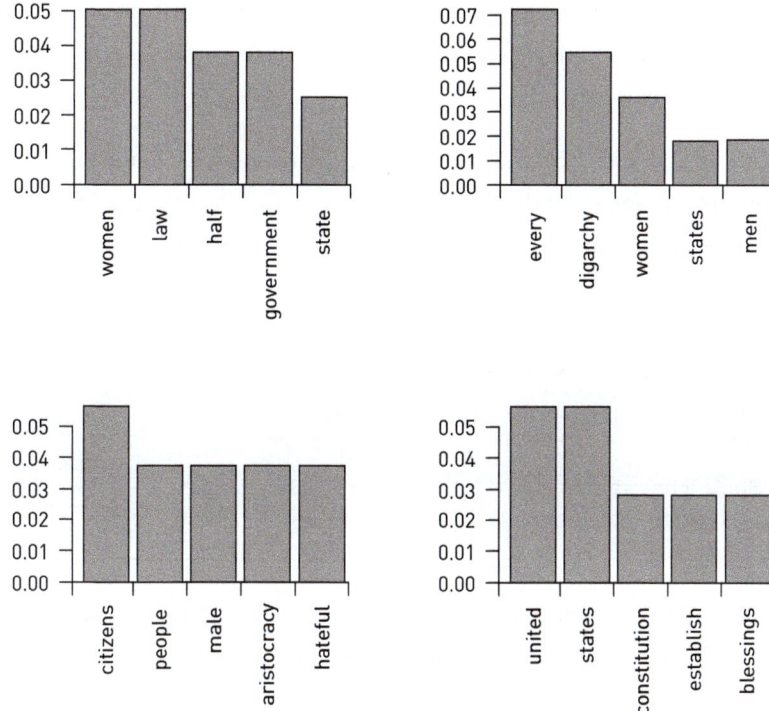

strongly that topic connects with that document. Ideally, each document has one strong gamma weight showing the topic that predominates, whereas all of the other gammas for that topic are much lower. Among other uses, we can access the gamma matrix to find out which document best represents each topic:

```
# Review one document that best fits each topic
for (i in 1:4) {
  bestDoc <- which.max(sbaModel@gamma[ ,i])
  print(sbaCorpus[bestDoc])
}
```

This "for loop" spits out four very long sentences. Rather than take up space with all of them on this page, here's the beginning of the fourth sentence: "We, the people of the United States, in order to form a more perfect union . . ." Recognize that? It's the preamble to the U.S. constitution. If you can now remember the five most influential words in topic four—united, states, constitution, establish, and blessings—the picture starts to fall into place. Topic four is made up of a profile of words that are very common in the short excerpt of the preamble that Susan B. Anthony used in her speech. When we probe topic four to find which document best represents it, we find that the sentence in her speech containing that excerpt from the preamble is the document that is most highly representative of topic four.

Try running the following code to find out more about topic four. The histogram shows that there are four sentences that have very high gamma values for topic four, whereas all the rest of the sentences have very low gamma values. This makes topic four a good topic—sentences either have it or they don't.

```
# Distribution of gamma for topic four
hist(sbaModel@gamma[ ,4])

# Show the sentences that fit topic four best
sbaCorpus[sbaModel@gamma[ ,4] > 0.75]
```

The second statement prints out the sentences that have those high gamma values. In addition to the preamble of the U.S. constitution, there are three other sentences in her speech that use very similar language to the preamble.

## OTHER USES OF TEXT MINING

Although we have focused on using text mining for sentiment analysis and topic modeling, there are many other uses for text mining. While space does not allow us to discuss all the different possible uses of text mining, let's explore three different scenarios where text mining might be useful. The first common example is to do text mining on tweets. When someone mines tweets, she can explore the frequency of a certain hashtag or how a specific tweet or hashtag can go viral (which is related to the phrase "trending on Twitter"). In addition, a company can use text mining to review tweets to get an understanding of how consumers view their product.

In a different example, text mining can also be used in call centers. For example, for an inbound call center (where people call into a call center with questions or to order a product), it is helpful to know what people are talking about on the phone. Using speech-to-text, an organization can generate text documents from the phone conversations, which can then be analyzed using text mining to create key words or topics representing various types of calls. The organization might show this list to the call center representative or the organization might focus on the frequency of the key words used. Armed with these data, the organization can then do analysis of what customers talk about during calls, potentially connecting the call topics to customers' satisfaction. In a related use of text mining, notes about repairs (e.g., by a manufacturer) could be analyzed to determine whether specific keywords (representing specific components in a manufactured system) are causing problems at a higher-than-expected rate.

In one last example, we can use text mining to do an analysis for a specific industry by text mining news feeds to extract the names of people, areas of focus, and companies that occur in the news—for example, those focusing on health care. The goal would be to try to infer who the key people are in that field or how different areas of focus change over time: for instance, although this year many people may be discussing measles, next year the main topic may be another respiratory disease.

To recap, in this chapter we explored sentiment analysis, a text mining technique that attempts to determine how positive or negative an unstructured text document is. We also reviewed a simple example of topic modeling, where we used a statistical analysis to create topics with unique word profiles and mapped those onto the documents in the corpus. We touched upon some other possible scenarios where text mining could be used, such as analyzing customer comments (via Twitter or other communication channels).

## CASE STUDY: CONNECTING TOPICS TO NPS

> `Case Key Points:`
> - `The customer survey contains many brief text comments`
> - `Customer comments may contain key words that are associated with either positive or negative net promoter score (NPS)`
> - `We can create a topic model and then analyze the gamma matrix to predict NPS—when a topic successfully predicts NPS, it can provide actionable information about operational improvements`

The foregoing chapter demonstrated how to use a corpus of documents to create topic models—create a set of statistical profiles of word frequencies. In the case study dataset, a subset of customer flight segments contains brief comments that customers wrote on their surveys. In the following analysis, we will generate a topic model to ascertain whether any topic will predict net promoter score (NPS). If there is a topic that does predict this outcome variable, we can examine examples of documents that represent this topic to obtain actionable insight about customer retention. First, let's read in the survey and keep only the rows (surveys) where a free-form text response was provided. We then include an additional action which is to create a vector of brief document titles and append it to the dataframe. These document titles can help with later diagnostics by summarizing a few pieces of information about the flight segment. In this case, we have used the partner airline code, the destination city, and the day of the month to create a short string for each row of our dataframe. This information will not be used as part of the topic modeling analysis, but will provide a human readable "handle" for referring to any particular comment in our dataset. Finally, we create a subset of the dataframe, with just the detractors. We are doing this so we can explore the free-form text for the people who were detractors—maybe there is some insight that can be gained by exploring their responses.

```r
library("quanteda")
library("topicmodels")
library("readr")
library("jsonlite")
library("tidyverse")

#read in the full survey
mydata.list <- jsonlite::fromJSON("completeSurvey.json")
surveyDF <- data.frame(mydata.list)

# just keep surveys with free form text
textSurvey <- surveyDF %>% filter(!is.na(freeText))

# Create a short document title for future reference
textSurvey$docTitle <- paste(textSurvey$Partner.Code,
                    textSurvey$Destination.City,
                    textSurvey$Day.of.Month,sep="_")

#first just focus on detractors
detractDF <- textSurvey %>%
                filter(Likelihood.to.recommend < 7)
```

The next step of this analysis involves creating a DFM from the comment data. Note that we added a few additional stopwords, such as southeast, flight and "s." We removed southeast and flight because using those words will not provide any value in this context, and we remove the word "s," since that word was created somehow via our parsing. Feel free to run the code without removing these additional stopwords!

```
# Convert to a corpus
flightCorpus <- corpus(detractDF $freeText,
            docnames= detractDF $docTitle)

# create a new set of stopwords to include
# southeast and flight as well as the word 's'
myStop <- c(stopwords("english"),
                    's', 'southeast', 'flight')

# Now convert the corpus to aDFM
flightDFM <- dfm(flightCorpus,
            remove_punct=TRUE,
            remove=myStop)
flightDFM

Document-feature matrix of: 282 documents,
2,123 features (98.9% sparse).
```

After creating the corpus with these document titles, we built a DFM that R reports as having 282 documents (same as the number of rows in our survey subset) and 2,123 features. Note that we have more than 14 times as many documents in our corpus than were in the Susan B. Anthony corpus, as well as more than 11 times as many features. This is a much more complex corpus and will require more topics to adequately analyze it.

First, let's visualize the overall frequencies of the terms in the corpus. We can do that with a ggplot chart, showing the most commonly used words in the free-form text of the detractors. Below, we store the words and their associated frequency into the wordDF dataframe, and then use some of ggplot's more advanced options to view the word frequencies.

```
#most frequent words used by detractors
wordDF <- flightDFM %>%
        textstat_frequency(n = 50) %>%
        select(word=feature, freq=frequency)

wordDF %>%
        filter(freq>20) %>%
        ggplot(aes(x = reorder(word, freq), y = freq)) +
        geom_point() +
        coord_flip() +
        labs(x = NULL, y = "Frequency") +
        theme_minimal()
```

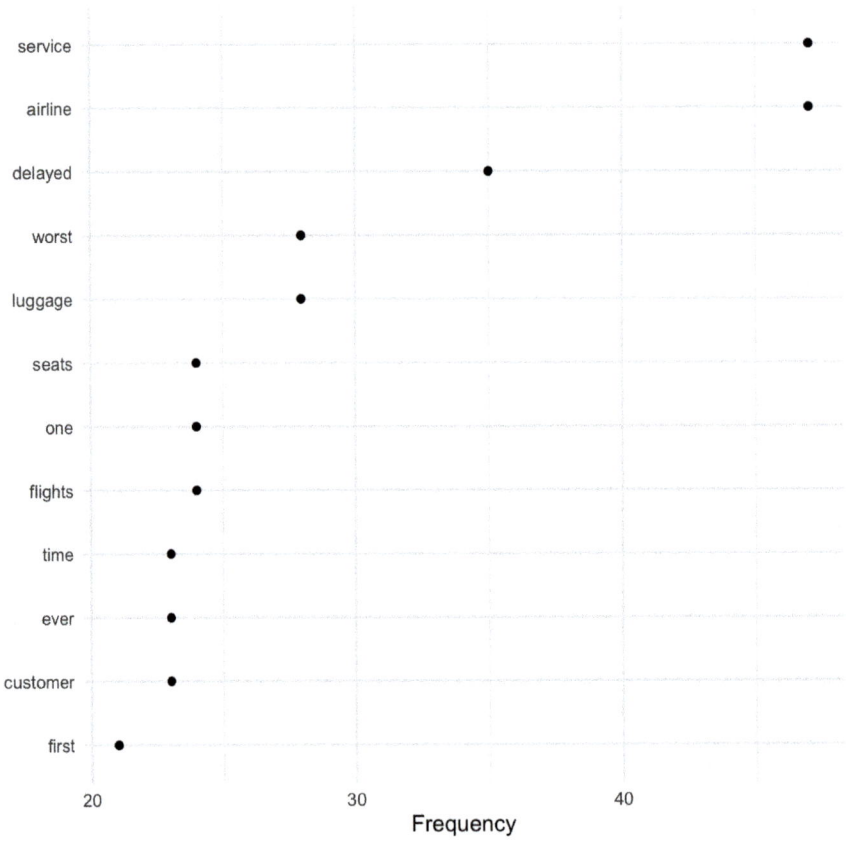

frequent words (DETRACTOR)

We can view the same data with a word cloud. Note that, as shown below, we used set. seed(11) to control randomization of the word cloud.

```
set.seed(11)
textplot_wordcloud(flightDFM)
```

Across both of these visualizations, the word "service" is seen as the most important word. Since this is for detractors, one might start to investigate if bad service is one key factor driving people to be a detractor (at least for the survey respondents who completed the free form part of the survey).

In the next set of steps, we will explore all the free-form responses (from detractors and others), with a goal of understanding some of the words that can help predict changes in the likelihood to recommend score. Specifically, we will create a topic model, and then use the gamma matrix from the topic model to build a new dataframe. We will use the dataframe to create a linear regression model where we predict the likelihood to recommend values from the gamma coefficients.

Below, we first use the set.seed to ensure repeatable results and then create our topic model:

```
#start with all the free form text
library("topicmodels")
set.seed(200)
flightCorpus <- corpus(textSurvey$freeText,
                        docnames = textSurvey$docTitle)


# Now convert the corpus to a document-feature matrix
flightDFM <- dfm(flightCorpus,
        remove_punct=TRUE, remove=myStop)


# Convert the DFM to the topic model class
flightTopics <- convert(flightDFM, to = "topicmodels")


# Create the topic model, while controlling
# randomization for a consistent result
flightModel <- LDA(flightTopics,
                        control = list(alpha = 0.1,
                                        seed=c(1:10),
                                        nstart=10), k=7)
```

After a little bit of experimentation, we settled on modeling seven topics. As mentioned earlier in the chapter, it is possible to use perplexity scores to empirically guide the number of topics, but in this case, we just used some trial and error. We next use the gamma matrix from the topic model to build a new dataframe.

```
# Add Likelihood.to.recommend to the gamma matrix
predMatrix <- cbind(textSurvey$Likelihood.to.recommend,
                        flightModel@gamma)
```

```
# Convert to a dataframe
predDF <- as.data.frame(predMatrix)

# Change the column labels to something more helpful
colnames(predDF) <- c("LTR", "Topic1", "Topic2",
                      "Topic3","Topic4", "Topic5", "Topic6",
                      "Topic7")
```

We will then use that new dataframe to create a linear regression model where we predict the likelihood to recommend value from the gamma coefficients. You will see below that when we model seven topics, we can only use six of the gamma scores. You may remember that for a given document, all the gamma scores add up to one. That's why we can loosely interpret each gamma score as the "percentage" of each topic in a given document. But the fact that the gamma scores always add up to one also means that any six of the scores can be used to exactly calculate the seventh score. If we tried to use all seven in a prediction equation, we would create a problem in the linear regression model. So, we must only use six of the topics as predictors. If you wanted to see the coefficient for Topic 7, you could temporarily drop Topic 1 from the analysis.

Note that, rather than using lm() directly, we use the caret package, and treat lm() like the other machine learning algorithms we used in Chapter 11.

```
library(caret)
model.lm <- train(LTR ~ Topic1 + Topic2 + Topic3 +
                               Topic4 + Topic5 + Topic6,
                  method = "lm",
                  data = predDF)


summary(model.lm)

Call:
lm(formula = .outcome ~ ., data = dat)

Residuals:
   Min      1Q   Median      3Q     Max
-7.2121  -1.8429  0.7882  1.7979  4.2694
```

```
Coefficients:
             Estimate Std. Error t    value    Pr(>|t|)
(Intercept)   7.1034     0.3812     18.635     < 2e-16 <
Topic1        0.3726     0.5456      0.683      0.49525
Topic2       -1.3784     0.5220     -2.641      0.00875 **
Topic3       -0.2385     0.5789     -0.412      0.68063
Topic4       -0.8230     0.5531     -1.488      0.13788
Topic5        1.1126     0.5220      2.131      0.03395 *
Topic6       -0.1003     0.5709     -0.176      0.86061
---
Signif. codes: 0 '<' 0.001 '**' 0.01 '*' 0.05 '.'
Residual standard error: 2.389 on 275 degrees of
freedom
Multiple R-squared: 0.09537
Adjusted R-squared: 0.07563
F-statistic: 4.832 on 6 and 275 DF, p-value: 0.0001042
```

Although the model only has an R-squared of 0.07, the results are nonetheless significant. Specifically, these regression results show that Topics 2 and 5 have an ability to predict likelihood to recommend. The way to interpret this is that if we contrasted two comments, and one had nothing for Topic 2 (gamma = 0), whereas the other was all Topic 2 (gamma = 1), the likelihood to recommend would on average be 1.37 points lower for the flight segment with the comment that was all Topic 2. That's quite a change: for example, if we compared a customer who gave an LTR of seven with a customer who gave an LTR of six, we would consider the second customer to be quite unsatisfied (i.e., a detractor). Note that for Topic 5, it is the reverse—the likelihood to recommend will increase by more than 1. So, let's open up Topics 2 and 5 and explore both topics.

```
#Create a function to generate the barchart
createTextBarchart <- function(topicNum) {
    topicDF <- data.frame(importance=
                exp(flightModel@beta[topicNum, ]),
            words=flightModel@terms)

  #sort / keep the top 10 rows (based on importance)
  topWordDF <- arrange(topicDF, desc(importance)) %>%
      slice(1:10)
```

```
    #display the most important words in this topic
    viz <- ggplot(topWordDF) +
      aes(x=reorder(words,-importance), y=importance) +
      geom_col() +
      xlab(paste0("Words in Topic", topicNum))+
      theme(axis.text.x =
                element_text(angle = 90, hjust = 1))
    retzurn(viz)
    }


vizTopic2 <- createTextBarchart(2)


vizTopic5 <- createTextBarchart(5)


library(gridExtra)
grid.arrange(vizTopic2, vizTopic5, nrow=2,
            top = "Exploring Important Topics")
```

The code first creates a function that given a topic number, creates a dataframe with the words and the importance of the word (for that topic). The function then sorts the words and keeps just the top 10 words (with respect to the importance of the word). Given these 10 words, we use ggplot to create the chart. We then use the function to create visualizations for Topic2 and Topic5. Finally, we use the gridExtra package to show both visualizations within one chart.

Now we can see that Topic2 seems to be about poor service and flight delays, whereas Topic5 seems to be focused on customers reporting good service and friendly staff.

We can explore the documents in Topic 2 by first creating a histogram with hist(flightModel@gamma[ ,2]). While we do not show the histogram (you can generate the histogram in R), it shows that about 40 documents where Topic 2 was predominant, while nearly all the 200+ remaining documents had no Topic 2: a nearly perfect analytical result. So, let's take a look at how many survey responses are in Topic 2 as well as looking at a representative survey response (the 10th response).

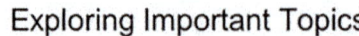

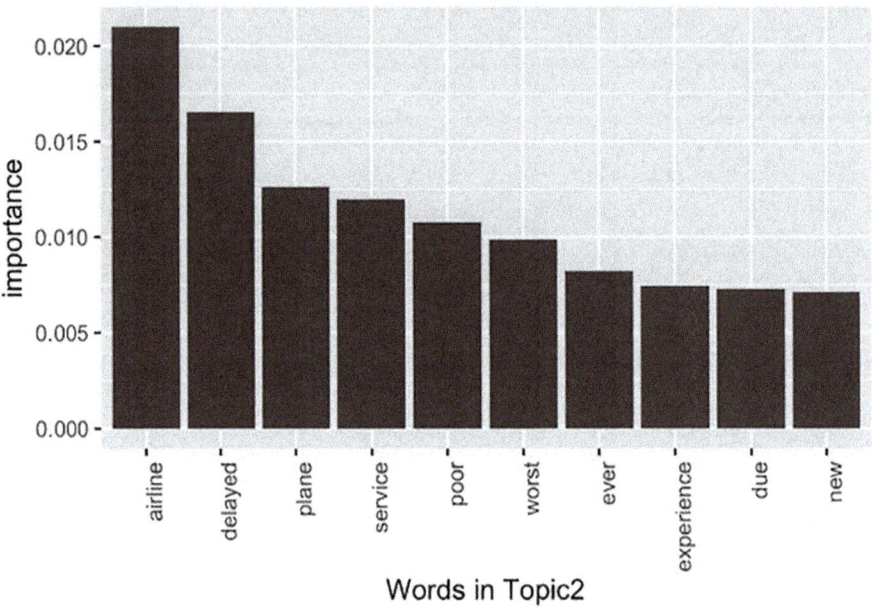

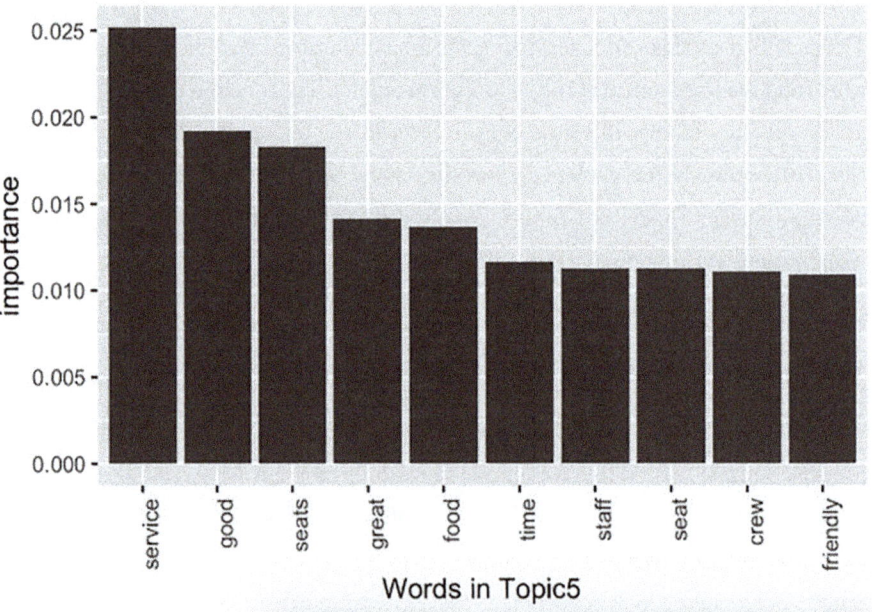

```
topic2Comments <- flightModel@gamma[ ,2] > .99
sum(topic2Comments)
[1] 40
```

```
flightCorpus[topic2Comments] [10]
   MQ_Chicago, IL_1
   "bad experience: i usually prefer another airline but
   is the only service provider to this location so they
   were my only option. my connection was delayed. and
   then delayed again before finally being told that it
   was cancelled after 2 hours due to lack of crew."
```

Wow, clearly this customer was upset about flight delays. Let's now explore topic5:

```
topic5Comments <- flightModel@gamma[ ,5] > .99
sum(topic5Comments)
[1] 41

flightCorpus[topic5Comments] [10]
   OU_Los Angeles, CA_18
   "flew many times.: taken many times before. this time
   it was just quick s but i've flown to other places
   as well. definitely a million times better than some
   other airlines. cleaner, more professional and just
   over all nicer planes. they have tv's at the back of
   every seat so you can see what you want."
```

Definitely a much happier customer!

These comments, and others like them, indicate customer experiences that could have a plausible effect on NPS. This example shows how it would be possible to use topic modeling as a way of directing our attention to customer comments that are indicative of problems with satisfaction. Note the brief document title shown just before each comment. This shows us the partner code, the destination city, and the day of the month. We can use this brief document title to refer to these comments in a presentation or search for the relevant row in the dataset.

We can also explore sentiment analysis with our survey responses. The following code first creates a dfm for each response (as opposed to before, where we created one dfm for all the responses). Then, using a for statement, it calculates the positive and negative counts (similar to how we previously did sentiment analysis in this chapter). So, although it looks like a lot of code, we are repeating techniques that we previously used in this chapter.

```r
#initial the positive and negative counts
textSurvey$freeTextNegCnt <- 0
 textSurvey$freeTextPosCnt <- 0

#loop through each free form text survey response
for (i in 1:nrow(textSurvey)) {
     print(i) #just for debugging

     # Convert the response to a corpus
     flightCorpus <- corpus(textSurvey$freeText[i],
        docnames = textSurvey$docTitle[i])

     # Convert the corpus to a document-feature matrix
     flightDFM <- dfm(flightCorpus,
                         remove_punct=TRUE, remove=myStop)

     #count negative words
     negDFM <- dfm_match(flightDFM, negWords)
     if(!is_empty(negDFM@x)) {
        negFreq <- textstat_frequency(negDFM)
        negFreq <- negFreq[negFreq$frequency>0, ]
        textSurvey$freeTextNegCnt[i] <-
                        sum(negFreq$frequency)

   }

     #count positive words
     posDFM <- dfm_match(flightDFM, posWords)
       if(!is_empty(posDFM@x)) {
          posFreq <- textstat_frequency(posDFM)
          posFreq <- posFreq[posFreq$frequency>0, ]
          textSurvey$freeTextPosCnt[i] <-
                           sum(posFreq$frequency)

     }
   }
```

Next, we calculate the sentiment for each response. We can then do a quick check to see whether the sentiment is different for detractors (as compared to others):

```
textSurvey$sentiment <-
  textSurvey$freeTextPosCnt - textSurvey$freeTextNegCnt
textSurvey$detractor <- as.factor(
                      textSurvey$Likelihood.to.recommend<7)

textSurvey %>%
      group_by(detractor) %>%
      summarize(mean(sentiment))
# A tibble: 2 x 2
    detractor `mean(sentiment)`
    <fct>              <dbl>
  1 FALSE               2.03
  2 TRUE               -1.41
```

Not surprisingly, detractors have a much more negative sentiment! Maybe we can use this information to build a model that can predict who will be a detractor, but we will leave that exploration as an exercise for the reader.

# Chapter Challenges

1. Read in a text file from the web using URLencode() and htmlTreeParse() as shown in this chapter. For example, you could read in the text of the speech by another suffragist, Elizabeth Cady Stanton, from this page: http://www.historyplace.com/speeches/stanton.htm. Note that if you encounter an error check that the URL has http and not https. Depending on the setup of your computer, htmlTreeParse() may not be able to read an https file.

2. Use the unlist() command as shown in this chapter to create a character vector from the html object you created. Review the elements of the character vector with head() and tail() to find out which elements contain the text of interest. For example, if you used the Elizabeth Cady Stanton file, only elements 6 through 14 contain her speech.

3. Use the corpus() command and the corpus_reshape() command from the quanteda package to organize your character vector by sentences. Report how many documents are in your corpus.

4. Convert your corpus into a DFM using the dfm() command from the quanteda package. Report how many terms and documents that the dfm contains. List the 10 most frequently occurring words using the textstat_frequency() command from the quanteda package.

5. Create a word cloud from your dfm using textplot_wordcloud() from the quanteda package.

6. Download a list of positive words from github by going to the following URL: https://gist.github.com/mkulakowski2/4289437. Click on the "Raw" button to get a text only version of the file that can be saved directly to your computer. Alternatively, you can download the zip file with positive and negative words from Dr. Bing Liu's website as shown earlier in the chapter. Use dfm_match() from the quanteda package to match your dfm from Problem 4 to the positive word list. Review and report on the result with textstat_frequency().

7. Convert your dfm to a topicmodels object and run the LDA() command (from the topicmodels package) on the result. Choose a four-topic model to start and feel free to change that number to improve your result. Plot the beta values (per word per topic probability) for the five most important words in each of the topics. Report a list of the words shown for any one topic and suggest what that topic might be about.

8. For the topic you described in Problem 8, find and show the text of the document that best represents that topic. Reinterpret your topic now that you have looked at a representative sentence.

# Sources

https://cran.r-project.org/web/packages/quanteda/quanteda.pdf
http://en.wikipedia.org/wiki/Document-term_matrix
http://en.wikipedia.org/wiki/Stop_words
http://en.wikipedia.org/wiki/Text_mining
http://www.jasondavies.com/wordcloud/

## R Functions Used in This Chapter

| | |
|---|---|
| as.character() | Coerces numeric or factor data into strings. |
| barplot() | Creates a simple graph where the height of a bar represents the values of a numeric variable. |
| cbind() | Binds columns together into one matrix. |
| colnames() | Reports or sets the names of columns in a data structure. |
| convert() | Changes a dfm object into an object suitable for use by a text analysis package other than quanteda. |
| corpus() | Creates a corpus of words (or bag of words). |
| corpus_reshape() | Reorganizes a corpus so that each sentence is a document. |
| data.frame() | Creates a dataframe from one or more other data structures. |
| dfm() | Creates a document-feature matrix. |
| dfm_match() | Creates a new dfm that matches an old dfm and a feature list. |
| filter() | Removes elements based on a criterion. |
| fromJSON() | Extracts data from a Java Script Object Notation (JSON) string and places it in an R variable. |
| ggplot() | Provides advanced graphics capabilities. |
| grid.arrange() | Organizes graphic objects. |
| group_by() | Organizes a dataset by groups. |
| head()/tail() | Shows the beginning or end of a vector or list. |
| hist() | Creates a histogram of a numeric variable. |
| htmlTreeParse() | Reads a web (HTML) web page. |
| names() | Extracts the name attribute from elements of a vector or list. |
| paste() | Concatenates elements into a string. |
| scan() | Reads a text file into a vector. |
| select() | Chooses a subset of variables. |
| set.seed() | Controls randomization. |
| sort() | Reorganizes a vector or list in alphabetic or numeric order. |
| sum() | Computes a sum of numeric values. |
| summarize() | Summarizes groups using mean() or another function. |
| textplot_wordcloud() | Creates a word cloud visualization. |
| textstat_frequency() | Shows the (sorted) frequency of occurrence of words in a dfm. |
| train() | Runs an analysis on a training dataset. |
| unlist() | Flattens a complex data structure into a list. |
| URLencode() | Processes a character string to ensure that it can be used as a URL. |
| xpathApply() | Parses an HTML file. |

This text includes access to datasets and select student resources. To learn more, visit sagepub.com

# 14

# SHINY® WEB APPS

## LEARNING OBJECTIVES

Build an interactive R application.

Deploy that application on the web.

Create a Shiny Web App within RStudio.

# CREATING WEB APPLICATIONS IN R

Sometimes, when we use R to solve a problem, it is helpful to actually create an interactive application, especially one that can be used from within a web browser. Fortunately, we can create interactive web applications in R using the Shiny package created by the folks at RStudio. Let's get started!

The first step, within RStudio, is to open a new file, but rather than an R source file, we want to click on the File menu, then New File, then create a "Shiny Web App . . ." When you see this dialog window, press the Create button.

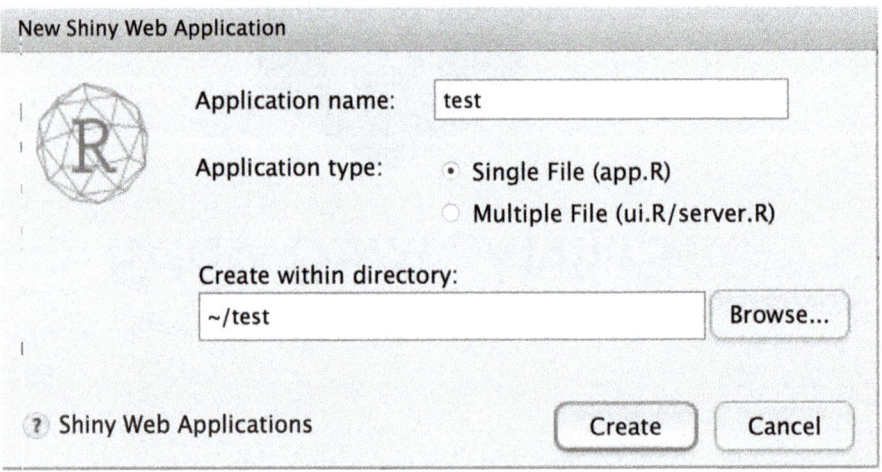

After creating a new app (select single file as the application type), an R file (app.r) will be created. This code will be visible as a tab in your R source RStudio window (i.e., in the upper-left-hand part of RStudio). Wow, a lot of code was created! Even though it looks complex, the Shiny package has done us a huge favor by creating a basic interactive application that already works. There are three main components of the code. The first is the user interface (ui) and the second is the code that does the R calculations (the server). The final, very small piece of code connects the ui and the server by calling shinyApp() to get the application started.

```r
library(shiny)
# Define UI for application that draws a histogram
ui <- fluidPage(
    # Application title
    titlePanel("Old Faithful Geyser Data"),
    # Sidebar with a slider input for number of bins
    sidebarLayout(
    sidebarPanel(
        sliderInput("bins",
                    "Number of bins:",
                    min = 1,
                    max = 50,
                    value = 30)
    ),
    # Show a plot of the generated distribution
    mainPanel(
        plotOutput("distPlot")
    )
  )
)
# Define server logic required to draw a histogram
server <- function(input, output) {
    output$distPlot <- renderPlot({
        # generate bins based on input$bins from ui.R
        x      <- faithful[, 2]
        bins   <- seq(min(x), max(x), length.out =
            input$bins + 1)
        # draw the histogram with the specified number
        # of bins
        hist(x, breaks = bins, col = 'darkgray', border
            = 'white')
    })
}
# Run the application
shinyApp(ui = ui, server = server)
```

As we can see, the first blue box contains the code that creates the user interface (this is the code that lets a user adjust the application, such as selecting an attribute). That code defines an object called "ui." The second blue box contains the code that runs on the server (think of this as the code that performs the functions needed to display the appropriate information on a web page). That code defines an object called "server." Finally, in the third blue box, one line of code gets the whole process started by identifying the ui and the server objects in a call to shinyApp(). It is important for this shinyApp() function call to be the last line in the file.

We can rename "ui" and "server" with any names we want to use. The call to shinyApp() lets R know the names of these two key components. For example, if we changed ui to myUI, the shinyApp would be changed to

```
shinyApp(ui = myUI, server = server)
```

Note that when you are examining or editing the Shiny application file in RStudio, the normal Run button does not appear. Instead, you can now see the "Run App" button. Since a working file of code has already been generated, you can press the Run App button and the code will run.

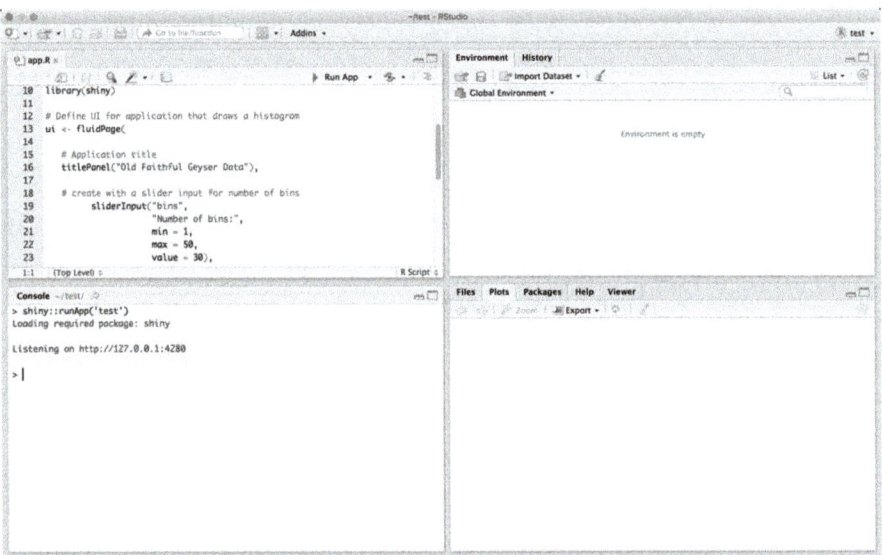

RStudio will launch the app in a new window, a window in your browser or in the viewer window (the lower-right window in RStudio). You can choose to have the app launch in

one of these by clicking on the small down arrow icon just to the right of the Run App button. RStudio will give you a pull-down menu to select how you want to display the app. Note that the output on the console says "Listening on http://127.0.0.1:4280." That shows that RStudio has invisibly created a temporary, local server on your computer. The "ui" portion of your app that appears in the web page will connect with this temporary server to do all of the behind-the-scenes work to show the histogram.

With our application running (e.g., in your browser or in your viewer window), we can change the number of bins used to create a histogram, and then the picture adjusts. One important note is that while this app is running in your web browser, it is not yet a "public" web application that other people can use (we will get to that later). For now, it is an interactive application, running locally on your machine.

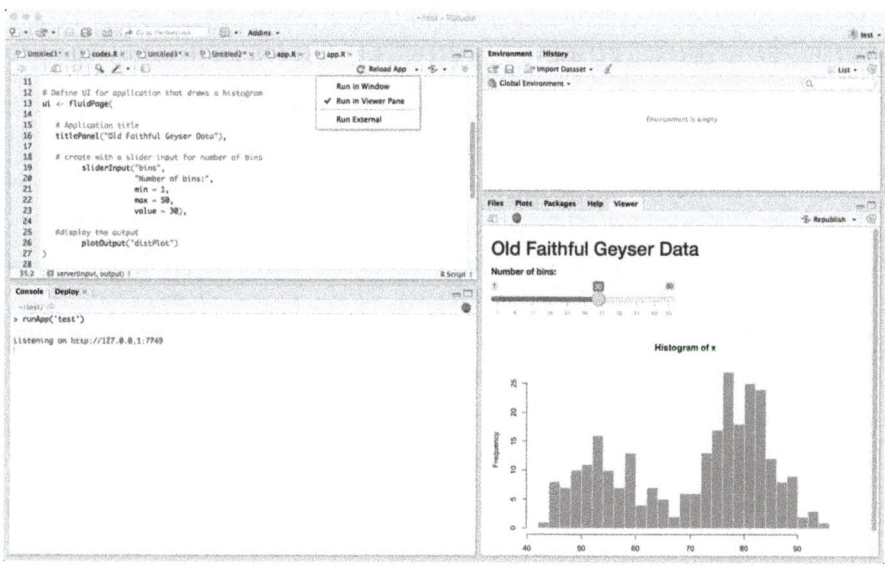

Occasionally, after closing the application window (e.g., the window tab in a web browser where the R code was running), RStudio might not terminate the server application. So, if you hit enter in the console of RStudio, you might not see the > prompt. If this is the case, then it is likely the case that the temporary R server is still running. If this happens, just click the Stop button, in the middle of the RStudio screen (in the upper-right part of the console window). This will cause RStudio to shut down the server and return control to the R console command prompt.

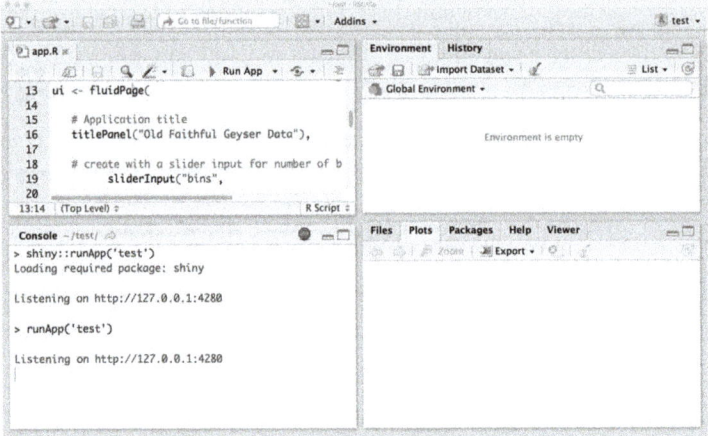

Now that we got the code to run and then stop, let's explore the code in more detail. Make sure to follow along by looking at app.R in your RStudio code window as you read the following explanations. First, within the ui, which is defined by a function called fluidPage(), we can see there are two areas defined: titlePanel(), which is just a space to put the title of the app, and sidebarLayout(), which is the space where all the activity happens. Within sidebarLayout, there is sidebarPanel(), which contains one interactive control called sliderInput(). This control defines the number of bins to be used. The sidebarLayout() also contains mainPanel() where we plot (draw) the histogram.

Next, move on to the block of code that begins with "server." Note that the function that we are defining for "server" has two arguments: input and output. In the ui, when we called sliderInput, we defined a data slot called "bins." As a result, the server now can access input$bins, to get the information from the slider. The server uses that value to help define the number of bins for the histogram in this line of code:

```
bins <- seq(min(x), max(x), length.out = input$bins + 1)
```

Next, looking back at the ui, when we called plotOutput() we specified the name "disPlot." As a result, the server code can now access a data object called output$distPlot. This data object stores the rendering of the histogram so that it can be shown within the web page. Let's make a couple of small changes to the server code to prove to ourselves how things work:

```
# Define server logic required to draw a histogram
server <- function(input, output) {
```

```
output$distPlot <- renderPlot({
  # generate bins based on input$bins from ui.R
  x     <- faithful[, 2]
  # draw histogram with the specified bins
  hist(x, breaks = input$bins, col = 'black',
       border = 'white')
  })
}
```

After you make this change, rerun the app to make sure everything works and see if you can spot any differences in the appearance of the page.

# DEPLOYING THE APPLICATION

Although this Shiny app runs within RStudio, and can be run in a local web browser, it is still not a web application. We still have to deploy our application to a public server if we want other people to use it. There are many ways to deploy the app, and one of the easiest is to use the hosting service available at http://www.shinyapps.io/, which is free for testing small applications.

What makes shinyapps.io so nice is that it is integrated with RStudio. In fact, we have already done almost all the work required to deploy a Shiny app. To get our interactive web page to work, we first need to create an account at shinyapps.io, and then follow instructions in RStudio, using the following screens:

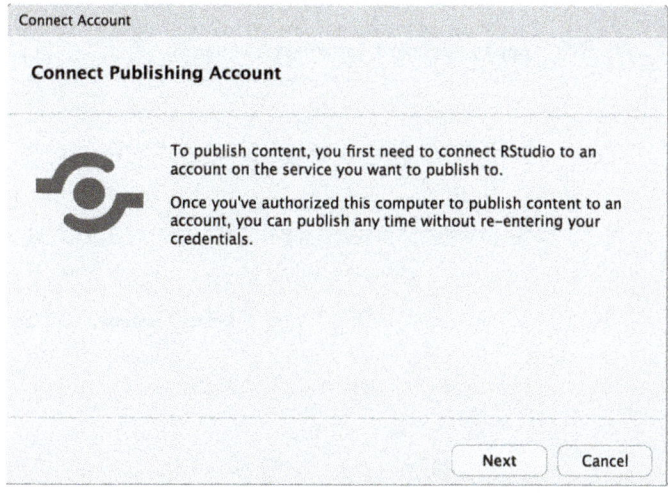

Typically, we want to select the ShinyApps.io service (i.e., the first choice shown below):

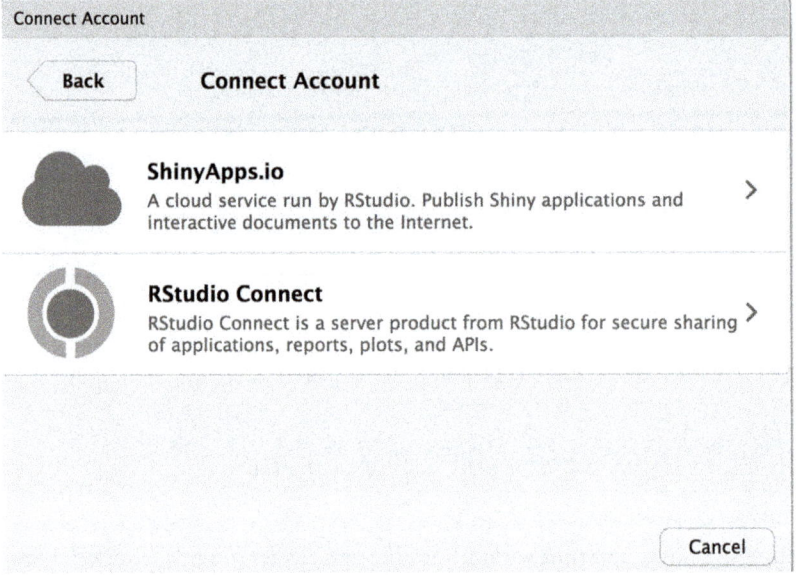

Next, we need some information from the shinyApps web site (via the account that you created).

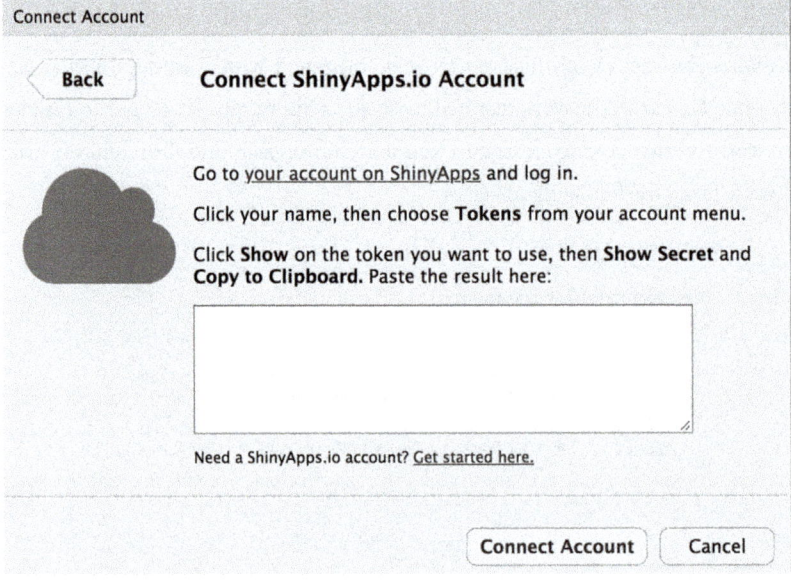

That's all the configuration that is required, and you only need to go through that process once. If you need more help configuring RStudio, this process is explained at http://shiny.rstudio.com/articles/shinyapps.html, which has a small shinyapps tutorial available. Once these steps are completed in RStudio, we can publish the application (instead of Run App). The Publish Application icon appears next to Run App, and is circled in the image below.

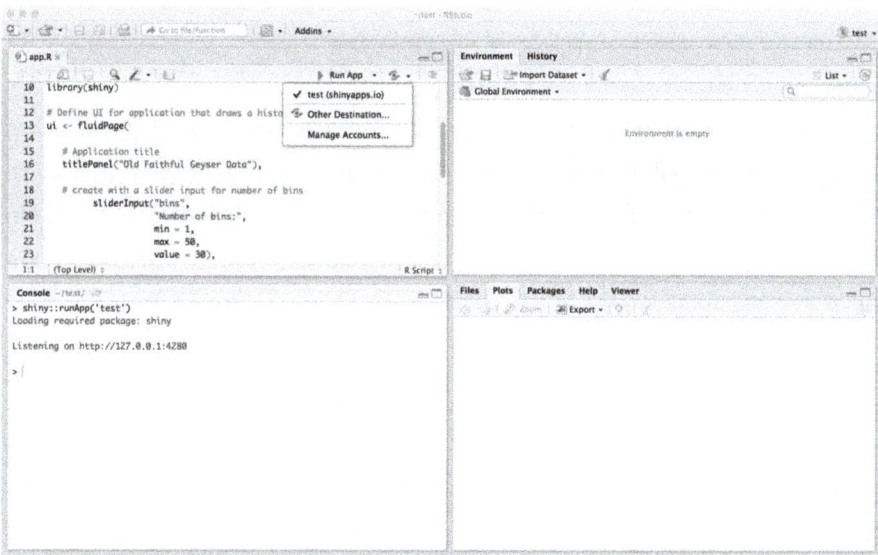

When we use Publish Application, RStudio will create a new tab in the lower-left window. Now, in addition to the console, there will be a Deploy tab. After publishing, you should see something similar to the following (in the deploy window):

Preparing to deploy application . . . DONE

Uploading bundle for application: 146349 . . . DONE

Deploying bundle: 655321 for application: 146349 . . .

Waiting for task: 317406782

building: Parsing manifest

building: Installing packages

building: Installing files

building: Pushing image: 645493

deploying: Starting instances

rollforward: Activating new instances

success: Stopping old instances

Application successfully deployed to https://xxx.shinyapps.io/test/

Deployment completed: https://xxx.shinyapps.io/test/

As you can see, we just deployed a public test of a simple R application. Note that when you deploy, the xxx will be replaced with your account. That's it! We now have a real web-based application. Of course, there are many ways to configure/define input within Shiny—a slider is just one possibility. Our small application was just a way to test how to deploy an application.

Let's build a slightly more-advanced application, using the map visualizations that we previously created. Within this new application, we will use a different input method to build an application that will allow the user to define how to color-code our map. For this input, we will have a predefined list of possible choices, so a choice menu makes the most sense. To do this, we need to create a new shiny app (from the File, New File, menu in RStudio).

Once we have this new application, the ui code is similar to our initial example, but rather than a sliderInput input, we have a selectInput (which will create a choice menu). When we create a choice menu, for each menu choice we define two items. The first item is what is shown to the user and can be any text string. The second item is the variable name we want to use in our R code. In this example, the choice menu is letting the user select a column in our dataframe, so the different choices have the appropriate column name as the second item for each choice selection.

The code to define the server function is somewhat more complicated, but is similar to the code that we have previously created to display the map. In fact, the only real difference is the use of input$variable to specify the column of data that we want to drive the color the map. Where previously we had coded that to be a specific column, now the user interface allows us to change columns, based on what the user selects. You may notice that we also use the exact same readCensus function. So, while this is a lot of code, almost all of it should look familiar.

```
library(shiny)
library(ggmap)
library(ggplot2)
ui <- fluidPage(
  selectInput("variable", "Variable:",
                c("july population" = "july11pop",
                  "region of country" = "region",
                  "change in population" = "popChange",
                  "Percent change in population" =
                  "percentChange")),
  plotOutput("plot")
)
server <- function(input, output) {
    dfStates <- readCensus()
    dfStates <- dfStates[dfStates$stateName !=
                    "District of Columbia",]
    dfStates$region <- state.region
    dfStates$stateName <-
              tolower(dfStates$stateName)
    dfStates$popChange <- dfStates$july11pop -
                                dfStates$july10pop
    dfStates$percentChange <-
        dfStates$popChange/dfStates$july10pop * 100
    us <- map_data("state")
    output$plot <- renderPlot(
      ggplot(dfStates, aes(map_id = state)) +
        geom_map(map = us,
            aes(fill=dfStates[,input$variable])) +
        expand_limits(x = us$long, y = us$lat) +
        coord_map() + ggtitle("state population") +
        guides(fill=guide_legend(title=input$variable))
  )
}
  # Numberize() - Gets rid of commas and other junk and
  # converts to numbers
  # Assumes that the inputVector is a list of data that
```

```r
  # can be treated as character strings
  Numberize <- function(inputVector)
  {
    # Get rid of commas and spaces
    inputVector<-str_replace_all(inputVector, "[,]","")
    #convert to a number and then return that number
    return(as.numeric(inputVector))
  }
#read in the census data set. This function
#is the same as the one previously defined
readCensus <- function() {
  u1 <- "http://www2.census.gov/programs-surveys/"
  u2 <- "popest/tables/2010-2011/state/totals/"
  u3 <- "nst-est2011-01.csv"
  urlToRead <- paste0(u1, u2, u3)
  #do the basic cleanup
  testFrame <- read.csv(url(urlToRead))
  testFrame<-testFrame[-1:-8,]
  testFrame<-testFrame[,1:5]
  testFrame$stateName <- testFrame[,1]
  testFrame<-testFrame[,-1]
  testFrame<-testFrame[-52:-58,]
  #remove the 'dot' from the state name
  testFrame$stateName <- gsub("\.","",
         testFrame$stateName)
  #convert columns to numbers and rename columns
  testFrame$april10census <-Numberize(testFrame$X)
  testFrame$april10base <-Numberize(testFrame$X.1)
  testFrame$july10pop <-Numberize(testFrame$X.2)
  testFrame$july11pop <-Numberize(testFrame$X.3)
  testFrame <- testFrame[,-1:-4]
  #remove the old rownames, which are now confusing
  rownames(testFrame) <- NULL
  return(testFrame)
}
```

```
# Run the application
shinyApp(ui = ui, server = server)
```

If you encounter an error when trying to execute the application, the shinyApp might generate a "Disconnected from Server" error (and then not show the web page). When this happens, or if you are just curious about how the app is doing, one trick is to look at the output log by typing the showLogs command within the R console:

```
rsconnect::showLogs('~/ShinyCensus/app.R')
```

You can see the double colons (::) between the rsconnect and the showLogs. This full line makes sure we are using the rsconnect's showLogs function. Since there might be other packages that use a showLogs function, explicitly telling R we want to use the function from the rsconnect package makes sure we get the function we wanted.

To recap, in this chapter we explored how to create web-based applications, written in R, that anyone can see with a web browser. These applications allow interactive R visualizations.

# CASE STUDY: VISUALIZING NPS BY KEY ATTRIBUTES

```
Case Key Points:
- Create a shiny application.
- Let the user select an attribute of interest.
- Visualize the attribute by generating a barchart of NPS
  across the values of the selected attribute.
- Also show the number of surveys represented by each bar.
```

The shinyApp below leverages the code and analysis that we previously used within our case analysis. Specifically, we read in the JSON survey, and then generate a bar plot of NPS, based on an attribute defined by the user. We also color encode the bars with the number of surveys with each of the defined attribute values.

```r
#
# This is a Shiny web application. You can run the
# application by clicking the 'Run App' button above.
#
# Find out more about building applications with Shiny
# here: http://shiny.rstudio.com/
#
library(shiny)
library(tidyverse)
library(ggplot2)
ui <- fluidPage(
    selectInput("attribute", "Attribute:",
            c("Age" = "roundedAge",
              "Origin State" = "Origin.State",
              "Destination State" = "Destination.State",
              "Partner Name" = "Partner.Name",
              "Arrive Delay" = "roundedArrivalDelay",
              "Big Arrival Delay" = "Big.Arrival.Delay",
              "Class of Travel" = "Class",
              "Type of Travel" = "Type.of.Travel",
              "Loyalty" = "roundedLoyalty",
              "Price Sensitivity" = "Price.Sensitivity",
              "Airline Status" = "Airline.Status",
              "Shopping Amount at Airport" =
                    "roundedShopping.Amount.at.Airport",
              "Eating and Drinking at Airport" =
                    "roundedEating.and.Drinking.at.Airport"
            )),
    plotOutput("plot")
)
# CalcNPS function - calculate a net promoter score
# ltr - a vector of likelihood-to-recommend values
# neutral - the range, below which someone
# is considered a detractor and above which
# some is consider a promoter (default is 7 to 8)
CalcNPS <- function(ltr, neutral=c(7,8)) {
    # create a new vector with just the promoters
    #  then calculate the length of the promoters vector
    promoters <- ltr[ltr > max(neutral)]
```

```r
    numPromoters <- length(promoters)
    # calculate the number of detractors
    detractorsTrueFalse <- ltr < min(neutral)
    numDetractors <- sum(detractorsTrueFalse)
    # calculate NPS, based on the length of ltr
    #   and the number of promoters and detractors
    total <- length(ltr)
    nps <- (numPromoters/total -
                numDetractors/total)*100
    #return the NPS value
    return(nps)
}
#generate a barchart, with fill color representing the
number of surveys
#and the user defining the attribute to be charted
server <- function(input, output) {
    survey <- readSurveyData()
    output$plot <- renderPlot(
        survey %>%
            group_by_at(input$attribute) %>%
            summarize(
                nps = CalcNPS(Likelihood.to.recommend),
                numSurveys = n()) %>%
            ggplot() +
            aes_string(x=input$attribute) +
            aes(y=nps, fill=numSurveys) +
            geom_col() +
            theme(text = element_text(size=16),
                axis.text.x = element_text(angle = 90,
                                            hjust = 1))
    )
}
#read in the json survey, similar to other chapters
readSurveyData <- function() {
    library(jsonlite)
    mydata.list <- fromJSON("completeSurvey.json")
    surveyWithNA <- data.frame(mydata.list)
    #Remove rows with'Likelihood.to.recommend' == NA
    survey <- surveyWithNA %>%
```

```
          filter(!is.na(Likelihood.to.recommend))
    #Was the arrival delayed a lot
    survey$Big.Arrival.Delay <-
        survey$Arrival.Delay.in.Minutes > 5
    survey$roundedAge <- round(survey$Age, -1)
    roundedDelay <- survey$Arrival.Delay.in.Minutes
    roundedDelay [roundedDelay > 300] <- 300
    survey$roundedArrivalDelay <- round(roundedDelay, -1)
    survey$roundedLoyalty <- round(survey$Loyalty, 1)
    survey$roundedShopping.Amount.at.Airport <-
        round(survey$Shopping.Amount.at.Airport, -1)
    survey$roundedEating.and.Drinking.at.Airport <-
        round(survey$Eating.and.Drinking.at.Airport, -1)
    return(survey)
}
# Run the application
shinyApp(ui = ui, server = server)
```

This code can be run at https://saltz.shinyapps.io/CaseStudyApp/, and an example screenshot is shown below. We can see that West Airways has the highest NPS value (out of any of the partner airlines), but there are not that many surveys from West Airways (either because West Airways flies fewer flights for Southeast, or due to some issue with respect to how the surveys were distributed).

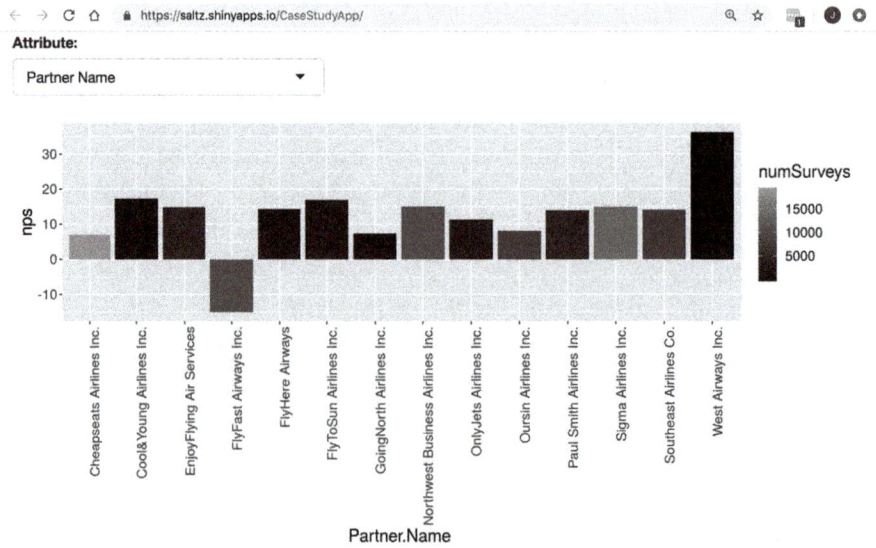

## Chapter Challenges

1.  Create a new Shiny app (this will be the default app that runs a histogram on the faithful built in dataset). Modify the server portion of the app so that it displays the first column from mtcars instead of the second column from faithful. Run the app and the number of bins to a value that causes no gaps in the display of histogram bars. Save a screenshot of the app with this setting.

2.  Change the range of the slider in the ui portion of the app so that the range goes from 1 to 12 instead of 1 to 50. Make sure to change the starting value from 30 to a number between 1 and 12. Run the app and set the number of bins to the maximum value on the slider. Save a screenshot of the app with this setting.

3.  Modify the server portion of the app so that it displays blue histogram bars with red borders. Run the app and save a screenshot with these new colors.

4.  Add a control to the sidebarPanel() area of the ui to let the user choose which variable should be used in the histogram. Allow five choices—mpg, hp, drat, wt, and qsec—in the selectInput() control. Run the app and save a screenshot that shows the new control with hp selected.

5.  Create a free account for yourself at shinyapps.io and deploy the modified app that you created in items one through four above. Run your app to test it and save the URL that other users will need to use your app.

6.  Create a scatterplot interactive application. In this application, use the mtcars built-in dataset, and let the user determine the choice of variables for the X-axis and the Y-axis. To do this, you will need multiple-choice menus, one for each selection the user needs to make.

## Sources

http://shiny.rstudio.com/articles/shinyapps.html
http://www.shinyapps.io/

## R Functions Used in This Chapter

| | |
|---|---|
| setAccountInfo() | Enables the creation of web-based hosted applications. |
| shinyApp() | Runs the shiny application, defining the ui and the server. |
| Run App | Is a new way to run an application, not just R code. |

This text includes access to datasets and select student resources. To learn more, visit sagepub.com

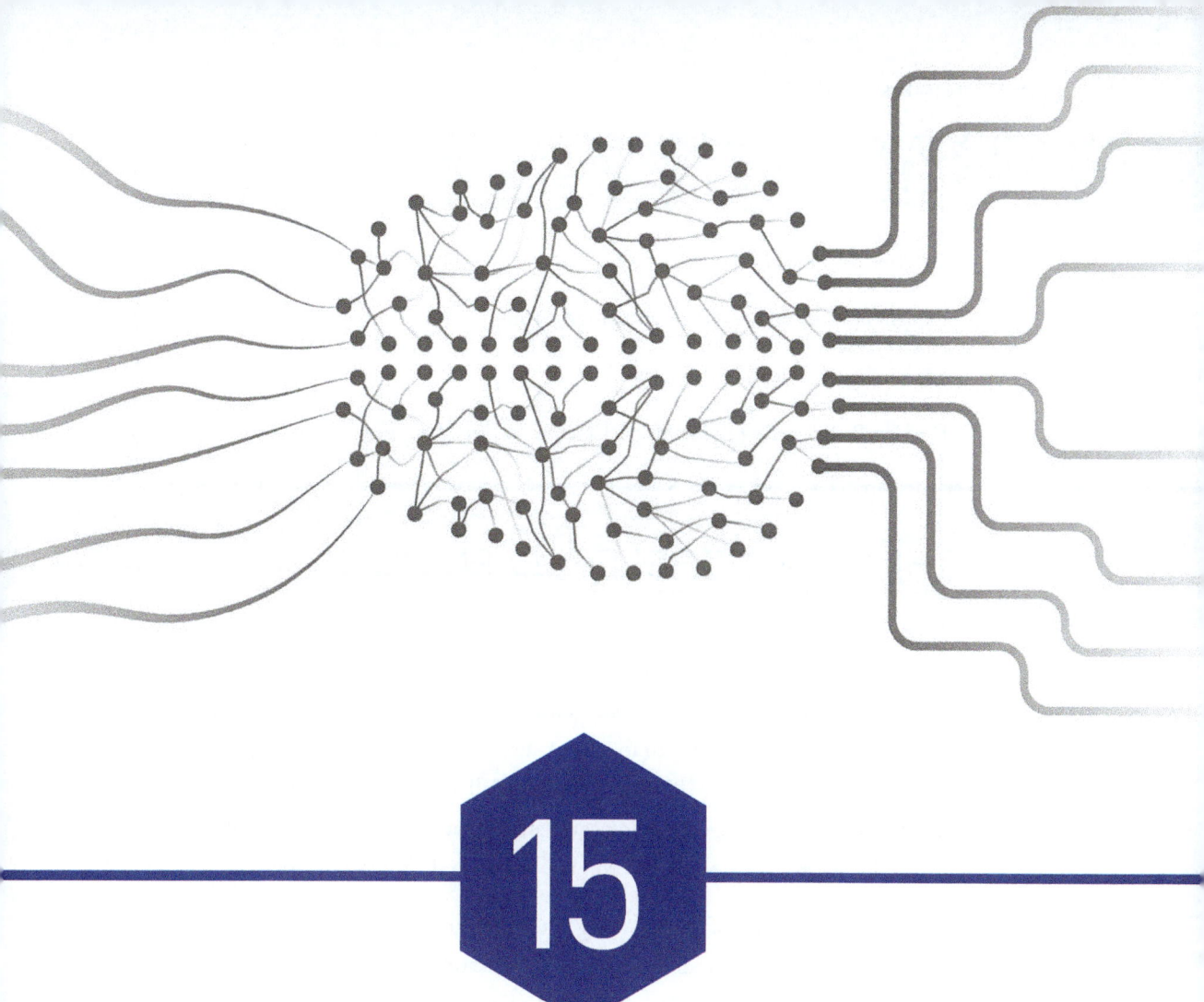

# 15

# TIME FOR A DEEP DIVE

## LEARNING OBJECTIVES

Describe the impact deep learning has had on the field of machine learning.

Explain how neural networks conceptually work.

Explain key deep learning concepts.

Develop R code, using the Keras package, to do Deep Learning.

# THE IMPACT OF DEEP LEARNING

Deep learning has had, and probably will continue to have, a huge impact on our lives. For example, it is the key machine learning technique that has enabled the development of self-driving cars! Although the basic ideas that underpin deep learning date back to the 1960s, the field really started to take off around 1999, when researchers began using graphics processing units (GPUs), which are specialized parts of a computer, to run some of the complex and time-consuming calculations that deep learning algorithms require (we explore deep learning in R, but will not be using GPUs, just our laptops).

To illustrate the power of deep learning, let's examine its impact on speech recognition. Before deep learning came along, computer applications could only achieve about 80% accuracy for speech recognition. This level of accuracy was far below what a human listener could do, which is around 95% accuracy. As shown in the figure below, which is our estimation of how the industry has evolved, this level of accuracy did not materially change until around 2013, when deep learning was first used to address speech recognition. Accuracy then rapidly improved to the point that, by 2017, deep learning algorithms could achieve essentially the same level of accuracy as humans. It is this deep learning technique that has enabled speech recognition to be used in apps such as Siri and Alexa.

Image recognition is another domain that has demonstrated the power of deep learning. Prior to 2012, having a computer system recognize a dog or a cat in a digital image was both difficult and error prone. However, similar to the speech recognition example, there was a rapid decrease in the error rates for identifying what was in the image starting around 2012, when deep learning started to be used for image recognition. As our ability

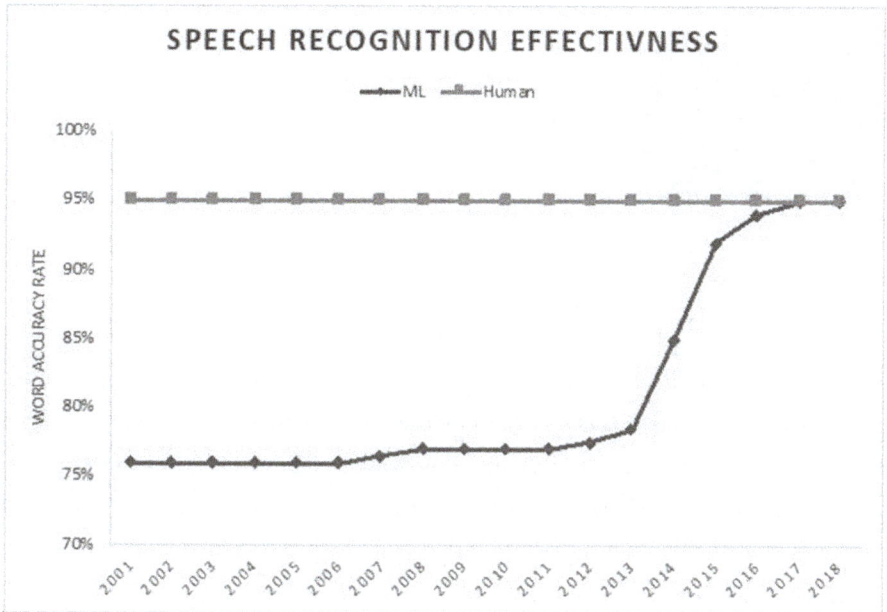

to use deep learning improved, deep learning systems have now become better than humans at identifying an object in an image.

# DEEP LEARNING IS SUPERVISED LEARNING

In Chapter 10 we discussed linear modeling, a supervised regression technique that uses input variables to predict a metric output variable. For example, we can use the weight of a vehicle and its engine horsepower to predict its fuel economy. After that, we examined classification supervised machine learning techniques, which can use input variables to predict a categorical outcome, such as whether a bank customer will default on a loan. Deep learning is a supervised learning technique that can address both prediction and classification problems.

To illustrate deep learning with a standard classification problem, let's walk through an example of recognizing numeric digits from digital images. We can use supervised machine learning (with deep learning or another algorithm) to examine thousands of examples of images that contain a digit. As the figure below shows, a rectangular grid of black and white pixels serves as the input data. The input is processed through the model, such as a deep learning model, and the results of the model indicate which numeric digit is most likely.

Image

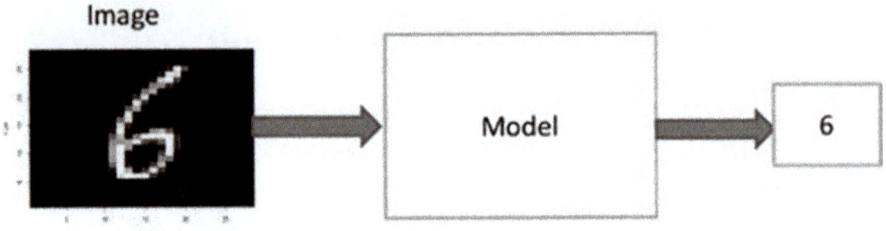

# HOW DOES DEEP LEARNING WORK?

Deep learning works by creating a network of artificial "neurons." Each artificial neuron can receive one or more inputs and can produce one or more outputs in response. The most interesting aspect of an artificial neural network is that each neuron can learn from training examples. As each neuron learns, the pattern of outputs it produces in response to a set of inputs will change to become more accurate. A system with only one neuron is pretty boring—in fact, it is a little bit like a simple linear regression prediction model. The power of deep learning comes from connecting neurons together. A group of neurons is called a "layer" and a deep learning algorithm generally has input layers, hidden layers, and output layers. When a deep learning model has one or more hidden layers, it begins to have the potential to tackle some very challenging prediction or classification problems.

To understand deep learning, we first need to explore the basic building block of a deep learning network—the neuron. Each neuron describes a calculation process with one or more input connections, a weight (or importance value) for each input, a transfer (or activation) function that combines the inputs in some way, and an output. Let's create a simple one-neuron model that predicts which car to buy. The neuron has three inputs (factors) that will be used to determine the output of the neuron. The neuron will produce an output score combining the three inputs. The table below lists the three factors (inputs) to our neuron, and the weight (importance) of each factor on a scale of one to five (i.e., how the different factors combine).

| Factor | Factor Description | Factor Weight |
|---|---|---|
| X1 | Is the miles per gallon (mpg) above 30 mpg? | W1 = 3 (high mpg is important) |
| X2 | Is the horsepower above 200 hp? | W2 = 2 (high horsepower is slightly important) |
| X3 | Is the transmission type auto? | W3 = 5 (an automatic transmission is very important) |

So, for example, a car with 32 mpg (which means that X1 = 1), 190 hp (which means that X2 = 0), and an automatic transmission (which means that X3 = 1), will create a sum of 8 (X1×W1 + X2×W2 + X3×W3 = 1×3 + 0×2 + 1×5 = 8). The figure below shows an example of a simple Activation Function for a neuron that outputs the value of 1 if the sum of the weighted inputs is greater than or equal to 5, or the value of 0 if the sum is less than 5. If the output of the neuron equals 1, then it would be a good idea to buy the car!

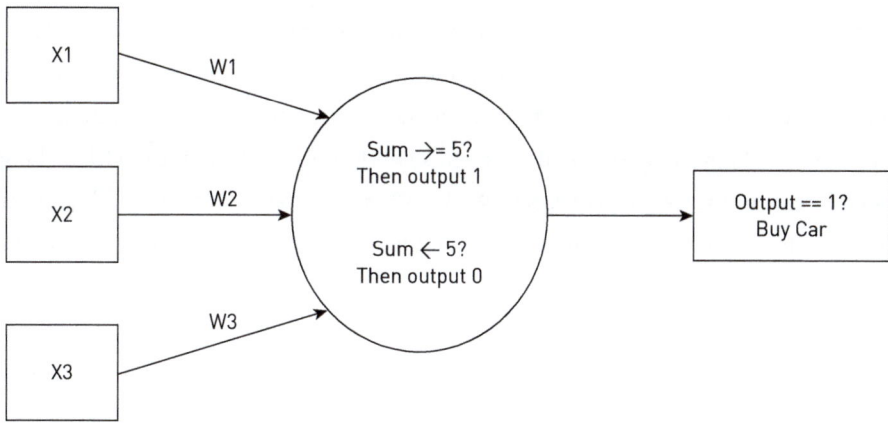

While this example had the weights defined, when doing supervised learning, the weights can be calculated by exploring many existing examples (e.g., which cars were bought or not bought).

A system with just one neuron is pretty limited in what it can accomplish, but as we add more neurons to a layer, we can get an improvement in predictive capability. However, neural networks with just one layer can only handle the simplest of regression and classification problems—basically just those situations where the outputs are a linear function of the inputs. In contrast, a *multi-layer* network can be used to solve much more difficult prediction problems. In this situation, the networks can learn complex, non-linear interconnections among the inputs that lead to different decisions about the output. For example, let's say we were trying to use deep learning to identify pictures of dogs. Perhaps we could address that problem with one hidden layer. The algorithm might look for pointy ears, fur, four paws, and a tail. This simple, one-layer model might make a mistake, however, when presented with a picture of a large cat, which also has pointy ears, fur, four paws, and a tail. In order to accurately differentiate between a small dog and a large cat, we could add more layers of neurons to our deep learning model.

We have examined one neuron and imagined several neurons working together in a layer, but how does the training process actually change the weights for each neuron? The answer is a procedure known as *back-propagation*. Back-propagation tunes the weights of a neural net, based on the errors that occur in the previous *epoch* of the training. An epoch is just a fancy name for one complete pass through the training process. The training process contains dozens, hundreds, or even more epochs to complete the training. The reason the tuning activity is called back-propagation is that changing the weights actually begins by comparing the results from the final layer (generally the output layer) to the true values that appear in the training data. After fixing up the weights for the output layer, we move to working on the hidden layer that precedes the output layer. After that we keep going backwards through all of the other layers in the model, making adjustments to the weights as needed. We keep running epochs until we reach a preset criterion for the amount of error of prediction that the deep learning model still contains. As with all supervised machine learning models, we must be careful not to "overfit" or we will create a predictive model that works fine with the training data, but that will not generalize to a novel set of data. You may remember from Chapters 10 and 11 that we can hold out some testing data or use a k-fold cross-validation strategy to prevent overfitting.

## DEEP LEARNING IN R—AN EXAMPLE

Training a deep learning network to identify an object in an image can take a very long time because the training model needs to process millions of images that are paired with correct identifications. Part of the reason that deep learning networks have become more practical is the decreasing cost of specialized processing chips known as graphics processing units (GPUs). However, actually using GPUs to create a deep learning model is more than we want to tackle right now. So, we can create and use a simpler deep learning model that works on most standard commercial laptops.

To start, let's use the "keras" R package. The word *keras* is Greek for "horn" and is also a literary reference about announcing the future—a very apt idea for a powerful predictive method. The keras R package is actually an interface to code that runs in Python. Your computer will need to have a working Python environment for the following code to work. Many systems have one by default. But, the code in this chapter might not run without installing some additional software (see the chapter challenges, at the end of this chapter, for an explanation on the required software). Furthermore, the code might require more memory than is provided on your laptop. In any event, if you are having trouble running the code in this chapter, you can run the code using a web-based R environment (for example, see: https://www.kaggle.com/jsaltz/kernel-intro-mnist).

After running install.packages() and library() on the keras package, we also use a special install_keras() command to configure the Python environment:

```
# Keras provides an R interface
# to the Python deep learning package Keras
install.packages("keras")


# Keras uses Tensorflow at backend to install
# both Keras and Tensorflow run following the
# following commands.
library(keras)
install_keras()
```

Let's start with a simple example, where we have three columns of input data, and one column of output data. The dataset has 10,000 observations in total, and the outcome variable, Y, is a binary class variable (values of 0 or 1) and nearly balanced between classes.

```
library(tidyverse)
library(caret)

df <- read_csv("testData.csv")
head(df, 5)
# A tibble: 5 x 4
    X1     X2     X3     Y
  <dbl>  <dbl>  <dbl>  <dbl>
1 0.308  0.665  0.882    1
2 0.258  0.0175 0.318    0
3 0.552  0.409  0.454    0
4 0.056  0.416  0.380    0
5 0.469  0.657  0.390    1
```

Examine the first few rows of the dataframe. Can you guess what pattern of X values tends to lead to Y==1 and what pattern leads to Y==0? In trying to figure out the pattern, many people take a guess by looking at the first few rows, and then update their ideas as they look at more rows. For example, maybe the first guess would be that one or more values (X1, X2, or X3) must be above 0.6. This rule seems to work for the first five rows. If we looked beyond the first five rows, we might find exceptions to this rule and have to refine our logic. This guessing and refining process is somewhat analogous to the back-propagation learning procedure that is used to create a deep learning network. Initial weights for the X variables are guessed at the start, and then refined after each epoch.

Our first next step is to create a test and train dataset, using the Caret package, just as we did earlier in the book when we ran a support vector machine (SVM) model.

```
#create test and train datasets
trainList <-
        createDataPartition(y=df$Y, p=.80, list=FALSE)

trainData <- df[trainList,]
testData <- df[-trainList,]
```

Now we can begin to define our model. Keras supports two major types of models: sequential and functional. In sequential models, each layer of neurons is connected only to the next layer, starting with the input layer, moving through hidden layers, and ending with the output layer. In contrast, a functional model can be much more complex: for example, a hidden layer could connect with many other hidden layers, rather than just the next one in sequence. For this model, we will use the simpler sequential method, so we start with a call to keras_model_sequential() to define the input layer and one output layer. The input layer takes three inputs (input_shape=3), has 64 nodes (neurons), and uses an activation function called "relu." Relu is an abbreviation for "rectified linear unit" and it produces an output value of zero if the value of the node was negative or the actual value of the node if that value is positive. The input shape is 3 because there are three input variables (X1, X2, X3). The output layer has one node for the predicted Y value and the activation function is now "sigmoid," an activation function that helps to produce a binary choice (i.e., 0 or 1).

```
# input_shape is the number of X inputs (we have 3 inputs)
# units is the number of neurons
# ReLU (rectified linear unit) is the typical activation
# function for intermediate layers,
# linear (identity) for positive values, and zero for
  negative
# sigmoid is used in the final layer for binary analysis
model = keras_model_sequential() %>%
    layer_dense(input_shape=3, units=64, activation="relu") %>%
    layer_dense(units=1, activation = "sigmoid")
```

Next, we compile the model. The loss= parameter determines the mathematical function that will be used to measure error. In this case, we have chosen an option called "binary_crossentropy," which is particularly suitable to a two-class (i.e., 0 or 1) output value. The keras model also needs our choice of a method of making the training process more efficient—an "optimizer." In this case we use optimizer_rmsprop(), a choice that works well when keras divides the training data into many separate batches (see below). Finally, we tell keras what metric to use to judge the goodness of a model: accuracy refers to the overall number of correct classifications divided by the total number of observations in the data. There is one unusual aspect of the call shown below to the compile() function: no object is returned from this function. Instead, we have supplied "model" as the first argument and keras modifies this object directly by adding the specifications we have described.

```
# loss == how to measure error.
#     Use categorical crossentropy in classification problems
#                where only one result can be correct.
# optimizer == how to optimize during iterations
#       optimizer_rmsprop is a good default
# metrics == List of metrics to be evaluated by the model
#       often use metrics='accuracy'
compile (model,
    loss = "binary_crossentropy",
    optimizer = optimizer_rmsprop(),
    metrics = "accuracy")
```

Next, we create a separate matrix of input values that only contains the X1, X2, and X3 columns from the trainData dataframe. There are three different ways to get this matrix, as shown below:

```
#pull the columns from the dataframe
#these are all functionally equivalent
x_data <- as.matrix(trainData[,1:3])
x_data <- as.matrix(trainData[c('X1', 'X2', 'X3')])
x_data <- trainData %>% select (c(X1, X2, X3)) %>% as.matrix()
```

Now that we have a compiled model, and the appropriate columns in a matrix, the last step is to actually fit the model to the training data. One notable aspect of the call to the fit() function is that we have specified a division of the training data. Recall that in the preceding code, we used the createDataPartition() function from the caret package to create separate trainSet and testSet dataframes. The call to fit() below performs another split of the training data—holding 20% of it aside for cross validation—as a strategy to avoid overfitting. We have also specified that we want 20 epochs, that is, 20 complete passes through the training process. Finally, we have asked keras to divide the data into batches of 128 observations. Each batch is presented to the training process as a complete "mini" dataset. The process of updating the weights is not undertaken until all of these mini datasets have been presented to the model within a given epoch.

```
# epochs: # times that the learning algorithm will work
#                  through the entire training dataset.
# batch_size: the number of samples to work through before
#                  updating the internal model parameters.
#                  --> 64, 128, 256 are typical default numbers
# validation_split: The % to validate the model
#                  (the rest is to train the model)
history = fit(model,
              x_data,
              trainData$Y,
              epochs = 20,
              batch_size = 128,
              validation_split = 0.2)
```

The two graphs below, which RStudio generates from the code above, visualizes the results of this training process. Notice that each graph shows 20 steps—one for each epoch. The top graph shows gradual decreases in the loss function (binary crossentropy) while the bottom graph shows increases in overall accuracy.

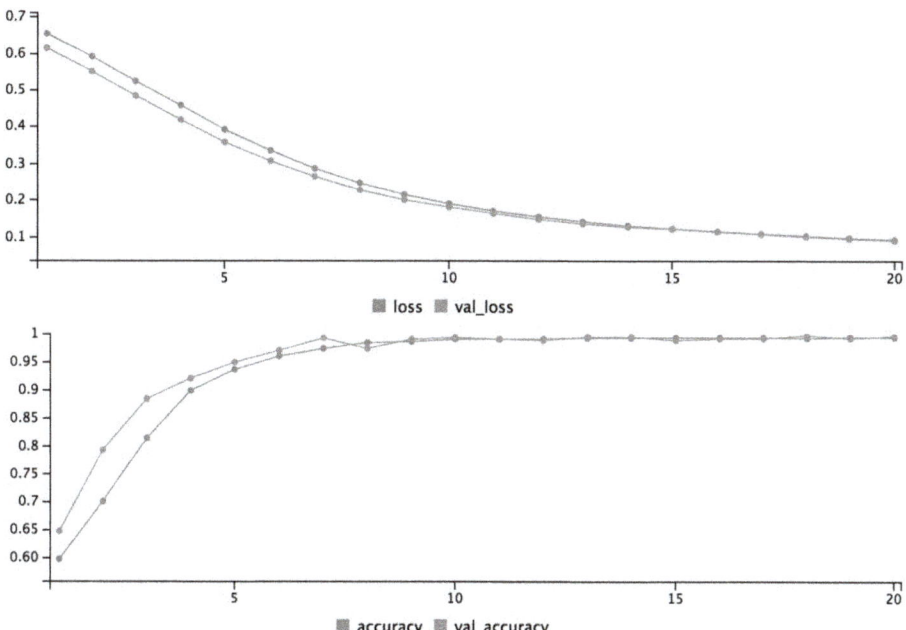

Each graph has two lines: one refers to the 80% of the training data that was actually used to train the model while the other refers to the 20% of the training data that was held back for cross validation. Ideally, and as shown in this case, those two lines converge for the final set of epochs. If cross validation accuracy is notably lower than training accuracy, the lines will diverge and we will have an overfitting situation.

Now it might be a little confusing, but keep in mind that we are still holding on to a small dataset that keras never saw, namely testData. We can use the trained keras model to make some predictions using the X values from testData and compare those to the actual Y values in testData. Then, just as we have done with other supervised learning algorithms, we can generate a confusion matrix, based on the test dataset.

```
x_data_test <- as.matrix(testData[,1:3])
y_data_pred=predict_classes(model, x_data_test)

#see how good the prediction was
confusionMatrix(as.factor(y_data_pred), as.factor(testData$Y))

Confusion Matrix and Statistics

          Reference
Prediction   0   1
         0 997   0
         1   4 999


          Accuracy: 0.998
```

This is an excellent model, with accuracy of 99.8%. For the sake of comparison, let's also try training an SVM with our training data and then comparing those results to the keras model. As the code below shows, SVM can also generate a very accurate model (in this case, 99%).

```
#run the SVM
trainData$Y <- as.factor(trainData$Y)
svm.model <- train(Y ~ X1+X2+X3, data = trainData,
    method = "svmRadial",
    trControl=trainControl(method = "none"),
    preProcess = c("center", "scale"))

#use the model on the test data
testData$Y <- as.factor(testData$Y)
predictValues <- predict(svm.model, newdata=testData)
confusionMatrix(predictValues, testData$Y)
Confusion Matrix and Statistics
                      Reference
Prediction 0 1
         0 992 8
         1 11 989
      Accuracy: 0.9905
```

If SVM is basically the same as deep learning algorithms, why use a deep learning approach? The most important reason is that the computational costs of training a deep learning model only increase as we add layers and neurons, whereas the computational cost of training an SVM algorithm grows very quickly with the size of the training dataset. This means that for larger datasets (e.g., images), a deep learning approach is much more efficient.

## DEEP LEARNING IN R—AN IMAGE ANALYSIS EXAMPLE

Let's now try a real-world example. Specifically, given an image, we would like to predict what handwritten digit is in the image (think about a bank trying to determine what is written on a check). We will use the MNIST dataset, which is publicly available and easy to access from the keras package. The MNIST data consists of 60,000 28×28 grayscale images of handwritten digits (check out the MNIST web site, http://yann.lecun.com/exdb/mnist/ for more information). The image below shows an example:

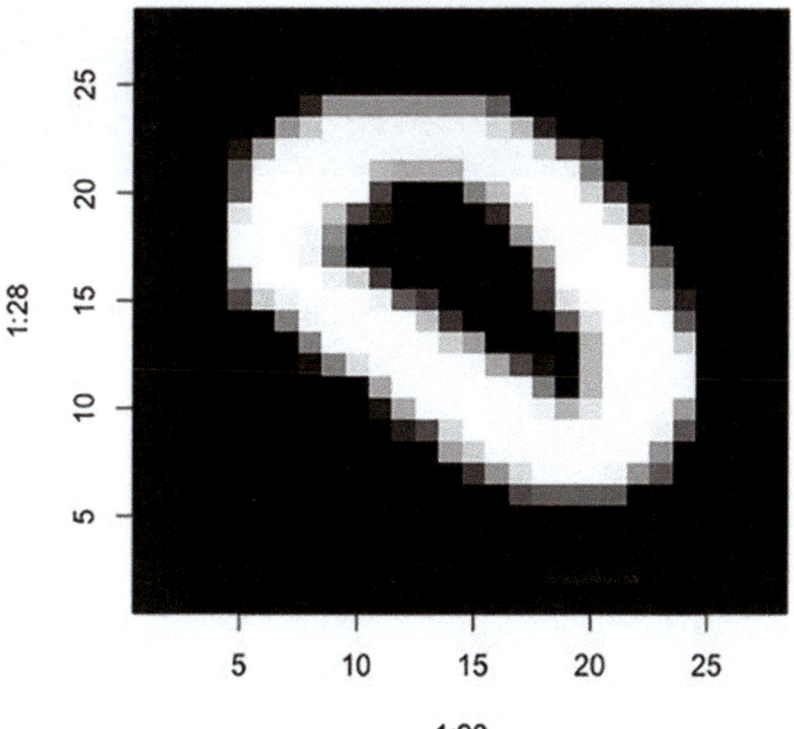

We want to use the many thousands of examples in the MNIST data to train a keras model to recognize these and other digits. At a high level, the code to do this training is similar to our previous example. But first, we need to load our dataset, which contains a list of images and the true digit (identified by a human) associated with that image.

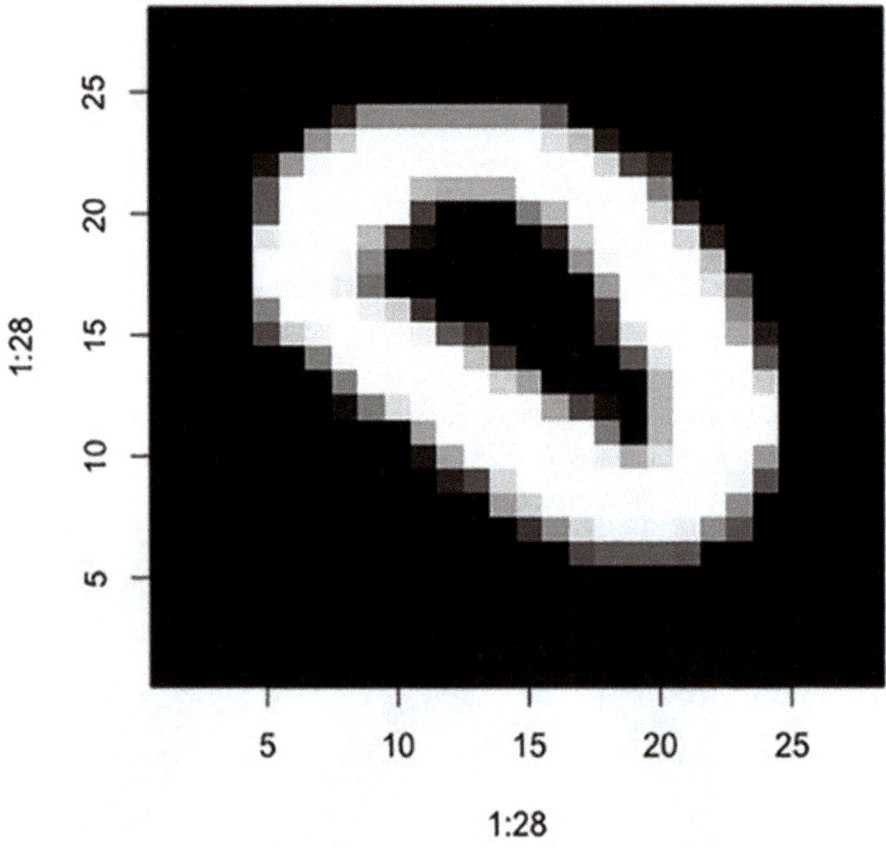

```
library(tidyverse)
library(keras)
library(caret)

# Load the images of digits: By default this will
# get the data from a Google repository. If you prefer
# to use a local version of the file, you will have to
# supply a full pathname.
mnist <- dataset_mnist()
```

Now that we have the data, let's look at an example image. As you can see, the image is a zero, and the y value (i.e., the supplied digit) is, not surprisingly, also a zero.

```
#look at an images (only 28x28) and the known value
img <- mnist$train$x[400,,]
image(1:28, 1:28, img, col = gray.colors(start=0, end=1, n=256))


#Output the training value
mnist$train$y[400]
[1] 0
```

Next, let's use the same set of steps that we previously used, this time, to create a model that can predict a digit that is within an image. In the second line of code, using layer_flatten(), we organize each 28×28 image into one vector of 784 numbers (28×28). Think of this layer as unstacking the rows of pixels in the image and lining them up—this layer only reformats the data. In the hidden layer, we use 128 neurons with the "relu" ("rectified linear unit") activation function. As noted above, this produces an output value of zero if the value of the node was negative or the actual value of the node if that value is positive. We have twice as many hidden neurons as in our previous example because this visual recognition task is much more challenging than the simple three-predictor model we developed before.

```
model <- keras_model_sequential() %>%
    # Flatten the square 28*28 image
    layer_flatten(input_shape=c(28, 28)) %>%

    #After the pixels are flattened, the network consists of
    #two layers. Starting with 128 units (neurons)
    layer_dense(units = 128, activation = "relu") %>%

    #The final layer is a 10-node softmax layer
    layer_dense(units = 10, activation = 'softmax')
```

Finally, for our output layer, we use 10 neurons with the "softmax" function. This setup allows us to identify the most likely of the 10 digits for each image we examine. For each image, this softmax layer will provide a list of 10 probability values that sum to one. The digit with the highest probability will be considered as the model's choice for that image. By having a complete list of 10 probability values, we can also see how sure the model is about that choice.

Next, we compile the model. Note that we now use "categorical_crossentropy" (rather than 'binary_crossentropy'), because we have 10 choices rather than just two choices.

```
#same code as previous example to compile the model, except
# we use 'categorical_crossentropy', since we have 10
   choices
# (not just two choices)
model %>% compile(
    loss = 'categorical_crossentropy',
    optimizer = optimizer_rmsprop(),
    metrics = c('accuracy')
)
```

Because we have more than two choices, we need to turn our categorical variable ("y," which is the digit) into a little vector. Rather than having one variable that can have any value between 0 and 9, this deep learning method requires a binary variable for each possible choice of digit. Engineers call this *one-hot encoding* because only one of the numbers in the list can be a one, the rest must all be zeroes. So, in our MNIST example, the categorical variable has 10 choices (0 through 9), so doing one-hot encoding, we will create 10 new variables, each representing one of the digits. For each record (observation), nine of the new variables will be 0, and the other new variable will be 1.

If you are curious why it's called one-hot encoding, the term is from the field of digital circuit design, where engineers set up a chip so that only one of its output wires is "hot" at any one time (i.e., it has a signal voltage on it). Another way to think about one-hot encoding is that we are creating a very small sparse matrix, where there are 0s for nine of the 10 columns, and a 1 in the column that represents the digit. The keras package gives us a simple function, called to_categorical() as a way of accomplishing this:

```
#create a matrix of choices
y_train <- to_categorical(mnist$train$y, 10)
```

Then we run the model:

```
#same code as previous example to run the model
history <- model %>% fit(
    mnist$train$x, y_train,
    epochs = 30, batch_size = 128,
    validation_split = 0.2
)
```

Hmmm. This isn't as good as our first example, in that our validation accuracy is getting worse as we continue to do more epochs (iterations). This is a classic sign of overfitting,

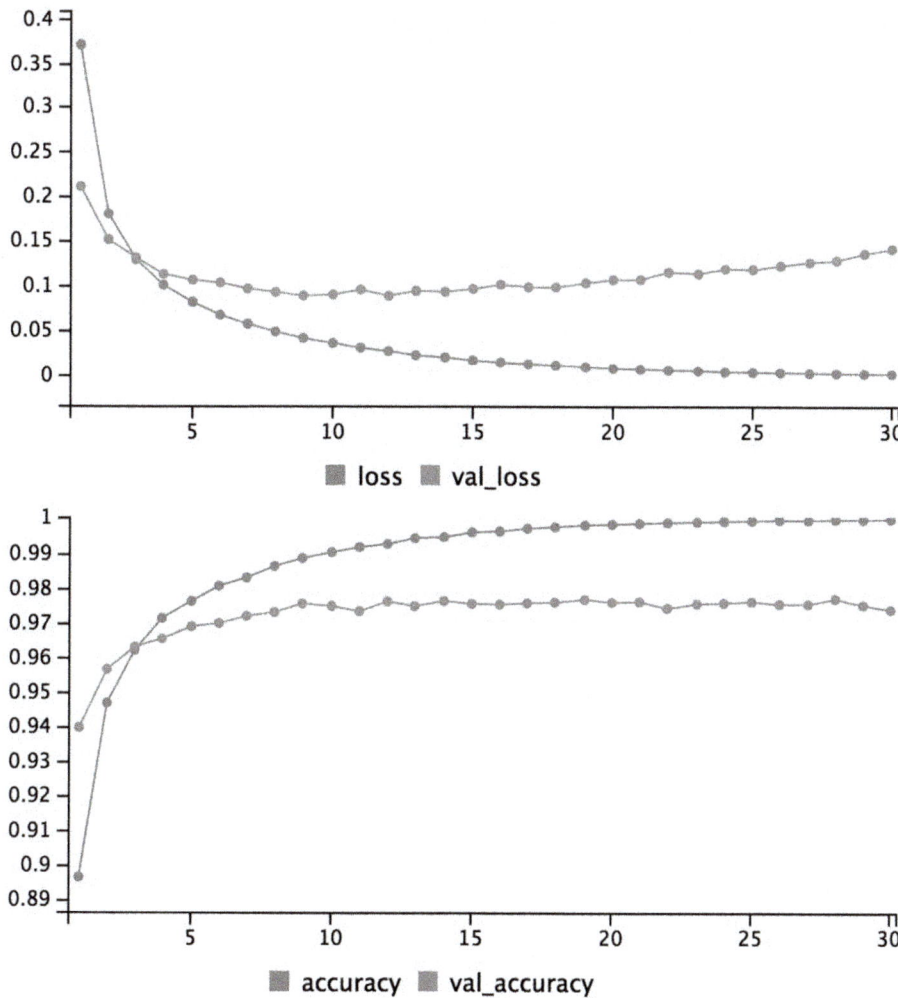

where the model becomes too specialized on the training dataset, and thus, does not do as well when used on other datasets (such as the validation dataset).

One way to try and avoid overfitting is to use a method called dropout regularization. Research has shown that this is an efficient method for preventing the training process from overfitting and developing a model that will generalize well to new data. The idea is very simple: in any given epoch, randomly choose some of the outputs from one layer and nullify their influence on the next layer. The way that we do this is to insert dropout layers in the model and then for each layer, specify the percentage of outputs that should be nullified. In the example below, we establish a new hidden layer with 128 neurons and place dropout layers both before and after that new hidden layer. We've set the dropout rate so that 40% and 30% of outputs are dropped at random within each epoch.

```
# Add a third layer of nodes (neurons)
# And add dropout layers-sets % of neuron weights to 0
   randomly)
model <- keras_model_sequential() %>%
    layer_flatten(input_shape=c(28, 28)) %>%
    layer_dense(units = 256, activation = 'relu') %>%
    layer_dropout(rate = 0.4) %>%
    layer_dense(units = 128, activation = 'relu') %>%
    layer_dropout(rate = 0.3) %>%
    layer_dense(units = 10, activation = 'softmax')
```

After defining this new model, we compile and run as before:

```
#same code as previous example to run the model
model %>% compile(
    loss = 'categorical_crossentropy',
    optimizer = optimizer_rmsprop(),
    metrics = c('accuracy')
)

#same code as previous example to run the model
history <- model %>% fit(
```

```
    mnist$train$x, y_train,
    epochs = 30, batch_size = 128,
    validation_split = 0.2
)
```

The figures below showed that we have reduced the overfitting problem from earlier. In particular, the accuracy and cross-validated accuracy levels in the lower pane of the figure track very closely starting at about the fifth epoch.

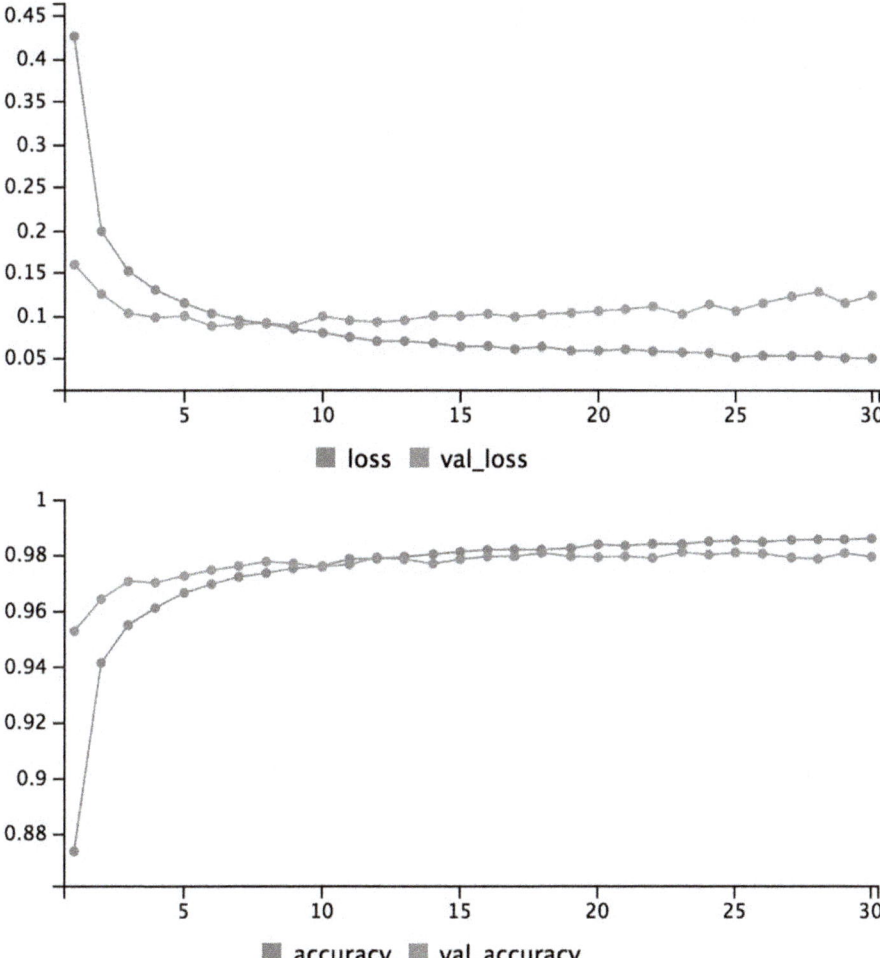

To explore model accuracy, we can use similar code to what was previously used. When this code is run, we can see that we have 98% accuracy.

```
# Explore model accuracy
pred.digit <- model %>% predict_classes(mnist$test$x)
confusionMatrix(as.factor(pred.digit), as.factor(mnist$test$y))
```

As with any machine learning model, we should take a little time to explore what causes the classification or prediction errors in the model. First, let's get a list of mistakes:

```
which(pred.digit != mnist$test$y)
  [1] 248 322 341 446 .... 9983
```

Next, we can pick one of these incorrect predictions. In our case, let's explore the last incorrect prediction (at index 9983).

```
pred.digit[9983]
[1] 6

mnist$test$y[9983]
[1] 5
```

We can see that the model predicted that the digit was a 6, but the true digit from the test data was a 5. Why did the model get this image wrong? Let's look at the image:

```
img <- mnist$test$x[9983,,]
image(1:28, 1:28, img, col = gray.colors(start=0, end=1, n=256))
```

Well, this makes it a bit more understandable why the model had difficulty with this example: looking at this image, it's somewhat ambiguous whether the digit is a 5 or a 6.

Let's compare the performance of our deep learning model to another machine learning technique, SVMs. Be careful—this model could take up to an hour and a half to run, depending upon the power of your computer!

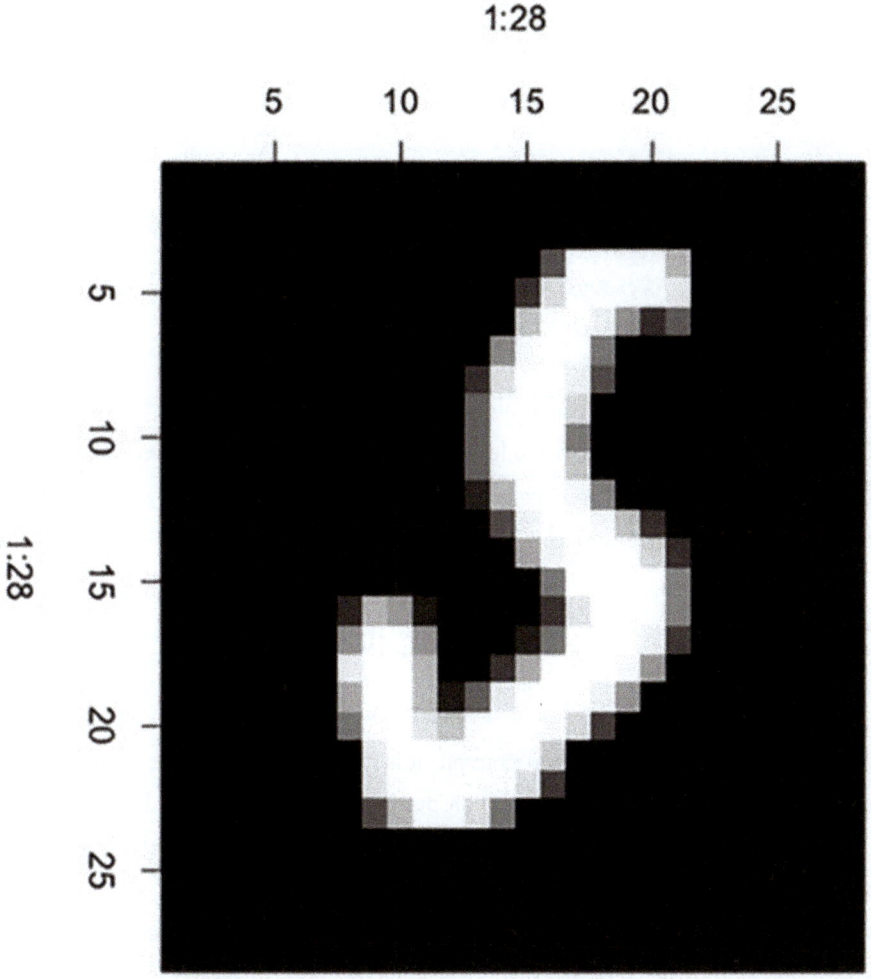

```
library(caret)
library(e1071)

#convert the input data (X image data) into something
   usable
x_train <- array_reshape(mnist$train$x,
                         c(nrow(mnist$train$x), 784))
trainData <- as.data.frame(x_train)
```

```
#add the digit value to the dataset
trainData <- cbind(trainData, digit=mnist$train$y)
trainData$digit <- as.factor(trainData$digit)

#run the SVM - takes about 20-90 minutes on a high end
   laptop
svm.model <- train(digit ~., data = trainData,
    method = "svmRadial",
    trControl=trainControl(method = "none"),
    preProcess = c("center", "scale"))
```

While the accuracy of this SVM model is roughly the same as the DL model, the scalability of the deep learning approach become apparent because of the very long run time required to build the SVM model.

# DEEP LEARNING IN R—USING A PREBUILT MODEL

While the MNIST example is a real example, it is still a somewhat simple example, insofar as the images are small (only 28 by 28 pixels), black and white, and we were only trying to predict a digit. ImageNet, which contains millions of images with thousands of categories, provides a more complex example. With ImageNet data, we need to predict not just a choice of 10 digits, but what is the main subject of the image, such as a cat or a ball. As noted on ImageNet's web site (www.image-net.org), ImageNet is an image database organized by a hierarchical group of 1,000 nouns, with each node (noun) having hundreds (or thousands) of categorized images.

Because this is a public dataset, researchers have created many machine learning models to predict the type of image in ImageNet. For example, Xception is an imageNet model that was trained on the ImageNet dataset. The training took 3 days, using 60 GPUs all working parallel. Rather than redoing that training ourselves (which would take a very long time, since we do not have 60 GPUs), we can use keras to import a pre-built model. You can also save models that you have trained for other people to use. For example, to save our MNIST model, we only need to use the "save_model_hdf5" command:

```
# After training completes, you can save your model
model %>% save_model_hdf5("my_model.h5")
```

Similarly, to read a model that was saved, we just need to use the 'load_model_hdf5' command.

```
# Call load_model_hdf5 to load the model
new_model <- load_model_hdf5("my_model.h5")
```

So, to load the Xception model, we just need to use the same code, but using the name of the downloaded model.

```
# Call load_model_hdf5 to load the model
# (once you have saved the file locally)
model <- load_model_hdf5("xception.h5")
```

After loading the model, we still need to compile the model, just as we have for our other deep learning models. Note that we use "categorical_crossentropy," since the model is predicting one of the 1,000 different image categories.

```
model %>% compile(
    loss = 'categorical_crossentropy',
    optimizer = optimizer_rmsprop(),
    metrics = c('accuracy')
)
```

Because there are 1,000 categories, we also need to write some code to easily know which category the model predicts (for a given image). In the code below, we read in a JSON file that has the names for each image category, and then create an array of names, where the index within the named categories represents the name of that category.

```
imageNames <- fromJSON("imagenet_class_index.json")
imageNamesDF <- as.data.frame(imageNames,
          stringsAsFactors = FALSE)
predictedImageNames <- as.character(imageNamesDF[2,1:1000])

predictedImageNames[1:3]
[1] "tench" "goldfish" "great_white_shark"
```

Now, let's try to use our retrieved model to do some image prediction.

```
#use the model on a test image (of a cat)
testImage <- "cat.jpg"

# first just display image using magick package
library(magick)
im <- image_read(imageName)
plot(im)
```

As you can see, we have a picture of a cat (we are showing the image in black and white, but if you run the code, the image will be in color). Now, let's use the model. Similar to the digit model, as the code below shows, we first load the image and then reshape the image into one large vector (which is called "x"). Then we pre-process the image input, make a prediction, and then map the prediction percentage with the image categories.

```
# Next load image, convert to array and reshape for our
  model
img <- image_load(testImage, target_size = c(299,299))
x <- image_to_array(img)
x <- array_reshape(x, c(1, dim(x)))

# xception_preprocess_input() is used for image
  preprocessing
x <- xception_preprocess_input(x)

# predict the type of image
predictions <- model %>% predict(x)

# create a dataframe of prediction % and the name of that
  animal
predsDF <- data.frame(predPercent=predictions,
            predictedImageNames)
```

Of course, now that we have the predictions, we can output the top predictions, which shows that there is a 55% chance that the image is a tabby cat, and a 21% chance that the image is a tiger cat.

```
# sort the predictions
predsDF <- predsDF %>% arrange(desc(predPercent))

# show the predictions
predsDF[1:5,]
predPercent      predictedImageNames
1 0.555413783          tabby
2 0.215213165          tiger_cat
3 0.047023088          Egyptian_cat
4 0.031442393          lynx
5 0.002431044          sock
```

# CASE STUDY: BUILDING NEURAL NETWORKS FROM THE SURVEY

```
Case Key Points:
- Using Deep Learning to predict Detractors
```

Let's apply our deep learning approach to our case study. We will use our data to predict who are the detractors. We can use the same attributes as we did when using SVM, specifically the airline status and type of travel attributes. Let's read in and do some basic cleaning as well as creating a detractor attribute.

```r
#load survey
library(jsonlite)
mydata.list <- fromJSON("completeSurvey.json")
surveyWithNA <- data.frame(mydata.list)

#Remove rows with'Likelihood.to.recommend' == NA
survey <- surveyWithNA %>%
    filter(!is.na(Likelihood.to.recommend))

#look for detractors - 1 is a detractor
survey$Detractor <- survey$Likelihood.to.recommend <7
survey$Detractor <- as.integer(survey$Detractor)
```

Next, we need to convert factors to numbers, so that we can use those columns within our deep learning network:

```r
survey$Type.of.Travel <- as.integer(survey$Type.of.Travel)
survey$Airline.Status <- as.integer(survey$Airline.Status)
```

We are ready to use deep learning, and the code will look very similar to our first example, when the algorithm was trying to predict Y based in X1, X2, and X3. We can put aside 20% of the data for cross validation and use the rest for training:

```
trainList <-
      createDataPartition(y=survey$Detractor,p=.80,list=FALSE)
trainData <- survey[trainList,]
testData <- survey[-trainList,]
```

Next, extract the two attributes we need from the dataframe, and store them in our 'x_data' matrix:

```
x_data <- as.matrix(
            trainData[,c("Type.of.Travel", "Airline.Status")])
```

Finally, we can create and run our deep learning neural network:

```
# Define the model
model <- keras_model_sequential() %>%
  layer_dense(units = 256, activation = 'relu',
                          input_shape = ncol(x_data)) %>%
  layer_dropout(rate = 0.4) %>%
  layer_dense(units = 128, activation = 'relu') %>%
  layer_dropout(rate = 0.3) %>%
  layer_dense(units = 1, activation = "sigmoid")

# Compile the model
compile(model,
        loss = "binary_crossentropy",
        optimizer = optimizer_rmsprop(),
        metrics = "accuracy")

# Run the model
history = fit(model,
              x_data,
              trainData$Detractor,
              epochs = 20,
              batch_size = 128,
              validation_split = 0.2)
```

After the model has been defined and run, we can use the model to predict detractors.

```
#do prediction
x_data_test <- as.matrix(
                testData[,c("Type.of.Travel", "Airline.Status")])
y_data_pred=predict_classes(model, x_data_test)


#see how good the prediction was
confusionMatrix(as.factor(y_data_pred),
                as.factor(testData$Detractor))
Confusion Matrix and Statistics


          Reference
Prediction     0     1
         0 11098  1921
         1  1328  3272
          Accuracy: 0.8156
```

The accuracy is very similar to what we obtained when we trained a model using SVM. In this situation, neither model can generate improved results because the survey does not include all the factors that may contribute to a person being a detractor. As an illustrative example, our dataset does not contain an indication of when a passenger's luggage was lost.

## Chapter Challenges

Note: Because keras requires a working Python environment that some students may have difficulty installing, the first eight of these Chapter Challenges use a simple neural network example with the nnet package (no Python required).

1. Run install.packages() and library() on the nnet package. Run help("nnet") and read the documentation. Describe the conditions under which nnet() runs a softmax model.

2. We will use the built-in iris dataset for the next few problems. Copy the species column from iris into a new variable called y. Copy the first four columns of iris to a matrix, like this: x <- as.matrix(iris[,1:4]). Run str() on the result and report what you see.

3. Run set.seed(1) to control randomization before starting this problem. Run the nnet() fitting procedure using the x matrix to predict y. Include only 12 neurons in the hidden layer, like this: netOut <- nnet(y ~ x, size=12, maxit=200). Make note of the comments printed on the console by the procedure. Describe how many back-propagation iterations the nnet() procedure needed to converge on a final set of weights.

4. In the previous problem, you stored the output object from the call to nnet() in an object called netOut. Type netOut at the console and describe what the object contains. What type of modeling did nnet() use for this problem and why?

5. Run summary(netOut) and describe the results. Many values are reported, with labels like "i1->h1." Explain what these values represent. The overall architecture of the neural net shows as "a 4-12-3 network with 99 weights." Explain what these numbers mean.

6. Examine the neural network model's predictions with predict(netOut, x). To improve the readability of the output, try embedding the call to predict() within the round() command. Try rounding to two or three digits of precision. Explain what you see.

7. Save the rounded prediction results to a data structure, like this: probTable <- round(predict(netOut, x),2). Then use the table() command to compare each column of predictions to the actual y values, like this: table(probTable[,1], y). Run a similar command to display tables for the second and third columns. Explain your results.

8. Rerun the code from problems 3 through 7, this time using only eight neurons in the hidden layer. How do the results change?

9. Install an up-to-date Python development environment on your computer if it does not already have one. One way to do this is to use the "conda" package management facility, an open source system for managing programming language installations. Some data scientists like "miniconda" because it minimizes the number of newly installed packages while providing the full set of conda package management capabilities.

10. Run install.packages() and library() on the reticulate package. This package provides a software interface between the R environment and your Python installation. Once reticulate is running, you can point to your Python installation by supplying the pathname to your Python executable with

the use_python() command. You can usually find the pathname for your new installation of Python by searching your computer for python3.X (where X is the version number). Make sure you use the option required=TRUE when you call use_python(), otherwise reticulate treats your pathname as a suggestion.

11. Using the keras package requires that your Python installation includes a recent version of the Python tensorflow module. Run tf <- import("tensorflow") to add the tensorflow module to your installation of Python.

12. Run install.packages() and library() on the keras package. Then run install_keras() as described at the beginning of this chapter. Note that if you installed the conda package management facility in item 9 above, make sure to use the option method="conda" when you call install_keras(). You also may need to supply a full pathname to your conda executable file. Note, if you see a variable called py3path in R's Global Environment, make sure it is set to the same pathname that you specified in problem 10.

13. Reproduce the keras deep learning model for detractors from the Case Study section of this chapter. Report whether your results match what was reported in the chapter.

14. Add the predictor "Age" from the case study survey to your list of predictors used in the keras deep learning model. To what extent does adding this variable improve the predictive performance of the model?

15. Choose another predictor from the survey and add that to your keras model. To what extent does adding this variable improve the predictive performance of the model?

## Sources

https://keras.rstudio.com
https://machinelearningmastery.com/how-to-reduce-overfitting-with-dropout-regularization-in-keras/
https://rstudio.github.io/reticulate/
https://www.datacamp.com/community/tutorials/keras-r-deep-learning

## R Functions Used in This Chapter

| | |
|---|---|
| array_reshape() | (reticulate) Reorganize the dimensions of an array/matrix. |
| compile() | Create a version of the keras model that is ready to train. |
| confusionMatrix() | Calculate a confusion matrix between predicted and actual outcome data. |
| createDataPartition() | (caret) Divide a dataset randomly into training and test sets. |
| fit() | Train the keras model. |
| image() | Display a digital image. |
| image_load() | Prepares an image for analysis by keras. |
| image_read() | (magick) Read in an image file. |
| install_keras() | Set up the various modules needed for keras. |
| keras_model_sequential() | Initiate a multi-layer model where each layer only connects to the next layer. |
| layer_dense() | Build a "densely interconnected" layer of neurons. |
| layer_dropout() | Use dropout regularization by creating a special layer that randomly drops outputs from the previous layer. |
| layer_flatten() | Using a rectangular matrix as input, flatten it to a vector that is supplied to a layer of neurons. |
| load_model_hdf5() | Reads in a pre-trained keras model for use in making new predictions. |
| predict_classes() | Predict classes with novel data on a trained keras model. |
| to_categorical() | Create a one-hot vector from a categorical variable. |
| train() | (caret) Train a machine learning model. |

This text includes access to datasets and select student resources. To learn more, visit sagepub.com

# INDEX